PAYING WITH THEIR BODIES

JOHN M. KINDER

Paying with Their Bodies

AMERICAN WAR

AND THE PROBLEM

OF THE DISABLED

VETERAN

THE UNIVERSITY OF CHICAGO PRESS *Chicago and London*

JOHN M. KINDER *is assistant professor of American studies and history at Oklahoma State University.*

The University of Chicago Press, Chicago 60637
The University of Chicago Press, Ltd., London
© 2015 by John Kinder
All rights reserved. Published 2015.
Printed in the United States of America

24 23 22 21 20 19 18 17 16 15   1 2 3 4 5

ISBN-13: 978-0-226-21009-4 (cloth)
ISBN-13: 978-0-226-21012-4 (e-book)
DOI: 10.7208/chicago/9780226210124.001.0001

Library of Congress Cataloging-in-Publication Data

Kinder, John M. (John Matthew), 1975– author.
   Paying with their bodies : American war and the problem of the disabled veteran / John M. Kinder.
       pages : illustrations ; cm
   Includes bibliographical references and index.
   ISBN 978-0-226-21009-4 (cloth : alk. paper) — ISBN 0-226-21009-X (cloth : alk. paper) — ISBN 978-0-226-21012-4 (e-book) — ISBN 0-226-21012-X (e-book) 1. Disabled veterans—United States—History. 2. Disabled veterans—Rehabilitation—United States—History. 3. War and society. I. Title.
   UB363.K56 2015
   362.4086'970973—dc23

2014029497

CONTENTS

ILLUSTRATIONS

FIGURES

In a great war for the right the one great debt owed by the nation is that to the men who go to the front and pay with their bodies for the faith that is in them.

—Theodore Roosevelt, *The Great Adventure: Present-Day Studies in American Nationalism* (1919)

INTRODUCTION

> When a man is wounded on the field of battle he becomes an immediate problem of pain and suffering to himself, a subsequent problem of support to himself and to his family, and in time a problem of cost to the taxpayers of his country. The problem of the disabled veteran is therefore humanitarian, economic, and political. At the outset he represents the strongest possible appeal to human sympathy, torn and bleeding flesh, mangled features, blinded eyes, missing arms and legs. At some later time he becomes an item in a column of government statistics.[1]
> — Richard Seelye Jones, *A History of the American Legion* (1946)

In the summer of 2006, US Army staff sergeant Christian Bagge, a twenty-three-year-old former National Guardsman and double amputee from Eugene, Oregon, made headlines when he joined president George W. Bush for a slow jog around the White House's south lawn (fig. 1). The White House Press Office commemorated the event in a series of glossy photographs—the two men shaking hands in the Oval Office, running together midstride, chatting with reporters—which were soon picked up by news agencies and websites around the country. For the Bush administration, increasingly under fire for its policies of "preemptive war," the photo op proved to be a publicity coup. It afforded the president an opportunity to reassure the American people that he would never forget the nation's wounded warriors. More important still, the spectacle of Bagge bounding along at Bush's side—the young soldier's metallic, comma-shaped prosthetics glinting in the afternoon mist— fed into a deeply entrenched yearning for that most utopian of martial ideals: a war without permanent casualties. To see Christian Bagge run was to witness the capacity of modern technology to replace what war had taken away.[2] Or so it would seem.

Since returning from Iraq, Bagge has consistently refused to sugarcoat war's effects on his body and life. At his Purple Heart ceremony, when military officials asked him to cover his stumps with long pants, he donned shorts, telling curious reporters: "They said they didn't want

1

FIG. 1. In June 2005, Christian Bagge lost parts of both legs when he was injured by a roadside bomb in the desert just south of Kirkuk in Iraq. In fulfilling a promise to run with president George W. Bush, he hoped to inspire other disabled veterans and draw public attention to their postwar struggles. Photo courtesy of the US Army. Photographer William D. Moss.

the public to be disturbed. They said they wanted it to be 'soft on the eyes.'" In addition to the months of phantom limb pain, he has faced an array of social hardships, including the daily frustration of being "trapped" in a non-wheelchair-accessible home.[3] Like many disabled Iraq War vets, Bagge has also struggled to come to terms with the political significance of his injuries. Asked by his hometown paper whether his wounds had been "worth it," he offered a notably ambivalent reply: "I want people to hear me say, 'Yes it was worth it.' But the honest part of me says I would do anything to get my legs back." As for the justification of the Iraq War, Bagge was no less circumspect: "[The Kurds] would say, 'My freedom is worth his legs.' I'm personally confused about the cost. First it was Afghanistan. Then it was weapons of mass destruction. Then it was Saddam Hussein. Then it was freedom. I have to pick one in mind."[4]

Christian Bagge is not alone. Since the start of the "Global War on Terror" in 2001, and the subsequent US invasion of Iraq two years later, tens of thousands of American service personnel have returned home with devastating physical impairments and mental trauma. They have been greeted by a steady stream of magazine articles, Internet videos, public pronouncements, and television newscasts dedicated to honoring their injuries and assuaging Americans' fears about the bodily toll of military intervention overseas. Thanks to a sympathetic media and the Department of Defense, ordinary Americans have grown intimately acquainted with the latest generation of body-mending technologies—anticlotting tourniquets, titanium prostheses, and biologically engineered skin grafts—designed to help war-disabled veterans return to productive life. At the same time, groups like the Wounded Warrior Project have made it their mission to "foster the most successful, well-adjusted generation of wounded service members in our nation's history."[5]

And yet, amidst the flag-waving and fanfare, the fate of disabled veterans remains both a source of national anxiety and fodder for political debate. In an era when "supporting the troops" has become something of a civic religion, many Americans struggle to make sense of the social, political, and personal legacies of war injury. What are the nation's obligations to those who fight in its name? Who is ultimately responsible for veterans' disabilities—the enemy combatants they faced abroad or the public officials whose policies put them in harm's way? And at what point does war's legacy of disability outweigh the nation's interests at home and abroad?

This book attempts to answer these questions by exploring the cultural history of disabled veterans from the Civil War era to the present day. Specifically, it charts the rise and fall (and rise again) of what came to be known as the *Problem of the Disabled Veteran*, a term I have chosen to capitalize throughout the text that follows.[6] The Problem of the Disabled Veteran was more than a description of disabled soldiers' postwar struggles. It was a perceived national crisis about the social, political, and foreign-policy implications of disabled veterans in modern American society. Before the mid-nineteenth century, disabled veterans were considered little more than an unfortunate by-product of battle. Venerated as icons of manly courage and patriotic sacrifice, they were expected to return to civilian life with few demands upon the state or the public. By the start of World War I, however, Americans' attitudes toward disabled veterans had changed. While disabled vets continued to be singled out for public praise, many in the United States came to associate war-related disability with a host of social ills: pathological dependency, compromised masculinity, and the crippling legacies of foreign intervention.

Since that time, disabled veterans have been at the center of two competing visions of American warfare. The first imagined the disabled veteran—and his successful reintegration into postwar society—as an index of the United States' ability to enter the global arena and return home functionally, if not aesthetically, unscathed. This vision would be most closely aligned with Victorian-era militarists and advocates of the soldiers' rehabilitation movement, which emerged during World War I and has served as the backbone of federal disabled veterans' policy ever since. Throughout the 1910s and 1920s, the US government embarked upon a massive campaign to "salvage" the nation's war-wounded and erase the painful memory of war from the American body politic. Despite the movement's early failures, Theodore Roosevelt and other rehabilitationists were confident that the "era of the disabled veteran" was quickly drawing to an end. Implicit in their arguments was an even more tantalizing promise: that future generations of political leaders could remove the social consequences of veterans' disabilities from the calculus of American war-making.

The second vision forecast a very different picture of the nation's future. Rooted in Progressive-era critiques of military intervention and empire, it cast disabled veterans as portents of a terrible new age of unparalleled violence. To pacifists, isolationists, and critics of American militarism in general, disabled veterans were object lessons about the lingering legacies of military adventurism. Although this vision was dramatically altered during World War II, it would nevertheless remain central to many Americans' understanding of the threat posed by foreign conflict, re-emerging like a repressed nightmare during the Korean War, the Vietnam War, and in the run-up to the United States' most recent military conflicts in the Middle East. Its dominant refrain: to leave US soil under arms was to risk mutilation, disfigurement, disability, and death.

Why World War I?

This book locates the high point of America's Disabled Veteran Problem in the decades surrounding World War I, and that's where we will be spending most of our time. With the conflict's centenary fast approaching, it has become fashionable to take stock of the "war to end all wars" and the human misery it produced. At academic conferences, I'm regularly assured by like-minded colleagues that World War I is now "back." (As evidence, they point to the popularity of the BBC's *Downton Abbey* or HBO's gangster drama *Boardwalk Empire*, whose cast of gun-toting villainy includes a former army marksman who wears a tin mask over his severely disfigured face.) After basking in the nostalgia-tinted afterglow of the "Greatest Generation," Americans are finally ready to take a hard look at the nation's first "bad" war. Anyone who visits Europe, Turkey, or the British Commonwealth recognizes that World War I never fully disappeared, of course. From London to Paris to Canberra, the Great War remains a part of living memory. The reasons are not difficult to understand. For many Europeans, World War I was fought on—and over—home soil (the "there" of Americans' "over there"). And then there are the casualties—more than sixteen million killed, another twenty million wounded—staggering figures even today.[7]

While the number of US dead and injured paled in comparison to those of other belligerents, the bodily cost of American participation is shocking nonetheless. Between April 6, 1917, when the United States entered the conflict, and November 11, 1918, when the Armistice was declared, more than 53,000 Americans died from combat-related injuries, a figure that becomes even more horrific if we consider that the majority of US troops spent only about two hundred days in the field. Tuberculosis, influenza, and other infectious diseases killed 63,000 more, many of whom perished in training camps or on transport ships, long before reaching European shores.[8] For the survivors, the Great War's physiological and psychological effects lingered well beyond its end. More than 224,000 Americans suffered battlefield wounds, among them 70,000 casualties of poison gas. Even those who managed to escape German artillery fire usually came home worse for the experience. Of the nearly 1.3 million Americans who served in combat zones, nearly all endured some kind of health ailment, from diarrhea and muscle fatigue to debilitating "shell shock." As a result, over 930,000 American service personnel had applied for disability benefits by 1923.[9] In the end, more than 200,000 Americans officially returned from the Great War permanently disabled.[10] Untold others would suffer from flashbacks, nightmares, and undiagnosed mental trauma for decades after the "war to end all wars" drew to a close.

The United States' high casualty rolls would have triggered alarms in any circumstances. But the rise of the disabled veteran as an object of national crisis cannot be explained by numbers alone. The brutality of the fighting, coupled with the Great War's unsatisfactory ending, inspired a period of intense public reflection about the bodily hazards of international engagement. Even as political elites championed a rapid "return to normalcy," well-publicized stories of veterans' suffering, coupled with scandals at Walter Reed Medical Center and other medical facilities, convinced many Americans that the Problem of the Disabled Veteran would not disappear any time soon. Newly formed veterans' groups such as the American Legion and the Disabled American Veterans fueled public concerns even further, waging massive publicity campaigns to carve out a privileged cultural and legal status for wounded soldiers and their families. By the early 1930s, Americans of all political stripes were wrestling with the broader implications of the Great War's mass production of injury. If World War I was any indication, what could the United States expect in its next military encounter overseas? Did the survival of so many US war casualties signal the victory of modern medicine over industrialized armaments? Or did it lay the groundwork for social upheaval for decades to come?

This book contends that the decades surrounding World War I marked the United States' most sustained examination of the relationship between disability and the nation's future military endeavors. In the eyes of many Americans, World War I had proven, beyond any doubt, that the United States was capable of mobilizing a war machine of tremendous destructive power. Less clear was whether the Great War—and policies of martial adventurism in general—was worth the high price in broken bodies and shattered lives. Within this context, and throughout much of the twentieth century, the fate of America's sick, wounded, and disabled soldiers took on a new and pronounced significance. More so than ever before, Americans looked to disabled soldiers to gauge the long-term legacies of military conflict in national life.

Diagnosing the Disabled Veteran Problem

When I began this study, my knowledge of disability history was limited primarily to my own personal experience. In the mid-1980s, after suffering a series of seizures, I was diagnosed with epilepsy, an umbrella term used to describe a spectrum of neurological ailments. To soften the blow, my neurologist gave me an illustrated pamphlet highlighting the Great Epileptics of History—the Apostle Paul, Julius Caesar, among others—in whose shuddering shadow I now walked. While the pamphlet was clearly intended to serve as a source of comfort, it offered few insights into the daily struggles of ordinary disabled people. Nor did it seek to explain why social conceptions of ability and disability remain relevant in highly industrialized nations such as the United States. Instead, I was encouraged to understand epilepsy simply as a medical problem—the product of a "natural" neurological defect—that could be successfully managed with proper medication and careful supervision.

In subsequent decades, I have come to recognize the limitations of the *medical* model of disability, which "assumes that pathological conditions are the primary obstacle to disabled people's social integration." Today, most scholars approach disability as a *social construction*, the product of interconnected government policies, societal arrangements, and public institutions. In the broadest sense, disability has less to do with physical or mental impairments than with the meanings a society assigns it.[11] These meanings, as pioneering historian Paul K. Longmore points out, are rarely static. Throughout US history, disability has "operat[ed] synergistically as public problem, cultural metaphor, social identity, and mechanism for managing social relations."[12] Both before and after World War I, Americans routinely turned to cultural notions of disability—or, at least, fear of injury—to make sense of the dangers of US military intervention abroad. At the same time, they grappled with how to define disability in an age of modern technology. Was being disabled a lifelong identity, as many veterans' groups would argue, deserving of recognition from the state? Or was it, like war itself, a transitory phenomenon, something that could be transcended with time?

Let me be clear. In highlighting the "constructed" or symbolic nature of disability, I don't mean to downplay the physical and mental hardships that accompany many disabled people's lives. Quite the opposite, in fact. War injury is by definition traumatic (*trauma* coming from the Greek, meaning "to wound"). Pain might very well be "inexpressible," as some philosophers have argued, but that makes it no less *real*, no less *felt*.[13] Thus, this book is guided by the principle that bodies matter—that bodily *matter* (blood, viscera, skin, organs) matters. If at times I linger on the horrific, it's only to remind readers—to remind myself—that wounds are more than metaphors. Modern war is about many things, but its most defining feature is the rupturing, wounding, and destroying of human bodies.

I also take seriously the idea that soldiers' injuries do not take place in a cultural vacuum. Throughout my research, I have spoken to disabled veterans, poured over their medical files, read their oral histories, and tried to understand their lives as much as possible. And much of the material I have found is contained in the pages that follow. But my central focus is how disabled vets are constructed as problems within American culture—problems to be solved, problems to be exposed, and problems to be ignored. To understand that, I turn my attention to other kinds of historical sources: magazine articles and prescriptive literature, Hollywood films and government propaganda, homecoming parades and antiwar art. I do so for two reasons.

The first is that, despite the mass production of injured bodies since the Civil War, most Americans' primary encounters with disabled soldiers do not come face-to-face; they are filtered through forms of culture, from movies and posters to stat sheets and photographs. The second reason is that the exercise and consequences of military power cannot be abstracted from mechanisms of cultural production. To quote historian Daniel Pick, "Words, ideas, images constitute the discursive support for military conflict; they should be understood not as though they are mere froth without consequences, but as crucial aspects of the destructive reality of violent conflict itself."[14] Simply put, one cannot begin to understand Americans' anxieties about war-produced disability without considering the ways language, cultural stereotypes, and modes of thinking have rendered disabled veterans dangerous or problematic in the popular imagination.

One additional note: In tracing how the disabled veteran became a Problem (with a capital P), this book invariably touches on issues of gender and race, though perhaps not as much as some readers would like. Disability cannot be abstracted from other categories of identity and power, and very often what it means to be disabled is determined as much by these aspects of social existence as by the nature of physical impairment. Put another way, no one is ever *just* disabled, not even disabled vets. (If you don't believe me, ask a disabled veteran of color whether his or her racial status disappears postinjury.) Gender and race enter this story in other ways as well. Although more than 2,000 US women left World War I with service-connected disabilities, gendered preconceptions about martial citizenship made it difficult for female vets to receive public and state recognition.[15] Likewise, race-based prejudices were woven into all aspects of the United States' experience in World War I, from wartime propaganda campaigns to postwar rehabilitation practices.[16] These are important histories, and they deserve to be told.

However, in the overwhelming majority of the posters, propaganda texts, newspaper articles, novels, and films I have examined for this book, the Problem of the Disabled Veteran was imagined in response to one type of casualty: young white men. This makes some sense, particularly given the racial and gender disparities of the US military at the time. White men were far more likely to wind up in combat roles and thus were more likely to suffer life-altering injuries. That said, Great War–era concerns about white male casualties also spoke to perceived links between whiteness, masculinity, and national economic health.[17] As many observers saw it, the primary *problem* of the (white) disabled veteran was not that he was injured or shell-shocked; it was that he would become a burden on postwar society, crippling the nation's economic growth and well-being. Indeed, from today's perspective, the Problem of the Disabled Veteran often appears to be little more than an opportunity for affirmative action—a chance to spend millions of dollars, millions of hours, and millions of words to shore up the social and economic privileges of white men.

Structure and Aims

In tracing the evolution of the Problem of the Disabled Veteran, this book follows a looping yet ultimately linear trajectory. Part I examines the conditions that led to the Problem of the Disabled Veteran, focusing on the United States' experiences in the Civil War and World War I. Part II carries the story forward, exploring the aftermath of the Great War, from the homecomings of 1918 to the rise of the soldier's rehabilitation movement. In Part III, I look at the attempts of several groups, including organized veterans and peace activists, to mobilize the disabled veteran for social and political gain. Part IV sketches an outline of the Problem of the Disabled Veteran from World War II to the present day. As we will see, public attitudes toward disabled veterans do not follow a neat line of progress, nor do they necessarily cohere into a single attitude at a single time. Following World War I, disabled veterans were both celebrated and reviled; they were both honored on holidays and urged to "deveteranize" and remove themselves from public life. Images of sick and injured veterans were used to promote both pro-war ideologies and movements for peace.

Indeed, because it was always symptomatic of a diverse set of fears, there never was a single Problem of the Disabled Veteran. For Progressives, the "problem" was that disabled veterans threatened to bankrupt the nation with high pensions and other costly demands from the state. For veterans' groups, the "problem" was that disabled veterans were being ignored, forgotten, or ill-treated in a culture that harbored deep suspicions about veterans as a class. For peace groups, the "problem" was not the disabled veteran himself, but the policies of militarism and foreign intervention that led to his existence. And, of course, for military propagandists and war planners, the "problem" was that no one wanted to come from battle missing a limb—or worse.

Beyond charting the history of the Problem of the Disabled Veteran, this book has several distinct aims. The first is to debunk the myth of the "lost generation," the notion that post–World War I Americans experienced a widespread loss of faith in progress, civilization, and national destiny.[18] The "lost generation" is a powerful term and I've used it myself many times, but it makes little sense when describing Americans' responses to World War I as a whole. To be sure, the postwar years witnessed disillusion with World War I (and war in general). But the United States' experience in the Great War prompted optimism as well, particularly within the first decade of the Armistice. Soldiers were optimistic they could use the lessons they learned "over there" to improve their lives once home. Veterans' groups were optimistic they could—to quote a popular American Legion slogan—keep the spirit of the war alive and heighten the public's awareness of veterans' sacrifices. Physicians, economists, and social planners were optimistic that rehabilitation could bring about the "end" of disability itself. And antiwar groups were optimistic that the horrors of World War I would lead to a permanent culture of peace in the United States and around the globe. Focusing only on

Americans' disillusion (which was substantial) belies a much more complicated story. Namely, it prevents us from understanding how World War I era set the template for how Americans think about, plan for, and accommodate themselves to the Problem of the Disabled Veteran today.

This leads me to a second and far more pressing aim: to provide historical context for today's Disabled Veteran Problem. Every time I sit down at my desk, it seems, I spot an Internet article about the newest medical technique, about the most recent veterans' hospital scandal, or about how—in this war—more soldiers are surviving their injuries. But, of course, none of this is new. As we will see, in the 1920s, Americans were awed by the same promises of "miracle medicines" and high-tech prosthetics; they were shocked by the same scandals of veteran neglect; and they were told to take comfort in the same promise of war's survivability. Although historians, cultural critics, gender scholars, and disability activists have made injury a site of intense investigation, there has been little effort to trace contemporary anxieties about disabled veterans back to Americans' first experiences with modern warfare. In turn, this book seeks to expand the field of disability studies by exploring the ways disability has served as a framework for understanding US foreign policy. Americans have routinely turned to cultural notions of disability to make sense of the dangers of US military intervention abroad. American isolationists in particular have a history of peppering their critiques of foreign intervention with references to injury, dependency, emasculation, and disfigurement.

My final aim is to help reshape the way Americans think about the nation's history of war. For far too long, disabled veterans have existed on the periphery of American warfare. Scan the pages of many bestselling war narratives and you would think that injured soldiers simply disappear once the final shots are fired.[19] But what happens if we move disabled veterans to the center of the American war story? As we shall see, the history of American war over the last century begins to look a lot different. We'll see that war is not a temporary phenomenon, something that can be easily left behind; rather, its human legacies are felt for decades, if not entire lifetimes. We will also see that war's cost in money, bodies, minds, and memory is far more substantial than most would imagine. (The United States did not stop paying benefits to World War I veterans until 2007.)[20] Further, moving the disabled veteran (and other war casualties) to the center of the war story makes it more difficult to use easy metaphors of "healing" and "closure" to describe war's immediate aftermath. Some bodies never heal; some wounds never close. In short, what emerges is a counternarrative to the traditional story of American warfare, a history of men and women—physicians and social workers, peace activists and veterans' organizers, rehabilitation aids and fiction writers—attempting to put together the damage left behind in war's wake.

––––––

Today, the idea of permanent warfare and a permanent military is taken for granted. But it didn't happen overnight. Well into the twentieth century, the fact that war produced large numbers of disabled veterans was considered a dangerous threat to the nation's future—a Problem that had to be solved. I believe that the Problem of the Disabled Veteran functions as an invaluable lens through which to explore Americans' attempts to come to terms with war's inevitable human damage. For some, the political and social benefits of military intervention overseas more than made up for war's mass production of disability and death. Many others, however, came to view the nation's participation in foreign conflicts as inherently dangerous and frequently disabling. These views informed American society and politics well before the United States' current campaigns in Afghanistan and Iraq. To understand how they first developed and how they have changed over time is now more important than ever.

THE INDUSTRIALIZATION OF INJURY

Thomas H. Graham

On August 30, 1862, Thomas H. Graham, an eighteen-year-old Union private from rural Michigan, was gut-shot at the Second Battle of Bull Run near Manassas Junction, Virginia.[1] One of 10,000 Union casualties in the three-day battle, Graham had little chance of survival. Penetrating gunshot wounds to the abdomen were among the deadliest injuries of the Civil War, killing 87 percent of patients—either from the initial trauma or the inevitable infection.[2] Quickly evacuated, he was sent by ambulance to Washington, DC, where he was admitted to Judiciary Square Hospital the next day. Physicians took great interest in Graham's case, and over the following nine months, the young man endured numerous operations to suture his wounds. Deemed fully disabled, he was eventually discharged from service on June 6, 1863.

But Graham's injuries never healed completely. His colon remained perforated, and he had open sinuses just above his left leg where a conoidal musket ball had entered and exited his body. As Dr. R. C. Hutton, Graham's pension examiner, reported shortly after the Civil War's end, "From each of these sinuses there is constantly escaping an unhealthy sanious discharge, together with the faecal contents of the bowels. Occasionally kernels of corn, apple seeds, and other indigestible articles have passed through the stomach and been ejected through these several sinuses." Broad-shouldered and physically strong, Graham attempted to make a living as a day laborer and later as a teacher, covering his open wounds with a bandage. By the early 1870s, however, he bore "a sallow, sickly countenance" and could no longer hold a job, dress his injuries, or even stand on his own two feet. Most pitiful of all, the putrid odor from his "artificial anus" made him a social pariah. Regarding Graham's case as "utterly hopeless," Hutton concluded, "he would have died long ago from utter detestation of his condition, were it not for his indomitable pluck and patriotism." Within a few months, Graham was dead, but hundreds of thousands lived on, altering the United States' response to disabled veterans for decades to come.

1

"TO BIND UP THE NATION'S WOUNDS"
How the Disabled Veteran Became a Problem

> With malice toward none, with charity for all, with firmness in the right
> as God gives us to see the right, let us strive on to finish the work we are
> in, to bind up the nation's wounds, to care for him who shall have borne
> the battle, and for his widow, and his orphan, to do all which may achieve
> and cherish a just and lasting peace among ourselves and with all nations.
> — Abraham Lincoln, Second Inaugural Address (1865)

War injury is as old as war itself. For as long as armies have taken up arms, combatants have returned home, their bodies and minds permanently marked by the traumas of battle. Very often such men—and, historically, the vast preponderance of disabled veterans have been men—have required some form of monetary or medical assistance upon leaving the service. In this sense, disabled veterans have always posed a problem for postwar societies, and they likely always will.

However, as it came to be defined in the late nineteenth and early twentieth century, the Problem of the Disabled Veteran can be traced to three sources in particular. The first was the Civil War, a conflict whose legacies included both the largest cohort of disabled veterans in American history and the first "system of national public care" for a single population of US citizens.[1] Less visible, though no less important, was Americans' growing ambivalence about the place of disabled people in modern society. While frequently celebrated as icons of national sacrifice, disabled Civil War vets returned home to a cultural climate increasingly hostile to all forms of physical and mental impairment. Finally, anxieties about the Problem of the Disabled Veteran would be closely linked to heated debates about the future of American warfare. By the 1890s, a number of political and military leaders touted the survivability of modern combat and the progressive nature of American military power. To critics of American imperialism, however, war's supposed benefits could not outw eigh its high cost in disability and death.

The Disabled Veteran: A Fractured History

To appreciate the emergence of the Problem of the Disabled Veteran, we need to take a quick tour through the history of disabled vets in the West. The first thing to understand is that the disabled veteran is a relatively modern figure on the historical stage. The term *veteran* (as in, an old or experienced soldier) didn't appear in English until the early 1500s, and *disabled* did not become a standard term of use until the twentieth century, when it began to replace words like *crippled* and *deformed* to describe people with physical and mental disabilities.[2] Terminology aside, the very concept of the disabled veteran—as a member of a coherent group or social category—would have been largely unfamiliar throughout large chunks of Western history.

The ancient Greeks, for example, did not recognize the disabled veteran as most industrialized societies would today. Military medicine was limited throughout the ancient world, and the fact that you didn't have to be in perfect physical condition to take up arms blurred the lines between disabled and nondisabled from the start. Though Greek myths told of unhealable wounds, medical textbooks recounted stories of spontaneous, miracle cures, leaving open the possibility that no war injury was permanently disabling.[3] In 594–593 BC, the Athenian statesman Solon declared that "persons maimed in war be maintained at the public charge," a position that would be championed by Plutarch and others in later centuries.[4] Despite such entreaties, Greek city-states were generally reluctant to accept the responsibility of caring for disabled veterans. According to historian Martha Edwards, the most militaristic societies in the ancient world had no "custom of valorizing men wounded in battle."[5] Severely injured hoplites were often abandoned by their comrades-in-arms, and few Greeks believed disabled vets should claim preferential treatment before the state. Destitute Athenians were eligible for modest food rations, but not necessarily as a reward for patriotic sacrifice; other impoverished citizens also received government support.

War-wounded Romans garnered a bit more recognition. During the late Republic (147–30 BC), it was customary for political hopefuls to boast about old war wounds when seeking elected office, and Caesar Augustus later set aside tracts of land for disabled legionaries on the empire's frontier.[6] Soldiers invalided out of service because of injury or disease received monetary pensions, calculated according to their length of time in uniform. (Disabled veterans who served more than twenty years were eligible for the same pension as men who managed to complete a twenty-five-year term.)[7] Even so, in a society that tended to scorn physical imperfection, many disabled Roman veterans were disqualified from full participation in civic life.[8] Those who escaped public stigma remained a hidden minority, socially invisible with little to distinguish them from the rest of the underclass (fig. 2).

In Europe, the disabled veteran did not begin to cohere as an institutionally recognized social category until the Early Modern period (c. 1500–1800), when the transition from "tenant-based armies to nationally raised forces" radically transformed the relationship between soldiers and the state.[9] In prior centuries, war had been fought with privately conscripted armies, and the upkeep of permanently injured veterans had fallen to individual feudal lords, local magnates, or the church. Disabled veterans unable to support themselves or secure private patronage had been forced to turn to extended family or religious monasteries for their daily survival.[10] With the rise of professional armies, the governments of Western Europe abandoned private charity schemes in favor of state-sponsored measures to care for the men injured in wartime service. Such efforts were not necessarily the product of national benevolence. In sixteenth-century England, home of "Europe's first state system of benefits for rank-and-file disabled veterans," the earliest relief laws were disciplinary in nature, meant not only to reward veterans' sacrifice but also to curb postwar mendicancy.[11] Whatever their motivations, a growing number of European states acknowledged an obligation to provide for the welfare of permanently injured combatants. In the process, they lay the groundwork for disabled veterans' emergence as a special class of "martial citizens," men whose claims of patriotic sacrifice and masculine service afforded them political considerations beyond those of their fellow countrymen.[12]

The earliest government measures on behalf of disabled veterans usually came in the form of pensions and soldiers' homes, the twin pillars of government disability policy from the Anglo-Spanish War to World

FIG. 2. Although disabled veterans have not always received special status, many cultures have viewed war injury as a sign of masculine courage and symbolic strength. This drawing (c. 1870s) by Four Horns of the Hunkpapa Lakota commemorates the military exploits of his nephew Sitting Bull (on the right), who has been injured by his Crow enemy. Four Horns copied this drawing from one originally made by Sitting Bull himself. National Anthropological Archives, Smithsonian Institution (MNNH-ms1929A_08584800).

War I. In 1593, England legislated the first pension scheme for disabled ex-servicemen.[13] Other European nations quickly followed suit, providing war-injured soldiers and sailors with food allowances and small monetary sums at the taxpayers' expense. Despite state recognition, most disabled veterans were geographically dispersed with little sense of group identity. That began to change in the late seventeenth century when large populations of disabled and indigent veterans were resettled into state-sponsored infirmaries, asylums, and residential homes.

The best-known soldiers' home of the Early Modern era was France's Hôtel des Invalides, a massive hospital and retirement facility that housed more than 4,000 sick, disabled, and aged veterans in central Paris. Constructed in the 1670s and renowned for its architectural splendor, Les Invalides supplied disabled veterans with all of their daily needs, including food and rudimentary medical care. However, such provisions came at a steep price. Although the institutional segregation of disabled veterans encouraged the growth of a collective political consciousness, it also contributed to their growing reputation as threats to public welfare. Residents were virtual prisoners, their behavior and movement regulated according to a strict set of military guidelines.[14] Beyond that, critics charged that soldiers' homes like the Hôtel des Invalides consigned their wards to lives of unmanly idleness—a pathetic end for men who gave so much in service to the realm.[15]

Although Americans did not construct ex-soldiers' homes of any significant size until the mid-nineteenth century, the colonial governments of the "New World" quickly adopted the European principle of pensioning disabled veterans. As early as 1636, Massachusetts Puritans established the English settlement's first lifetime pensions for invalid vets. Other colonies offered similar provisions, including free medical care for injured soldiers and monthly payments for the dependents of fatal casualties. In 1776, the Continental Congress adopted the nation's first pension law, promising disabled soldiers half pay for life.[16] Following the Revolutionary War, the cash-strapped legislature restricted government assistance to amputees and men whose injuries prevented them from earning a living. Adding insult to injury, the United States' first pension scheme instituted a two-tiered hierarchy of veterans' benefits based upon military rank. While incapacitated officers typically received half their usual pay, disabled privates and noncoms had to settle for five dollars per month.[17]

Over the next seventy years, as invasion and expansion added fresh bodies to the nation's casualty rolls, the United States liberalized its disability pension laws and adopted new measures to compensate permanently disabled veterans for their wartime injuries. In lieu of monetary payments, many ex-soldiers received grants of public land, a policy that both relocated disabled veterans to the hinterlands and helped secure US control of the North American continent. And yet, as historian David A. Gerber has argued, disabled veterans of the American Revolution, the War of 1812, and the Mexican-American War "had little long-lasting effect on American society." Dispersed across the continent, with no formal organizations to bind them together, "they lacked a consciousness of themselves as a defined group with specific needs."[18] Put another way,

Table 1. US participation and casualties in major wars, 1775–1975

Conflict	Served	Battle deaths	Other deaths	Wounded
Revolutionary War	> 200,000*	6,900*	18,000*	8,500*
War of 1812	286,730	2,261	17,500*	4,500*
Mexican War	115,906	1,733	13,000*	4,152
Civil War				
Union	2,000,000*	112,000*	250,500*	277,500*
Confederacy	750,000*	94,000*	167,000*	194,000*
Spanish-American War	306,760	385	3,000*	1,662
Philippine-American War	126,468	1,004	3,161	2,911
World War I	4,734,991	53,402	63,114	224,089
World War II	16,112,566	291,557	113,842	671,846
Korean War	5,720,000	33,651	> 8,000*	103,284
Vietnam War	8,744,000	47,364	10,797	313,616

*Estimate
Sources: The figures and format of this table are taken from Allan R. Millet and Peter Maslowski, *For the Common Defense: A Military History of the United States*, rev. ed. (New York: Free Press, 1994), 653. The number of soldiers wounded in World War I is from John Maurice Clark, *The Costs of the World War to the American People* (New Haven: Yale University Press, 1931), 182.

disabled veterans were a growing population (table 1), but they failed to rank as a national Problem.

The United States of Injury

The turning point came in the mid-nineteenth century, when a confluence of factors thrust disabled veterans into the public consciousness. By far the most traumatic was the American Civil War (1861–1865). Though today clouded in romantic myth, the war of "brother against brother" inaugurated a frightening new age of industrialized slaughter. Armed with a rifle-bore muskets, exploding artillery shells, and canister (tin cans filled with grape-sized bullets designed to shred human flesh at close range), the armies that fought at Antietam and Gettysburg mass-produced injured on a previously unimaginable scale. The fact that so many troops could be outfitted at once—464,500 for the South; up to a million for the North—virtually ensured that casualty rates would be high.[19] It also meant that, for all the talk of war's glory, the lives and bodies of individual soldiers were largely expendable. According to historian

John Ellis, the war's mechanized wonders led to a "new emphasis . . . on the material ability to kill as many men as possible. . . . The days were now gone when it was sufficient to win one big battle to win a war."[20] Instead, generals waged long series of inconclusive firefights, some designed to do little more than bleed their enemies dry.

The resulting carnage has no parallel in the annals of American warfare. Over four years, 620,000 Americans died because of the conflict, more than in all of the twentieth-century wars combined. Although the majority of fatalities died from disease (typhoid, dysentery, yellow fever, and malaria were endemic on both sides), over 110,000 Union soldiers and 94,000 Confederates succumbed to battlefield injuries.[21] Another million men were wounded in action, many with bodily damage so disfiguring in appearance and incapacitating in function they had little hope of permanent recovery. The primitive state of medicine hardly helped matters. The *materia medica* of the average wartime physician consisted of "herbal and mineral concoctions similar to those used since the time of Hippocrates," and surgeons practiced their craft with no knowledge of bacteriology or antisepsis.[22] A half century after the war's end, famed Philadelphia surgeon William Williams Keen recalled, "We operated in old blood-stained and often pus-stained coats . . . with undisinfected hands. . . . If a sponge or an instrument fell on the floor it was washed and squeezed in a basin of tap water and used as if it were clean."[23]

It should come as no surprise that the Civil War's signature disability— the "empty sleeve"—was more a product of the surgical tent than the battlefield. Schooled in "heroic medicine," physicians on both sides were notorious for chopping first and asking questions later, the results of which could be found in the heaps of limbs that greeted visitors to Civil War field hospitals. While statistics remain imprecise, Union and Confederate sawbones performed some 60,000 full- and partial-limb amputations over the course of the war. The approximately 45,000 patients who survived their operations accounted for the largest number of war amputees in US history. However, their cultural visibility far outranked their actual numbers. Despite the fact that amputees represented a relatively small minority of Civil War casualties, they would become the public stereotype of disabled veterans over the next century.[24]

Besides their physical injuries, veterans returned home suffering the effects of mental illness and psychological trauma. Although the field of military psychiatry did not emerge until the early twentieth century, Civil War physicians could not help but notice the war's emotional toll on the men who took up arms. Diagnosed under such terms as "acute nostalgia," "nervousness," or "general insanity," Civil War–era psychiatric casualties exhibited a wide array of psychosomatic symptoms, from bodily tremors and paralysis to "soldier's heart" (severe cardiac palpitations) and a crippling longing for home. Military leaders typically viewed psychiatric casualties as "malingerers," lacking in the stamina and character necessary for the manly art of nineteenth-century warfare. Early in the war, it was Union policy to muster out "nostalgic" soldiers, leaving frightened and psychologically unstable men to wander the countryside. By 1863, the US government had converted St. Elizabeth's Hospital in Washington, DC, into the first American institution to deal exclusively with mentally ill soldiers. That same year Union forces initiated the world's first psychiatric screening program of potential recruits.[25]

But such measures did little to diminish the long-term mental anguish of the most severely traumatized men. Haunted by their wartime experiences, countless veterans endured paranoia, chronic depression, and debilitating flashbacks for years afterward. Many former soldiers practiced a crude form of psychopharmacology, turning to alcohol or commercial opiates to dull their memories of war's horrors.[26] Although most psychologically damaged men found shelter with friends and family, violent or deranged veterans were locked up in local jails or insane asylums, sometimes indefinitely. An untold number took the route of Newell Gleason, a brevet brigadier general who suffered a mental breakdown during the war, was temporarily committed to an Indiana insane asylum, and killed himself in 1886.[27]

Those who survived the fighting faced an uncertain future once discharged from service. Jobs promised in the heat of wartime fervor failed to materialize, and thousands of men were forced to rely upon local charity organizations to make ends meet.[28] By 1865, cities across the United States teemed with indigent, uniformed vets peddling almanacs, pencils, and cheaply printed regimental histories. In an era in which economic independence and good citizenship were closely aligned, jobless vets—including disabled ones—often came to be seen as "bummers, suckers, loaders, or beats." Government officials were hopeful that soldiers' postwar hardships were only temporary, and that even severely disabled men would soon transition back to their prewar lives. In its "Four Rules for Discharged Soldiers" (1865), *The Army and Navy Journal* advised "mutilated" soldiers to "learn the strategy of new muscular habits" in the wake of war-produced disability: "What you have lost in body, try and make up in energy, decision, and mental vigor." However, such admonitions could not change the social and material conditions facing disabled veterans. Even in the North, whose industrial landscape had survived the war virtually unscathed, vets returned to a crowded labor market, an economy in ruin, and "secret distrust of the soldier" on the part of many employers. Mentally vigorous or not, tens of thousands of disabled soldiers left the service economically diminished, lacking either the resources or the physical vitality to assume their culturally prescribed roles as workers and heads of households.[29]

Building the Veteran's Welfare State

Anticipating a postwar crisis, government officials and civilian experts introduced a number of plans to assist disabled veterans and their families. John Ordronaux, a professor of medical jurisprudence and author of a well-regarded book on military surgery, believed that disabled vets should help settle the West as "military agriculturalists."[30] Others favored the legal establishment of veterans' preferences in civil service employment, a practice that eventually relocated large numbers of them to the nation's capital.[31] The US Sanitary Commission, a relief society organized by Northern women, called for an informal program of community-centered relief, combining both federal pensions and family or communal care.[32] Whatever the plan, all agreed that the federal government had a moral and legal duty to compensate the men who had suffered in its defense.

In 1862, Congress took the first step to meet that duty, authorizing the provision of "general pensions" for all service-disabled Union veterans.[33] Under the 1862 scheme, pension rates for "totally disabled" men "ranged from thirty dollars per month for high-ranking officers to eight dollars for privates or common sailors."[34] Shortly thereafter, Union amputees were granted additional allowances for the purchase of braces or artificial limbs ($50 for an arm or foot, $75 for an entire leg). In 1866, the federal government extended amputees' benefits even further, providing them with free transportation to get their prosthetics fitted and replaced.[35] Confederate veterans were ineligible for any of these benefits. Considered traitors, they had to rely upon local charities and meager payouts from their individual states.

Cloaked in the mantle of scientific authority, the disability pension system was nonetheless inconsistent in its decisions, relying upon subjective criteria to determine which soldiers received federal assistance. Disabled veterans seeking government support not only had to prove their injuries were service-connected; they needed to convince federal officials of their "honorable reputations, good work ethics," and strong moral fiber. Potential pensioners were required to supply at least two character witnesses to testify on their behalf, an arduous task given the social dislocation that characterized many veterans' postwar lives.[36] Moreover, federal pension boards employed a crude, mechanistic definition of disability based upon veterans' inability to perform manual labor. Severely disabled men who earned their living by other means were often disqualified, as were African Americans and psychologically traumatized veterans whose bodies revealed no visible sign of injury.[37] In turn, pension examiners used vaguely defined social and aesthetic norms when evaluating veterans' potential for self-support, frequently citing the "disgusting" and "offensive" nature of soldiers' injuries as evidence of their disabilities.[38]

In the decades following the war's end, Union veterans organized to consolidate their gains, lobbying whomever would listen to liberalize veterans' benefits and eliminate red tape. Under pressure from the partisan Grand Army of the Republic, which urged its 400,000 members to "vote as they shot," Republican politicians passed a series of increasingly generous pension measures for war-injured veterans and their families. In 1879, the Arrears Act backdated disability claims to the date of discharge, providing thousands of vets with large cash payouts.[39] A decade later, the 1890 Dependent Pension Act extended federal benefits to all soldiers who had served a minimum of ninety days in the Union forces, effectively transforming the disability pension system into a social security network for aging vets. By 1893, the United States was spending 41.5 percent of its annual budget on the benefits of its 966,012 pensioners.[40] Even as Union veterans died off in droves, payments to wives and dependents continued unabated. Between 1918 and 1941, Civil War pensions cost American taxpayers more than three billion dollars.

By the time the United States entered World War II, it had spent more than $8 billion on Union pensions, with no end in sight.[41]

Besides monetary support, tens of thousands of Union vets received long-term shelter at state and federal soldiers' homes.[42] Conceived in the waning days of the war, the nation's largest network of soldiers' homes was the National Home for Disabled Volunteer Soldiers (NHDVS). At its peak, the NHDVS operated eight separate branches, from the flagship Central Branch outside Dayton, Ohio, to the Southern Branch near Hampton Roads, Virginia. (In keeping with the prevailing ideology of racial segregation, the latter was built as a sanctuary for African American veterans.) The finest NHDVS facilities resembled sprawling country estates with beautiful gardens, ornate architecture, and well-manicured lawns. Residents wore uniforms and were expected to follow military discipline and share a common barracks. Building and maintaining federal soldiers' homes did not come cheaply, despite the fact that veterans themselves provided for much of the upkeep. Between 1866 and 1930, when the NHDVS was consolidated into the Veterans Administration, its total cost topped $250 million. Yet most officials considered the money well spent, if only as a prophylactic measure. Constructed in rural areas, soldiers' homes were designed to shield war-injured veterans from the "temptations of city life." More important still, they served as material reminders of the nation's social contract with its former warriors.[43]

Taken together, the federal pension system and the NHDVS encompassed the United States' first large-scale response to the Problem of the Disabled Veteran. The pension system in particular represented a dramatic expansion of the veterans' welfare state, one that was meant to deliver on the mission Abraham Lincoln set forth in his Second Inaugural Address (1865): "to bind up the nation's wounds, to care for him who shall have borne the battle, and for his widow, and his orphan."[44] Among other legacies, Civil War pensions underscored "the restricted and male character of martial citizenship" and elevated disabled veterans' status as a special class of the body politic.[45] No less important, they affirmed the notion that caring for the wounded was a necessary part of national healing.

Predictably, federal programs for disabled veterans brought their fair share of critics. Skeptics worried that the massive expenditures for disabled vets could bankrupt the nation, which was already facing decades of costly Reconstruction. As the war years receded, moreover, there was a growing consensus that the federal pension system had become corrupted by greed and partisan politics. Many Americans believed that able-bodied veterans—including former "deserters," "malingers," and "bounty-jumpers"—were selfishly manipulating public sympathy for disabled vets to win benefits for themselves, a practice that threatened to undermine the public reputation of veterans as a whole. Speaking for a number of critics, congressman Henry Warner Slocum (D-NY), a former Union general and lifelong veterans' advocate, warned: "There is great danger if we allow the pension-claim agents to represent the soldiers as a body of cormorants who are discontented with what they have received, that sooner or later we shall kill the goose that lays the golden egg."[46] By the late 1890s, the excesses of the federal pension system had become a national scandal (fig. 3). In the eyes of many Americans, there was little distinction between permanently disabled soldiers and the "professional patriots" getting fat on government largesse. Although federal examiners went to great lengths to weed out deadbeats and fakers, all Civil War pensioners (even those with "visible" disabilities) were suspect cases.[47]

Stigmatizing Disability in Victorian America

Despite growing discomfort with the financial burdens of the federal disability system, many postwar Americans adopted an idealized view of disabled veterans. Steeped in chivalric myths of martial valor, they viewed war injury as a sign of manly courage and physical endurance, more prized than any medal or military commendation. Popular poetry such as W. E. Credesly's "The Tale of the One Armed" and R. L. Cary, Jr.'s "The Story of the Empty Sleeve" portrayed permanently disabled Union veterans as paragons of civic virtue and patriotic sacrifice. For their part, disabled vets often echoed such sentiments.[48] In "Good-Bye, Old Arm," a broadside published in 1866, one recovering amputee reflected on his missing limb: "Understand I don't regret its loss, it has been torn from my body that not one State should be torn from this Glorious Union."[49]

Well after the war's end, the public continued to associate wounded or disabled veterans with the highest ideals of the republic. In his bestselling 1895 novel, Stephen Crane famously celebrated soldiers' wounds as "red badges of courage," cementing the link between war injury and

FIG. 3. In one of a series of antipension covers for *Harper's Weekly*, cartoonist W. A. Rogers depicts "pension fraud" as a grossly corpulent politician crushing both a disabled veteran and Uncle Sam beneath his swollen gut. "An Intolerable Burden," *Harper's Weekly*, January 15, 1898.

manly experience for generations to come.[50] Like their Roman counterparts two millennia earlier, a number of Civil War vets—including
governors Lucius Fairchild (R-WI), Francis R. T. Nichols (D-LA), and
James H. Berry (D-AR)—traded upon their wounded-hero status to win
high political office.[51] As the hostilities of war receded, romanticized
depictions of soldiers' injuries became part of the vision of national
reconciliation (the desire to "bind up the nation's wounds") that dom-

FIG. 4. Following the Civil War, race-conscious artists used idealized images of disabled soldiers to demonstrate African American men's willingness to sacrifice on the nation's behalf. In a pair of images from August 1865, Thomas Nast contrasts white Southerners' demands for pardon with the nation's reluctance to grant African Americans the full rights of martial citizenship. Thomas Nast, "Pardon" and "Franchise," *Harper's Weekly,* August 5, 1865.

inated postwar political discourse. To quote historian Robert I. Goler, "In order to move beyond the high costs and ambiguous results of the conflict, Northern politicians [began] to focus less on the social and political differences that motivated the conflict and more on the noble sacrifice of both sides." Against a backdrop of racial antagonism, partisan anger, and environmental devastation, "the wounded veteran . . . became a ready symbol of sacrifice for the good of the nation"[52] (fig. 4).

At the same time, Civil War veterans returned home to a cultural climate that stigmatized disabled bodies, characterizing them as economically burdensome, psychologically unstable, and socially objectionable. Disability scholars have identified the mid-nineteenth century as a pivotal moment in the invention of disability as a social category and a public problem.[53] Even as the violence of industrialization was quite literally mutilating the bodies of thousands of working men and women every year, disabled people were increasingly cast as dangerous threats to public welfare and national health.

Victorians' hostility toward physical and mental disability sprang from several sources. One source was Americans' growing investment in the concept of the *normal body*. Before the Enlightenment, Western cultures had yet to establish rigid demarcations between "normal" and "abnormal" human forms. During the mid-nineteenth century, however, the rise of statistics and eugenics led to increased pressure to standardize bodily function and appearance.[54] Among Americans, the best known architect of the normal body was Dudley A. Sargent, a circus performer turned athletics director who served as director of Harvard's Hemenway Gymnasium from 1879 to 1919. Over his tenure, he measured the bodies of thousands of students, plotting his findings on easy-to-read reference tables, which young people could use to chart their physical development vis-à-vis the "normal standard."[55] Like many nineteenth-century scientists, Sargent initially equated normalcy with a statistical mean or average, in this case, the bodily attributes shared by the largest number of subjects. But as historian Douglas C. Baynton points out, the normal body very quickly lost its connotations of ordinariness; instead, it functioned as an ideal in its own right, one that "excluded only those defined as *below* average."[56]

Disabled populations were also targets of rapidly shifting ideals of health and public respectability. At a time when physicians equated total health with physical and mental wholeness, people with disabilities were frequently diagnosed as emotionally unbalanced and sexually ambiguous.[57] Henry Maudsley, a pioneer of psychosomatic medicine, observed that "the forms and habits of mutilated men approach those of women," while American neurologist S. Wier Mitchell famously described the "phantom limbs" of Civil War amputees in the gendered language of female hysteria.[58] Given such concerns, large numbers of disabled people found themselves physically and visually segregated from mainstream society (fig. 5). For some disabled people, including Garret Rozell, a Union soldier who had much of his face torn away by shell fragment at Chapin's Farm, Virginia, segregation was voluntary. Although his wounds would eventually heal, Rozell's visage was so disfigured that,

FIG. 5. Published in an August 1865 issue of *Harper's Weekly*, Winslow Homer's woodcut "Our Watering Places—The Empty Sleeve at Newport" captures the feelings of confusion and thwarted masculinity felt by many newly disabled male veterans. In the accompanying story, a returning amputee soldier struggles to come to terms with his wife's newfound independence, particularly her ability to drive the family horse and buggy. *Harper's Weekly*, August 26, 1865.

according to his pension examiner, he would remain "an object of pity, and unable to gain a living except in seclusion from society."[59] Very often, however, the aesthetically disabled had little choice in the matter. In many cities, de facto "ugly laws" prohibited unsightly citizens from defiling the public sphere with their presence. More commonly, the sick, disabled, and "insane" were confined to rural poorhouses and asylums, out of sight and out of mind.[60]

Antagonism toward disability was especially pronounced in the burgeoning white-collar commercial sectors of urban America, where the state of one's bodily façade could mean the difference between success and failure. As early as the 1860s, aspiring businessmen were encouraged to "cultivate an appearance of probity and industry" and to disguise their physical flaws whenever possible.[61] Forty years later, A. A. Marks Company, a major prosthetics manufacturer, echoed such beliefs, warning prospective clients: "Any deficiency of the body that becomes conspicuous will attract attention and invite comment and sympathy. No person who maintains his self-respect, no matter what his disability may be, cares to be constantly reminded of it, and the commiseration of others, above all things, is the most abhorrent."[62]

Though companies like A. A. Marks had an obvious financial stake in stigmatizing bodily deviance, their rhetoric was shared by a range of Victorian social critics who considered the disabled body an affront to the increasingly refined sensibilities of modern Americans. In an *Atlantic Monthly* article published at the height of the Civil War, famed physician and essayist Oliver Wendell Holmes, Sr., set the tone for a generation of Victorian moralists: "Misfortunes of a certain obtrusiveness may be pitied, but are never tolerated under the chandeliers." In an "age when *appearances are realities*," gross bodily deformities and impairments had no place in the "decent classes" of American society.[63]

Above all else, anxieties about disability were fueled by growing concerns about *economic dependency*. Before the industrial era, dependency was understood mainly in socioeconomic terms. "To be dependent," write Nancy Fraser and Linda Gordon, "was to gain one's livelihood by working for someone else. . . . Dependency, therefore, was a normal, as opposed to a deviant, condition." During the mid-nineteenth century, however, dependency came to designate a kind of "individual character trait," a marker of one's failure to meet the full demands of capitalist citizenship.[64] Economic dependency was considered particularly shameful among working-age men, who were expected to pull their own weight no matter what obstacles lay in their path.[65] By the 1890s, two broad understandings of dependency had become fully entrenched in American society: "a 'good' household dependency, predicated of children and wives, and an increasingly 'bad' (or at least dubious) charity dependency, predicated of recipients of relief."[66]

Where did disabled veterans fit within this dynamic? For hundreds of thousands of men, the answer was not always clear. Veterans' groups like the Grand Army of the Republic proved highly successful at persuading policy makers to distinguish disabled vets from other "dependent" populations. Indeed, even at the height of the pension scandal, few Americans challenged the underlying social contract of the veterans' welfare state: the exchange of bodies and minds in times of war for monetary and institutional assistance in times of peace.

Nevertheless, disabled veterans were not safe from social stigma. To a growing number of observers, ex-soldiers' reliance upon government assistance figured them as inadequately independent and, by extension, insufficiently manly. Although revered as icons of masculinity in their own right, many disabled veterans lacked the physical stamina or economic resources to set up households on their own. As triumphal memories of the war began to wane, the aging residents of federal soldiers' homes appeared less like permanent warriors and more like public wards. In an era that conflated economic autonomy and good citizenship, the dependency of disabled veterans—upon the state, their relatives, and their communities—threatened to undermine their status as national heroes.

Rationalizing Injury

For all of war's destruction, many Americans and Europeans remained confident that the Civil War's legacy of disabled bodies would prove to be the exception and not the rule. Beginning in the mid-nineteenth century, physicians, arms manufacturers, industrialists, and social scientists led a concerted effort to develop what might be described as a *rationalist* approach to war injury, one that sought to predict, manage, even curtail, the crippling effects of combat-related trauma.[67] Symptomatic of a larger project to reconcile the human body to the speed and violence of industrial modernity, the rationalization of war injury was premised on two broad principles. The first was that *war was knowable*, and that with knowledge came control. Poets might speak of war's "chaos," but modern combat was the sum of discrete processes and patterns— the physics of a bullet's trajectory, the biology of wound infection, the phenomenology of human terror—which, once understood empirically, could be bent to serve their masters' ends. The second principle was that the injuring of soldiers' bodies in wartime was a *mass* phenomenon. Eschewing romanticized visions of the combat experience, which often represented war injuries in individualized terms, a rising class of Victorian wound experts viewed collective and indiscriminate injury as the sine qua non of modern combat. It did not matter if individual soldiers were brave or cowardly, fanatically committed, or merely desperate to survive: on the machine-age battlefield, men were bound to get hit.

Victorians' confidence in their ability to limit the aftereffects of war injury stemmed from several sources, chief among them advancements in antisepsis and military medicine. Joseph Lister's development of antiseptic surgery in the late 1860s ushered in a new era of wound treatment, saving the lives of countless fighting men. Seventeen centuries after Galen praised suppuration—the appearance of milky-white "laudable pus"—as a welcome part of the healing process, physicians adopted a variety of measures to contain and even eliminate the spread of infection, the main cause of postoperative fatalities. The results were nothing short of revolutionary. Armed with the germ theory of disease, surgeons increasingly denounced conservative techniques such as amputation in favor of more radical practices to save soldiers' limbs. Although some military physicians resisted the "clean surgery" movement, deaths from hospital gangrene and other pre-antiseptic scourges dropped dramatically in the second half of the nineteenth century. By 1900, additional advances in wound examination, electronic bullet location, and X-ray imaging, as well as pharmacology and sanitation, made it possible for soldiers to survive—and in some cases fully recover from—injuries that would have been fatal only a few decades earlier.[68] For the first time in history, it seemed that humans' capacity to heal was catching up with their aptitude to destroy.

No less encouraging were the remarkable designs produced by American prosthetics manufacturers eager to tap the growing market of disabled soldiers and industrial workers. Between 1861 and 1873, the prosthetic industry exploded in the United States, as American companies introduced dozens of artificial limbs, feet, hands, and eyes.[69] In their promotional materials, limb makers presented their products as marvels of technological and aesthetic ingenuity, scientifically calibrated (and mass produced) to restore amputees to a state of social and mechanical normalcy. Less than a decade after the Civil War's end, physician Stephen Smith remarked of the newest prosthetics: "In our time, limb-making has been carried to such a state of perfection that both in form and function they so completely resemble the natural extremity that those who wear them pass unobserved and unrecognized in walks of business and pleasure."[70] Designed both for appearance and mobility, the latest generation of prosthetics promised disabled veterans something that no prewar peg leg ever could: the fiction of wholeness. As a result, growing numbers of Victorians viewed the prosthetically re-engineered bodies of war amputees as evidence of technological progress—visible proof of industry's power to put back together what modern weaponry had rent asunder.[71]

Parallel efforts to limit war-related disability were taking place in the field of wound ballistics, the study of the physiological trauma produced by modern projectile weapons.[72] Achieving quasi-scientific status in the mid-nineteenth century, the field was led by a small cohort of European and American military physicians, surgeons, and arms manufacturers eager to fine-tune the production of bodily damage. Much of their research involved firing ammunition into gelatin, human cadavers, or the carcasses of recently slaughtered horses or dogs (in some cases, live animal targets were also used). Through statistical analysis of the resulting trauma, ballisticians sought to determine the immediate and long-term impact of different armaments on various parts of the body.[73] Two issues were of special concern: the "explosive effect" of high-velocity projectiles on human tissue and the "stopping power" of modern weaponry (i.e., the combination of mass and velocity necessary to knock an opponent *hors de combat*). Steeped in Victorian race science, most ballisticians believed that the indigenous populations of Africa, Asia, and South America lacked the refined "nervous systems" of whites and, thus, were undeterred by even the most horrific of wounds. As one leading ballistics expert explained, "'Stopping power' in a rifle-bullet is only a real necessity in a fight against a fanatical savage enemy, who will advance as long as he is physically capable of doing so; the civilised soldier does not act in a similar manner, and 'stopping power' in Continental warfare is only required against cavalry and artillery horses."[74]

Ultimately, ballistics experts hoped to capitalize on the perceived sensitivity of Anglo-European combatants by developing a new line of "humane" armaments, weapons designed to limit the bodily trauma of combat casualties. The desire to produce humane armaments arose as an outgrowth of a broader cultural fantasy to "civilize" war among Western industrialized nations. Anticipating a day when arbitration would supplant armed combat as the primary means of conflict resolution, industrialists, social philosophers, and others hailed the development of "less lethal" ordnance as a tremendous leap forward for international cooperation and world peace.[75] Receiving special praise were the latest generation of high-velocity, "self-cauterizing" bullets which—if they did not kill a soldier on impact—were thought to leave only clean, symmetrical wounds with little chance of permanent damage. In future wars, predicted Paul Bruns, a prominent German authority on war injury, "cure will be easier, and fewer men will be mutilated and crippled."[76]

In the United States, the central clearinghouse on the science of war injury was the Army Medical Museum in Washington, DC.[77] Founded by surgeon general William Hammond in 1862, the museum was the first American institution to document, inventory, and analyze battlefield injuries on a mass scale. Its first curator, John Hill Brinton, was assigned the grim task of collecting medical specimens from nearby battlefields and shipping them back to Washington in kegs of diluted whiskey or brine. In addition to amputated limbs, ruptured organs, and skeletal remains, the museum's early holdings included medical paraphernalia, surgeons' field notes, weapons, and projectiles removed from the bodies of the wounded. At the war's end, the museum was relocated to the newly remodeled Ford's Theatre, scene of Abraham Lincoln's assassination, where it became something of a national shrine. As one curator declared somberly in 1871: "What nobler monument could the nation erect to [Lincoln's] memory than this somber treasure-house, devoted to the study of disease and injury, mutilation and death?"[78]

Its morbid appeal notwithstanding, the Army Medical Museum lent an air of scientific credibility to the emerging federal bureaucracy dedicated to parceling out benefits—medical and otherwise—to disabled vets. Working closely with the Surgeon General's Record and Pension Office, located just two floors below the exhibition space, museum staff produced thousands of photographs and clinical illustrations of Civil War veterans' injuries (fig. 6), which were then copied and distributed to medical schools and military installations across the Western world.[79] More important still, the museum's collections formed the backbone of one of the most exhaustive medical research projects of the nineteenth century: the 6,000-page *Medical and Surgical History of the War of the Rebellion* (1870–1888). Tracking some veterans' cases for nearly two decades, the *History* scrupulously recorded the injuries, treatments, and follow-up evaluations of thousands of Civil War casualties, including Thomas H. Graham. A trove of patients' testimonies, anatomical description, and medical photography, the *History* represented the first attempt to capture, and render intelligible, the totality of modern war's human trauma for the benefit of future generations. It was also a tribute

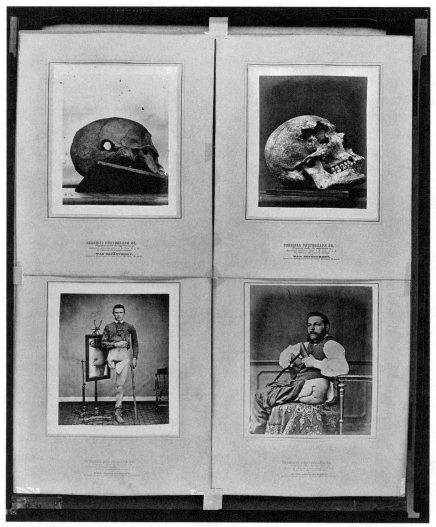

FIG. 6. Photography played a vital role in nineteenth-century efforts to understand—and ultimately manage—the production and long-term effects of war injury. Prepared by the Army Medical Museum, these surgical images (c. 1861–65) document the skulls of two fatal casualties, including that of Edward Volk (*upper right*), and two soldiers with amputated legs: Eben Smith (*lower left*) and John Schranz (*lower right*). Library of Congress, Prints & Photographs Division, LC-DIG-ppmsca-10106.

to the growing belief that, one day, the United States might be able to eliminate combat-related disability altogether.

Progressive Militarism and Its Discontents

Although the United States avoided wars of national mobilization between 1865 and 1917, the future of modern warfare was never far from the national consciousness. Throughout the final decades of the nineteenth century, scarcely a month went by when US soldiers, sailors, and marines were not called upon to take up arms in the nation's name. Little of this activity resembled war in the traditional sense. US troops were deployed as strikebreakers, emergency aid workers, and—in the reconstructed South—de facto police. The most prolonged military conflict took place along the nation's western frontier. Between 1865 and 1891, the US Army fought in ten campaigns against Native American populations, engaging with Indian forces on 1,067 separate occasions and, in the process, effectively ending five centuries of violent resistance to white settlement.[80] At the same time, US troops began to flex their military muscles overseas, conducting punitive campaigns in such faraway places as Kangwa Island, Korea (1871). Meanwhile, intense press coverage of armed conflicts in France, South Africa, and elsewhere spurred highly publicized debates about the "nature and place of war in the modern world."[81] By the century's end, two visions of armed conflict circulated widely in American culture. One minimized future traumas and portrayed modern warfare as a path to physical and spiritual regeneration. The other predicted modern war would soon become so destructive it would be impossible to pursue in good faith.

The first vision is associated with the rise of militarism in Western societies. Originating as a pejorative in the mid-nineteenth century, *militarism* can be best understood as a catchall description for the impingement of military ideals and practices on foreign policy and public life.[82] Scholars of nineteenth-century militarism have tended to emphasize its antimodern tendencies—namely, its nostalgic celebration of chivalry and the warrior ideal. Yet, as it came to be promoted by American and European elites, militarism had a decidedly progressive cast, closely aligned with ideas of civilization, modernization, and industrial order.[83] In his essay "The Place of War in the Civilization of the Twentieth Century" (1900), Teunis S. Hamlin echoed many Progressive-era militarists, who argued that war continued to serve as a necessary, albeit painful, means of spreading Western values to the "uncivilized" world. Citing two contemporary conflicts, he noted: "Present wars in the Philippines and in South Africa [between the British government and Boer settlers] will establish pure, righteous and stable government over peoples that have never known these blessings. Could any other means than war bring these beneficent results? The history of all high civilization on the globe seems to answer, No."[84]

By far the most vocal supporters of American militarism were a small group of expansionist-minded politicians and thinkers, including such Progressive-era luminaries as naval theorist Alfred Thayer Mahan, statesman John Hay, Senator Henry Cabot Lodge, and secretary of war Elihu Root.[85] Yet militarist attitudes proliferated well beyond a handful of bellicose nationalists. In the decades following the Civil War, a diverse cohort of philosophers, theologians, social critics, and ideologues embraced the idea that war or military life could play a positive role in America's future. Above all else, militarists asserted that overseas fighting could serve as a tonic for physical and psychic renewal—bitter tasting, perhaps, but necessary if the United States hoped to maintain long-term national health.

In their public statements, militarists made little effort to disguise their martial enthusiasm. Outlining war's benefits in the *North American Review* (1891), Stephen B. Luce, the "father" of the modern US Navy, breathlessly proclaimed, "War arouses all the latent energies of a people, stimulates them to the highest exertion, and develops their mental and material resources." A purifying "malady" sent from heaven above, war had all the features of a sociopolitical colonic: "It stimulates national growth, solves otherwise insoluble problems of domestic and political economy, and purges a nation of its humors."[86] Along similar lines, militarists celebrated war as a necessary antidote to the degenerate influence of peacetime society. Among many late nineteenth-century writers, peace was synonymous with national stagnation, effeteness, and physical decline. Militarists frequently cast their critiques of peace in the racialized discourses of social Darwinism and Victorian anthropology, both of which attributed to different nations or "civilizations" varying degrees of racial development. At their most alarmist, American militarists promoted a vision of the United States (and the Western world in general) on the verge of racial and spiritual collapse. Without the regular exercise that only war could provide, they argued, the body politic would become corrupted, neurasthenic, and impotent.[87]

For the individual soldier, war was said to offer numerous benefits, none more potent than the adrenaline-fueled euphoria that only came in the heat of battle. As Horace Porter explained in his widely read "The Philosophy of Courage" (1888): "In the excitement of a charge, or in the enthusiasm of approaching victory, there is a sense of pleasure which no one should attempt to underrate."[88] Other war supporters played up the numerous physical or remasculinizing rewards of military service. Some physicians, for instance, believed that even the briefest periods of soldiering produced stronger, more vigorous men than decades of civilian abundance. Summarizing this view in an 1892 issue of *Forum* magazine, John S. Billings argued, "No form of mechanical labor, and still less of clerical or mercantile employment, is so well adapted to [build healthy male physiques] as the systematic training of the body produced by military drill and discipline."[89] The fact that, beginning in the 1890s, military service might involve stints overseas only added to its body-hardening appeal. While American servicemen justifiably complained about the poor food, tempestuous weather, and personal hardships associated with foreign assignments, militarists idealized overseas war-making as an opportunity to recreate the hardened, frontier bodies of the United States' mythic past.

To militarism's critics, modern war was not a path to individual and national regeneration—it was a recipe for disability and death on an unprecedented scale. Like its pro-war counterpart, the antimilitarist camp represented a mixture of constituencies, from traditional isolationists and anti-imperialists to socialists, women's groups, and peace-oriented internationalists.[90] Rising in prominence at the beginning of the twentieth century, they were united not only by a deep skepticism about war as an instrument of US foreign policy, but also by an acute awareness of modern warfare's devastation of combatants' bodies and minds.

One of the hallmarks of turn-of-the-century antimilitarist discourse was its emphasis on the human costs of industrialized warfare.[91] Eager to combat militarist cheerleading, antiwar writers, artists, and religious figures sought to publicize the broken bodies America's military endeavors inevitably left behind. Speaking before the annual convention of the

Protestant Episcopal Diocese of New York in October 1898, the Reverend Henry C. Potter saw the future of the "race for empire" not in the United States' newly won imperial possessions but in the "gaunt and physically wrecked sons and brothers by tens of thousands at home."[92] Pacifist eugenicists such as Canadian writer William Restelle advanced similar arguments, pointing to the poor health of war's survivors (combatants and noncombatants alike) as a reason to curb militarist tendencies. "Far from perfecting a fine physique in the race," Restelle observed in 1906, modern warfare led to racial and national "degeneration." According to Restelle and others, industrialized war was tantamount to race suicide, destroying the "best blood of the nation" while leaving the "idle, the incompetent, the immoral, [and] the diseased" alive to repopulate the body politic. Unless such conflicts were abolished, eugenicists argued, Western nations would devolve into cesspools of deviance and widespread disability.[93]

In their campaigns to debunk war's allure, American and European antimilitarists frequently drew upon the writings of Polish banker and industrialist Jean de Bloch. A conservative critic of modern war, Bloch published the most influential antiwar tract of his era, *The Future of Wars* (1898), a six-volume treatise on the looming "impossibility" of industrialized warfare.[94] More so than any of his contemporaries, Bloch offered readers a horrifying vision of modern war, one devoid of any semblance of heroism or romance. As he saw it, war had become "more and more a matter of mechanical arrangement. Modern battles will be decided, so far as they can be decided at all, by men lying in improvised ditches which they have scooped out to protect themselves from the fires of a distant and invisible enemy." A decade and a half before the start of World War I, Bloch predicted that military conflicts between industrialized nations would devolve into protracted scenes of mass butchery. He also divined an unhappy fate for the next generation of cannon fodder. Not only would future wars see a sharp rise in the number of soldiers killed or seriously wounded on the battlefield, but the wholesale adoption of long-range artillery, smokeless powder, and high-power rifles by industrialized armies would make it nearly impossible to escape the battlefield unscathed.[95] For all his pessimism, Jean de Bloch remained hopeful that the era of "Great Wars" was near its end. Like many in the antimilitarist camp, he was confident that, when presented with the specter of mass casualties, the "civilized" nations of the West would abolish war as a matter of foreign policy.[96] In his mind, the "dimensions of modern armaments" and the political realities of modern states had combined to make decisive warfare between Western nations "impossible except at the price of suicide."[97] Still, he conceded that not all forms of military conflict would be relegated to the dustbin of history. Given the irreconcilable racial and ethnic differences between the civilized West and its seemingly backward neighbors, industrialized nations would fight "frontier brawls" and conduct punitive operations against "semi-barbarous peoples" for years to come.[98]

"The Splendid Little War"

Both sides got a glimpse of what the future of American war might entail during the United States' twin conflicts with imperial Spain. Dubbed a "splendid little war" by future secretary of state John Hay, the Spanish-American War (April 21 to August 21, 1898) began after the USS *Maine*, a battleship sent to Havana to safeguard American expatriates, mysteriously exploded on February 15, 1898, killing more than 260 crewmembers.[99] Madrid denied responsibility, and President McKinley, himself a Civil War veteran, was initially reluctant to commit US troops. However, calls for revenge, amplified in the yellow press, soon proved impossible to ignore. On April 21, the US Navy began its blockade of Cuba, and Spain officially declared war on the United States two days later. After weeks of preparation, the hastily mobilized force of US regulars and volunteers landed on Cuban soil in late June, quickly overcoming Spanish troops first at Las Guásimas on June 24 and then, eight days later, at El Caney, San Juan Hill, and Kettle Hill. By July 16, Santiago capitulated, the Spanish fleet was in shambles, and the war in Cuba was effectively over.

At the time, many military professionals and popular commentators touted the Spanish-American War as a medical triumph—and an example of how much war had progressed since the killing grounds of Gettysburg and Antietam. American troops suffered only 379 combat-related deaths, and thanks to the introduction of antiseptic field dressings and surgical techniques, the mortality rate of wounded soldiers (6.7 per 100) was less than half of what it had been during the Civil War.[100] One reporter noted, "The man who is struck receives a clean-cut wound which, while it disables him for fighting, heals quick and leaves him in a few weeks almost as sound as new."[101] No less promising was the fact that the hastily assembled volunteers appeared healthier and more physically uniform than earlier generations of fighting men. Prior to enlistment, the US military weeded out thousands of would-be recruits, including men with poor eyesight, "faulty physiques," epilepsy, venereal disease, and other potentially disabling conditions.[102] The soldiers who left for Cuba were, in one observer's words, a "splendid spectacle of physical symmetry and proportion"—the ultimate embodiment of national health.[103]

However, as the campaign evolved from military conquest to imperial occupation, militarist fantasies about less-lethal warfare began to fade. In the aftermath of the main fighting in Cuba, American forces systematically claimed what was left of Spain's crumbling empire, including Guam, Puerto Rico, and the Philippine Islands, where a second conflict erupted between US troops and Filipino nationalists in February 1899. Unwilling to exchange Spanish colonialism with the purportedly more benign model offered by the Americans, Filipino revolutionaries led by Emilio Aguinaldo waged a three-year guerilla war against the US occupiers. This time the fight was far from easy. By the time president Theodore Roosevelt declared the United States "victorious" on July 4, 1902, roughly 4,200 Americans had been killed in the fighting.[104] The Filipino dead numbered more than 200,000, a figure that would continue to rise as indigenous Moros of the southern Philippines periodically clashed with US troops over the next decade.[105]

To war's advocates, the Spanish-American War's legacy of disability and disease proved equally unsettling. Because of ineffectual planning and a tacit faith in their own invulnerability, US forces made little provision for blankets, medical supplies, or food for their wounded and dying. In Cuba, 2,565 American servicemen died from typhoid fever, malaria, yellow fever, and other tropical diseases—seven times the number killed by Spanish bullets. Countless more suffered the lingering effects of wartime illness for months, years, even decades after the Spanish surrender.[106] Moreover, the damage produced by modern armaments—including high-power bullets traveling faster than the speed of sound—struck many observers as anything but "humane."[107] Military spokesmen attempted to downplay the war's legacy of disability and its implications for future military adventures (fig. 7).[108] Nevertheless, for those hoping to sell a vi-

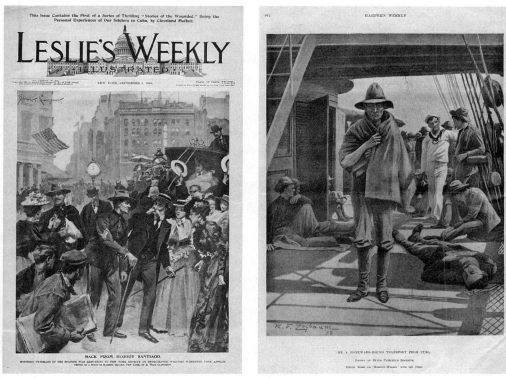

FIG. 7. Following the Spanish-American War, popular magazines conveyed mixed messages about the conflict's legacy of disability and disease. For example, B. West Clinedinst (*left*) paints wounded soldiers as heroic figures, deserving of public accolades and female admiration. By contrast, Rufus Fairchild Zogbaum (*right*) highlights the degenerative effects of overseas warfare. In this particular image, Zogbaum sketches a disease-ridden "living Lazarus" on his way home from Cuba. Clinedinst, "Back from Bloody Santiago," *Leslie's Weekly Illustrated*, September 1, 1898; and Zogbaum, "On a Homeward-Bound Transport from Cuba," *Harper's Weekly*, September 17, 1898.

sion of benign military intervention, devoid of casualties and long-term health problems, the Spanish-American War did not fit the bill.[109]

"Unhappy, Most Unhappy"

When the nineteenth century began, disabled veterans were marginal figures in American life. By the century's end, the twin forces of industrialization and imperialism had transformed the face of American war and the lives of the soldiers who survived it. To complement its expanding overseas empire, the United States boasted a massive pension roll, a network of federally funded soldiers' homes, and a cohort of scientists eager to "rationalize" the production of war injury. In many Americans' eyes, the growing attention given to those with "honorable scars" was a sign of national progress, undisputed evidence of a generous social contract between citizens and the state. Yet a growing number of observers worried that rising rates of war-related disability portended a looming crisis. Left unchecked, they warned, war's wounded survivors would threaten the United States' economic and political health for decades to come.

Even the Spanish-American War's most visible hero, Theodore Roosevelt, was deeply torn about the implications of US casualties for the nation's future. TR rose to fame as the leader of the Rough Riders, the voluntary cavalry regiment whose dramatic assault on San Juan Heights helped cement the US victory over imperial Spain. Despite his fierce hatred of all forms of physical disability, a hangover from his asthmatic childhood, Roosevelt fetishized war injury as emblematic of manly courage and patriotic valor. Like his fictional contemporary, Henry Fleming, the hero of Stephen Crane's *The Red Badge of Courage*, TR openly envied the battle scars of his fellow comrades, telling one reporter: "I have always been unhappy, most unhappy, that I was not severely wounded in Cuba . . . in some . . . striking and disfiguring way."[110]

Throughout the rest of his life, Roosevelt's writings and speeches reflected a similar attitude toward "disfiguring" war wounds and the men who sustained them. In his best-selling war memoir, *The Rough Riders* (1899), TR waxed poetic about the "self-reliant spirit" of the wounded soldiers under his command.[111] However, even in the flush of victory, Roosevelt recognized the threat modern warfare could pose to both the nation's military effectiveness and the long-term health of American society. Shortly after Santiago's surrender, he wrote highly publicized letters to his commanders demanding the removal of US troops from yellow fever areas and raging against the military's failure to attend to the basic needs of US casualties.[112] Once home, the Progressive reformer began to outline measures to help disabled veterans fully reintegrate into postwar society. "When these men come home, or at least when those of them who escape death come home," Roosevelt would later write of the next generation of disabled vets, "I believe that they will demand, and I know that they ought to demand, a juster type of life, socially and industrially, in this country." Unwilling to relegate disabled veterans to a life of dependency, TR called for the wholesale "training of the disabled and the crippled returning soldiers, so that they may become, not objects of charity, but self-supporting citizens."[113]

Roosevelt's experiences in the Spanish-American War eventually led him to become a spokesman for the soldier's rehabilitation movement during World War I. Equally important, it left him convinced that, if the United States hoped to retain its status as a military power, it could not ignore the legacy of injured bodies that modern warfare left in its wake. In TR's mind, disabled veterans were heroes for sure, but they were also potential powder kegs of social unrest that had to be defused at all costs.

Arthur Guy Empey

For American readers during World War I, no contemporary account offered a more compelling portrait of life on the Western Front than Arthur Guy Empey's autobiography, *"Over the Top," by an American Soldier Who Went* (1917).[1] Disgusted by his own country's refusal to enter the Great War, Empey had joined the British army in 1916, eventually serving with the Royal Fusiliers in northwestern France. Invalided out of service a year later, the former New Jersey National Guardsman became an instant celebrity, electrifying US audiences with his tales from the front lines. Despite nearly dying on several occasions, Empey looked back on his time in the trenches with profound nostalgia. "War is not a pink tea," he reflected, "but in a worthwhile cause like ours, mud, rats, cooties, shells, wounds, or death itself, are far outweighed by the deep sense of satisfaction felt by the man who does his bit."[2]

Beneath the surface of Empey's rollicking narrative, however, was a far more disturbing story. For all of the author's giddy enthusiasm, Empey made little effort to hide the Great War's insatiable consumption of soldier's bodies, including his own. During a nighttime raid on a German trench, Empey was shot in the face at close range, the bullet smashing his cheekbones just below his left eye. As he staggered back toward his own lines, he discovered the body of an English soldier hanging on coil of barbed wire: "I put my hand on his head, the top of which had been blown off by a bomb. My fingers sank into the hole. I pulled my hand back full of blood and brains, then I went crazy with fear and horror and rushed along the wire until I came to our lane." Before reaching shelter, Empey was wounded twice more in the left shoulder, the second time causing him to black out. He awoke to find himself choking on his own blood, a "big flap from the wound in my cheek . . . hanging over my mouth." Empey spent the next thirty-six hours in no man's land waiting for help.[3]

As he recuperated in England, Empey's mood swung between exhilaration and deep depression: "The wound in my face had almost healed and I was a horrible-looking sight—the left cheek twisted into a knot, the eye pulled down, and my mouth pointing in a north by northwest direction. I was very down-hearted and could imagine myself during the rest of my life being shunned by all on account of the repulsive scar." Although reconstructive surgery did much to restore his prewar appearance, Empey never recovered entirely. Like hundreds of thousands of Americans who followed him, he was forever marked by his experiences on the Western Front.[4]

"THE HORROR FOR WHICH WE ARE WAITING"
Anxieties of Injury in World War I

> We have not yet had, thanks to the God of Battles, a casualty list. That is
> the horror for which we are waiting, knowing it will soon come. And when
> it comes it will electrify the country into an energy capable of all the things
> of which America is capable.[1]
> — Charles Dana Gibson (January 1918)

Beginning in August 1914, World War I marked the start of a new era in
the history of war-produced disability, both in the United States and
around the globe. Known as the Great War, the conflict exposed Western nations' willingness to abandon all pretense of moderation on the
battlefield. Having perfected the techniques of mechanized destruction
in colonial settings, European armies quickly turned the machinery of
genocide—poison gas, automatic weaponry, aerial bombing—upon
themselves, with devastating results. More than 600,000 combatants
were killed in the first four months alone: some obliterated entirely, va-
porized in the artillery barrages that preceded infantry assaults; others
violently dismembered, their once seemingly impenetrable physiques
mutilated beyond recognition.[2] Those who survived their initial traumas
returned home to nations ill equipped to provide for their long-term
care. By the close of 1916, many believed that modernity's technosci-
entific triumphs—railroads, telegraphs, automated assembly lines, industrial discipline, medicine—had made possible a future of unprecedented human destruction.[3] With its mountains of corpses and endless
production of disabled bodies, the Great War was more than a military
conflict. It was, in one US observer's words, "the greatest holocaust the
world [had] ever known."[4]

Among the enduring myths of World War I is the notion that Americans had little sense of the bloodshed awaiting them across the Atlantic.

To quote historian Page Smith, US citizens had "only the most superficial notion of the grimmer realities of the war. Stories of German atrocities abounded . . . but little or nothing of the reality of men in combat, in part because it was in fact incommunicable, but even more because the Allied propaganda agencies did not wish to have it communicated."[5] In the immediate aftermath of World War I, former war supporters, including some ex-soldiers, would invoke similar arguments to disavow their own complicity in the Great War and, in turn, justify their subsequent disillusion.

Yet the American people were hardly the innocents of popular imagination—at least not when it came to the Great War's human carnage. From the conflict's opening shots until well after the Armistice was signed, injured soldiers occupied a conspicuous place in American life. Eager to glimpse war's horrors, Americans poured over newspaper casualty reports, flocked to injury-themed movies, and engaged in heated debates about war-related injury and its implications for America's future. Such debates would help set the parameters by which the Problem of the Disabled Veteran would be understood over the course of the twentieth century. On one side were critics of US military intervention, including antiwar artists and isolationist-minded politicians who sought to highlight the bodily dangers facing US fighting men; on the other, a nebulous coalition of former soldiers, self-professed experts, and military officials eager to downplay the Great War's consumption of combatants' bodies.

With the United States' official entrance into World War I in April 1917, the nation's propaganda ministry, the Committee on Public Information (CPI), emerged as the loudest voice in the wartime disability debate. Charged with transforming a brutally fought, ideologically ambiguous, and decidedly unromantic war of attrition into a noble crusade to save civilization, CPI officials deployed a massive media apparatus to assuage—and exploit—Americans' anxieties about war-produced disability. But even at the height of the government's propaganda campaign, there was little consensus about the meaning of combat injury or the likely fate of war's sickened or disabled survivors. Were war wounds material proof of courage under fire, or were they evidence of modern warfare's indiscriminate brutality? Was technology making war "safer" for America's fighting men, or did it only accelerate the production of mutilated bodies? Should civilians feel pity for disabled veterans, or should they elevate them above those who escaped the war unscathed?

Embodied Isolationism

At the time the Great War began, tens of thousands of Americans could not wait to get in on the action. As early as August 1914, hordes of journalists, filmmakers, military and medical observers, and would-be heroes were already scrambling for passage overseas. Joining them was a vanguard of youthful volunteers, most recruited from New England prep schools and Ivy League universities, eager to take part in the "Great Adventure" awaiting them across the Atlantic. This early cohort would be largely responsible for establishing the narrative of romance turned disillusion that continues to dominate American accounts of World War I. Future "lost generation" writers John Dos Passos, E. E. Cummings, and Ernest Hemingway drove ambulances; other volunteers, including as many as 25,000 women, handed out care packages or bandaged war wounds in hospitals and Red Cross clinics.[6] A smaller contingent enlisted in the French Foreign Legion or the famed Escadrille Américaine (later renamed the Lafayette Escadrille), a squadron of American pilots with the French Aviation Service. Although many volunteers expressed deep sympathy for Great Britain and France, some were remarkably ambivalent about which side to choose. "It mattered little to me which of the warring nations I would join," admitted one American aviator, "and finally I chose to throw in my lot with the army possessing the largest number of aeroplanes."[7]

The vast majority of Americans proved to be reluctant warriors, however. Underlying much of the antiwar sentiment in the early war years was a renewed faith in military isolationism, the notion that the United States should avoid being drawn into foreign conflicts.[8] The nation's recent imperial adventures notwithstanding, many Americans believed that policies of neutrality and nonintervention were key to the United States' national security and long-term health.[9] As the war progressed, critics of US intervention increasingly framed their arguments in bodily terms, relying upon tropes of injury and disability to highlight the dangers of overseas combat. In a conflict where tens of thousands could be wounded in a single day, a growing number of Americans felt that isolationism was the only sure-fire way of protecting the nation's youth from the fate of their European counterparts. More than a political philosophy, isolationism came to seen as kind of prophylactic measure, a necessary strategy for protecting the nation's boys from war's inevitable sickness and slaughter.

Fueling Americans' fears was the flood of injury-filled war reports streaming in from across the Atlantic. Thanks to advancements in transoceanic communication, curious spectators in the United States could follow the conflict more or less as it happened, a phenomenon that would radically transform Americans' attitudes toward combat casualties throughout the twentieth century. Though much of the news US audiences received was either heavily censored or propagandistic in design, the conflict's spectacle of human misery proved overwhelming. Writing his congressman in 1917, Michael Joseph Curley, a Roman Catholic bishop from Florida, raged against the Great War's obscene waste of human life. For three years, he lamented, the "flower of Europe's manhood [had been] laid low, mangled, shattered, unrecognizable, consumed by flame, riddled by shot and shell, hurdled and huddled by tens of thousands into graves far from loved ones."[10] As many Americans saw it, the onset of World War I presented the United States with a stark choice: embrace isolationism or sentence American boys to disability and death.

This discourse of *embodied isolationism* found its most visceral expression in the work of antiwar filmmakers and writers, many of whom commanded large audiences in the years prior to US intervention. Convinced that showing the "male body in fragments" would keep the United States out of World War I, war's critics inundated American audiences with nightmarish scenes of bodily destruction, filling their wartime polemics, short stories, poetry, and films with pitiful *mutilés* and mangled corpses.[11] In 1914, future American Socialist Party presidential nominee George Ross Kirkpatrick set the tone, republishing *War— What For?* (1910), an encyclopedic survey of war's horrors replete with gruesome descriptions and photographs from earlier conflicts in South Africa and Manchuria.[12] Other war skeptics quickly followed suit, bolstering their cris de coeur against military adventurism with shocking images of dismembered combatants. Written to illuminate the causes of the Great War for American audiences, Henry T. Schnittkind's stage play *Shambles: A Sketch of the Present War* (1915), for example, chronicled the return of a dying, legless veteran to his family home, the man's mangled body contrasting sharply with romanticized visions of war's glory.[13] In 1916, Thomas Ince struck a similar chord in his pacifist epic *Civilization*, a film often credited with helping to re-elect Woodrow Wilson on his platform of nonintervention.[14] Best known today for its elaborate fantasy sequences—including one in which the film's protagonist, an inventor and submarine commander, descends into hell to witness the suffering wrought by war—Ince's cinematic fable combined religious symbolism with graphic scenes of bodily destruction, a formula that would be repeated by antiwar and isolationist polemicists for decades to follow.

That same year, Ellen N. La Motte, a professional nurse from Baltimore who had served at a privately established surgical hospital near Ypres, published the ultimate testimonial to war's bodily destruction: *The Backwash of War: The Human Wreckage of the Battlefield as Witnessed by an American Hospital Nurse* (1916). Unlike most wartime accounts of hospital work, La Motte's book did not sentimentalize the wounded or the American women working on their behalf. Instead, it presented a searing portrait of the Great War's human detritus, detailing the anguish of suicidal shell-shock victims, multiple-limb amputees, and other "weak, hideous, repellent" young men whose lives had been permanently transformed by war injury. Reprinted several times before it was banned in August 1918, *The Backwash of War* forced readers to confront one of modern warfare's darkest truths: that "the science of healing stood baffled before the science of destroying."[15] More important, the book's fourteen vignettes gave Americans a glimpse of what would happen to their own sons if the United States joined the fight.

Not all war observers shared La Motte's pessimism. Throughout the war years, vocal supporters of military preparedness and US intervention continued to celebrate what George Mosse has called the "myth of the war experience," the belief that war's emotional and spiritual rewards far outweigh its risks of injury and death.[16] Though they occasionally paid lip-service to the cliché that "War is hell," pro-war forces sought to shift the nation's focus away from war's material consequences—the disfigurement, sickness, and disability experienced by countless fighting men—to its immaterial dividends—fraternity, psychic regeneration, and personal fulfillment. Western novelist Owen Wister called World War I the "greatest spiritual opportunity" its participants would ever encounter, a sentiment that would be repeated in recruitment posters, pamphlets, and public speeches throughout the spring and summer of 1917.[17] Wister's friend and fellow martial enthusiast, Theodore Roosevelt, whose youngest son Quentin would be killed in northern France in 1918, was no less effusive. At the onset of the conflict, TR mused, "our gross ideals were shattered and the scales fell from our eyes, and we saw things as they really were. Suddenly in the awful presence of death we grew to understand the true values of life."[18]

Anxieties over the bodily cost of intervention came to a head on April 2, 1917, when Woodrow Wilson stood before a packed special session of Congress and made his case for war against imperial Germany. Convinced that US neutrality was no longer an option, Wilson asked the American people to "spend [their] blood" not for "conquest" but in defense of political principles: democracy, self-determination, and "the privilege of men everywhere to choose their way of life and of obedience."[19] Although no disabled veterans spoke out during the three-day debate that followed, the specter of mass casualties loomed large over the proceedings. Nebraska Republican George W. Norris, one of only six senators to vote against the war resolution, urged his colleagues to weigh the president's abstractions against the "terrible consequences" of entering such an "unholy and unrighteous" conflict. Mass death and bloodshed were just the beginning, he thundered. "Upon the passage of this resolution, we will have joined Europe in the great catastrophe and taken America into entanglements that will not end with this war, but will live and bring their evil influences upon many generations yet unborn."[20]

In the House, a hotbed of Republican isolationist sentiment, opponents of intervention were even more determined to put a soldier's face—and body—on the war debate. Illinois representative Frederick A. Britten argued that no political dispute could "justify the loss of untold thousands of lives, the crippling and maiming of our American boys, nor the suffering and anguish which is bound to follow our flag to Europe." Fellow Republican William La Follette of Washington agreed; assenting to war, he proclaimed, would mean "the maiming and dismembering of thousands of our noble boys and the deaths of thousands more." Ohio's Isaac R. Sherwood, one of the few Democrats to reject the war declaration, drew upon personal history to explain his objection. Reflecting upon the "indescribable agony" he felt watching his "maimed, mangled, and dying" comrades six decades earlier, the former Civil War officer declared: "I can not vote to send the brave and stalwart sons of my beloved country into the horrid slaughter pens of Europe, to enter the most useless, brutal, and criminal war in all history."[21]

For war supporters, such arguments bore little weight. Henry Cabot Lodge, for decades a leading champion of US imperialism, declared that "some things [are] worse for a nation than war": "national degeneracy," "national cowardice," and racial division, among others. "Whatever suffering and misery war may bring," he promised his fellow senators, "it will at least sweep these foul things away." Sixty-two-year-old Mississippi senator John Sharp sounded a similar note, dismissing concerns about the imminent slaughter of American youth as "cowardly nonsense." Other pro-war politicians were not quite so flippant. A strong supporter of soldiers' causes, New York congressman James W. Husted acknowledged "the dreadful toll that war exacts of human life, shattered bodies, sightless eyes, and broken hearts." Nevertheless, he threw his weight behind the president's war resolution, citing the need to preserve liberty and "uphold the cause of civilization."[22]

As the House debate entered its final hours, Missouri Democrat Perl D. Decker rose to his feet and, in perhaps the session's most prescient moment, wondered aloud how Europe would react if the assembled body defeated the war resolution. What would they say—the English, the Italians, the "proud, haughty" Germans—if Congress exercised its constitutional authority and said no to war? "They might not say it to-night when the blood lust is on," Decker predicted.

> But after the war is over I think I know what they would say. After they begin to stagger home with eyes that can not see, begin to stagger home with bodies partly shot away, begin to stagger home to firesides where the chairs are empty, when they begin to take up the burdens of this war I think I know what they would say. They would say, "Would to God that we, too, had lived in a Republic like America, where the American Congress before it voted for war kept in mind the wishes and welfare of the people who have to do the dying when the war has come."[23]

Decker's question ultimately went unanswered. On April 6, 1917, shortly after 3:00 in the morning, the House of Representatives passed the war resolution by a vote of 373 to 50. Appeals to national honor and political ideals had trumped concerns about "shattered bodies, sightless eyes, and broken hearts." Officially, the war debate was now over, but public battles over the social significance of war injury—and the bodily toll of foreign intervention—were just heating up.

The Compensations of War

Americans' concerns about future casualties did not disappear overnight. In the weeks following the US war declaration, pacifists, socialists, and other war critics took to the streets, staging mass demonstrations against Congress's decision. Over the next two years, thousands of protesters, including former presidential candidate Eugene V. Debs, were jailed for challenging US war policies in person or in print.[24] Yet, amidst an atmosphere of hypernationalism and hardening conformity, most Americans put aside their misgivings—at least publicly—and rallied behind the war banner. Leading the way was a vocal chorus of politicians and ideologues eager to tout war's "compensations" for the nation and its fighting men. Nativists, including future leaders of postwar veterans' groups, hailed US intervention as a grand experiment in Americanization, promising that military service would "yank the hyphen" out of the nation's unassimilated immigrants. Progressive reformers like Walter Lippmann and John Dewey threw their weight behind the war effort as well. Abandoning their earlier skepticism, pro-war Progressives viewed World War I as an opportunity for social engineering and political reorganization, one whose long-term benefits would offset the inevitable cost in bodies and blood.[25] Other Americans found ready inspiration in Woodrow Wilson's crusade to make the world "safe for democracy," a call that would be echoed by later administrations to justify American military commitment overseas. To the war's most fervent supporters, "the United States was going to war not simply against Germany but against Europe itself, against the very *idea* of Europe and all that Europe historically represented in the American mind: coercive government, irrationality, barbarism, feudalism."[26] If all went smoothly, the United States would emerge at war's end among the world's great powers—a beacon of freedom and the savior of civilization.

For millions of would-be *doughboys*, the nickname soon attached to American soldiers in World War I, the prospect of overseas fighting held tangible appeals as well. Many recruits were primed to see the "war to end all wars" as a chance to escape the stultifying influence of peacetime society. As future historian William L. Langer reminisced about his World War I comrades,

> One would think that, after almost four years of war, after the most detailed and realistic accounts of murderous fighting on the Somme and around Verdun, to say nothing of the day-to-day agony of trench warfare, it would have been all but impossible to get anyone to serve without duress. But it was not so. We and many thousands of others volunteered. . . . Most of us, I think, had the feeling that life, if we survived, would run in the familiar, routine channels. Here was our one great chance for excitement and risk. We could not afford to pass it up.[27]

To a generation of thrill-seekers, facing a future dominated by the rhythms of the corporate workplace, war seemed to offer an "antidote to the effete routine of modern life."[28] If anything, the bodily dangers of the Great War battlefield only added to war's allure as a once-in-a-lifetime experience.

Above all else, the Great War promised to transform doughboys into "better men"—both physically and mentally—than they could ever become in civilian life. For all their prewar trepidations, many Americans continued to view wartime military service as an important passage of manhood. In retrospect, the notion that masculinity that can be achieved only by exposing young men's bodies to the vicissitudes of modern weaponry appears absurd. By any measure, Great War armies were far more adept at destroying male youth than preparing them for adulthood. However, many at the time took a different view. There was a growing consensus that American men had "gone soft" after decades of prosperity and peace. In the eyes of numerous observers, only the hardships, discipline, and sacrifice of war could fast-track a generation of weaklings on the path to physical and mental maturation.[29]

As early as 1917, US military recruiters made warrior masculinity a central part of their enlistment campaigns. Posters trumpeting the slogan "The United States Army Builds Men," accompanied by images of heavily muscled soldiers, were plastered anywhere young men were thought to congregate. Government propagandists promised that returning veterans would barely resemble the boys their parents sent away. Hardened by war and military fitness regimens, the Great War's survivors would march home "strong in body, quick and sure in action, alert and keen in mind, firm and resolute in character, calm and even-tempered."[30] To those who questioned war's masculinizing power, Major George W. Crile, an American surgeon who served with the British during the early years of the war, testified: "I've seen these sallow, pasty young clerks get out and turn into Men! I've seen young chaps who were little more than flabby human jellyfish transformed by their life in the trenches into husky fellows that were grit clean through."[31]

Few touted war's compensations more loudly than the first wave of returning disabled veterans, several of whom achieved celebrity status stumping on behalf of war's physical and spiritual benefits. Although the vast majority of war-wounded doughboys would not begin to trickle back until 1919, wartime America was inundated with scores of disabled soldiers from Great Britain, Italy, France, and elsewhere—many eager to spread war's good news, often for a profit, to US audiences. North America's most famous disabled spokesman was Harold R. Peat, a Jamaican-born infantryman from Alberta, Canada (fig. 8). A fixture on the northeast lecture circuit, "Private Peat" (as he came to be known) was the subject of a best-selling autobiography, a 1917 Hollywood film (starring himself), and countless flattering articles in the US press. His claim to fame occurred in the spring of 1915, when, at the Second Battle of Ypres, he "got plugged" by German machine-gun fire while returning to his trench with ammunition. The bullet tore through his right shoulder and exploded out of his back, carrying with it bits of soft tissue and bone. After spending two days on the battlefield awaiting evacuation and more than four months in the hospital recovering from his wounds, Peat was eventually discharged with a useless right arm and what he deemed "one and a fraction" lungs.[32]

Despite his disabling injuries, Peat was adamant that the pain and suffering he endured in service had only made him "more of a man." In his mind, war instilled in combatants a level of self-respect and physical stamina that peacetime society could never provide. Writing in the *American Magazine* in March 1918, Peat predicted that, at war's end, American soldiers would "come smiling out of Hell." The rigors of combat would give them a "post-graduate course" in courage, loyalty, self-

FIG. 8. Invalided out of the Canadian Army in World War I, Pvt. Harold R. Peat ("Private Peat") became a household name in the United States lecturing and writing about the man-making virtues of combat and war injury. After the war, he evolved into a sharp critic of modern war, joining the stage with Smedley Butler and other luminaries of the 1930s peace movement. Library of Congress, Prints & Photographs Division, LC-DIG-ggbain-25867.

sacrifice, and faith—the values upon which they would build a better tomorrow. More importantly, he assured US readers that war's valuable lessons would not be wasted on the dead. "Almost without exception, the men in the trenches are a hundred percent stronger physically than they were when they enlisted," he promised. "And we don't die easy. We're mighty hard to kill."[33]

Selling the Safe War

Private Peat was not the only wartime spokesman to proclaim the rising survivability of modern warfare. As the nation girded itself for battle, scores of newspapers, magazines, and military publications offered up a similar message: that the Great War was, in fact, becoming safer and that, by the time US troops entered the line of fire, combat would be little more dangerous than civilian life.[34] Led by military physicians, government pundits, and pro-war journalists, the campaign to frame World War I as a "safe war" was part of a larger ideological crusade—emerging in the late nineteenth century and culminating in the postwar rehabilitation movement—to eliminate mass casualties from the ledger of American war-making. Convinced that the public had been misled about the dangers awaiting US servicemen overseas, safe-war advocates sought to cast the nation's anticipated injuries in the best light possible, downplaying the threat of death and disability and highlighting soldiers' prospects of escaping the conflict intact.

Belief in the rising survivability of modern combat stemmed from several sources. Some safe-war proponents held fast to the gospel of "humane" warfare, the Progressive faith that advancements in technology, ballistics, and transportation would limit war's lethality. Even in the face of the Great War's undeniable carnage, military enthusiasts continued to tout the life-saving potential of modern weaponry, asserting that machine guns and other body-rending technologies ultimately saved more lives than they extinguished.[35] Others contended that battlefield conduct had become far more "rational" since the war's early days, a development that promised to drastically reduce doughboys' likelihood of disability or death. According to safe-war disciples, the mass confusion and undeniable waste of life that characterized the Great War's first few years had been an aberration—the product of untested leadership, wartime hysteria, and a failure of military tactics. By 1917, they argued, the United States' newest allies were "fighting with their heads as well as with their arms, and the result [was] greater security" for all involved.[36]

Safe-war advocates also staked their confidence on the body-healing power of military medicine and applied science. In the nearly three years prior to the US war declaration, both Allied and Central Powers physicians had made tremendous advances in disease prevention, antiseptic surgery, skin grafting, bone plating, and emergency triage—all of which, safe-warriors insisted, greatly improved American troops' chances of escaping combat-related disability and death.[37] The *Ladies Home Journal*, a popular venue of safe-war boosterism, reassured its female readership that "modern surgery and modern ingenuity" had all but eliminated the word "cripple" from the "languages of society."[38] Interviewed in the March 1918 edition of the *American Magazine*, US Army surgeon general William C. Gorgas echoed a similar refrain, telling writer Mary Mullet that "more lives will be saved by preventive medicine and modern sanitation than will be lost in the actual fighting." Gorgas was no armchair general. He had made his reputation battling mosquito-borne diseases in US-occupied Cuba and Panama, an experience that left him well aware of soldiers' susceptibility to contagion and ill health. Still, like many military physicians of his generation, Gorgas believed modern weaponry was no match for medical science. While some battle casualties were inevitable, he insisted that "the most distressing by-products of war"—including disease, wound infection, and battlefield insanity—were on the decline.[39]

Ultimately, safe-war advocates cast themselves as level-headed realists, their reassuring proclamations an antidote to the "wild stories of danger and death" circulated by war's critics. In their eyes, pacifists and German propagandists (the two were often conflated) had deliberately exaggerated the bodily risks awaiting US soldiers overseas.[40] As a corrective, safe-warriors frequently attempted to ground their arguments in the purportedly objective discipline of comparative statistics. In a September 1917 report, for example, the Minnesota Commission of Public Safety told soldiers' parents not to worry if their sons were drafted: "Fifteen men out of every sixteen in the Allied armies have been safe through three years of fighting. During the past year not more than one man in thirty has been killed. The death rate from disease is less than in peace times. Only one man in five hundred loses a limb—a chance not greater than that in hazardous occupations at home."[41]

Similar figures found their way into newspapers and magazines across the country, as safe-war advocates urged the American public to look past war's "horrors" and consider the cold hard facts. Citing a recent claim by Babson's Statistical Organization, a prominent investment advisor, *Outlook* reported that—except during an infantry assault—a soldier on the Western Front was "statistically, almost as well off as in the streets of New York."[42] In July 1918, writer Judson D. Stuart went a step further, arguing that "the fighter in the trenches is in less danger of death than the baby in its mother's arms." By Stuart's calculations, the fatality rate for infants in US hospitals was four and a half times higher than that of all Allied soldiers—indisputable evidence, he believed, that military service in the Great War was no more a death sentence than birth itself.[43]

Even as federal officials publicly testified to war's safety, the government launched a new program aimed at limiting taxpayers' liabilities for sending men into battle: war risk insurance. Established by Congress in September 1914, the Bureau of War Risk Insurance was initially authorized to provide affordable insurance coverage to American cargo ships (and later their crews) facing the "unknown and uncertain new risks of naval submarine warfare."[44] Following the US war declaration, treasury secretary William G. McAdoo quickly drew up plans to provide similar provisions to troops in the field. A fierce critic of the federal pension system, McAdoo nonetheless believed the federal government had a responsibility to give US troops a chance to reduce the economic risks of military service.[45]

Drafted by Julian Mack, a federal judge and life-long Democrat, the War Risk Insurance Act of October 1917 "introduced the principle of insurance as part of the contract of employment between the government of the United States" and its men and women in uniform.[46] Specifically, the act allowed US service personnel to purchase short-term insurance policies in case of disability or death (this on top of the death and disability compensation already provided by the federal government). Policies ranged in amount from $1,000 to $10,000, and because the US Treasury bore the cost of administrative expenses and excess claims, the price of premiums was minimal (roughly $6.50 a month on a $10,000 policy).[47] Service personnel deemed permanently disabled could expect monthly installments of $5.75 for every $1,000 of insurance for 240 months; beneficiaries of the dead were allotted similar amounts.[48] Although opposed by the insurance industry, the scheme won wide support among Progressives, who—like McAdoo and Mack—hoped it would eventually replace the pension system as the primary means of addressing the economic burdens of war injury.[49] By the war's end, the federal government had issued more than $40 billion in term insurance.[50] As far as the War Risk Bureau was concerned, American soldiers might not escape the dangers of modern warfare, but they could rest assured that their financial future was secure.

The concept of war risk insurance marked a significant development in the federal response to the Problem of the Disabled Veteran. Like the pension system before it, war risk insurance affirmed a social contract between disabled veterans and the state. But it also redefined the government as an employer and shifted much of the responsibility for securing disabled veterans' long-term livelihood to the injured parties themselves. This message of personal responsibility was at the heart of *His Best Gift* (1918), a two-reel melodrama designed to warn doughboys-in-training about the perils of entering the war zone uninsured. Produced by the Army Signal Corps and required viewing for countless enlisted men, the film tells the story of Jack Harris (played by William Sherwood), a newly married soldier who—against the urging of his wife, his buddies, and an army insurance officer—puts off buying his policy until it is too late. Wounded in the eyes during a snowy trench battle, Jack returns home a blind invalid with no means of supporting his despairing wife. Luckily for the film's hero, it is all a dream, and Jack awakens in his tent to discover his vision miraculously restored. Given a second lease on life, he immediately rushes out to buy his insurance, the "best gift" a departing doughboy can leave his dependent spouse.

Its upbeat ending notwithstanding, *His Best Gift* acknowledged what many safe-war advocates sought to dispel: that life-altering injury was an inevitable feature of modern warfare. The most a US soldier could do, the film suggests, was anticipate his body's destruction and plan accordingly. Once insured, the nation's fighting men could rest assured they would not be "CHARGED FOR THE EXTRA RISK OF WAR." Less comforting was the film's other message: that without adequate coverage, the nation's disabled vets could look forward to a lifetime of alienation and economic insecurity.[51]

The Dreadful Toll

As members of the American Expeditionary Force (AEF) soon discovered, the Great War bore little resemblance to the orderly realm predicted by safe-war enthusiasts. Packed to the gills and lacking adequate ventilation, US transport ships were rife with scarlet fever, diphtheria, and measles, which soldiers dispersed upon landing.[52] Although the AEF was largely spared the chronic outbreaks of "trench diseases" that had plagued their European counterparts, open latrines and a shortage of clean water left 70 percent of American troops sick with dysentery and diarrhea.[53] Body lice (or *chats*) were an unrelenting menace, breeding in the seams of uniforms and leaving itchy, red bite marks on soldiers' skin. In summer, clouds of flies descended upon any exposed food, and the ground was slippery with maggots and frogs. Gorging on corpses, swarms of huge black rats—numbering in the tens of millions—contaminated food supplies, spread infective jaundice, and bit men while they slept. Even the mud was a threat to good hygiene. Fertilized by manure and decaying bodies, the soil of France was rich in gas-forming anaerobic bacteria normally found in the intestines of horses. When exposed to traumatized tissue, the bacteria released gases and poisonous toxins, killing the flesh and producing a deadly form of wound infection known as gas gangrene.[54]

Once under fire, the AEF faced additional dangers. The combination of industrially administered violence and an "ideology of the offensive" resulted in a battlefield of unprecedented lethality and human devastation.[55] Although US drill instructors continued to tout the relevance of hand-to-hand combat, doughboys rarely met their enemies in close quarters. They were far more likely to be injured by exploding shells, shrapnel, and "unspecified" gunshots, which collectively were responsible for over half of all battlefield casualties.[56] Upon impact with human flesh, the cone-shaped bullets used by Great War combatants tumbled end-over-end, leaving behind ragged holes and dragging bits of clothing deep into the body. Thanks to improved transportation and medical care, doctors were able to limit much of the damage caused by modern weaponry. (Despite the fact that more than 50 percent of soldiers' wounds occurred in the extremities, only 4,403 doughboys returned home missing all or part of a limb.[57]) Even so, from the moment the AEF entered the war zone, the threat of sudden, anonymous violence was a constant companion.

No weapon epitomized the Great War's indiscriminate terror more than poison gas. Sprayed in amorphous clouds, gas attacked soldiers on the molecular level, turning their bodies' own defense systems against them. Over the course of the war, US forces suffered 70,552 gas-related casualties, including 1,221 fatalities.[58] Men gassed with chlorine succumbed to violent coughing, vomiting, or shock; in fatal cases, death from asphyxiation or drowning could take days. Inhaling toxic phosgene, introduced by the French in 1915, was more lethal still.[59] The gas's reaction with moisture in the lungs could lead to pulmonary edema, respiratory failure, and death within hours.[60]

The most feared of all Great War "gases" was not a gas at all, but an oily, colorless liquid dispersed as an aerosol by bursting shells. Named for its noxious odor, mustard gas could burn flesh to the bone. It was most deadly when swallowed or inhaled, destroying the mucous membrane of the lungs and bronchial tubes and leaving survivors susceptible to secondary infections, pneumonia, and tuberculosis, sometimes years after the initial trauma. Unlike other World War I–era gases, which dissipated quickly, mustard gas remained in the soil for weeks after an attack. Many a doughboy was seriously burned after sleeping in contaminated trenches or defecating on gas-soaked grass. "I got that damn mustard stuff on both my backside and my testicles," one US infantryman recalled. "Christ, did it burn! My rear end still looks like it's petrified."[61] By the war's end, 27,711 American soldiers had been hospitalized because of mustard gas wounds. Nearly 600 died; thousands of others would suffer the effects of gassing for the rest of their lives.

From the earliest days of the conflict, stories filtered back to the United States about a "new type of casualty," one whose debilitating symptoms stemmed from the "stress and special horrors of modern warfare."[62] At first many specialists believed that battlefield neurosis—commonly known as *shell shock*—was a neuropathological condition caused by the concussive effects of heavy armaments. By 1917, most military psychiatrists felt that war neuroses were primarily psychosomatic in origin—the product of battlefield stress, individual soldiers' predispositions for mental illness, and combatants' unconscious instincts for survival. Whatever the cause, nearly all physicians agreed that the "terrible conditions of modern war" were an indispensable catalyst for the creation of this "novel disease entity." Writing in 1920, the British psychiatrist C. Stanford Read argued that "war neurotic states have an intimate relationship with the conditions under which this great war was fought—the enormously high explosives, special trench warfare, poison gases, and horrors that were not present to any extent in previous wars."[63]

To the untrained eye, soldiers in the grip of shell shock were terrifying to behold. Men who had previously behaved courageously under fire would twitch, whimper uncontrollably, or scream in terror. Some suffered from paranoia and hysterical blindness; others went into convulsions at loud noises, complained of amnesia, or lost the power of speech. Shell shock did not necessarily result in permanent disability. A regimen of warm food, bed rest, and exercise was often enough to restore troops' capacity to fight. Unfortunately, large numbers of shell-shock victims failed to recover—at least in the short term. Of the more than 100,000 US soldiers evacuated for psychological or neuropsychiatric ailments, nearly two-thirds never returned to their units, and more than 40,000 doughboys received disability discharges because of psychiatric complaints. Thousands more developed debilitating symptoms after the war was over.[64] In 1921, US veterans' hospitals housed over 9,000 "war neurotics," with numbers continuing to rise over the next decade.[65]

Doughboys faced other risks as well. During the official war period (April 1, 1917, to December 31, 1919), more than 168,000 US soldiers were discharged from the army because of physical or mental illness. A large number of these men had slipped through the weeding-out process during enlistment only to develop pathological or disabling symptoms once in uniform (of the 22,390 troops discharged because of tuberculosis, 90 percent never made it to the war zone). Within the first months of their training, thousands of recruits were invalided home due to undiagnosed (or incurable) cases of epilepsy, venereal disease, alcoholism, and drug addiction.[66] Others fell victim to *nonbattle* injuries, both at home and overseas. According to the Surgeon General's Office, over 5,000 US servicemen were killed by "external causes," a blanket category covering everything from plane crashes and auto accidents to suicide and murder.[67]

Ironically, for all of the gross lethality of industrial age weapons, accidents and training camp mishaps resulted in tens of thousands more casualties than German armaments. Between 1917 and 1919, 10,511 American soldiers were officially discharged for nonbattle injuries.[68] One doughboy, Harry Iverson of New York City, suffered a hernia scaling a wall during boot camp at Fort Leavenworth, Kansas. Another, Roy Moore of Avon, Pennsylvania, fractured his arm crank-starting an ambulance in France. Following the ceasefire, the injury toll continued to add up. On March 13, 1919, John Evans, a company cook, was carrying an armful of meat back to camp when he was hit by a speeding car. The collision left him with a fractured back, and as of 1924, he was living on a government stipend of $20 per month.[69]

Interpreting Injury

What did wartime Americans make of doughboys' injuries? The answer often depended upon the observers' proximity (or lack thereof) to the battlefield. Those looking on from afar were more likely to glorify war injury and the men who sustained it. Poet Charles Hanson Towne compared America's crippled veterans to architectural "ruins," claiming that both were more picturesque in their decrepitude than in their whole and spotless youth.[70] An aging Theodore Roosevelt, the nation's leading disciple of the cult of war injury, went further, ascribing deep moral and political significance to soldiers' bodily trauma. In his mind, doughboys' wounds were "proofs of their high devotion to their country and to the cause of civilized mankind."[71] From the safety of US soil, many saw soldiers' injuries as little more than abstractions: symbols of manly courage, national valor, and the righteousness of American intervention.

Closer to the front, soldiers' wounds lost much of their romantic aura. Many senior military commanders tried to remain detached from the Great War's human carnage, particularly when it came to drawing up orders for attack. As Evan Andrew Huelfer has shown, Great War generals viewed mass casualties as an unfortunate but inevitable consequence of attrition warfare. Trained at a time when "military success meant accomplishing the mission, regardless of the cost," America's top brass were willing to sacrifice thousands of dead, wounded, and hospitalized men if it secured an Allied victory.[72] From the military's perspective, soldiers' physical and mental ailments represented one thing above all else: a drain on the nation's fighting strength. During the war, disease alone accounted for more than sixty-two million days "lost" because US troops were too ill to report to duty.[73] At times, senior leaders displayed great sympathy for the sick and injured. (The AEF's senior commander, major general John J. Pershing, famously broke drown and cried after visiting a ward of battle-maimed doughboys.) But they were expected to adopt a cold, even calculating, attitude toward soldiers' injuries, weighing the number of "acceptable" casualties against the likelihood of battlefield success.[74]

For soldiers and medical personnel stationed near the war zone, the daily spectacle of injury was typically met with bewilderment and disgust. The eminent American surgeon Harvey Cushing confessed in his wartime diary that

> it is difficult to say just what are one's most vivid impressions: the amazing patience of the seriously wounded, some of them hanging on for months; the dreadful deformities (not so much in the way of amputations, but broken jaws and twisted, scarred faces); the tedious healing of the infected wounds, with discharging sinuses, tubes, irrigations, and repeated dressings—so much so that grating and painful fractures are simply abandoned to wait for wounds to heal, which they don't seem to do.[75]

While medical professionals like Cushing could take refuge in an idiom of clinical description, many soldiers and volunteers struggled to find words to make sense of the slaughter.[76] "I could hardly tell you of the awful horrors of the front," one soldier wrote to his parents, "that is if the whiffing away of strong lives and the mangling of strong bodies comes under the heading of horrors."[77] For the normally articulate Guy Emerson Bowerman, a Yale graduate working with the US Ambulance Service, the Great War's human devastation seemed to defy linguistic signification altogether. Reflecting upon a young German soldier whose leg had been amputated earlier in the day, Bowerman noted in his diary: "As we lifted him into the ambulance his huddled body expressed far better than words his—I know not what—could I describe what I saw there I would be a writer—I only know that I saw something tragic, more than tragic something I cannot put into words."[78]

As for the wounded soldiers themselves, eyewitness accounts reported an assortment of responses. When first hit, many Great War soldiers experienced feelings of shock, fear, or indifference.[79] Once stabilized, their attitudes ranged from boundless euphoria to unrelenting despair. This diversity of feelings can be attributed to several factors, including the fact that being wounded was—and remains—a highly subjective experience, the personal implications of which can take years to comprehend. In the mind of the wounded soldier, wrote one anonymous war casualty in the September 1917 issue of *Living Age* magazine, "There is a continuous, insensible shifting of the perspective from the moment that he feels the thud made by the arrival of the bullet to that when he realizes one day at the end of his convalescence that he is well again. The gradual changes are so subtle, the inability to reproduce any one state of consciousness when in the next is so complete that the most introspective must hope for nothing better than confused reminiscence."[80] More important still was the nature of soldiers' injuries and their prospects of recovery. Historian Mark Meigs notes that doughboys' attitudes toward their wounds—and toward the war itself—tended to reflect their likelihood of permanent disability or disfigurement.[81] Raised in a culture that associated disability with state dependency and compromised masculinity, many newly injured warriors sank into long bouts of depression, unwilling to accept their new identities as disabled men. For doughboys like John L. Golob, a US infantryman severely wounded in the thigh during the Meuse-Argonne Campaign, the ultimate nightmare was not being injured; it was returning home a "broken piece of furniture."[82]

Even as their comrades were mowed down in droves, many hospitalized doughboys continued to fetishize war injury, exhibiting the bullets and shrapnel dug from their bodies as prized souvenirs.[83] Getting hit also meant a reprieve—if only temporary—from the dreadful conditions of the front lines. Among war-weary troops, few things were more cherished than a "Blighty" wound, British slang for an injury that permanently knocked a combatant out of action.[84] Speaking for countless front-line soldiers, Harold W. Pierce, a rifleman in the 28th Division, admitted, "As for me I would welcome a wound, even a foot or a hand off, just so I am not going to be horribly mangled. . . . I can understand now why a man is so happy when a bullet hits him in the arm or leg. A blight is about the best a doughboy can look for in this war."[85]

Blighty wounds notwithstanding, Great War soldiers subscribed to a hierarchical vision of war injury, drawing subtle distinctions between honorable and dishonorable wounds. If injured, the very best a doughboy could hope for was a small flesh wound or scar—corporeal confirmation of his time under fire but without the physical and social burdens of permanent disability. Beyond that, the meanings doughboys attached to war wounds were largely determined by two criteria: the bodily location of injury and the circumstances in which it was received. Despite rapid advances in plastic surgery, disfiguring wounds to the face were especially feared, as were injuries to the abdomen, genitals, and spinal column—and not just because all were likely to result in permanent impairment. More than a lost hand or "lame" leg, such injuries threatened soldiers' ability to live up to social codes of masculinity and sexual virility, a fate many men believed was worse than death itself. Similarly, soldiers evacuated for nonbattle wounds (or for injuries incurred in minor excursions) were viewed as less heroic than their combat-wounded counterparts.[86]

Further down the wound hierarchy were casualties of disease and so-called invisible wounds, including victims of gas attacks. Unlike the "red badges of courage" worn by gunshot victims, invisible wounds were sustained inside the body and were thus undetectable by the naked eye. Sympathetic observers complained that invisible injuries were devalued within the military and the image-conscious popular culture:

> Among the wounded, the empty sleeve and the sightless eye, the visible scars, are bound to be more or less of a compensation in themselves. Where is there a heart that does not swell with gratitude toward the soldier bearing the outward signs of his war sacrifices? And even when the injuries are hidden by the clothing, the wound chevron on the right sleeve tells the story and stirs the heart. . . . Ask the mother of the boy who developed tuberculosis in the army. To her his wound is as real and as glorious as that of her neighbor's boy.[87]

Without visible signatures of their wartime sacrifice (either on their skin or sewn onto their uniforms), sick and invisibly wounded soldiers could not be distinguished from ordinary civilians. While such men might be "just as honorable as their brothers who [were] obviously handicapped," both their fellow soldiers and the public were reluctant to view such injuries as "real" wounds or to afford them equal status.[88] After all, no one sang songs about the honor of coming home with chronic bronchitis or a tubercular heart.

At the bottom of the wound hierarchy were a small group of pitiful, even shameful, injuries. Combat-induced shell shock, for example, was difficult to reconcile with wounded soldiers' heroic image. Throughout the Great War, battle neuroses continued to be associated with weakness, malingering, and pathological insanity. Although few front-line officers publicly disputed its existence, many equated battlefield collapse with old-fashioned "yellow fever" (cowardice) and were loath to have formerly shell-shocked men under their command. Debilitation because of negligence or "willful misconduct" was considered more reprehensible still. Writing his father from Camp Hancock in 1918, one soldier recalled a memorable lecture outlining the difference between noble battle wounds and the scars of venereal disease: "It was a picture [the lecturer] drew before us in our minds of men who were terribly wounded. Not by shells or bayonets but by the young man's greatest sin, disease. He pictured how these men wanted to die, couldn't face home, with a body wrecked of manhood. . . . Then the picture of the wounded and crippled who were proud of their wounds. Why? Because they were inflicted in honorable battle."[89]

The least honorable type of injury a soldier could receive was a self-inflicted wound. In the eyes of military officials, the act of intentionally damaging one's body—especially for the purpose of escaping front-line duty—was tantamount to treason. Some hospitals kept men recovering from self-inflicted wounds in separate wings so they would not demoralize the rest of the patients. When this proved impossible, they hung posters reading "S.I.W." above the beds of men with self-inflicted wounds. The goal was not only to humiliate such men but also to prevent visitors from mistaking them for "genuine" battle casualties.[90]

Publicizing Injury

Back at home, the task of publicizing the war—and the wounds suffered by American servicemen—fell to the Committee on Public Information (CPI) and its charismatic chairman, newspaper editor George Creel. Created by executive order on April 13, 1917, the CPI represented an unprecedented attempt to shape public opinion on a national scale. From its Washington headquarters, the propaganda ministry deployed every means of communication available—from posters and pamphlets to traveling slideshows and films—to sell the war to the American people.[91]

When it came to wounded soldiers, Creel and company pursued a two-pronged strategy, aimed at both alleviating Americans' anxieties about war casualties and appropriating the disabled soldier as a pro-war icon. To the first end, the CPI went to great lengths to erase the worst of American injury from official wartime culture. Overseas soldiers were forbidden from mentioning war casualties in their correspondence, and the CPI authorized a blanket prohibition against publishing graphic descriptions and images of injured doughboys. According to historian Susan Moeller, CPI "censors, editors, and some photographers intentionally misled readers with spurious captions and robbed many images of their gritty impact by the heavy-handed use of the retoucher's brush."[92] Journalists who failed to practice self-censorship could be denied access to official communiqués and photographs from the front lines. More ominous still, under Title I of the 1917 Espionage Act, any person who made statements "with intent to interfere with the operation or success of the military or naval forces" could be punished with a $10,000 fine and a twenty-year jail sentence.[93]

Government officials defended such practices by pointing toward the "depressing effect" of war casualties on public morale. In the words of one government official, visual evidence of America's war-wounded "caused needless anxiety to those whose friends and relatives were at the front, and tended to foster the anti-war spirit that was always so persistently cultivated by the enemy. Accordingly the general policy was adopted of withholding such views from the public—although as a matter of fact only a bare handful of such pictures reached this country."[94] On the rare occasions it addressed medical topics, the army newspaper *Stars and Stripes*, which had over 70,000 single subscriptions in the United States, scrupulously avoided any mention of soldiers' pain and suffering.[95] Even more telling, the CPI's 320-page *War Cyclopedia: A Handbook for Ready Reference on the Great War* (1918) contained only one entry on America's war-wounded, a brief quotation from secretary of war Newton Baker reprinted under the heading "War, Low Death Rate for Casualties."[96]

However, government propagandists were not averse to stoking public interest in war casualties when it suited their needs. In fact, by the Great War's end, representations of wounded and disabled soldiers were thoroughly integrated into a number of propaganda and fundraising campaigns. As one might expect, many casualty-themed CPI productions, including the 1918 documentary *If Your Soldier's Hit* (1918), were aimed at assuaging Americans' lingering fears about the bodily threat of overseas combat (fig. 9). Others sought to highlight the cheerfulness of America's war-wounded or to reaffirm the connection between war injury and spiritual growth.

FIG. 9. In keeping with the "safe war" ideology promoted by the US Army Surgeon General's Office, the CPI film *If Your Soldier's Hit* (1918) was designed to reassure the American public that wounded doughboys would be able to survive their injuries. Rare Book Collection, Wilson Library, University of North Carolina at Chapel Hill.

Typical of this trend was Alan Crosland's *The Unbeliever* (1918), a feature-length melodrama about an elite snob who learns to discard his class prejudices after he is seriously wounded on the battlefield. Produced by Thomas Edison Studios in conjunction with the US Marine Corps, the film was a public relations coup. In San Francisco, street parades accompanied every day of *The Unbeliever*'s two-week run. In Denver, more than two hundred fans joined the Marines at a makeshift recruiting booth set up in the theater lobby.[97] Productions like *The Unbe-*

liever promoted what would become a core belief among postwar veterans' groups: that wounded or disabled soldiers had a special authority to speak about war and its broader significance.

The CPI considered disabled veterans ideal spokesmen, their injuries conferring upon them a sense of gravitas that no politician or matinee idol could hope to match.[98] Prominent among its cast of real-life heroes were C. W. R. Bowlby, a Canadian corporal wounded at the Somme and Arras; Roberto de Violini, an Italian lieutenant blinded in one eye by a rifle shot; and Leslie Vickers, a British cavalryman and former preacher living in New Jersey—all three of whom toured the country delivering upbeat speeches at Liberty Loan rallies and Red Cross fund-raisers.[99] Disabled veterans proved so popular as inspirational speakers and rabble-rousers that the CPI's Speaking Division could barely keep up with public demand. Writing to George Creel in September 1917, the head of one American high school issued a telling request: "We would like to secure a man, American or Ally, who had been in the trenches and who has a story to tell. . . . If this man were crippled and an officer it would not make much difference whether he was a great speaker or not. The human touch would 'Get him by.'"[100] For many audiences, the actual message delivered by veteran speakers mattered little; being "crippled" was impressive enough.

Ironically, most propaganda images of disabled veterans bore little resemblance to the soldier-heroes of CPI speaking campaigns. Government artists tended to figure war injury within what disability scholar Rosemarie Garland Thomson has called a "visual rhetoric of sentimentality," representing wounded soldiers as helpless figures in need of public support.[101] Of all war-related organizations, the American Red Cross was especially adept at using sentimental images of disabled veterans to evoke monetary contributions from their viewers. The group's most famous World War I poster, Alonzo Earl Foringer's *The Greatest Mother in the World* (1917) (fig. 10), featured a white-robed giantess cradling a diminutive, bandage-wrapped soldier in her arms like a helpless infant. Similar illustrations and magazine advertisements featured wounded soldiers as metaphorical poster children, wholly dependent upon female assistance for their everyday care. At war's end, such imagery would be repudiated by advocates of the rehabilitation movement, who viewed sentimentality as an explicitly "feminized" approach to understanding (and representing) war injury. Nevertheless, the Red Cross and other groups made the suffering soldier one of the most widely reproduced visual icons of the Great War era.[102]

Even as government censors picked through photographs of wounded soldiers, Creel's propaganda machine urged its artists and writers to conjure gruesome scenarios featuring US war casualties. In its weekly bulletins to cartoonists, the CPI regularly stressed the need to keep the Great War's bodily destruction at the forefront of the American imagination. "The appeal of the wounded soldier must be heard by all," one bulletin declared.[103] Another encouraged patriotic cartoonists to depict "the hundreds of young men who have been cruelly wounded and gassed, or who have made the supreme sacrifice. And then ask your readers what they are doing in comparison with those men."[104] When invoking the specter of US casualties, CPI propagandists rarely mentioned actual, flesh-and-blood men and women. Rather, they filled their gore-filled stories with what Christina Jarvis calls a "generalizable wounded body," an anonymous and wholly generic figure whose pain and suffering was meant to stand in for that of all war-injured troops.[105]

No branch of the CPI did more to shine a rhetorical spotlight on the mutilation of American soldiers than the Four-Minute Men, a group of 75,000 government-sponsored speakers who delivered propaganda messages to movie and theater audiences in 1917–1918. Named after the minutemen of the Revolutionary War (as well as the length of time it took film projectionists to change reels), the Four-Minute Men were famed for ability to move listeners to tears with nightmarish invocations of life on the front lines. During Red Cross Week in June 1917, they asked theatergoers to imagine "a great engagement, with long trenches of men writhing in torture from poison gas or from liquid flame" and "soldiers smashed and disfigured by shell wounds—their lacerations as indescribable as their heroism is undaunted." Without the "generosity of the public," the speakers reminded their captive audiences, this "purgatory of pain" would never diminish.[106]

A model speech composed for the Third Liberty Loan drive the following year transported listeners to the war zone, drawing a stark contrast between the safety of the home front and the bodily dangers confronting US troops:

FIG. 10. One of the most widely circulated illustrations of the Great War era, with some ten million copies distributed across the United States, A. E. Foringer's Pietà-themed *The Greatest Mother in the World* epitomizes the sentimentality inherent in most Red Cross and CPI representations of wounded soldiers. Removed from the theater of battle, this bandaged soldier is a helpless, infantilized figure, completely reliant upon his Red Cross "mother." Library of Congress, Prints & Photographs Division, LC-USZ62-76884.

So, while we are sitting here, all comfortable, well fed, secure, our boys are standing in the trenches, down in the mud. Shells are bursting over their heads—right—now—there's fire in one place—roaring cannon—poisonous gases creeping through the trenches.

Perhaps a moment ago while I was talking a giant German bomb struck a squad of our men—some are dead, others dying, mangled bodies are being taken away in stretchers. Yes, that's what is happening perhaps *right now*.

If it's not *now*, as we *imagine*, then, as we *know*, it was yesterday, will be again to-morrow, and the day afterwards. Every day now our American boys are being shot at, wounded, gassed, mangled, killed.[107]

The goal of such speeches was not to hide the Great War's horror but to magnify it: to remind those who stayed at home of the wounding, gassing, and mangling "over there." If the CPI was worried about the "depressing effect" of wounded soldiers on public morale, it also understood their value—as symbols and spokesmen—in the information war at home.

The Final Casualty

In the Great War's calculus of suffering, it is tempting to say that the United States got off easy. Only in the Meuse-Argonne Campaign of late 1918—where 26,000 Americans were killed and 95,000 wounded—did US forces approach the casualty rates sustained by other belligerents. French troops suffered some 300,000 dead and 600,000 wounded within the first four months of fighting; by the war's end, almost two million French soldiers had been killed and five million wounded, including hundreds of thousands of *grands mutilés* with missing eyes and limbs. British casualty rates were similarly high, with nearly one million "Tommies" killed and another 750,000 permanently disabled in fifty-two months of bloody fighting. In terms of raw numbers, the German war generation sustained even greater damage: over two million men died of battle injuries, while another four million were severely wounded.[108] By comparison, the bodily destruction of American troops—some 120,000 dead from injury or disease, another 224,000 wounded in battle—appears almost negligible.

However, it would be a mistake to rely on statistics alone when gauging Americans' deep concerns with war injury and its significance for the nation's future. Throughout the war years, the Problem of the Disabled

Veteran was never far from Americans' minds. Even as isolationists and antiwar groups attempted to frame war-related disability as an obstacle to military intervention, their ideological opponents made a cult of war injury, valorizing combat wounds as signs of manliness and evidence of spiritual growth. After April 1917, concerns about wounded soldiers were renewed with even greater urgency, as the US propaganda agency carefully manipulated public exposure to the nation's mass casualties to maximize support for the war effort. Yet, as the CPI itself came to understand, the horrific realities of war injury defied even the strictest of censorship measures. Despite the federal government's virtual monopoly on all information emanating from the front lines, the "dreadful toll" of sick, wounded, and permanently disabled soldiers would have been impossible to hide forever.

On October 2, 1919, the United States suffered what many considered to be its final Great War casualty when Woodrow Wilson, exhausted after leading a prolonged campaign on behalf of the fledgling League of Nations, collapsed with a massive stroke, leaving him paralyzed and partially blind. Though few Americans knew the full extent of his disability, the president's incapacitated state came to symbolize the Great War's dire legacy of destruction—a foreign policy in tatters, political division at home, and a new generation of disabled vets. The recently formed Disabled American Veterans of the World War would elect Wilson an honorary member for life, pronouncing him as much a "casualty of the war as any doughboy wounded on the battlefields of France."[109] Another wounded veterans' group, the California-based Under-Fire Veterans Association, went even further, excoriating Wilson's Republican opponents for failing to make good on the president's dream of a world without war. On the eve of the 1920 elections, the group seethed, "Our own wounds throb anew in pain, our minds burn in angry resentment at even the thought of such treachery, faithless betrayal and national dishonor on the part of selfish souled politicians."[110]

But by that time, most disabled veterans had other matters on their minds. They were far too busy trying to get back to "normal" life.

THE AFTERMATH OF BATTLE

Elsie Ferguson in "Hero Land"

In the immediate afterglow of World War I, Americans welcomed home the latest generation of wounded warriors as national heroes—men whose bodies bore the scars of Allied victory. Among the scores of prominent supporters was Elsie Ferguson, a Broadway actress and film star renowned for her maternal beauty and patrician demeanor.

During the war years, "The Aristocrat of the Silent Screen" had been an outspoken champion of the Allied effort, raising hundreds of thousands of dollars for liberty bonds through her stage performances and public rallies. After the Armistice, she regularly visited injured troops at Debarkation Hospital No. 5, one of nine makeshift convalescent facilities established in New York City in the winter of 1918. Nicknamed "Hero Land," No. 5 was housed in the lavish, nine-story Grand Central Palace, and was temporary home to more than 3,000 sick and wounded soldiers recently returned from European battlefields.

Unlike Ferguson's usual cohort, who reserved their heroics for the big screen, the patients at No. 5 did not resemble matinee idols—far from it. Veterans of Château-Thierry, Belleau Wood, and the Meuse-Argonne, many of the men were prematurely aged by disease and loss of limb. Others endured constant pain, their bodies wracked with the lingering effects of shrapnel and poisonous gas.

Like most observers in the early days of the Armistice, Ferguson was optimistic about such men's prospects for recovery. Chronicling her visits in *Motion Picture Magazine*, she reported that the residents of Hero Land received the finest care imaginable. Besides regular excursions to hot spots throughout the city, convalescing vets enjoyed in-house film screenings and stage shows, and the hospital storeroom (staffed by attractive Red Cross volunteers) was literally overflowing with cigarettes, chocolate bars, and "all the good things waiting to give comfort and pleasure to the men who withheld nothing in their giving to their country." The patients themselves were upbeat to a man and, in Ferguson's view, seemed to harbor no ill will about their injuries. Reflecting upon a young marine from Minnesota, now missing an arm and too weak to leave his bed, she echoed the sentiments of many postwar Americans: "The world loves these fighting men and a uniform is a sure passport to anything they want."[1]

Still, the actress cautioned her readers against expecting too much, too soon. The road to readjustment was a long one, and Ferguson warned that the United States would never be a "healed nation" until its disabled doughboys were back on their feet.

3

"THINKING AHEAD OF THE CRIPPLED YEARS"
Carrying On in an Age of Normalcy

> Down the street, with a lilting swing,
> Each so bright that never a thing
> Seems to harass, so proud were they,
> One leg gone, but their hearts were gay.
>
> Clickety clack, went the crutches' tune
> God! How can they be brave so soon!
> Brave, when I can not keep back the tears,
> Thinking ahead of the crippled years.
> — Elizabeth R. Stoner, "The Crutches' Tune" (1919)[1]

In November 1918, militarists and other supporters of an aggressive US foreign policy had reason for excitement. The United States had accomplished what was previously unthinkable: wage a successful ground war on European soil. Despite a long tradition of military isolationism, Americans had eventually embraced the war effort, supplying cash and bodies in record numbers. The US economy had shifted to a war footing seemingly overnight, and though there had been many problems along the way (strikes, mass jailings, the suspension of civil liberties, to name but a few), they were considered temporary, soon to disappear in the wake of battle. Best of all, the America Expeditionary Force (AEF) had escaped the conflict relatively unscathed. World War I had not been the "safe war" that some newspaper commentators had promised, but by the time US troops saw action, the days of suicidal trench warfare were mostly over. If the United States had entered World War I as a minor player on the global stage, it emerged well on its way toward international preeminence.

However, one nagging problem did not look to disappear any time soon: the disabled veteran. Feted upon their demobilization, war-injured doughboys returned to an increasingly hostile social climate marked by widespread unemployment, political intolerance, and growing ambivalence about the costs of American victory. Within months of the ceasefire, lurid stories of veteran mendicancy and violence fueled mounting concerns that wartime service had transformed the finest specimens of American manhood into mentally deranged criminals and idle cripples. By the early 1920s, rising pension costs and widespread fraud at the newly established Veterans' Bureau further soured Americans' opinion of the Great War and its legacy of bodily destruction.

As a result, disabled Great War veterans found themselves torn between two competing visions of postwar American life, both of which resonate to this day. On the one hand, they were urged to embrace what future president Warren G. Harding deemed a "return to normalcy." Rather than dwell upon the past, disabled veterans were encouraged to put the war behind them and to set their minds (and bodies) to the business of domestic readjustment. On the other hand, there was a growing sense—among policy makers, the public, and former soldiers—that disabled veterans could not easily set aside their wartime traumas. Haunted by shell shock, their bodies debilitated by injury and disease, many returning vets were condemned to "carry on," reliving war's horrors for the rest of their natural lives. Over time, large numbers of Americans concluded that, as long as disabled veterans continued to suffer, the nation's "return to normalcy" would remain incomplete. As a columnist for the *Shreveport Times* explained in 1921, "The war is not over for those veterans discharged 'with disability' . . . And until the war is over with them, with the last one of them, it can not be entirely over for the rest of us."[2]

Heaven, Hell, or Hoboken before Christmas

On November 11, 1918, the banner headline of the *New York Times* left no room for doubt: ARMISTICE SIGNED, END OF THE WAR! BERLIN SEIZED BY REVOLUTIONISTS; NEW CHANCELLOR BEGS FOR ORDER; OUSTED KAISER FLEES TO HOLLAND.[3] Although false reports of the Armistice had circulated for several days before the ceasefire went into effect—prompting riotous celebration in cities across the country—few Americans were prepared for the announcement that "the war to end all wars" was over. In New York City, crowds of soldiers and sailors, some bearing the scars

FIG. 11. World War I was barely over before critics of martial internationalism resurrected the disabled soldier as an isolationist icon. In this image, renowned editorial cartoonist Winsor McCay suggests that joining the League of Nations would lead to a fresh wave of US casualties. Interestingly, McCay seems to single out Great Britain—caricatured as a rotund John Bull—as the primary force behind the United States' military misadventures. Winsor McCay, "If We Were in the League of Nations" (c. 1920). Library of Congress, Prints & Photographs Division, LC-USZ62-85742.

of recent battle, gathered around the *Times* building, unable to comprehend what had happened. For thousands of late draftees, including many already en route to France, the news brought the disheartening realization that they would never experience the thrills and terror of battle firsthand. Soldiers closer to the action expressed a range of emotions, from relief that the war was over to guilt that they had survived the conflict while others had not. Meanwhile, in the nation's capital, word of the ceasefire unleashed a torrent of activity, much of it aimed at returning the United States to a peacetime footing as quickly as possible. Even as Woodrow Wilson laid the groundwork for the League of Nations (fig. 11), the War Department and other federal agencies began to dismantle the United States' vast wartime bureaucracy, canceling contracts, rerouting shipments of munitions and material, and returning entire industries to private hands.[4]

From the public's point of view, the most pressing issue facing postwar America was the demobilization of the armed forces.[5] On the day the Armistice was signed, the United States had an emergency army of nearly four million men—half of them serving overseas—suddenly without a war or a purpose. While a few thousand soldiers would be required for a postwar army of occupation, the vast majority of US troops had little to do besides exercise, drill, and wage a relentless battle against boredom. In their minds, and in the minds of Americans stateside, the nation's doughboys had performed their duty: they had thwarted German militarism and, in the process, made the world "safe for democracy." Now it was time for them to come home. Luckily, for the rawest of US servicemen, home was rarely more than a few hours away. The minute the Armistice went into effect, secretary of war Newton D. Baker immediately halted all troop trains, and thousands of recently inducted draftees were dismissed by nightfall. Within four months of the ceasefire, the nation's training camps were virtually empty, and more than 1.3 million "home service" veterans were once again civilians.[6]

The task of dismantling the American Expeditionary Force (AEF) posed a far greater set of challenges. To begin, there was the logistical problem of repatriating millions of US soldiers. With the war's end, foreign troopships, which had ferried more than half of the AEF to France, were no longer available, and it would take months before the United States could assemble a flotilla of cargo transports, ocean liners, and warships to take their place. No less vexing was the question of demobilization's impact on the postwar economy. Although the War Department, the War Labor Policies Board, and other federal agencies rejected the British plan of mustering out men by industry or trade, they worried about flooding the domestic labor market with millions of former soldiers.[7] Restless, underskilled, and flush with a sense of their own importance, who knew what kind of trouble such men could sow, particularly if they maintained their wartime allegiances? But such concerns mattered little to the soldiers stationed abroad or to their friends and families waiting at home, who rallied under the slogan "Heaven, Hell, or Hoboken before Christmas." Faced with mounting civilian pressure (and highly publicized entreaties from members of Congress), the War Department soon abandoned its reservations about rapid demobilization of the troops. By December 1918, the French coastal cities of Brest, Bordeaux, and Saint-Nazaire began to swell with doughboys awaiting passage home. When the demobilization effort peaked in June 1919, more than 340,000 soldiers were returning from Europe every month.[8]

For those lucky enough to escape the war unhurt, demobilization was a remarkably efficient process. Whenever possible, overseas soldiers were mustered out by military units, a decision intended to expedite doughboys' transition to civilian life. Upon leaving France, most US troop transports crossed the Atlantic in about two weeks, arriving in one of four landing ports—Hoboken, Charleston, Newport News, and Boston—located along the Eastern Seaboard. Once on shore, soldiers were marched to nearby debarkation camps, where they were stripped naked and deloused in kerosene baths, their uniforms cleaned and pressed in gigantic steamers. From there, members of the AEF began the final leg of their journey as military personnel, traveling by rail to one of the thirty-three newly established demobilization centers. Camp commanders had marching orders to discharge all soldiers within forty-eight hours of their arrival, so there was little opportunity for ceremony or sentimental reflection. Besides their overseas pay ($30 a month for a buck private), departing men received a modest travel allowance and a cursory physical and psychiatric inspection. Early reports of ex-soldiers begging in uniform prompted Congress to authorize an additional payment to all discharged men. Starting in February 1919, former doughboys received a $60 bonus (enough to buy a set of civilian clothes) upon their release from service.[9]

The demobilization of seriously ill, convalescing, or wounded soldiers, on the other hand, proceeded on a case-by-case basis. While thousands of US troops were invalided out of front-line service before the war was over, only a small percentage of them—those deemed "permanently disabled"—were sent back to the States prior to the ceasefire. Military leaders were reluctant to devote precious cargo space to shipping home injured men, and many believed that even partially recuperated soldiers could still play some role in the war effort. When the war ended, men who were healthy enough to return with their units did so, but for tens of thousands of doughboys, rapid demobilization was out of the question. Troops discovered to be carrying acute infections—including venereal diseases—could not return to the United States until cured, a policy that tarred some late-arriving casualties with the brush of wartime sexual impropriety. Other hospitalized soldiers were simply too weak to survive the trip home, and were forced to wait months until they were fit enough to travel.

Unlike their able-bodied comrades, most sick or injured soldiers were not discharged soon after reaching US shores. Armed forces policy dictated that wounded soldiers could only be released after achieving a maximum point of "physical reconstruction," which meant that men with serious injuries were typically among the last doughboys to sever their ties with the armed forces. For patients recovering from severe burns or lost limbs—both of which usually required multiple surgeries and lengthy recuperation periods—the wait could seem interminable, with men shuttled from hospital to hospital for years on end. When soldiers, sailors, and marines showed no further chance of recovery, they were examined by military disability boards and prepared to reenter the world as civilians. As was the case throughout the World War era, federal examiners assigned disability ratings as a percentage of diminished earning power (a soldier rated 50 percent disabled, for example, was determined to have lost half of his earning power).[10] Many cases of latent sickness or future disability were not diagnosed until this final phase of demobilization, much to the chagrin of the men themselves. Upon learning that disability was an obstacle to their release, some doughboys even feigned healthiness, signing away future claims of compensation and relief. Those who did so would later regret their decisions, but in 1919, many vets weren't thinking about their long-term prospects. All they wanted was to get home as quickly as possible.

When the Boys Came Home

From the moment they made landfall, returning doughboys were accompanied by civilian well-wishers, eager to greet them as conquering heroes. Throughout the early months of the Armistice, local reception committees, some from as far away as California, made daily visits to East Coast landing ports, waiting for AEF troopships to pull into harbor. As US troops disembarked, cheering crowds waved signs, sang songs, and pelted the war-weary men with oranges, chocolate bars, and other symbols of peacetime abundance.[11] Public exhibitions of gratitude only intensified once veterans reached their final destinations. Across the United States, local politicians and civic boosters held lavish banquets and testimonial dinners for recently returned doughboys, showering them with praise and tokens of community affection. More than a decade after the Great War's end, Roger Burlingame, an officer in the 308th Machine Gun Battalion, waxed nostalgically on civilians' homecoming efforts: "The welcome they gave us was beyond all dreams of welcome in the history of America, if not of the world. We were paraded, feted, dined, wined, kissed, spoken and written about in terms that defied rhetoric and frequently abused it."[12] In the eyes of many Americans, nothing was too good for the nation's fighting men—and it was important for them to know it.

As always, some commentators worried about civilians' excessive displays of appreciation toward Great War vets. Critics argued that too much hero-worship would turn former doughboys—particularly wounded or disabled ones—into "professional patriots" who expected to leech off public sympathy for years to come. Instead of handing out flowers and medals to returning soldiers, one *Chicago News* cartoonist urged patriotic citizens to give them "A Welcome They Would Appreciate": namely, jobs with which they could begin a new life.[13] At the same time, many veterans abhorred the thought of returning home a public spectacle—to be gawked at, eulogized, and put on display for the admiration of all. Writing to his priest from a hospital bed in Fort Snelling, Minnesota, John L. Golob spoke for countless of his war-injured comrades: "The average soldier hates the word 'hero,' that's a fact. . . . Recognize us as men, men's men, and lay low on the sentimental stuff and we'll be satisfied."[14] By most accounts, the majority of World War I veterans wished to slip back into civilian life quietly and without ceremony.[15]

Unfortunately, returning soldiers rarely had a choice in the matter. More than mere by-products of demobilization, homecoming events were rituals of deep cultural significance, designed as much to mediate the collective fears and desires of civilians as those of soldiers returning from abroad. On one level, such displays offered communities a chance to demonstrate their gratitude toward soldiers' wartime service and make a grand patriotic gesture before taking up the business of peace.

Just as important, celebratory dinners and other homecoming events allowed communities to release pent-up anxieties about the dangers facing US troops "over there." According to Harold Hersey, an army public relations officer and author of the popular guidebook *When the Boys Come Home* (1919), homecoming fantasies pervaded wartime national consciousness, to a degree bordering on obsession:

> *When the boys come home!*
>   The entire nation is thinking of the day. It is the burden of speeches, the refrain of song, the subject of stories, the background of our daily lives . . .
> *When the boys come home!*
>   There is something holy in the very thought. It transcends all other mental things. It quiets the lonely heart of everyone who waits with longing. It amounts almost to a religion in the American home. No gathering omits reference to that greatest day of all—the day "when the boys come home."[16]

If soldiers' homecoming was a national religion, its signature ritual was the victory parade. As historian Mary Ryan has shown, the public parade emerged in the mid-nineteenth century as "the characteristic genre of American celebration."[17] Unlike fixed memorials, parades conveyed a sense of perpetual motion—of history moving forward and leaving the past behind. In the first year of the Armistice, some 200,000 US servicemen marched in more than 500 separate parades (fig. 12). The largest homecoming parades were filmed as newsreels and screened in movie theaters across the United States.[18] New York City alone hosted six massive processions, with thousands of uniformed veterans marching up Fifth Avenue through the Victory Arch, past the Court of the Heroic Dead, to the Tower of Jewels at 59th Street, where "a cluster of thirty thousand crystals flashed all the Allied colors in iridescent splendor."[19]

Parade watchers learned to spot wounded soldiers by the gold chevrons they wore on their uniforms ("naturally the most prized in the army," according to one veterans' newspaper).[20] Convalescing and disabled doughboys were singled out in other ways as well. When the 27th Division paraded through New York City on March 25, 1919, for instance, the wounded rode in open cars, wearing roses and carnations in their overseas caps. The practice of segregating war-wounded men from other

FIG. 12. Returning World War I soldiers march through a temporary victory arch in Minneapolis, Minnesota in 1919. Among other functions, homecoming parades served as temporal markers, dividing the time of war and the time of peace. Library of Congress, Prints & Photographs Division, LC-USZ62-78370.

parading troops had a twofold effect. From a purely logistical perspective, it made Great War casualties easier to identify. This was especially critical because, with the exception of amputees, burn victims, or men in wheelchairs, most disabled soldiers looked virtually the same as their fellow doughboys. More importantly, it reinforced the notion that disabled vets were in fact exceptional. Here amidst the crowds of olive green was a special class of American citizen, men whose bodily sacrifices made them deserving of extraordinary recognition.

In some parades, disabled troops were the sole attraction. One of the most spectacular precessions of disabled vets took place on a warm Saturday morning in September 1919, when more than 2,000 Great War soldiers—some on canes and crutches, others in wheelchairs or ambulances—filed past ecstatic crowds in downtown Chicago (fig. 13). Billed as the greatest public display of convalescing veterans in US history, the parade was but the opening stage of a citywide celebration honoring Illinois' "wounded heroes." Veterans from local hospitals were treated to lunch at the grand Auditorium Hotel, a trip to a White Sox baseball game, and an open-air dance on Michigan Avenue.[21] Chicago's Honor Day was not a "homecoming" parade in the traditional sense. At day's end, the patients would return to their hospital beds, some awaiting months, if not years, of medical care. For many of these men, the effects of the Great War would never disappear—at least, not as far as their bodily health was concerned.

Postwar parades were not meant to inaugurate a new era of veterans' appreciation. They functioned instead as *rites de sortie*—rituals of separation and closure. Their central message was that the war was over and it was time to go home. Even as the lines of doughboys filed past, paradegoers were urged to anticipate the day when America's fighting men removed their uniforms and rejoined the civilian ranks. But what kind of "home" were Great War veterans returning to? And what would they do when they got there?

Home—Then What?

In May 1919, Leon Schwarz, a US Army captain, sought to answer those questions—or, at the very least, keep his troops mentally occupied until they were sent back to the States. With the help of other officers, he organized an essay contest asking soldiers still stationed overseas to describe their plans once home. The collected volume of entries, entitled *Home—Then What?* (1920), promised readers an inside peak into the "mind of the doughboy." Essays touched on a range of topics, but two themes ran throughout. The first was that World War I vets had been changed by their experience—and, if the essayists were to be believed, changed for the better. "While soldiering our blood has reddened, our muscles have hardened," explained one soldier. "We are heavier, we are taller, we are stronger, and returning, we will infuse the iron of our blood in the nation and give her vigor." Just as prevalent was the conviction that World War I was the start of a larger moral crusade. "Problems confront us, the world, at every hand," another essayist warned, from Bolshevism abroad to disease at home. Veterans had a duty to continue

FIG. 13. Illustration of Chicago's "Honor Day" celebration for locally hospitalized disabled vets. Note the tension between the smiling faces of the participants and the line of wheelchairs, crutches, and empty sleeves that literally stretches into the horizon. "The Advance on Grant Park," *Fort Sheridan Recall*, September 27, 1919.

the fight, and they were not about to back down now.[22] According to John Kendrick Bangs, who wrote the book's forward, the collection was a blueprint for a revitalized nation. In the simple language of ordinary men, readers would find the "Soul of our New America, born in the muck and mire of War, and bred in the blood of an unselfish devotion to the highest ideals of Service."[23]

Although such optimism did not fade overnight, the climate at home was unreceptive to a fresh dose of veteran idealism. The AEF returned to a nation in the midst of social and political upheaval. Few could ignore the resurgence of racial nationalism, manifested most visibly in a wave of violence against blacks, Jews, and "hyphenated Americans." On July 17, 1919, the city of Chicago erupted into a race riot after an African American teenager accidentally swam in front of a "whites only" beach; when the violence subsided thirteen days later, thirty-eight people (mainly black) had been killed, and more than a thousand poor African Americans had lost their homes. From 1917 to 1919, the number of lynchings doubled, and a resurgent Ku Klux Klan practiced its unique brand of terror and political fundamentalism across the South and Midwest. The Armistice also ignited a revival of labor militancy as workers battled to retain gains won during the war. Nineteen-nineteen was among the bloodiest years of industrial strife in US history, with upward of four million workers walking off the job. In February, striking workers in Seattle brought the city to a standstill, prompting mayor Ole Hanson to raise the specter of a general workers' revolution. Adding to the climate of unease was the deadliest plague since the Middle Ages. The influenza pandemic of 1918–19 killed between 50 and 100 million people worldwide, including some 675,000 in the United States. Among those struck down by the disease were 57,000 US soldiers and sailors, roughly 4,000 more than had died in the actual fighting.[24]

Veterans who survived the disease faced a no less daunting challenge: finding a job. The vast majority of US doughboys had entered the armed forces with little work experience, and they returned home to a labor market already glutted with well-trained war workers and federal employees dismissed at the conflict's end. Within a few months of the Armistice, the US economy had slipped into recession, and more than three million Americans were unemployed. By April 1919, the War Department estimated that 41 percent of ex-soldiers were out of work.[25]

Initially, many jobless vets turned to social welfare groups and religious organizations for help. In some towns, the American Red Cross and Jewish Welfare Board functioned as de facto employment agencies for Great War vets. Larger communities organized local "reception committees" to help hometown soldiers make a fresh start.

In Minneapolis, for example, the local Citizens Welcome Committee distributed colorful pamphlets outlining veterans' services available in the Twin Cities. Local vets could wash up and make free phone calls at the committee's downtown headquarters, book a room at the Soldiers and Sailors Inn, or head over to the Army and Navy Club to shoot a game of pool with other ex-servicemen. The club's Bureau of Advice and Information helped vets track down job openings and plan their postwar futures. "Every man, woman, and child in Minneapolis is grateful to you," the Welcome Committee assured Minnesota's vets, "SO TALK UP AND MAKE YOUR WANTS KNOWN."[26] Although local welcome committees invoked public gratitude when explaining their efforts, they were also inspired by fears of a veteran population with nothing to do and no place to go. The faster ex-doughboys were off the streets, city leaders reasoned, the faster everyone could return to normal life.

Many state governments adopted a similar approach to the jobs crisis. As early as May 1919, the California legislature appropriated funds for the immediate financial assistance of indigent veterans. Connecticut provided small "separation allowances" to ex-servicemen, while Illinois established a special commission "to obtain employment and the necessaries of life" for returning soldiers. Within a few years of the Armistice, state governments passed a wide range of veteran-friendly legislation. In some states, former doughboys were given preferences for civil service jobs; other states provided veterans with free notary service and hunting and fishing licenses. As one might expect, sick and disabled veterans were beneficiaries of the most relief. In Massachusetts, disabled veterans and their families received small cash payments to supplement their incomes. Nebraska's disabled veterans were offered free admission to the state home for soldiers and sailors; likewise, Wisconsin provided convalescing veterans up to thirty dollars per month until they had recovered.[27]

On the federal level, complaints about the dire economic climate facing Great War veterans usually found their way to the desk of colonel Arthur D. Woods. A former New York City police commissioner and propaganda officer in the CPI, Woods headed the War Department office responsible for helping former soldiers make the hard transition to peacetime life. In his mind, the government's reemployment efforts were not a "charity" or a "kindness" but a "moral . . . [and] technical obligation to those who have served it so heroically."[28] His office was also motivated by growing suspicion that mass unemployment and veteran-led labor unrest could spark a homegrown Bolshevik uprising. Although many Americans were sympathetic to socialist ideals, the Russian Revolution of 1917 and the formation of the 3rd Communist International (Comintern) two years later, with its expressed goal of fomenting popular uprisings abroad, sparked one of the most pernicious Red scares in the nation's history. The US Justice Department waged a national witch hunt, deporting immigrants, jailing union organizers, and vilifying those who dared stand in their way.

As it turned out, Great War veterans were frequently at the forefront of antiradical activity. Regional veterans' publications such as the *"Over Here" Digest* and the *National Warriors Magazine* were filled with Red-baiting articles, and some veterans championed violent measures to quash would-be revolutionaries (the United States' most famous wounded vet, Arthur Guy Empey, once declared that "the tools for dealing with communists could be found in any hardware store").[29] On November 11, 1919, in Centralia, Washington, members of the American Legion attacked the headquarters of the radical Industrial Workers of the World (or "Wobblies") labor union. In the ensuing fracas and its aftermath, four Legionnaires were killed, one IWW member was lynched by local citizens, and thousands of Wobblies were arrested statewide.

Nevertheless, US vets had a difficult time shaking public suspicions that they harbored communist tendencies. Soldiers' participation in the Russian Revolution, along with the emergence of veteran-led political uprisings across postwar Europe, convinced many that it was a short road from disgruntled doughboy to armed militant. More paranoid critics worried that the armed forces' emphasis on collective behavior fostered a "mob mentality." Severely wounded or disabled soldiers were considered especially at risk—if not of becoming infected with Bolshevism, then of succumbing to an unhealthy dependence upon the state.

During the first few months of the ceasefire, Woods's office was inundated with letters, postcards, and wire messages from veterans seeking work. Some men sent in full resumes complete with detailed lists of their qualifications and vocational interests. The saddest missives told of veterans revisiting their old firms only to discover that they were no longer considered qualified or that former underlings had now become their superiors.[30] In March 1919, Woods created the Emergency Employment Committee, consisting of former soldiers, college professors, and experts in the fields of business, management, and law. Over the next nine months, the committee sponsored job classes, promoted public works projects, and distributed thousands of engraved citations to businesses that hired out-of-work veterans. Recognizing the importance of good publicity, Woods launched a multimedia propaganda campaign to convince hesitant employers that ex-soldiers were, in his words, an "excellent buy."[31]

Despite Woods's efforts, veterans with disabling injuries or mental impairments remained vulnerable to the dramatic contraction of the postwar economy. Many of the private-sector jobs promised in the flush of victory never materialized, and government placement officers struggled to persuade employers that permanently disabled men could hold their own alongside their nondisabled counterparts. In some cases, veterans' unemployment (or underemployment) was a result of recurring war-related illnesses or old wounds that refused to heal. Hit by a piece of shrapnel in the Argonne Forest, Ralph V. Anderson, a carpenter from Harwick, Pennsylvania, was forced to quit his job after only four months because of insomnia, post-traumatic nervousness, and chronic necrosis (his head wound did not stop draining fluid until 1922).[32] Others had been unhealthy upon enlistment and, despite incurring no actual wounds, were mustered out of service physically and mentally incapacitated. When he joined the Navy in July 1917, Francis Burke, an electric crane operator from Philadelphia, already suffered from painful varicose veins in his legs and a possible case of pulmonary tuberculosis. Aggravated by his service, his symptoms grew progressively worse, as near daily bouts of nausea and vomiting were compounded with night sweats, weight loss, and a relentless hacking cough. By the time Burke was finally discharged for disability in April 1919, he was spitting blood and too weak to return to the factory.[33]

In desperation, small numbers of disabled veterans sought to capitalize on their war-hero status before public interest lapsed. Across the United States, recently blinded doughboys opened up shops with official government seals verifying their disabled status. Others resorted to less scrupulous measures. Press reports from the early years of the Armistice describe an epidemic of veterans panhandling in uniform, including countless able-bodied men masquerading as "war cripples" to win public sympathy.[34] Some men simply begged or passed the hat on behalf of their disabled comrades. More often, they sold cheap trinkets and memorabilia, including war-themed magazines, commemorative books, and "authentic" souvenirs (e.g., German helmets, Iron Crosses) gathered from behind the front lines.

By mid-1919, the problem had become so pervasive (at least, in the public imagination) that the federal government launched a nationwide campaign to curb the "commercialization" of the uniform. Many cities passed ordinances restricting veteran panhandling and refused to issue business licenses to men in uniform. In a letter to Woods, who was also in charge of the War Department's antipeddling efforts, Newton D. Baker complained that the sight of panhandling soldiers sent the message that "the country is failing to provide suitable and proper places of employment for discharged men."[35] By Woods's own estimate, roughly 80 percent of vets had gone straight home after demobilization. The remaining 20 percent, however, had chosen to remain in the big cities, where they joined roving bands of vagrants and hustlers looking to prey upon patriotic sentiment.[36] In some cities, an underground industry sprang up to provide street fakirs with service stripes and medals. Government officials were especially worried about growing numbers of "Hun Cooties," professional con artists who hired veterans (or uniformed imposters) to hawk their wares and then pocketed the profits.

Although War Department spokesmen maintained that their "delousing" campaign was aimed at "Hun Cooties" and not down-on-their-luck vets, the connection between former soldiers and social deviance persisted well after the war's end.[37] Within two months of the Armistice, newspapers at home and overseas began to spread sensational reports of a looming "crime wave" perpetrated by ex-soldiers. Headlines about rising numbers of assaults, rapes, and murders within the AEF and among veterans at home fostered a climate of hysteria about the brutalizing impact of military life. Popular studies such as Benjamin Malzberg's "Demobilization and the Crime Rate" (1919) and Clarence Darrow's *Crime: Its Cause and Treatment* (1922) added a measure of scholarly weight to the frenzy, linking ex-soldiers to everything from rising numbers of bank robberies to sexual violence.[38] Phillip Gibbs, an influential British journalist who observed similar fears in the UK, proclaimed that combat and military discipline had transformed the nation's conscripts into sexually starved "ape-men" whose first impulse was to kill, maim, and destroy. While most soldiers were not "envenomed by the gospel of hate," Gibbs explained, there was no telling when a former soldier might suddenly revert to wartime barbarism.[39]

As would be the case following later conflicts, stories of veteran criminality after World War I were based more in fantasy than in fact. While former soldiers did represent a higher proportion of prison inmates than the general population, most vets were driven to crime because of unemployment, changing social conventions, and poor mental or physical health—in other words, the same reasons as everyone else.[40] But that mattered little to many postwar Americans, who continued to view disabled veterans as a potential menace.

Of all Great War veterans, none inspired greater fear and fascination than victims of shell shock.[41] Newspapers printed hundreds of articles on the lingering effects of psychological injury, often depicting shell-shocked men as deranged lunatics prone to violence and fits of hysteria.[42] While US popular culture tended to depict shell shock as a temporary phenomenon, mentally injured veterans were a common scapegoat for critics of postwar cultural change.[43] Some commentators described war neuroses as forms of moral contagion, seeping from shell-shocked carriers into an unsuspecting populace. Florence E. Allen complained, "The [post-Armistice] war neurosis was not limited to soldiers in the field. It spread throughout their families. From the family it spread throughout the entire civilian population and corrupted the growing boy and girl." Citing rising divorce rates and sexual promiscuity during the 1920s, one former general contended that soldiers' "shattered nerves" and "barbaric habits . . . lead directly and inevitably to . . . free love on a large, elaborate and ever-expanding scale."[44]

Meanwhile, recently returned veterans often felt like strangers in a strange land. Visiting a Chicago hospital in September 1919, former nurse Maude Radford Warren observed that the convalescing soldiers exhibited a "suspended" point of view, trapped between the horrors of the past and the banalities of the present.[45] Although many vets were simply glad to be home, others grew increasingly bitter, particularly because of what they saw as civilians' tendency to leave the war behind. Returning from Europe six months after the war's end, one wounded vet recalled, "I remember I met a girl I knew and I thought she would treat me like a hero. She acted as though she had seen me the day before."[46] A few months later, a reporter in Bridgeport, New York, described a similar scene. Though "Welcome Home" signs were "thickly scattered throughout the congested streets," the Great War was quickly losing its mystique. Gone were the "red, white and blue Columbias and Libertys" from the local cabarets. The writer even recalled spotting "a group of kiddies . . . mocking the jerky gait of a disabled ex-soldier, who was hobbling along in civilian clothes."[47]

Disabled Veterans and the Politics of Normalcy
The man who would be tasked with leading the nation through the postwar turmoil was former newspaper publisher and Ohio senator Warren Gamaliel Harding. A critic of faddish reform at home and military entanglements overseas, the white-haired Republican conveyed an image of calming stability after years of war and upheaval. The central theme of his 1920 presidential campaign was a "return to normalcy," a phrase popularized following Harding's address to the Home Market Club in Boston on May 14 of that same year. Despite the recent upsurge in "racked" nerves and "irrational" thinking, he told the assembled businessmen: "America's present need is not heroics, but healing; not nostrums, but normalcy; not revolution, but restoration; not agitation, but adjustment; not surgery, but serenity; not the dramatic, but the dispassionate; not experiment, but equipoise; not submergence in internationality, but sustainment in triumphant nationality."[48]

A few months later, Harding would clarify his by-then infamous catchword, explaining to a group of reporters: "By 'normalcy,' I do not mean the old order, but a regular, steady order of things. I mean normal procedure, the natural way, without excess."[49] As a campaign slogan, the "return to normalcy" resonated with war-weary voters who blamed Wilson-era internationalism for derailing the United States' tradition of peaceful progress.[50] The heart of its appeal was Harding's assurance that World War I—indeed the entire Progressive era of government reform and international military engagement—had been a period of exception, whose worst legacies were soon to fade away.

As the campaign stretched into summer, it was not entirely clear where disabled veterans fit within Harding's vision of postwar normalcy. Although several of the *buts* in his May 14 speech—"healing," "restoration," "adjustment," "sustainment"—were buzzwords within the burgeoning rehabilitation movement, the Republican senator tended to be critical of big government solutions to social problems. At the same time, Harding seemed to have a personal affection for Great War veterans and often felt the need to acknowledge their hardships, even if it also meant acknowledging the lingering consequences of the war itself. Accepting his formal nomination from his home in Marion, Ohio, Harding declared, "It is not only a duty, it is a privilege to see that the sacrifices made shall be requited, and that those still suffering from casualties and disabilities shall be abundantly aided and restored to the highest capabilities of citizenship and its enjoyment."[51] Voters believed him, and when they went to the polls in November, Harding defeated his Democratic opponent, governor James M. Cox of Ohio, by a margin of nearly two to one.

But by the time the new president took office the following March, federal relief efforts for disabled veterans were in disarray—and they would only get worse. With no central hub in Washington, responsibility for veterans' care was scattered across multiple governmental agencies, leading to bureaucratic inefficiency and administrative delays. In 1920, *New York Evening Post* reporter Harold Littledale released the first of a series of articles detailing systemic problems throughout the Federal Bureau of Vocational Education, the US Public Health Service, and other government agencies charged with veterans' care.[52] Because of government mismanagement, Littledale declared, tens of thousands of disabled veterans were "still waiting, exploited, neglected, forgotten, for the draft of honor to be redeemed."[53] A congressional investigation that same year found evidence of disabled men living on pennies a day, and of fraudulent vocational schools siphoning off government funds while leaving disabled veterans undertrained and out of luck.[54]

Littledale's reports ignited a firestorm in the national press. According to the *Birmingham Age-Herald*, "Disabled war-veterans are dying from neglect and the families of incapacitated soldiers are starving because they cannot get the compensation due them."[55] George Gillen, head of the National Disabled Soldiers' League, declared that 70,000 "insane" doughboys were languishing in county jails, a claim that would be repeated by experts and laymen alike.[56] When writer Helen Ledyard Birch visited the Washington headquarters of the Bureau of War Risk Insurance, she discovered disabled vets "at the point of suicide"; malnourished and penniless, America's fighting men had to wait weeks, even months, before their claims for compensation were heard.[57] Echoing the sentiments of many in the press, the *Pittsburgh Dispatch* observed, "If one-half of what is being told about the failure to provide for [disabled veterans] is true, it is cause for national abasement."[58]

The fervor surrounding the scandal reached a boiling point in the spring and summer of 1921. Across the nation, veterans' organizations joined muckraking journalists and citizens' groups in condemning the treatment of the war wounded. In New York City, Cornelius W. Wickersham of the American Legion chaired a series of public hearings at City Hall on the plight of disabled veterans. Hospitalized vets testified about endless red tape, indifferent staff, supply shortages, and inadequate medical care. Ally Hubelick, a patient at Fox Hills Hospital on Staten Island, recounted being physically abused by one of the hospital nurses (she had doused him with milk and gruel), while Frederick T. Albright described widespread neglect at the government's tuberculosis asylum at Saranac Lake, New York. Other men reported that their pensions had been slashed for no reason and that they were bullied into accepting unwanted surgeries or treatment regimes (often under the threat that refusal would result in the loss of all monetary compensation).[59]

On April 4, John Pershing delivered the keynote address at a mass meeting called "Justice for the Wounded" at Carnegie Hall. According to Pershing, the treatment of America's war wounded had been characterized by widespread mismanagement and incompetence. He told the assembled crowd of 4,000:

> It was the original purpose of our people, and is now, that all men suffering from wounds or illness incident to their splendid service should receive every consideration at the hands of the nation for which their sacrifices were made. But we continue daily to move

about in the enjoyment of peace and happiness while daily they who protected us suffer physical pain or physical incapacity from wounds which might be ours. They find themselves often helpless and beggared among those who escaped the risks of war, many of whom profited financially by its turmoil.

The former AEF commander urged his audience to "imagine the feelings of the neglected soldier toward a Government for which he offered his life. No government is worthy of its name that fails in sympathy and care for the men made helpless in fighting its battles." Like many champions of disabled vets, Pershing believed that the establishment of a single government agency would alleviate much of the bureaucratic entanglement and waste hindering disabled veterans' relief. Still, the fact that the United States' most trusted soldier was willing to criticize government efforts signaled a dramatic shift from the optimism of the early days of the Armistice.[60]

The emotional climax of the hearings came on April 5, when a delegation of Gold Star Mothers arrived to corroborate the veterans' stories of ill treatment and neglect. The group's name referred to the gold stars the women wore in memory of their dead sons. Revered for their personal sacrifice, many of them volunteered in government-run hospitals and rehabilitation centers following their sons' deaths.[61] According to the mothers' spokeswoman, what they found in New York area hospitals was even worse than veterans had described. Sick men ate from dirty dishes, slept in soiled sheets, and waited hours for even minimal treatment. Tears flowing down her face, Meta Steur told the audience, "On behalf of the Gold Star Mothers of the Union Hill, N.J., Chapter of the American War Mothers, I want to say that we gold-star mothers are 100 times gladder that our boys made the supreme sacrifice so quickly on the battlefields of France rather than that they should have been compelled to suffer the agonies that these poor boys are suffering in trying to get help and compensation."[62] Her message was emphatic: Great War veterans were better off dead than disabled.

That same day, a presidential committee led by banker (and future Republican vice president) Charles G. Dawes met in Washington to lay out plans to reorganize veterans' services under one roof. The committee reported its recommendations to Harding two days later, and after a summer of legislative wrangling in Congress, the United States Veterans' Bureau (USVB) was formally established on August 9, 1921. At the time, the USVB was considered a massive victory for veterans who had been agitating for just such an organization since the war's end. From its DC headquarters, the USVB wielded an annual operating budget of $450 million and an army of 30,000 employees. It offered America's veterans an institutional home within the federal government—a place to air their grievances, apply for monetary compensation or vocational training, and seek long-term medical assistance. Most important, the creation of the Veterans' Bureau ushered in a new "normal" in American political culture. From 1921 forward, the federal government recognized veterans' needs as a permanent problem requiring a permanent base of operations.[63]

Unfortunately, the paint had barely begun to dry before the Veterans' Bureau was mired in the very sort of negligence and misconduct it was meant to curtail. Traditionally, much of the blame has been placed on the bureau's first director, Charles R. Forbes—and rightly so. Forbes was an engineer and former Army administrator whose appointment was due more to his friendship with President Harding than his organizational skills. Under Forbes's direction, the Veterans' Bureau squandered $33 million appropriated for new hospitals while adding only two hundred new beds; it sold government property for pennies on the dollar and funneled kickbacks and lucrative contracts to Forbes's friends and business partners. Forbes himself was notorious for hosting elaborate drinking parties, running up massive hotel bills, and touring the country in luxury—all at the taxpayers' expense. According to one conservative estimate, the monetary outlay of waste and graft during Forbes's brief tenure exceeded $225 million dollars.[64] When Forbes resigned in February 1923, more than 200,000 letters from veterans and their families remained unanswered.[65] He was eventually convicted on charges of defrauding the US government, and he spent a year in Leavenworth federal prison for his crimes.

Of all the Veterans' Bureau's schemes, one of the most ill fated took place in the woods of eastern Minnesota. In 1922, District 10 of the US Veterans' Bureau and the University of Minnesota School of Agriculture sponsored a program to establish a series of farm colonies for disabled veterans and their families. The five colonies—Argonne Farms, Veteransville, Silver Star, Onamina, and Moose Lake—were modeled on the small, intensive farms doughboys had encountered while stationed in wartime France. Supporters of the plan believed that cooperative farming would offer disabled veterans both a chance for economic independence and a much-needed sense of community. By April 1923, Minnesota farm colonies were home to more than 130 disabled veterans, most of whom had taken out substantial loans to purchase their individual plots of land. Ex-soldiers built log cabins, dug wells, and sold raspberries through a collective trade association. In theory, the plan should have worked, but poor planning—and, in veterans' minds, shady real estate agents—doomed the project from the start. Much of the land proved unsuitable for cultivation, and few vets had the physical strength or agricultural background to operate a farm. Some colonists tried to stave off foreclosure by using government training stipends, but with cutbacks in veterans' funding, 75 percent of the farms were abandoned within the first decade. At present, visitors to the region would be hard-pressed to find any public reference to the colonies beyond the anachronistically named Argonne Village strip mall in Lakeville, Minnesota.[66]

Down and Out in the Jazz Age

It is at this point that the story of disabled veterans disappears from most treatments of the 1920s. In their seminal book, *The Wages of War*, historians Richard Severo and Lewis Milford argue that scandals at the Veterans' Bureau and other veterans' organizations failed to elicit a "national feeling of disgust." Concerns about disabled soldiers, they suggest, were swept away in the speed and greed of Jazz Age exuberance.[67] Today, the decade that followed World War I exists largely in the form of caricature: a time when would-be "It" girls bobbed their hair, sharp-suited Harlemites invented a "New Negro," and fast-talking gangsters tommy-gunned their way to the American Dream. Thanks to an insurgent mass culture, the decade's heroes and villains remain household names ninety years later: Charles Lindbergh and Babe Ruth, Charlie Chaplin and F. Scott Fitzgerald, Bonnie Parker and Clyde Barrow. However, throughout the Roaring Twenties, newspapers, magazines, and novels continued to prime the public imagination with searing portraits of disabled vets.

In some cases, media attention centered on the experiences of "celebrity" veterans. By far the most beloved disabled doughboy was former New York Giants pitcher Christy Mathewson. A member of the founding class of the Major League Baseball Hall of Fame, Mathewson had volunteered for overseas service at age thirty-eight. Shipped to France in the waning months of the war, he served—alongside Ty Cobb and future Dodgers' manager Branch Rickey—as an instructor in the hastily organized Chemical Warfare Service, a unit designed to teach soldiers how to respond to gas attacks. The work was dangerous, and Mathewson was exposed to poisonous gas on multiple occasions. He spent Armistice Day in the hospital, his lungs weakened by influenza and "residual deposits of mustard gas."[68] Plagued with a hacking cough, Mathewson briefly returned to the Giants as a coach but soon retired to a tuberculosis sanatorium in Saranac Lake, New York, where he eventually built a home. Mathewson's death on October 7, 1925, at the age of forty-five, made headlines across the country, and World Series rivals Pittsburgh Pirates and Washington Senators wore black armbands in his honor.

Yet most journalistic accounts of disabled veterans focused on the trials of ordinary men: the sick, the dying, the down-and-out. Throughout the 1920s, newspapers regularly printed stories of disabled Great War vets pushed to the brink of survival—or worse. In December 1923, for example, the *New York Times* carried the story of Ludwig Szymanski, a former butcher from Syracuse, New York. While serving near Château-Thierry, Szymanski had been shot in the abdomen and right thigh by a German machine gun; a burst from a high-explosive shell knocked out his teeth, and while awaiting rescue, he had been gassed, leaving him nearly blind. Upon demobilization, Szymanski was declared permanently disabled and awarded compensation of $80 per month. When his allowance was inexplicably slashed, he embarked on a futile crusade to verify his disability entitlement. According to the report, all attempts to win an audience with the Veterans' Bureau director were denied, and Szymanski was threatened with an insane asylum if he did not vacate the premises of the USVB headquarters. Once the embodiment of national will, the disabled doughboy was now a victim of bureaucracy, waging a quixotic battle against red tape and his own infirmities.[69]

Disabled veterans were also a staple of 1920s American fiction. No doubt the best-known book about a disabled veteran from this period was Ernest Hemingway's *The Sun Also Rises* (1926), whose male protagonist, Jake Barnes, struggles to find love and masculine identity in the English-speaking expatriate community of postwar Paris. Hemingway was not particularly interested in grappling with the everyday challenges faced by disabled veterans. Consequently, Jake Barnes's trauma-induced impotency functions largely as a metaphor of Lost Generation disillusionment and betrayal. However, other 1920s novelists took a different approach, examining the psychological, physical, and social obstacles that impeded disabled veterans' postwar adjustment once home.

In this regard, two novels deserve special attention, though for very different reasons. In 1921, best-selling Western novelist Zane Grey published *The Call of the Canyon*, a romantic pulp Western about a shell-shocked doughboy who regains his sanity in the American Southwest. Embittered by a government that "left [him] to starve, or to die of [his] maladies like a dog," Glenn Kilbourne flees his fiancée and New York City to a wilderness cabin near Flagstaff, Arizona. There, amidst the red rock canyons and picturesque waterfalls, he is physically and spiritually revived. Through hard work (he takes up pig farming), Kilbourne gains a renewed self-confidence and faith in the nation for which he fought. By the end, his fiancée has abandoned her Eastern home to join him in the frontier West. At its heart, *The Call of the Canyon* is a paean to traditional American ideals of rugged individualism and masculine authority. Critical of everything from feminism and war "slackers" to materialism and jazz, it suggests that—in Harding's words—disabled veterans don't need "revolution" or "experiment" to regain their past confidence. All they need is a pioneer spirit and a good woman at their side.[70]

Laurence Stallings' autobiographical novel *Plumes* (1924), on the other hand, offered a grimmer take on the causes and longevity of veterans' hardships.[71] Stallings was one of the most prominent literary figures of the postwar era, coauthoring the Broadway smash *What Price Glory?* (1924), writing numerous screenplays, and editing the award-winning collection *The First World War: A Photographic History* (1933). Steeped in Civil War history as a child, Stallings joined the Marines in 1917, eventually winning a Croix de Guerre and Silver Star. On the final day of the battle for Belleau Wood, he was leading a charge on a German machine-gun nest when a bullet shattered his right leg, tearing off his kneecap. Although surgeons were able to forestall amputation, the young author was never the same. In 1922, after slipping on a patch of ice, Stallings was hospitalized at Walter Reed Medical Center, where his right leg was removed. Four decades later, his left leg was amputated as well, a final

casualty of old war wounds and countless stumbles on his wooden prosthetic.[72]

Plumes traces the life of Richard Plume, a college-educated South-
erner whose dreams of battlefield glory lead him to enlist in World War I.
The latest in a long genealogy of family members disfigured or killed in
combat, Plume begins the novel a paragon of healthy manhood—"Flat
hips, and shoulders of a Rodin mode, with a shock of burnished hair
topping a wild, happy face"—only to be wounded seven times in the leg
and shipped home a grotesque reflection of his former self.[73] Shortly
after reuniting with his family, he embarks on a mission to "find out
why this thing happened to me" and to protect his young son from a
similar fate.[74] Along the way, Plume is forced to assimilate into a hostile world, where prejudices against disability trump pseudo-patriotic
promises, and where seemingly everyday tasks are fraught with danger.
Fitted with a heavy leg brace at Walter Reed, Plume is nearly assaulted
after accidentally bumping into a woman on a streetcar. During a job in-
terview at a Washington, DC, drug store, Plume is told to "drop back in
about six months" after the store manager notices his cane.[75] Estranged
from his wife and child, Plume eventually lands a job in a government
laboratory alongside Kenneth Gary, a crippled hunchback who served
with the Anzacs at the Battle of Gallipoli. In the novel's climax, Plume
clashes with a group of obnoxious, uniformed veterans at a political rally
at which Gary is a featured speaker. During the tussle, Plume reinjures
his leg, necessitating its amputation. He ends the book a tragic figure,
disenchanted with war yet helpless to do anything about it.[76]

What distinguishes *Plumes* from countless antiwar screeds featuring
disabled doughboys is Stallings's attention to the social and political context in which Great War vets attempted to piece together their lives. In the
novel, the economic downturn following the war's end, combined with
the cronyism of the Harding administration, has created an "economic
abyss" in which disabled veterans, former war workers, and political
appointees compete ruthlessly for a dwindling number of jobs.[77] While
businessmen enjoy an "orgy of normalcy," postwar Washington swarms
with an "army of disabled disgruntled."[78] The lucky ones are recruited
by politicians and put on display for their "vote-getting qualities."[79]
The rest are homeless or living in flophouses, forced to peddle issues of
the *Wounded Doughboy* magazine to make ends meet. Not surprisingly, the

Veterans' Bureau is the target of particular condemnation in Stallings's novel. While sharing a household with seventeen other disabled vets, Plume observes, "Their contempt and loathing for this departmental activity was beyond their power of expression. Criticism of the Veterans' Bureau usually ended in a tumbling tower of profanity"[80] Though Richard Plume might long to be "normal" once again, his desire is thwarted at every turn—by the federal government, his fellow citizens, even other vets. Outside of suicide, his only option is to carry on as best he can.

Carrying On

If the "return to normalcy" was the dominant cultural imperative of post–World War I America, disabled veterans' need to "carry on" represented a kind of subversion, an embodied protest against the notion that life after World War I could ever be "normal" again. The phrase "carry on" gained popularity during the war years when it was used to convey a sense of heroic stoicism and commitment to duty. Soldiers included it in their letters home to family, and it featured prominently in CPI propaganda and government fund-raising campaigns. A Liberty Loan advertisement from 1918 declared, "The fighting slogan in France, gathering inspiration and significance as the conflict grows more violent and more desperate, is 'Carry On.' On land, on sea, in the air, it rings sharp and clear." The Red Cross enjoined home-front civilians to send in money so that Red Cross workers could "carry on" helping doughboys with "parching throats and throbbing wounds." The phrase fed into popular myths of American exceptionalism and national valor, and was a special favorite of politicians looking to pay homage to the country's martial spirit.[81]

At war's end, "carry on" would take on darker meanings. Specifically, it came to be associated with disabled veterans' ongoing battles against physical impairment and bureaucratic indifference. The government's premier rehabilitation journal was named *Carry On*, and "Carry On Clubs" providing temporary living and communal space for disabled veterans popped up in cities across the country.[82] In later years, this and similar phrases would be used to describe the unique burden carried by disabled veterans: their inability to put the war behind them. While their fellow citizens returned to "normalcy" or lost themselves in Jazz Age reveries, disabled veterans were forced to "carry on," confronting the Great War's consequences on a daily (and lifelong) basis.

In this sense, the very concept of the permanently disabled veteran challenged the idea that World War I really was over—or that it ever could be. In her book *War Time*, legal scholar Mary L. Dudziak argues, "The onset of war is not seen as a discreet event, but as the beginning of a particular era that has temporal boundaries on both sides. Built into the concept of wartime is the assumption of an inevitable endpoint."[83] On November 11, 1918, Americans had celebrated just such an endpoint, and they would continue to mark the end of the fighting in homecoming celebrations and victory parades for months afterward. But every soldier and sailor who "carried on" was a tangible reminder that wars do not have neat beginnings and endings, particularly for those who fight them.

A decade after Warren G. Harding's promise of a "return to normalcy," the lingering costs of the Great War (and of "carrying on") continued to add up. Writing in *Commonweal* in 1931, Joseph Conrad Fehr lamented, "Year after year the ultimate figures expressed in terms of broken bodies, deranged minds, orphaned children, and millions of dollars for hospitals, training and compensation, have been mounting to new heights."[84] By the early 1930s, rising numbers of veterans with "neuropsychiatric disabilities" threatened to swamp government facilities, and more than 25,000 mentally traumatized veterans were under permanent guardianship of the state.[85] Not that the annual price tag of the war would decline any time soon. During the mid-1920s, the United States continued to pay hundreds of millions of dollars a year to veterans of the Civil War, a conflict that had been fought six decades earlier. In 1931, economist John Maurice Clark estimated that the total cost of caring for disabled veterans and their families over the next century could reach as high as $25 billion.[86]

Faced with such a future, large numbers of Americans saw the outlines of a new standard of "normalcy," one that included large outlays for veterans' services, a sprawling (and permanent) government bureaucracy for ex-soldiers, and an ever-expanding population of war-disabled citizens. Still, many continued to dream of a world in which disabled veterans (and the social, political, and economic problems they came to represent) did not have to "carry on." In 1924, this fantasy took celluloid form in *The Enchanted Cottage*, a film about a disfigured World War I veteran, played by Richard Barthelmess, who takes refuge within a secluded New England cottage (fig. 14). When he falls in love with the cottage's homely female caretaker, the couple's respective disabilities

FIG. 14. John S. Robertson's *The Enchanted Cottage* (1924), starring Richard Barthelmess and May McAvoy, tapped into widespread desires for the immediate disappearance of veterans' disabilities. Based upon a play by Arthur Wing Pinero and refilmed in 1945, it equated physical impairment in men with lack of beauty in women, offering up both as obstacles to happiness and social integration.

magically disappear, both in their own eyes and in the eyes of the audience. *The Enchanted Cottage* drew upon a widespread longing to erase the bodily consequences of World War I—indeed, to erase all forms of disability and aesthetic imperfection—from American life. And yet, a powerful contingent of military physicians and social reformers believed that the United States already had the means of eliminating the Great War's legacy of disability. In fact, they predicted that the United States was on the precipice of a post-disability era—an era in which war cripples did not need enchanted cottages to be seen as normal.

Sunday at the Hippodrome

On the afternoon of Sunday, March 24, 1919, more than 5,000 spectators crowded into New York City's Hippodrome Theater to attend the
culmination of the International Conference on Rehabilitation of the
Disabled. The purpose of the conference was to foster an exchange of
ideas about the rehabilitation of wounded and disabled soldiers in the
wake of World War I. Earlier sessions held the week before at Carnegie
Hall and the Waldorf-Astoria, had been attended primarily by specialists
in the field, among them representatives from the US Army Office of the
Surgeon General, the French Ministry of War, the British Ministries of
Pensions and Labor, and the Canadian Department of Soldiers' Civil
Re-Establishment. But the final day was meant for a different audience.
Part vaudeville, part civic revival, it was organized to raise mass support
for the rehabilitation movement and to honor the men whose bodies
bore the scars of the Allied victory.[1]

The afternoon's program opened with the debut performance of the
People's Liberty Chorus, a hastily organized vocal group whose female
members were dressed as Red Cross nurses and arranged in a white
rectangle across the back of the theater's massive stage. As they belted
out patriotic anthems, an American flag and other patriotic symbols
flashed in colored lights above their heads. Between songs, the event's
host, former New York governor Charles Evans Hughes, introduced inspirational speakers, among them publisher Douglas C. McMurtrie, the
foremost advocate of soldiers' rehabilitation in the United States. In
his own address, Hughes paid homage to the men and women working
to reconstruct the bodies and lives of America's war-wounded. He also
extended a warm greeting to the more than 1,000 disabled soldiers and
sailors in the audience, many transported to the theater in Red Cross
ambulances from nearby hospitals and convalescent centers.

The high point of the afternoon's proceedings came near the program's end, when a small group of disabled men took the stage. Lewis
Young, a bilateral arm amputee, thrilled the onlookers by lighting a cigarette and catching a ball with tools strapped to his shoulders. Charles

Bennington, a professional dancer with one leg amputated above the knee, danced the "buck and wing" on his wooden peg, kicking his prosthetic high above his head. The last to address the crowd was Charles Dowling, already something of a celebrity for triumphing over his physical impairments. At the age of fourteen, Dowling had been caught in a Minnesota blizzard. The frostbite in his extremities was so severe that he eventually lost both legs and one arm to the surgeon's saw. Now a bank president, Republican state congressman, and married father of three, he offered a message of hope to his newly disabled comrades:

> I have found that you do not need hands and feet, but you do need courage and character. You must play the game like a thoroughbred. . . .
> You have been handicapped by the Hun, who could not win the fight. For most of you it will prove to be God's greatest blessing, for few begin to think until they find themselves up against a stone wall.

Dowling stood before them as living proof that with hard work and careful preparation even the most severely disabled man could achieve lasting success. Furthermore, he chided the nondisabled in the audience not to "coddle" or "spoon-feed" America's wounded warriors: "Don't treat these boys like babies. Treat them like what they have proved themselves to be—men."[2]

4

"THE CRIPPLE CEASES TO BE"
The Rehabilitation Movement in Great War America

In August 1918, Curtis E. Lakeman, an official with the Red Cross, noticed a disturbing trend. "The constantly growing tide which for over a year has set steadily to the East has begun to send back its ebb of war-broken men," he wrote, "bringing at last to our shores visible evidence of the terrible reality of war."[1] Things would only get worse. By the Great War's end, more than 224,000 US service personnel had been seriously wounded in combat, with thousands more suffering the residual effects of disease, war neuroses, and "nonbattle" injuries. Americans had dealt with large numbers of war casualties before, but a growing cohort of Progressive reformers, business leaders, and military officials saw the makings of a crisis. Unless something could be done to "restore" US war casualties, they warned, American taxpayers would be saddled with expensive pensions and hospital bills for decades to come. As one writer put it, "[The disabled soldier's] wounds . . . will be 'glorious' for a time at least—but what then? How long before he will cease being a hero, and become just a cripple?"[2]

Thankfully, there was reason for hope: rehabilitation. Adopted with varying levels of enthusiasm by all of the Great War's belligerent nations, rehabilitation was an integrated program of physical and social reform combining orthopedics, vocational training, psychological counseling, and industrial discipline.[3] Its goal was seductively simple: to help disabled veterans reintegrate into postwar society as productive citizens. Supporters touted the rehabilitation movement as a "modern" alternative to Civil War–era models of veterans' relief, which they believed relegated disabled vets to lives of unmanly idleness. To its most fervent disciples, rehabilitation marked the start of a new historical epoch, one in which disability itself would soon disappear. In October 1917, the US Army Surgeon General's Office predicted, "Probably one of the strangest as well as one of the best things that will come to our country through this war, if its duration is of sufficient length, is that from now on the cripple ceases to be."[4]

Today, the basic tenets of Great War–era rehabilitation programs are so imbedded in US policy toward disabled veterans that it is almost impossible to imagine a time when they were new. In addition, predictions of disability's demise have become a staple of wartime political discourse and popular culture. From World War II–era paeans to the "miracle" of plastic surgery to recent headlines about Iraq War quadruple amputee Brendan M. Marrocco's double arm transplant, Americans have long been inundated with "evidence" that war's traumas can be— and soon will be—erased. However, Great War rehabilitationists' predictions of the "passing of the cripple" proved overly optimistic. Plagued by difficulties from the start, rehabilitation not only failed to solve the Problem of the Disabled Veteran, it fueled impossible fantasies about Americans' capacity to avoid war's consequences.

"The Problem of the Crippled Soldier"

The 1919 Hippodrome rally was not the first public forum on the challenges posed by disabled soldiers. Four years earlier, a group of college professors, surgeons, and businessmen met at the Summer School of Scientific Management in Providence, Rhode Island, to discuss what they called "the problem of the crippled soldier." The Summer School was the brainchild of Frank B. Gilbreth, the noted American efficiency expert and former student of Frederick Winslow Taylor. Gilbreth and his wife, Lillian Gilbreth, an industrial psychologist and writer, had first gained prominence with their "motion studies" of bricklayers and other workers.[5] At the start of World War I, Frank Gilbreth was in Berlin, studying the mechanical efficiency of German surgeons. Horrified by the carnage he encountered, and cognizant of public interest in war-related topics, he soon turned his attention to disabled soldiers and their reintegration into the European workforce.[6]

By the time the Summer School convened in August 1915, over two million combatants had been permanently disabled, and daily thousands more suffered severe injuries. Writing in *Scientific American Supplement* that December, Gilbreth asked, "What is to be done with these millions of cripples, when their injuries have been remedied as far as possible, and when they are obliged to become again a part of the working community?" The belligerent nations lacked the funds to provide pensions for so many wounded men, and even if they could have, Gilbreth believed that no pension system could provide incapacitated soldiers with the "occupation" necessary to living a meaningful life. "The great problem that faces the world to-day," he concluded, "is immediate and permanent provision for enabling these millions of crippled soldiers to become self-supporting."[7]

An ocean away, European military physicians expressed similar concerns. Even as wounded bodies continued to pour in, front-line observers fretted publicly about the looming challenges of peace. In a 1915 study, Maurice Bourrillon, director of the National Professionnel des Invalides de la Guerre in Saint-Maurice, France, declared: "The immense number of mutilated and infirm soldiers whom the modern methods of warfare will return to civil life in such condition that they will be totally or partially incapable of earning a living by their own industry, gives rise to a social problem of the highest importance, and the future of these glorious victims is a woeful question."[8]

Like Bourrillon, many early students of the "crippled soldier problem" credited large armies and modern weaponry for the sudden uptick of disabled combatants.[9] But other factors proved just as important. Advancements in ground transportation and triage care allowed medics to remove combatants from the battlefield in a matter of hours, while improved surgical techniques widely expanded the range of survivable injuries. The Western Front was the largest medical laboratory the world had ever known, and military physicians took advantage of the daily crop of wounded bodies. By 1918, enthused one writer, surgeons were "patching the human body in ways almost undreamed of five years ago."[10]

Within months of the United States' entrance into World War I, speculation about the nation's postwar disability crisis had already reached a fevered pitch. At that time, the Problem of the Disabled Veteran was primarily conceived as a matter of unemployment. Wartime commentators worried that the US economy would be unable to absorb large numbers of permanently weakened or disabled soldiers, and that the lost labor force would represent a significant financial burden for decades to come. Specialists working with the first wave of returning wounded soldiers only added to such fears. According to T. B. Kidner, vocational secretary of Canada's Invalided Soldiers' Commission, many wounded veterans had become so unaccustomed to caring for themselves that they lacked the competitive instincts to survive in the capitalist marketplace. Soldiers who failed to be "de-militarized," he warned, were prone to delinquency, criminal behavior, and a host of other social ailments.[11]

Never far from the minds of many American commentators was the aftermath of the Civil War. Fifty years after Appomattox, the "halo and pension" approach to veterans' relief had become a source of national embarrassment.[12] As one War Department official conceded in 1918, "The disabled hero of past campaigns, fortified alone by a Victoria Cross or some other badge of honor, was awarded a niggardly pension on which he could not live, and left to a life of idleness and dependence, if not mendicancy. About the best the crippled soldier could hope for in the war of employment was a job as doorman, night watchman, or street vendor."[13] Critics derided the high costs of nineteenth-century pension schemes, pointing to the millions "wasted" on soldiers who escaped the fighting unscathed. In turn, they argued that post–Civil War largesse had spawned a public menace: "the querulous, complaining, utterly idle pensioner, refusing to make the most of his remaining capabilities, indifferent alike to his dependents, his community, and himself."[14]

To an increasing number of Americans, World War I demanded a modern approach to the Problem of the Disabled Veteran. That approach was rehabilitation.

The Appeals of Rehabilitation
While the rehabilitation of disabled soldiers would garner support from a wide swath of policy makers and social critics, the movement's chief advocates came from several overlapping camps. Leading the charge were Progressive reformers, many of whom had either championed the US entrance into World War I or had welcomed the conflict as an opportunity for social engineering. Mobilizing the language of Progressive militarism, Theodore Roosevelt proclaimed, "The same efficiency that must be exercised in the making of our army and navy, in the building of ships to hurry men and supplies to our allies overseas, must also be applied to the rehabilitation of the wounded soldier and sailor—not a stone must be left unturned to restore these men to fields of usefulness and self-support."[15] As with previous Progressive campaigns, the rehabil-

itation movement was animated by a deep faith in the power of technology and government planning to resolve the social problems of industrial modernity. Rehabilitation also sought to inculcate ex-soldiers in the values Progressives believed most critical to national well-being: social responsibility, economic independence, and middle-class propriety.[16]

Progressives were joined by union and business leaders, many of whom championed rehabilitation on pragmatic grounds. Writing in September 1918, American Federation of Labor president Samuel Gompers argued that labor supported rehabilitation not only for "social reasons" but also because of the "detrimental economic consequences that would result from failure to return [disabled soldiers] as resourceful, able members of society."[17] The Red Cross, the Army Medical Department, and the Surgeon General's Office also embraced the cause of rehabilitation, as did a number of orthopedic surgeons and industrial physicians, all of whom hoped to raise their professional and institutional status by rebuilding America's wounded doughboys.[18]

In the United States, rehabilitation's most prolific spokesman was bibliographer and typeface designer Douglas Crawford McMurtrie. A graduate of the Massachusetts Institute of Technology, McMurtrie had no formal training in orthopedic medicine—or any disability issue for that matter. He first became interested in the plight of disabled people in 1910 after a chance encounter with an associate of the newly formed Society for Crippled Children. Within a few years, the legendary autodidact was considered an authority in the field, serving as both the editor of the *American Journal for the Care of Cripples* (1912–1919) and the president of the Federation of Associations for Cripples (1915–1919). During World War I, McMurtrie traveled abroad to study rehabilitation techniques in Europe and Canada, and he wrote scores of articles on such varied topics as disability in Western art and the construction of farms for disabled Panama Canal workers. Perhaps his most noteworthy achievement came in 1919, when he published *The Disabled Soldier*, one of the first book-length studies of injury and rehabilitation.[19]

For McMurtrie and others, rehabilitation had numerous selling points, especially when compared to the prevailing "pension and soldier's home" school of veterans' relief. First, rehabilitation promised to turn disabled soldiers into useful citizens. For white men in particular, being useful was understood to mean one thing in particular: achieving a sense of economic autonomy. In the words of one American rehabilitation officer: "The ultimate object [of rehabilitation] is the refitting of the disabled soldier to take his place in the world as a useful citizen, trained by the best instructors to make a good living for himself, to restore him to civil life not only sound in body but better equipped mentally to succeed in his calling than before his entrance into the service of his country."[20]

Thanks to government training programs, rehabilitated veterans would no longer be "victims" of physical impairment, wrote surgeon general William C. Gorgas in July 1918. Instead, they would be empowered to "enjoy the freedom and happiness afforded by world wide democracy for which [they have] given [their] all."[21]

Similarly, rehabilitation promised to remasculinize America's wounded warriors, saving them from lives of shameful dependency.[22] According to *Carry On*, the flagship government rehabilitation journal, the "Creed of the Disabled Soldier" was "Once more to be useful—to see pity in the eyes of my friends replaced with commendation—to work, produce, provide, and to feel that I have a place in the world—seeking no favors and giving none—MAN among MEN in spite of this physical handicap."[23] In forecasting disabled soldiers' return to manhood, rehabilitation's supporters often drew sharp distinctions between the economic and physical consequences of traumatic injury. Advancements in the fields of orthopedics, cosmetic surgery, and prosthetic mask design allowed reconstructive specialists to hide many (but by no means all) of the most socially disabling scars of war. Nevertheless, rehabilitationists believed that advances in science and industry meant that men no longer needed physically powerful bodies to avoid the stigma of charity. "In this age of specialization and diversification," opined one industrial specialist, "arms and legs are really incidental in the game of earning a livelihood by one's own labor."[24] By conceiving of disability—and, by implication, manhood—almost entirely in terms of socioeconomic independence, rehabilitationists were confident that successfully rehabbed vets would be able to "take up their burdens as normal human beings."[25]

At their utopian moments, rehabilitation's supporters argued that rehabbed vets were actually better off than those who escaped the war unhurt. In an article aimed at the parents of war-disabled doughboys, Gelett Burgess, a popular poet and one of many writers associated with the rehabilitation movement, highlighted the unique opportunity available to their sons:

> Think what that means—a free technical education for your boy! Perhaps he was a machinist. With efficient instruction that he could not before afford, he may fit himself to be a foreman in his old shop. If before he was wounded, he was only a "hand," he may be taught enough to make him an expert. Before the war he took any job he could get. Under the supervision of the best available vocational teachers, he will be trained for the job for which he is best adapted or most inclined.[26]

Burgess's faith that rehabilitation could transform laboring "hands" into supervising "experts" reflected the middle-class value system at the heart of much rehabilitation ideology. And his sentiments were by no means unique. Writing in the *Red Cross Magazine*, Samuel Hopkins Adams proclaimed that the "ideal result of reconstruction" was "to give the [disabled] man higher status than he had before" he was injured.[27] Indeed, the process of class mobility both men described was central to rehabilitation's most audacious claim: that severe war injury could be a soldier's best chance at a better life.

As its supporters were quick to point out, rehabilitation's appeals were not limited to veterans alone. By cutting down on the long-term costs of veterans' pensions, the practice promised to save taxpayers millions of dollars. Rehabilitationists also believed that veterans' training programs would serve as a prophylactic against the problems of delinquency and criminality long associated with unemployed vets. Thomas Gregory predicted that unlike "the army of tramps that infested the United States after the Civil War," disabled doughboys would help usher in a new era of American productivity and economic growth.[28] Equally important, rehabilitation would help eliminate that most dreaded of Progressive era scourges: *waste*. Concerns about different forms of waste permeated turn-of-the-century American culture, animating a wide range of reform movements designed to improve efficiency and conserve the nation's material and symbolic capital.[29] As an attempt to salvage America's lost labor power, soldiers' rehabilitation was not only an extension of these earlier movements but their apotheosis. In the words of the Office of the Surgeon General, "Perhaps . . . one of the greatest consequences of the present war is the *new attitude toward the war cripple*—a human waste product at last coming to be utilized" (emphasis in original).[30]

In theory, rehabilitation seemed to provide the answer to all of the problems of disabled veterans. Whether it actually worked was another issue entirely.

The Practices of American Rehabilitation

When World War I began, the United States had little firsthand practice rehabilitating diseased and disabled soldiers. Although primitive orthopedic hospitals dated back to the 1860s, the rehabilitation of American doughboys was largely an experiment, one initially fraught with disorganization and bureaucratic infighting. Some of the first studies of disabled soldiers' rehabilitation were conducted by the Federal Board for Vocational Education (FBVE), which had been created in February 1917 to promote vocational education for disabled workers and so-called congenital cripples. Later that year, the Office of the Surgeon General and the Bureau of War Risk Insurance established their own programs to help disabled veterans secure long-term medical care and employment upon discharge from service. In January 1918, representatives from the Surgeon General's Office, the US Army, the Red Cross, the American Federation of Labor, and other interested parties assembled in Washington, DC, to determine the scope of US rehabilitation practices. Out of their efforts came the first comprehensive legislation authorizing the physical, social, and economic rehabilitation of disabled vets.

The Vocational Rehabilitation Act of June 1918 provided extensive physical treatment and vocation training for all disabled ex-servicemen. Qualified applicants received expenses for school tuition, free medical care, prosthetics or orthopedic apparatuses, and a monthly monetary compensation equal to that of their last month of active-service pay. The act also institutionalized a division between the two main phases of the rehabilitation process: *physical reconstruction* and *vocational rehabilitation*. Soldiers undergoing physical reconstruction, which might include everything from orthopedic surgery to the application of prosthetic appliances, remained in the hospital under military supervision and discipline. Once discharged, they fell under the supervision of the Federal Board for Vocational Education, which was charged with retraining disabled veterans for a future occupation (fig. 15).

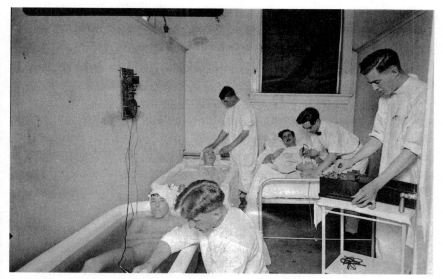

FIG. 15. As part of their physical reconstruction regime, these former doughboys are undergoing hydrotherapy at VA Hospital No. 37 in Waukesha, Wisconsin. 15-VR-3F-1, National Archives, College Park, MD.

In practice, it was often unclear when reconstruction ended and vocational training began. Months before the Vocational Rehabilitation Act became law, military physicians and orthopedic surgeons were already integrating preliminary forms of vocational education into their reconstructive regimens. Patients at Walter Reed Army Medical Center in Washington, DC, the largest in the War Department's network of rehabilitation hospitals, could choose from prevocational courses in agriculture, printing, mechanical and electrical work, drafting, leatherwork, and machine repair.[31] Eventually, the surgeon general designated more than forty-five military hospitals for reconstruction work, each of which had extensive facilities for technical and academic courses.

To cut down on delay and expense, the FBVE initially decided to use preexisting training facilities rather than build its own. By April 1922, the federal government had contracts with over 3,500 colleges, universities, commercial schools, and correspondence programs, along with 30,000 individual businesses, to provide vocational education and apprenticeships for rehabbing veterans. For soldiers already mustered out of service but physically unable to join other vocational courses, the government provided training opportunities in public health service hospitals, private sanatoriums, soldiers' homes, and tubercular communities. Beginning in the fall of 1921, the newly formed US Veterans' Bureau (USVB), which had taken over the job of administering soldiers' rehabilitation, established forty-eight all-veteran vocational schools across the United States.

From the start, American rehabilitation programs drew heavily upon the experiences of similar programs in Canada and Western Europe. Officials from the Surgeon General's Office (OSG) studied Belgian rehabilitationists at Port-Villez, France, where disabled soldiers were taught to produce supplies for the Belgian army. From the British, they learned that disabled students performed best when segregated from their nondisabled classmates, and that when it came to motivating disabled soldiers, "no one can be so helpful to a cripple as another cripple."[32] By far the most important lesson US rehabilitationists took from their Allied colleagues was that America's Disabled Veteran Problem could not be handled on a state-by-state basis; it required a national response, akin to that instituted by the Canadian Hospital Commission. The OSG calculated that for every million men sent overseas, 100,000 would return permanently disabled, with nearly 30,000 in the hospital at any one time.[33] Even so, American rehabilitationists were so confident they could learn the lessons of Europe—and then some—they dismissed the long-term social implications of war injury, even before the bulk of the disabled doughboys had returned to US shores. As rehab booster Herbert Kaufman put it, "The remarkable achievements of retinkered European soldiers indicate that the only hopeless cripple is a deliberate shirker."[34] Those who worked hard and listened to their counselors were virtually assured material success.

Despite later efforts to streamline the treatment of the war-disabled, there was no single route from disability to rehabilitation. The actual process of evacuating, transporting, hospitalizing, and training severely injured servicemen—known euphemistically as the *career* of the disabled soldier—was highly flexible, contingent not only upon the extent of an individual soldier's injuries but also his general health, former vocation, level of education, and willingness to undertake rehabilitation work. Some soldiers required extensive physiotherapy and orthopedic surgery before they could even begin their vocational training. Others recovered far more quickly and were able to begin prevocational training while still under doctor's care (fig. 16).

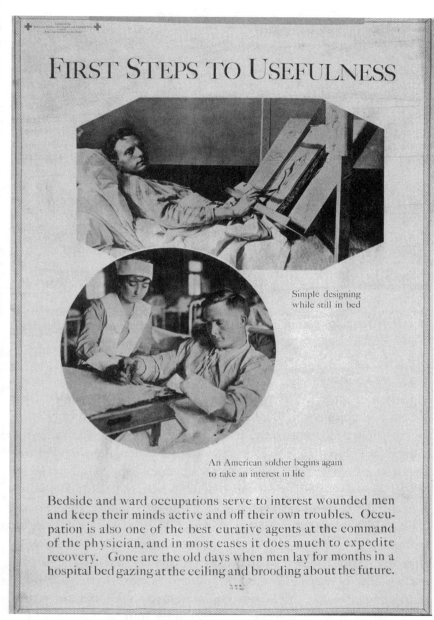

FIRST STEPS TO USEFULNESS

Simple designing
while still in bed

An American soldier begins again
to take an interest in life

Bedside and ward occupations serve to interest wounded men
and keep their minds active and off their own troubles. Occupation is also one of the best curative agents at the command
of the physician, and in most cases it does much to expedite
recovery. Gone are the old days when men lay for months in a
hospital bed gazing at the ceiling and brooding about the future.

FIG. 16. Produced by the Red Cross Institute for Crippled and Disabled Men and the Red Cross Institute for the Blind, this exhibit poster portrays bedside occupational therapy as the first step in returning disabled veterans to a state of "usefulness." Library of Congress, Prints & Photographs Division, LC-USZC4-7383.

FIG. 17. Many rehabilitation experts argued that mentally traumatized or "shell-shocked" soldiers needed to be separated from the "physically" wounded. This group of catatonic veterans was recovering at USVB Hospital No. 24 in Palo Alto, California. 15-VR-1-C-1, National Archives at College Park, College Park, MD.

Throughout this process, military and government officials made a concerted effort to segregate certain groups of disabled soldiers from the general population. Shell-shock cases, for example, were typically sent to General Hospital No. 30 at Plattsburgh Barracks, New York, while soldiers with tuberculosis recovered at General Hospital No. 16 in New Haven, Connecticut. General Hospital No. 11 in Cape May, New Jersey, hosted men with damaged hearing and speech, and blinded soldiers were shipped to General Hospital No. 7, a converted plantation in Roland Park, Maryland. This taxonomic approach to soldiers' reconstruction was meant to stimulate a sense of camaraderie among men with similar types of disabilities, but it also came from a belief that certain kinds of war casualties—war neurotics and blinded men in particular—had a depressing effect on general hospital morale (fig. 17).[35] In a 1922 report, Charles R. Forbes, the director of the Veterans' Bureau, authorized that Camp Sherman (along with five other USVB training facilities) would only accept "cases of a general medical or surgical nature." Men suffering from pulmonary or neuropsychiatric ailments were not welcome. In drawing such distinctions, Veterans' Bureau policy not only reaffirmed stereotypes about "worthy" and "shameful" injuries but also undercut one of the central tenets of rehabilitation: that all disabled vets could be made normal through training. Nevertheless, Forbes remained adamant: Camp Sherman "must not be used as a dumping ground for undesirables."[36]

While rehabilitation normally proceeded on a case-by-case basis, several principles pervaded all government-sponsored rehabilitation work. First, vocational specialists believed that rehabilitation needed to begin as early as possible. Soldiers were expected to take part in some form of exercise or occupational therapy as soon as their conditions had stabilized. Second, a soldier's decision to pursue vocational training had to be voluntary. According to Douglas C. McMurtrie, "The unwilling and rebellious pupil learns but little, the earnest and ambitious one makes rapid progress. The man must be persuaded, therefore, to take up instruction; the future advantages of being a trained workman in some skilled trade should be pointed out, and the practical arrangements to be made for him during the course of instruction carefully explained."[37]

The task of explaining the goals and advantages of rehabilitation fell to federal vocational counselors, who were responsible for guiding potential trainees toward the most appropriate courses of training. In their meetings with would-be trainees, vocational counselors discouraged disabled soldiers from pursuing "temporary war jobs" or occupations requiring the use of "specialized apparatuses." Instead, they pointed vets toward "standard trades" with the potential for long-term employment.[38] Whenever possible, vocational counselors tried to build on soldiers' former job experiences when helping them decide their future careers. If the trainees had little work experience (as was the case with the vast majority of America's war-wounded), vocational counselors were instructed to consider the men's aptitude, physical condition, and "character" when providing career advice. Ultimately, however, the individual soldier was responsible for choosing his own course of training.[39]

One of the most significant features of post–World War I veterans' programs was their emphasis on treating the "psychology of the cripple."[40] Rehabilitationists worried that, more than any physical ailments, soldiers' feelings of self-pity and inadequate masculinity would prove to be the biggest obstacles to their successful reintegration into civil society.[41] In a letter to the Surgeon General's Office, one disabled civilian stressed the importance of "kill[ing] the idea of helplessness almost as soon as it is born." The author advised government rehabilitation workers to screen "moving pictures of men who are crippled enjoying themselves in normal ways, dancing, skating, paddling a canoe, swimming, playing billiards, rolling cigarettes, and hundreds of things they cannot or do not know about."[42] Anticipating such concerns, the US government employed a number of "cheer-up men"—usually economically successful disabled civilians—to raise the spirits of the war-wounded and introduce them to the benefits of rehabilitation.

During the peak years between 1921 and 1923, roughly 156,000 World War veterans took part in government-sponsored rehabilitation work.[43] Many graduates went on to use their training to secure better-paying employment. After being shot in the left thigh near Verdun, John Aaron, a subsistence farmer from Haleyville, Alabama, was retrained as a tailor and dry cleaner, eventually landing a position at a clothes shop for a hundred dollars a month. Before the war, Fred Doucette of Malden, Massachusetts, worked as a chauffeur; gassed at Château-Thierry, he completed business school and found work as a jewelry salesman. Charles Rushford's only prewar job experience was as a receiving clerk making fifty dollars a month; after suffering from measles and a gas attack while in service, he was retrained as a mechanical draftsman at twice his prewar salary.[44]

Louis W. Jones of Starkville, Mississippi, epitomized rehabilitation's promise of upward mobility. Jones was a twenty-seven-year-old agricultural student at Mississippi A&M College when he enlisted in the US Army. An explosion in France left him deaf in one ear, and he spent twenty-three weeks in the hospital recovering from his injury. Returning to school in May 1919, he was declared rehabilitated three years later and quickly landed a teaching job at a salary of $2,000 per year. In its summary report of Jones's case, the Veterans' Bureau cast the newly minted teacher as living proof of rehabilitation's power to help veterans transcend class boundaries:

> As a result of his training, instead of "going back to the farm," [Jones] has begun to climb the ladder of success, and those who are intimately connected with his training, predict that he will be a suc-

cess and go much higher in his profession. Instead of doing manual labor himself, as he would probably have done had he not entered the service and received his handicap, he is now teaching others the best and most improved methods of farming, and receiving more than he would otherwise have done.

. . . Through the training received under the supervision of this Bureau, he has not only acquired the ability to do higher class work, but, in addition to having become capable of commanding a salary, he has developed a character which anyone might be proud of, and he is such a man as any community feels honored to claim as a citizen.[45]

Government records make it difficult to determine what happened to men like Jones later in life. Fully rehabilitated veterans were expected to break their ties with the state and take up their lives as "normal" civilians. It's likely that many vets continued to "climb the ladder of success," using the skills acquired in rehabilitation training to forge better lives for themselves and their families.

However, it's equally clear that rehabilitation had its limitations, particularly for those whose physical reconstruction remained incomplete. A case in point was the unhappy "career" of Sylvester Howland, a former textile worker from Waterford, New York. Shot in the left leg near Ronssoy, France, on September 29, 1918, Howland was immediately evacuated to the British hospital at Trouville, where emergency medical workers performed the first of many operations to help stave off long-term impairment. Over the next year and a half, surgeons continued to remove pieces of necrotic tissue and bone from the wound before finally amputating his foot on March 13, 1920. When the stump refused to heal, he was sent to Walter Reed, where his leg was re-amputated seven and a half inches below the knee.[46]

Upon his discharge in September 1920, Howland's vocational counselor advised him to pursue a course in watch making, a career that would require little in terms of formal education (Howland had left school after the sixth grade). But the new veteran disagreed and began training as an auto mechanic at a garage in his hometown. After an ill-fitting artificial leg and other medical problems delayed his progress, Howland was finally declared rehabilitated by the Veterans' Bureau in June 1924, nearly six years after suffering his initial wound. Despite his new designation, however, he struggled to find suitable employment. Rated 52 percent disabled, Howland continued to draw a monthly pension and he remained dependent upon government transportation whenever his prosthetic leg needed replacement or repair. By 1930, he had given up on his three years of auto repair training and was back inside a mill—this time working as a foreman.[47]

Roadblocks to Rehabilitation

For all his medical difficulties, Sylvester Howland was one of the luckier rehabilitation cases. Many disabled soldiers encountered even greater roadblocks to recovery. The process of transforming "helpless cripples" into "useful citizens" was notoriously inefficient. For the first eight months of the Armistice, disabled soldiers were not eligible for vocational training until they had first been awarded compensation by the Bureau of War Risk Insurance and had undergone rigorous screening by the US Public Health Service. The rapid rate of wounded soldiers returning home from Europe—23,000 per month in early 1919—soon outpaced the government's ability to handle their claims. A report published in the *New York Times* estimated that, as of June 28, 1919, fewer than 4,000 disabled veterans were training in government-sponsored vocational programs. Worse still, it concluded, "The long delays to which the crippled and disabled men have been subjected, the entanglements of red tape, and the worry over money matters while they waited, in many instances with nothing to live on and no way to make a living, have seriously affected their morale. This is apparent even among those under hospital treatment."[48] In July 1919, Congress tried to cut down on the backlog by transferring all responsibility for veterans' training to the FBVE. Two years later, under pressure by disabled vets and an outraged public, Warren G. Harding established the US Veterans' Bureau, effectively placing all aspects of disabled veterans' rehabilitation under one roof. But for many disabled veterans such responses came far too late. Frustrated by government bureaucracy, thousands of rehabilitation candidates gave up on vocational training before setting foot in the classroom.[49]

Those who actually entered vocational training found it to be a long and grueling process. Countless veterans' training was interrupted by extended periods of illness and physical incapacitation. In some cases, men endured months, even years, of training only to abandon their original course of study because of chronic pain or lingering injuries. Many tubercular soldiers could not train indoors for more than an hour at a time, while shell-shocked men often found it difficult to work near loud machinery without reliving their psychological trauma. Vets from rural areas often traveled long distances to reach the nearest federally contracted training facility, and many husbands were forced to live apart from their wives and families due to a shortage of housing for married trainees.

Rehabbing veterans also had to worry about being declared rehabilitated too early. Because rehabilitation was primarily a restoration of disabled veterans' economic viability, the success or failure of any rehabilitation regimen was contingent upon a host of factors beyond both veterans' and rehabilitation officers' control. A tumultuous economic climate, changing attitudes toward disabled people in the workplace, the return of past symptoms—all could undermine even the best-trained veteran's career goals. Still, many vets accused the Veterans' Bureau of booting them from training programs before they were ready to succeed on their own. In 1924, Joseph Ray, an African American cornet student at a federal music school in Chicago, vehemently protested his "rehabilitated" status. Despite four and a half years of instruction, he felt the government had failed to provide the training necessary to ensure economic independence. What was worse, he argued that his white instructors' decision to end his program was inspired by racial prejudice and not by his competence as a musician.[50]

Given the pervasive racism in early twentieth-century American society, Ray's fears were no doubt well founded. In its effort to "make the world safe for democracy," the United States had fought the Great War with a racially segregated army. Racist assumptions about blacks' innate mental deficiency and unwillingness to fight permeated the armed forces, and African American doughboys had to contend with race riots and violence from their white counterparts both at home and overseas.[51] Military officials were eager to convey an impression of racial harmony within rehabilitation programs, and they frequently made half-hearted attempts to allay concerns about discrimination without upsetting the racial status quo. Asked to clarify the government's policy toward rehabilitating African American soldiers, colonel Frank Billings, director

FIG. 18. Although many rehabilitation facilities were racially segregated, some vocational education courses were open to veterans of all races. Taken at the East Side YMCA in New York City on May 2, 1922, this photograph shows an integrated class of disabled vets training for future careers in the commercial arts. Photo: C. Feldman, B. Barclay, CCNY photo class. 15-VR-2G-3, National Archives at College Park, College Park, MD.

of the Office of Surgeon General's Division of Physical Reconstruction, declared, "No differentiation is made between the white and colored as to the hospitals in which they are treated." Yet Billings also made it clear that "equal" treatment did not necessarily imply racial integration. In areas with high African American populations—such as the South—black veterans were rehabilitated in racially segregated clinics and vocational centers (fig. 18).[52]

Despite Billings's assurances, race-based discrimination was rampant in both military hospitals and federally contracted rehabilitation schools.[53] Some facilities refused to accept African American trainees altogether or drastically limited their access to equipment, recreational facilities, or medical care. The USVB Vocational School at Silver Spring, Maryland, placed "Negroes" (along with epileptics, "imbeciles," "idiots," and men with communicable diseases) on its list of "undesirable" cases.[54] After receiving one black veteran's inquiry about training as a mechanic, E. W. Beatty, assistant manager of an auto repair school in Detroit, explained that they did not accept African American students "on account of the fact that we have students from all sectors of the USA and we have not been able to overcome the prejudice of having colored men and white men in the same class."[55] At Georgia's Fort McHenry, the Red Cross hut was officially off-limits to black trainees except between 12:30 and 2:00 in the afternoon (whites could come and go as they pleased all day). When pressed by African Americans to justify the policy, Red Cross staff initially claimed that it was a health measure but eventually admitted, "The [white] Boys like to be with their own race."[56] Not surprisingly, conditions at segregated facilities in the Jim Crow South proved to be particularly appalling. Surveying one Alabama trade school, P. H. Roney, a government official charged with placing rehabilitated African American veterans, concluded that the men should be removed at once. The barracks was a firetrap, the roof leaked during storms, and many buildings lacked windowpanes. A breeding ground for disease, the school had only one water faucet, and the local doctor refused to see African American patients.[57]

In December 1922, Dr. J. R. A. Crossland, former US ambassador to Liberia and an expert in charge of "Negro Training" at the Veterans' Bureau, embarked upon a tour of African American rehabilitation facilities in the Midwest and Deep South. What he found was worthy of national scandal: gross incompetence, systemic neglect, and persistent racial prejudice against African American trainees. The low point of the tour came in Prairie View, Texas, home of the A&M State Normal School. Due to a lack of housing and dining facilities on campus, rehabbing men were forced to walk seven miles every morning and evening for food and shelter. In nearby Hempstead, white residents treated the disabled vets with open hostility, and former soldiers were frequently harassed or imprisoned on petty charges. At the school itself, training facilities were filthy and students had to pay for their supplies out of pocket. The "commercial department" consisted of nothing more than two tables and a typewriter. Worst of all, the school's practice of graduating undertrained veterans made a mockery of the government's commitment to providing vets with thorough training. "Men have been put there and allowed to stay a few weeks and sent away 'rehabilitated,'" Crossland reported.[58]

Letters addressed to Crossland's office only confirmed his findings. According to C. A. Greer, an African American dentist in Chicago, government regulations made it nearly impossible for rehabbing black veterans to receive proper dental care.[59] Others complained that white instructors were taking advantage of their black trainees or failing to recognize the seriousness of their injuries. Writing from the Kentucky State Normal and Industrial School, Buster Sunter protested that his vocational program had been inexplicably slashed from four years to just two. More troubling still, although Sunter remained physically weakened, school instructors had him out working the farm as if he were completely healthy.[60] Perhaps the most common complaint was that whites did not give disabled African American veterans the respect and fair treatment afforded to their white counterparts. James E. Sanford of the Hampton Institute explained that African American veterans experienced constant intimidation and abuse throughout the rehabilitation process. In Hampton, Virginia, white doctors refused to give African American patients prescriptions and routinely made them wait for hours until all of the whites had been seen. "The fact is that," Sanford concluded, "we are invarible [sic] received and treated as a colored man and not as a disabled soldier."[61]

Despite their racial privileges, whites too had legitimate complaints. While conditions varied from school to school, many private facilities were little more than fly-by-night diploma mills, undersized and lacking adequate equipment and provisions. Qualified teachers and administrators were always in short supply, and trainees argued that rehabilitation schools were more interested in taking their money—through inflated prices for room and board—than preparing them for future employment. Making matters worse, archival records reveal deep-seeded distrust between rehabilitation agents and the men in their charge. Some military and civilian rehabilitation workers patronized their trainees, characterizing them as spoiled children or "mental semi-adults" in need of constant supervision.[62] In a letter to the head of the US Veterans' Bureau, George R. Kelton, commander of a disabled veterans' group in Waynesville, North Carolina, charged the staff at a nearby rehabilitation school with ineptitude and impartiality; he accused the teachers of enforcing rules in a haphazard fashion, and holding grudges against trainees who disobeyed their orders.[63]

Unhappy vets did not limit their grievances to angry letters. On June 3–4, 1921, students at the federal rehabilitation school in Pascagoula, Mississippi, staged a two-day strike to protest the poor living conditions on campus and the indifference of the staff. According to a list of grievances they submitted to the FBVE, the men's living quarters were unsanitary, the school lacked adequate recreational facilities, and the food served at the campus hotel (where the trainees were required to dine) was "unsuitable" for Southern palates. The men also complained that the staff was negligent in its duties, and that the camp's director had placed strict regulations on the trainees' behavior, especially when it came to liquor and women. Questioned by FBVE representatives sent to investigate the strike, the school's top administrator admitted that current services were inadequate and that attempts to impose military discipline had precipitated the strike. However, he felt that the trainees were equally at fault, if not more so. E. H. Hale, one of the FBVE representatives, reached a similar conclusion. At a student assembly not long after the strike, Hale dismissed the "alleged charges" leveled by the strikers and scolded them for failing to voice their objections through proper channels. He went on to accuse the strike's ringleaders of forsaking "American ideals," telling those who remained dissatisfied to take their disabilities and go home.[64]

Hale's response to the problems at Pascagoula typified the attitude of many rehabilitation workers, who believed that trainees often lacked the mental acumen and educational background to pursue their chosen professions. One-third of all American soldiers were functionally illiterate, and few had any formal job training prior to enlistment.[65] Entranced by visions of future wealth and respectability, men with elementary school educations ignored their counselors' advice and entered vocational courses in engineering, business, and commercial work, only to fail miserably or bounce from program to program for years on end. When he returned to Pascagoula four months after the strike, E. H. Hale concluded that many of the men had not given the "slightest thought" to their future, and had only signed up for the course in order to keep their monthly stipends.[66] However, as historian Jennifer Keene has shown, vocational counselors' assessments of trainees' potential relied heavily upon racist army intelligence tests and other culturally biased criteria. The result was that trainees usually wound up categorized with "others with a similar class, ethnic, or racial background."[67]

Two additional obstacles were especially worrying to government rehabilitationists. The first concerned the presence of women. Women were highly valued in government rehabilitation programs, serving as nurses, reconstruction aides, occupational therapists, and instructors at vocational schools. Even so, many men within the rehabilitation movement considered women an unhealthy distraction.[68] After inspecting a Baltimore vocational school, Edward P. Chester, a specialist in industrial training, recommended that women employees and teachers be replaced as soon as possible.[69] Major W. H. Henderson, the morale officer at a Maryland hospital, offered a similar view, arguing that the "feminization" of reconstruction work not only lowered patient morale but also convinced the wounded man that "his entire convalesce is a sentimental matter in which he wears a radiant halo."[70] Along similar lines, male critics warned against the "promiscuous entertainment" provided by female visitors.[71] In a memo to the chief of the Morale Branch of the Surgeon General's Office, James E. Baylis railed against the "viciousness" of allowing "over sympathetic women" free access to wounded soldiers while under government care. Baylis charged that female coddling "destroys [the soldier's] discipline and causes [him] to get a distorted idea of his importance and what his rights are now and should be in the future."[72]

The second obstacle was the idolization of wounded soldiers in general. Instead of encouraging disabled veterans to pursue a life of manly usefulness, lamented Douglas C. McMurtrie, "The first reaction of the public to the returning man is hero-worship of the most empty type— described coldly, it usually consists in making a fool of the man and entertaining him in inappropriate and hurtful ways."[73] Rehabilitationists warned that too much "ill-considered kindness" would weaken the moral fiber of the war-disabled, leaving them unprepared for the struggles of everyday life.[74] Unless Americans developed a "new psychology toward the handicapped," disabled Great War vets were doomed to the same cycle of dependency and uselessness as their Civil War forebears.[75]

Preaching the Gospel of Rehabilitation

To prevent this from happening, supporters both inside and outside the federal government launched a broad campaign to "reconstruct public attitudes" toward disabled vets.[76] Leading the way was the Committee on Public Information (CPI), the government's propaganda arm throughout World War I. CPI artists designed posters and newspaper cartoons on the many benefits of vocational training, while government-sponsored displays on military medicine and physical reconstruction were exhibited at state fairs throughout the fall of 1918. Privately produced films, such as Gaumont-Mutual's *New Legs for Soldiers* (1917), Gaumont Graphic's *New Vocations for Disabled Soldiers* (1919), and the Red Cross–General Film Company's *Rebuilding Broken Bodies* (1919), screened at theaters across the country. Meanwhile, magazine articles promoting government rehabilitation work regularly appeared in such varied publications as *Illustrated World*, the *American Journal for the Care of Cripples*, the *Red Cross Magazine*, *Scientific American*, *Survey*, *World's Work*, and the *Ladies' Home Journal*. Many such articles were prepared (or ghostwritten) by employees of the Office of the Surgeon General (OSG), which created a special section devoted to producing rehabilitation-themed "educational propaganda." In October 1917, the OSG released "The Passing of the Cripple," one of its first official statements about the benefits of soldiers' rehabilitation. Over the next six months, OSG officials toured the country lecturing on the appeals of rehabilitation and laying the groundwork for publicity campaigns to come.[77]

In June 1918, the OSG debuted its most ambitious publicity organ, *Carry On: A Magazine on the Reconstruction of Disabled Soldiers and Sailors*. Modeled on analogous productions in Great Britain and France, *Carry On* featured brief articles, essays, and speeches describing government rehabilitation programs, as well as humorous anecdotes, poetry, fictional stories, and excerpts from a number of regional publications. Each issue was also packed with prescriptive cartoons, lithographs, and black-and-white photographs depicting disabled veterans in various stages of reconstruction and training. As one might expect, the magazine's message was invariably upbeat (fig. 19). Veterans' wounds were kept strategically out of view, and *Carry On*'s writers avoided any reference to problems within the rehabilitation process. Instead, the magazine inundated readers with images of men at work, their active and upright bodies proof of their successful return to masculine independence. Unlike professional journals, *Carry On* was expected to appeal to as broad an audience as possible, reaching both general readers and the growing community of soldiers, orthopedists, nurses, and military officials active in the rehabilitation of disabled veterans. Because civilians were encouraged to donate old issues of *Carry On* to Army and Navy hos-

FIG. 19. Published in *Carry On*, John T. McCutcheon's cartoons illustrate what rehabilitationists believed was the underlying social contract of martial citizenship. If American men were disabled in wartime, Uncle Sam was duty bound to provide them "physical reconstruction," "vocational training," and a "good job" once they came home. John T. McCutcheon, "Standing by Each Other" and "Uncle Sam Will Not Desert the Man Who Didn't Desert Him," *Carry On* 1:3 (September 1918): 18, 19.

pitals, its total readership remains uncertain (although one contributor claimed that its monthly circulation exceeded 100,000 readers).[78]

Ford Motor Company and other private businesses also jumped on the rehabilitation bandwagon.[79] A fervent supporter of soldier's rehabilitation, Henry Ford worried that disabled veterans could be a drag to postwar economic recovery. Explicitly aimed at employers, Ford's 1918 film *Disabled Veterans Working in Industry* showed disabled men assembling cardboard boxes, working at sewing machines, running elevators, and laboring alongside their nondisabled peers. According to the film's intertitles, "There should be a place in our industries for every cripple returning from the war, except those totally disabled. It will not be necessary to create jobs for them. Suitable jobs exist. The real problem is to get employers of labor to interest themselves in the welfare of the cripple."[80]

Two years later, the company released another prorehabilitation film, *The Reawakening* (1920), as part of its Ford Educational Weekly series. Set largely at Fort Sheridan, Illinois, the documentary followed disabled vets through every stage of the rehabilitation process—from emergency evacuation to vocational training. Like nearly all prorehabilitation productions, *The Reawakening* offered a decidedly cheery vision of soldiers' return to productivity, carefully avoiding any visual evidence of corruption, discrimination, or disciplinary problems within the rehabilitation process. Aside from a few amputees, the disabled bore no visible signs of their injuries, and were shown either happily at work or smiling for the camera. The film ended with an accelerated sequence of a blossoming flower, symbolic, the viewer was told, of disabled soldiers' reemergence into productive life.[81]

No organization was more dedicated to "preaching the gospel of rehabilitation" than the Red Cross Institute for Crippled and Disabled Men.[82] Located at the corner of 23rd Street and 4th Avenue in New York City, the institute was founded in early 1917 as the nation's first training school for amputees and men with damaged limbs. Along with a shop for manufacturing prosthetics, it housed a trade school and employment office, and it sponsored athletic meets and "cripple parties" for disabled men in training (fig. 20).[83] The institute's most significant contribution to the rehabilitation movement came in the field of propaganda. Under the direction of Douglas McMurtrie, it produced over fifty different pamphlets, broadsheets, and monographs on rehabilitation work within the first year of the Armistice. In 1918, the institute distributed six million copies of McMurtrie's flyer *Your Duty to the War Cripple* in New York customers' utility bills. Red Cross staffers delivered hundreds of lectures and lantern slideshows on rehabilitation topics, and by 1920, its publicity service had amassed one of the largest collections of disability-related material in the world.[84]

Although rehabilitationists hoped to reach all sectors of the American public, their publicity campaigns targeted a few key groups in particular. One of the most important demographics included the factory heads, hiring agents, and business owners who would eventually provide soldiers with employment.[85] Rehabilitation propaganda sought to convince potential employers that hiring rehabilitated soldiers made good business sense, as they were likely to be better educated, better trained, and better motivated than their nondisabled counterparts. At the same time, rehabilitationists hoped to discourage businesses from taking on disabled soldiers out of a sense of sentimental obligation. In the pamphlet *What the Employers of America Can Do for the Disabled Soldiers and Sailors* (1918), the FBVE warned that the "grateful employer will do the injured man and society an ill service if he lets his heart run away

FIG. 20. Sam Luzofsky (one leg) and Lon Young (one arm) spar in a boxing match at the Red Cross Institute for Crippled and Disabled Men in New York City. Library of Congress, Prints & Photographs Division, LC-USZ62-68171.

with his head." Instead of setting aside a few "charity" positions for the nation's wounded heroes, employers were asked to consider the long-term consequences of adding disabled soldiers to the workforce. Would disabled veterans have opportunities for promotion? What would happen to them if the market turns sour?[86]

Rehabilitationists considered the cooperation of disabled soldiers' families—especially their mothers, fiancées, and wives—equally vital to their mission's success. As early as 1917, poet Herbert Kaufman asked American women how they would greet the "men with wood-and-wire arms, faces masked with celluloid, patched ears, pieced-out noses and make-shift jaws" soon to return home from the battlefield:

Shall you commit their dauntless souls to life-long torture, with shudders of repulsion? Shall you make them hate the light of day and invoke torments of humiliation surpassing any agony war can devise? Shall you rip agape the healing wounds and leave them to bleed and pulse incurably, by breaking betrothals and abandoning dear friendships?

Or shall the magic eyes of love transfigure every scar into a badge of honor?[87]

Rehabilitation propaganda urged women to take a sensible approach toward the war-wounded. Instead of fawning over disabled soldiers or turning away in disgust (the only two responses male rehabilitationists imagined women could have), female family members were instructed to provide constant encouragement throughout the rehabilitation process. Above all else, it was their job to make sure disabled veterans understood the benefits of rehabilitation and stuck with their training until the very end.[88]

Of course, the primary audience for rehabilitation-themed propaganda was disabled veterans themselves. In their campaigns to attract trainees, rehabilitations mobilized every form of media available at the time, from cartoons and posters to photographs and newsreels. Two themes ran throughout virtually all Great War–era rehabilitation campaigns. The first echoed back to the promises of nineteenth-century militarists such as Theodore Roosevelt. It was the belief that war could serve as a vehicle for self-improvement, that even the severely disabled could emerge from war's horrors as "better" men. According to its supporters, rehabilitation offered the disabled soldier a chance to "find his way back to industrial and social life, intellectually and financially stronger than when he left it."[89]

The second theme was that disabled veterans had a civic responsibility to make the most out of their opportunities for advancement. After a brief tour of US rehabilitation facilities in 1919, Maurice Bourrillon reiterated this argument in an open letter to America's disabled vets: "I firmly believe that just as our French soldiers have done you will understand that it is your duty both to America and to yourselves to put into the reconstruction of your lives the same ardor and courage which you gave evidence of when you came to the aid of France."[90] Those who failed to do so—whether because of laziness or self-pity—were derelict in their duties as soldiers, men, and American citizens.

Rehabilitating Modern War

In retrospect, one of the most remarkable features of the rehabilitation movement was the way it reinserted the United States' experience in World War I into a narrative of national (and bodily) progress. Measured in terms of lives lost and monies spent, the Great War was the most murderous and wasteful conflict in world history to that time. In the AEF's two hundred days under fire, the US death toll from accidents, disease, and combat-related injuries topped 100,000.

However, American rehabilitationists proclaimed that World War I marked a historical transition—the passing of an era of ignorance and indifference. According to one postwar elegist, the disabled soldier, hobbled by injuries and dependent upon government charity, would soon be as "obsolete as the old soldiers' home, and other institutions and practices that world progress is leaving in its wake."[91] For all of its horrors, rehabilitationists believed the Great War had spawned a new awareness of human suffering and a new commitment—on the part of governments and individuals—to help war's victims forge a better life. "Possibly no single fact so illuminates the vast strides in civilization . . . as the scientific forethought that the Government of countries at war are [sic] exercising on behalf of their mutilated men," opined Gertrude Atherton, a popular novelist, in November 1918. "War is damnable and death is the least of its tolls. But at least the blind and maimed are no longer in the hideous predicament of a century ago."[92]

Why were Atherton and others so confident? Part of their optimism stemmed from their faith that rehabilitation's mission of education and uplift would long outlive the immediate veterans' crisis. Once the Problem of the Disabled Veteran had been solved, rehabilitation techniques would be used to "salvage" other so-called problem populations: congenitally crippled children, illiterate African Americans, senior citizens, and disabled industrial workers.[93] Rehabilitation had implications for foreign policy as well. In his essay "The Meaning of Rehabilitation," John L. Todd went to far as to predict that rehabilitation work would usher in a new age of international harmony: "Rehabilitation will bring nearer the liberty of thought, the equality of nations, the brotherhood among men, which France long ago placed before mankind as an ideal."[94] Speaking to an audience of would-be occupational therapists in Ohio one week before the war's end, Dean Burris concurred, proclaiming that just as [the Allied] nations have stood by each other in battle, just so should they stand by each other in the work of reconstruction in all of its many phases, and nothing can do more in effecting a permanent alliance in defence of common ideals for which we have accepted such supreme sacrifices, than hearty cooperation among the allied governments in the work of rehabilitating the disabled defenders of our liberties. The work of the war will not be over until the last one of those has had our best efforts in assisting him to become self-reliant, free from haunting fears of dependence upon the bounty of others, and readjusted to civil life.[95]

For Burris and others like him, rehabilitation work was an extension of the war itself. The rebuilt bodies and lives of the war-disabled were a testimony to the "common ideals" for which the war had been fought.

Ultimately, rehabilitation represented the culmination of a decades-long campaign to reconcile industrialized nations such as the United States with the inevitable bloodshed of modern warfare. Whereas many turn-of-the-century observers had warned that war was simply too dangerous to pursue, the rehabilitation movement forecast a different future—a vision of American war without American war cripples. Today, wrote a representative of the OSG in October 1917, "the horror and despair [of war injury] are largely removed and the greatest possible optimism becomes our rightful possession."[96] The dead would remain dead, but rehabilitationists were certain that the disabled could "sink back into the mass of the people as though nothing ha[d] happened." In a very real way, rehabilitation operated as a means of making war not only more socially palatable but also easier to pursue—and leave behind. Eventually, Gertrude Atherton predicted, America's disabled veterans would "look back upon the war as an evil dream out of which a few blessings took material shape."[97]

Yet at least one rehabilitationist was willing to acknowledge what so many left unspoken: that in their efforts to salvage war's human wreckage, rehabilitationists were actually complicit in the production of later generations of disabled veterans. In an article in the December 1915 issue of *Export American Industries*, H. M. Kahler worried that, without a strong commitment to wiping out the root causes of war injuries, rehabilitation only served to make modern war that much more likely in the future. Surveying the landscape of European rehabilitation work, he observed:

> Salvage is always a dreary business. Even when, as in this instance, it is noble and unselfish and intelligent, it only serves to emphasize the sadness of the conditions which call it into being. Except for its object-lesson in practical community of interest and action, we should be the better if we had to watch our crippled soldiers starve and freeze. So much the sooner would we open our eyes to the criminal idiocy which made them what they are—the lesson which of all its unlearned truths this half-awake society of ours most needs to learn.

Kahler was optimistic that disabled veterans need not "starve and freeze" in order for the public to comprehend war's horrors. He believed that current rehabilitation practices already exhibited an "indication of a dawning intelligence" about why future wars must be avoided.[98]

Unfortunately, overwhelming evidence suggests that Kahler gave his peers far too much credit. Aside from a few generic complaints about the high casualty rates of the Great War, the architects of American rehabilitation were notably silent on the "criminal idiocy" of industrialized warfare. In the hundreds of pamphlets, films, photographs, books, and cartoons issued to publicize the soldiers' rehabilitation movement, American rehabilitationists approached war as if it were an inevitable feature of modern life. Its dangers could be predicted, compensated for, and ameliorated, but they could not be avoided.[99] Put another way: for all its progressive tenor, rehabilitation was at its heart a reactionary movement, one that engaged the Problem of the Disabled Veteran after it arose and not before.

Conclusion: "The Problem of Paying the Human Cost"

By the late 1920s, the United States' efforts to rehabilitate disabled veterans through vocational education had effectively ended. According to government officials, 180,000 Great War veterans—nearly one-half of the 330,000 deemed eligible for rehabilitation—had engaged in some form of training. Eventually some 128,000 "legless, armless, sightless, and otherwise crippled or physically handicapped men" were deemed rehabilitated by experts in their chosen fields.[100] As the first widespread movement to reintegrate war-injured soldiers into postwar society, the rehabilitation movement of World War I marked a major turning point in the development of the veterans' welfare state. It institutionalized the federal government's obligation to restore disabled veterans to a state of masculine productivity, and emerged as a distinctly modern alternative to the expensive and bloated pension programs of the nineteenth century. In their attempts to "reconstruct public attitudes" toward war-wounded veterans, rehabilitationists were among the first groups to approach disability as a social construction. More important still, the rehabilitation movement's efforts to reintegrate disabled soldiers into postwar society would play a key role in ameliorating the long-term legacies of warfare in twentieth-century America.

Despite all of this, it's hard to judge the United States' first mass experiment with soldiers' rehabilitation a triumph. Not only did the movement fail to bring an "end" to disability, the bureaucratic entanglements and mismanagement associated with veterans' care led to disappointment among veterans and nonveterans alike. Writing in 1923, Stanley Frost identified two broad standards by which soldiers' rehabilitation could be judged:

> One is that the Bureau's duty was no more than to provide a fair chance for each veteran, leaving it to him to make what he could out of it. On that basis the only serious failure has been in the poor quality of some of the schools.
>
> The other view, more paternalistic, is that the Bureau owed it to the veterans to give them, not merely a chance, but a state in life; to see that they made use of their opportunities and were in the end ready for successful independence. This is the attitude usually taken by Bureau officials, who seem to fall back on the first points of view only when excusing some failure.
>
> On this standard the failure is very great.[101]

Frost was not alone in his pessimism. In 1931, the eminent economist John Maurice Clark noted that, although rehabilitated veterans typically earned more money than they had before World War I, the increase was not enough on average to keep pace with rising inflation and wage rates. When it came to their socioeconomic independence, disabled veterans' "handicaps were not completely overcome, and one can only conjecture to what extent they were mitigated."[102] As a cost-cutting measure, moreover, the rehabilitation movement was a greater failure still. Federal spending on veterans' pensions, social relief programs, and medical care skyrocketed after World War I. The US government's total expenditures for disabled veterans topped $400 million in 1927 alone; one year later, the Veterans' Bureau's outlays exceeded half a billion dollars, much of which was spent on monetary compensation for disabled Great War vets.[103]

Even high-ranking government officials tended to look on rehabilitation as a qualified victory at best. Speaking on Armistice Day in 1928, Frank T. Hines, then head of the US Veterans' Bureau, admitted that the "problem of paying the human cost" of World War I loomed as large as ever. Despite the best efforts of military psychiatrists, the number of men suffering war-related "mental afflictions" continued to increase, and government hospitals and outpatient clinics treated upward of 800,000 former doughboys for various ailments every year. Although convinced that the American people would honor their "obligation" to "those who paid with life and limb, blinded eyes and twisted minds, the first and greatest cost of war," Hines had few illusions about the long-term implications of the US intervention in the Great War: "We shall not pay the full price of our participation in the World War in less than fifty years."[104]

It was a lesson that disabled veterans themselves knew all too well, one that left many convinced that if they were going to survive, they would have to stick together.

III

MOBILIZING INJURY

The Sweet Bill

On December 15, 1919, representatives of the American Legion, the United States' largest organization of Great War veterans, gathered in Washington, DC, for the first skirmish in a decades-long campaign to expand federal benefits for disabled veterans. They had been invited by the head of the War Risk Insurance Bureau, R. G. Cholmeley-Jones, to take part in a three-day conference on reforming veterans' legislation. Foremost on the Legionnaires' agenda was the immediate passage of the Sweet Bill, a measure that would raise the base compensation rate for war-disabled veterans from $30 to $80 a month. Submitted by Representative Burton E. Sweet (R-IA) three months earlier, the bill had passed by a wide margin in the House but had yet to reach the Senate floor. Some members of the Senate Appropriations Committee were put off by the high cost of the legislation (upward of $80 million a year); others felt that the country had more pressing concerns—such as the fate of the League of Nations—than disabled veterans' relief.[1] Meanwhile, as one veteran-friendly journalist lamented, war-injured doughboys languished in a kind of legislative limbo: "Men with two or more limbs gone, both eyes shot out, virulent tuberculosis and gas cases—these are the kind of men who have suffered from congress [sic] inaction."[2]

After an opening day of mixed results, the Legionnaires reconvened on the Hill the following afternoon to press individual lawmakers about the urgency of the problem. That evening, leading members of Congress hosted the lobbyists at a dinner party in the Capitol basement. Before the meal began, Legionnaire H. H. Raegge, a single-leg amputee from Texas, caught a streetcar to nearby Walter Reed Hospital and returned with a group of convalescing vets. The men waited as the statesmen praised the Legionnaires' stalwart patriotism; then Thomas W. Miller, the chairman of the Legion's Legislative Committee, rose from his seat and introduced the evening's surprise guests. "These men are only twenty minutes away from your Capitol, Mr. Chairman [Indiana Republican senator James Eli Watson], and twenty minutes away from your offices, Mr. Cholmeley-Jones," Miller announced to the audience. "Every man has suffered—actually suffered—not only from his wounds, but in his spirit, which is a condition this great Nation's Government ought to change." Over the next three hours, the men from Walter Reed testified about the low morale of convalescing veterans, the "abuses" suffered at the hands of the hospital officials, and their relentless struggle to make ends meet. By the time it was over, according to one eye-witness, the law-makers were reduced to tears. Within forty-eight hours, the Sweet Bill—substantially amended according to the Legion's recommendations—sailed through the Senate, and on Christmas Eve, Woodrow Wilson signed it into law.[3]

For the newly formed America Legion, the Sweet Bill's passage represented more than a legislative victory. It marked the debut of the famed "Legion Lobby," whose skillful deployment of sentimentality and hard-knuckle politics have made it one of the most influential (and feared) pressure groups in US history. No less important, the story of the Sweet Bill became one of the group's founding myths, retold—often with new details and rhetorical flourish—at veterans' reunions throughout the following decades.[4] Its message was self-aggrandizing, but it also had an element of truth: in the face of legislative gridlock, the American Legion was the best friend a disabled veteran could have.

5

"FOR THE LIVING DEAD I WORK AND PRAY"
Veterans' Groups and the Benefits of Buddyhood

> The war did not end with Armistice Day,
> I am not yet free from care;
> For the living dead I work and pray,
> I am a legionnaire.
> — American Legion chaplain H. A. Darche (1932)

At the end of World War I, veterans' groups faced an uphill battle if they hoped to win widespread support. Many Americans had grown suspicious of organized veterans and their influence on peacetime society. In part, their misgivings were rooted in the ancient principle that military service was a civic duty and that former soldiers had no special claim on public sentiment. Once war's fanfare had subsided, Americans expected their citizen-soldiers, in the words of historians John Lax and William Pencak, to "conform to the Roman Republic's hero Cincinnatus, who asked nothing of his country but returned to his fields after saving the nation."[1] On top of that, past veterans' organizations had a dubious record when it came to swapping arms for ploughshares. During its heyday in the 1890s, the Grand Army of the Republic (GAR), the nation's preeminent association of Union Civil War veterans, earned a notorious reputation for exploiting their wartime service. Waving the "bloody shirt," the GAR led crusades against Southern Democrats, lobbied Congress for universal military education, and won costly pensions and civil service preferences for more than 450,000 Union veterans.[2] Critics worried that Great War veterans' groups—potentially millions of members strong—would try to trade upon their warrior status for selfish or partisan gains. At the same time, the notion of veterans maintaining their wartime affiliations seemed at odds with the rigorous demands of "normalcy" that pervaded postwar American culture.

Despite such obstacles, the years following World War I witnessed an explosion of veteran organization and activism. By one count, the Great War spawned more than 175 veterans' groups in the United States, from small-town fraternal orders and ex-servicemen's clubs to large military societies.[3] Disabled veterans could pick between three types of veterans' organizations: *mixed* groups, such as the Veterans of Foreign Wars (VFW), which were open to the disabled and able-bodied alike; *composite* groups, such as the Disabled Emergency Officers of the World War, which were open to veterans with different kinds of impairments; and *single-population* groups, such as the National Blind Veterans, which were open to veterans with similar injuries or illnesses.[4] Multiple affiliations were common, and nearly all Great War–era veterans' groups were dedicated to helping disabled veterans in some capacity or another. In their induction ceremony, members of the VFW, for example, swore a solemn oath to protect their "wounded comrades" from additional harm, a sentiment shared by veterans across the political spectrum.[5]

Of the nearly two hundred organizations that took up the mantle of disabled veterans' relief after World War I, two groups stood out above the rest: the American Legion and the Disabled American Veterans of the World War (DAV). The American Legion was the loudest, richest, and most powerful veterans' lobby of the Great War era. At a time when many Americans were eager to return to "normalcy," Legionnaires were stubbornly determined to keep the spirit of the war alive, adopting the disabled veteran as both a source of inspiration and a cause to be defended. Often working in the Legion's shadow, the DAV represented the largest composite group of disabled veterans in the United States. It offered war-injured veterans a sense of identity and spiritual camaraderie rooted in a shared experience of disability. Together, the two groups mobilized their impressive cultural authority and material resources to carve out a separate, even preferential, legal status for disabled veterans. In the process, they frequently yoked disabled veterans' relief to a broader conservative political agenda—which the Legion deemed "100% Americanism"—aimed at spreading military values in civilian life.

Like the Grand Army of the Republic before them, the American Legion and, to a lesser extent, the DAV attracted their fair share of detractors. Critics accused veterans' groups of exploiting disabled veterans for political or monetary gain. Indeed, public responses to the American Legion and the DAV reveal divisions in post–World War I society about the social meaning of war injury and the nation's obligations to its former fighting men. While many Americans venerated the disabled veteran as an icon of military masculinity and embodied citizenship, others believed veterans' ultimate goal was the restoration of the nineteenth-century veterans' welfare state that rehabilitationists had tried so desperately to avoid. Such divisions came into especially sharp relief in 1932, when a far less organized veterans' group, the Bonus Expeditionary Forces, launched its dramatic march on Washington, DC. The Bonus March reenergized public debate about the high cost—both monetary and human—of the United States' intervention in World War I. It also illustrated the extent to which all members of the Great War generation came to be viewed as disabled by military service.

Keeping the Spirit of the War Alive

Founded by an elite cadre of AEF officers in 1919, the American Legion quickly established itself as a singular force in American politics and cultural life. Open to all US veterans of 1917–1918, including those who had served stateside, the Legion had 843,013 members (roughly 18.5 percent of all Great War veterans) within its first year. In 1931, the organization's membership rolls topped a million, peaking nine years later when a quarter of all eligible Great War vets were Legionnaires.[6] By that time, Legionnaires sat on key committees in the House and Senate, and the group boasted one of the most expansive organizational networks in the United States, including more than 10,000 local posts and a massive limestone headquarters in downtown Indianapolis.[7]

Although avowedly nonpartisan, the early Legion was governed by a militantly patriotic ideology known as "100% Americanism," a cocktail of hypernationalism, anticommunism, and civic responsibility. According to one early Legion insider, 100% Americanism was "real patriotism in its broadest sense—a clean body politic; a clean national soul and a clean international conscience."[8] The majority of the Legion's Americanism programs focused on socializing youth in the values of good health and military citizenship. However, 100% Americanism also authorized Legionnaires to take more drastic measures to protect the "body politic" from ideological and social contamination. Long after the Red scare of 1920–1921, the Legion censored school textbooks, supported immigration restrictions, and fought "Bolshevism"—both real and imagined—wherever the group encountered it. Above all else, 100% Americanism stressed the need for veterans to assume a position of collective leadership and moral authority in the postwar era. At the Legion's first Continental Congress in May 1919, former Dallas mayor Henry D. Lindsley assured the assembled men: "It is going to be within your power to say yes or no to many of the great problems of the United States."[9]

In the minds of early Legionnaires, one problem loomed above all others: the disabled veteran. As the United States' largest veterans' organization, the American Legion believed it had a sacred charge to protect disabled doughboys from government indifference and public neglect. In what would become something of a mantra in Legion circles, national commander Hanford MacNider proclaimed, "The first duty of The American Legion is to see that those men who came back from their service, blinded, maimed, broken in health and spirit, who must live through the war forever in their homes through the country, get a square deal from the Government they fought for."[10] Legionnaires typically framed their responsibility toward disabled veterans as an expression of the ideals they had learned in service (loyalty, comradeship, etc.). In turn, the Legion saw its work on disabled veterans' behalf as a central part of its ideological mission. As one Legion commander put it, the ultimate goal of 100% Americanism was "to keep old and young alike impressed with the sacrifices in blood and tears made in war and in peace."[11] More than any other figure, the disabled veteran exemplified the spirit of personal sacrifice, military service, and heroic masculinity Legionnaires hoped to keep alive in postwar America.

As the American Legion rose to national prominence, disabled veterans formed their own coalitions. Their reasons for coming together varied. Some men sought help securing federal disability benefits, while others hoped to find employment or raise money for their fellow vets. A number of groups coalesced around government rehabilitation centers, where disabled veterans spent their off-hours smoking cigarettes and discussing the hardships to come. The United States' largest disabled veterans' organization, the Disabled American Veterans of the World War, was born in Cincinnati, Ohio. During the early months of the Armistice, the city was home to a pair of self-help groups for disabled veterans: the Ohio Mechanics Institute for Disabled Soldiers, made up of students from a local industrial school, and a smaller group of disabled veterans from the University of Cincinnati. On December 25, 1919, about one hundred disabled veterans met at the Sinton Hotel and Lyric Theater for a night of Christmas entertainment. According to DAV lore, talk quickly turned to the prospects of setting up a national organization, and before the evening was over, plans for the DAV were starting to take shape.[12]

The party's host, Robert S. Marx, deserves much of the credit for shepherding the organization's early development. A charismatic Jewish attorney, with movie-star good looks and a knack for showmanship, Marx had served as an infantry officer in the final push of the Meuse-Argonne campaign. Hours before the ceasefire, he was severely wounded by a German artillery shell and spent months recovering in a French hospital. Upon his return to Cincinnati, he was promptly appointed to the Ohio Superior Court, a position he held for five years. Like many of his war-disabled cohort, Marx believed the federal government had failed to live up to its compact with disabled veterans and their families. Moreover, despite his own successes, he feared that many disabled veterans would be unable to assimilate smoothly into postwar society. Even with government assistance, Marx often reflected, "a man could not go through that conflict and come back and take his place as a normal being."[13]

During the spring of 1920, local vets met at Marx's courthouse office or at nearby Memorial Hall to discuss their progress. On September 25, 1920, they joined delegates from disabled veterans' groups across the country for the first official meeting of the Disabled American Veterans of the World War.[14] The following summer around 1,400 "comrades" (as DAV members came to be called) gathered at Detroit's Hotel Tuller, where Marx was elected national commander. The DAV never approached the American Legion in terms of its size and influence, but the scale of its operations was impressive. Riding a wave of early enthusiasm, the DAV attracted more than 25,000 members within its first two years. By the 1930s, the DAV had established more than 1,200 local chapters and state offices across the country. From its two headquarters—one in Cincinnati, the other in Washington, DC—DAV leaders oversaw a broad spectrum of rehabilitation, legislative, and social welfare initiatives. Eager to foster a feeling of camaraderie among members, the DAV founded a "fun-making" society known as the Trench Rats and sponsored hundreds of club rooms and recreational facilities for war-injured vets and their families. Though membership declined in the late 1920s (thanks in part to chronic financial setbacks), it rebounded during the Great Depression, topping 42,000 in 1936. In 1932, amidst a wave of cutbacks in veterans' benefits, the DAV joined the GAR, the VFW, and the American Legion as one of only four veterans' associations to receive a federal charter.[15]

From the start, the DAV went to great lengths to differentiate itself from more inclusive veterans' groups. Unlike the American Legion, whose rosters were open to all honorably discharged vets, the DAV restricted its membership to Great War veterans who had been "wounded, gassed, injured, or disabled by reason of service."[16] The DAV's membership requirement was crucial not only to the group's organizational identity, but also to its hierarchical understanding of military citizenship. According to the DAV, disabled veterans had met a higher standard of personal sacrifice and patriotism than their nondisabled peers, a standard that deserved special recognition. One recruiting ad told potential comrades: "YOUR service connected Disability is a distinction and a 'badge of honor' that entitles you to join this organization."[17] To some outside observers, such rhetoric smacked of self-aggrandizement; indeed, in trolling for new members, the DAV frequently traded in gendered stereotypes about the manly courage of war's disabled survivors.

However, the group's early leaders were adamant about the need to organize beneath a common banner. Speaking before Congress in 1921, Robert S. Marx justified the DAV's existence by pointing out the unique challenges faced by disabled veterans:

> The injured man is in a totally different situation from that of the uninjured veteran. The injured veterans have the common problem of medical treatment and hospitalization; they have the common problem of vocational training; they have the common problem of compensation; and they have the common future life problem ahead of them, namely, the problem of the physically handicapped man. Every member of our association, almost without exception—although there are exceptions, but they are few—will come into contact with an agency of the United States Government during the course of the

year; some of them daily, and practically all of them monthly. That is true of the membership of no other association of World War veterans, whether it be the Veterans of Foreign Wars, the American Legion, my own division association, or the other divisional associations.[18]

Beyond the "distinction" of injury, Marx believed DAV comrades' shared experience of disability set them apart from the great mass of ex-servicemen, including the vast majority of Legionnaires. Equally significant, he contended that disabled veterans' collective experiences and struggles bound them together in a common future, a future characterized foremost by veterans' regular, and at times fractious, encounters with the bourgeoning welfare state. If for no other reason, disabled vets needed a group of their own.

Ultimately, the DAV insisted that America's war-disabled could not—and should not—depend upon their able-bodied counterparts to secure their long-term well-being. Their rationale was both practical and political. Because of their relatively small number, DAV comrades worried that their unique insights into the Problem of the Disabled Veteran might go unnoticed in more inclusive veterans' organizations. Just as important, the DAV believed that organizational independence was necessary if disabled veterans ever hoped to achieve political agency and masculine self-worth. Invoking the democratic rhetoric of the early republic, Marx recalled, "We assembled from hospitals and homes and started this organization 'By, of, and for the disabled,' and we came there in order that we might alleviate the sufferings of our comrades who were in the hospitals and in Government vocational training schools, who were waiting for the compensation and war-risk insurance promised them."[19]

Given their significant differences, it is tempting to frame the American Legion and DAV as rivals—and not just in matters related to disabled vets. The early Legion was dominated by establishment WASPs who mingled freely in the upper echelons of American political power.[20] Its first elected national commander, forty-two-year-old Franklin D'Olier, had spent the war as an officer in the Quartermaster Corps before assuming a position on the General Staff. A Princeton graduate and, according to one Legion insider, a "conservative in almost everything," D'Olier eventually became president of Prudential Insurance and chair of the US Strategic Bombing Survey during World War II.[21] Like D'Olier, many Legion "king makers" made little effort to hide their affiliations with big business and chauvinistic politics. In the run-up to the 1920 convention, one of the group's principle founders, Theodore Roosevelt, Jr., championed his father's old friend general Leonard Wood, prompting some speculation that the Legion was simply a front for Republican elites. In comparison, DAV members tended to be more diverse in social origins and, because of their disabilities, more alert to the inequalities of privilege and power. For its first chaplain, the DAV selected Michael Aaronson, a Jewish rabbi blinded in France—a bold choice in an era of rising anti-Semitism. Even the "Father of the DAV," Robert S. Marx, frequently bucked political trends. During the presidential election of 1920, the life-long Democrat crisscrossed the nation stumping for liberal reformer James M. Cox and his young running mate, Franklin Roosevelt.[22]

Nevertheless, it would be a mistake to view the two groups' relationship as adversarial. Like the American Legion, the DAV eschewed party affiliations, and although the two groups occasionally scuffled over specific priorities, they worked closely on a variety of issues. No less a proponent of militant nationalism, the DAV supported a number of Legion-sponsored Americanism campaigns. It denounced communists, pacifists, and radicals of all stripes, and when it served the group's purpose, it forged close ties with white supremacists and anti-Semites, most notably John E. Rankin (D-MS). Although both groups were ostensibly open to veterans of all races, the American Legion and DAV tended to mirror the separate-and-unequal logic of early twentieth-century race relations. Throughout the United States, African Americans and other vets of color were often restricted to small, segregated "Negro" posts, a practice that reaffirmed their second-class status within the public imagination.[23] Overall, because of its relatively small size and modest budget, the DAV tended to adopt the Legion's political agenda as its own. In their public speeches, DAV leaders referred to the American Legion as "our big brother organization," and membership between the two groups overlapped widely.[24] By 1930, as many as 90 percent of DAV members were also Legionnaires (Robert S. Marx was a founding member of the American Legion's National Rehabilitation Committee).[25] Together, the two groups—along with their more militant brothers in the VFW—presented a largely united front on disabled veterans' behalf.

Representing Disabled Veterans

When it came to helping America's war-disabled, the matter of representation was a top concern. For Great War veterans' groups, representing disabled veterans involved two distinct but often conflated sets of practices. The first centered on propaganda and public education. The American Legion and DAV hoped not only to "awaken the public conscience" to the problems facing disabled veterans, but also to frame war-related disability as a civic ideal.[26] Equally important, both groups sought to cultivate their authority as disabled veterans' chief advocate in matters of politics and social policy. Rejecting the notion that government officials or rehabilitationists could ever represent disabled veterans' best interests, the American Legion and DAV attempted to use the mass media to secure their dominance as the nation's leading voice on veterans' affairs.

The American Legion made propaganda and public relations a high priority from its inception. In June 1919, it hired corporate publicist Ivy Lee, sometimes dubbed the "Father of Public Relations," to mount a massive publicity campaign to introduce the Legion to veterans and nonveterans alike. Under Lee's direction, the American Legion Publicity Committee flooded the nation's newspapers with editorials and advertisements, and distributed 300,000 copies of the Legion's first mass-produced poster, Ernest Hamlin Baker's *Let's Stick Together*, an iconic image of veteran solidarity. In the meantime, the American Legion began to develop its own mass-media outlets. On July 4, Legion headquarters released the first issue of the *American Legion Weekly*, whose pages would become a much-read source of information about disabled veterans throughout the post–World War I era.[27] Within a few years, the American Legion's media apparatus—including its News Service, Press Association, National Radio Committee and broadcasting stations, and film service—was among the largest in the United States.[28]

Much of early Legion propaganda focused on the continued suffering, both physical and economic, of disabled veterans. Lost in the Great War's aftermath, declared one Legion report, was "a fact that should have been outstanding—that the war was won by bloody sacrifices; at a fearful cost of lives, limbs, lungs, and minds."[29] No veteran leader did more to publicize the "fearful cost" of US victory than Frederic Galbraith, Jr. A former ship captain turned business leader, Galbraith was over forty when he enlisted as an infantry officer in the Ohio National

Guard. Wounded in the cheek by German shrapnel, Galbraith served as American Legion national commander from September 1920 to June 1921, when he was killed in an automobile accident near Indianapolis. Like other prominent Legionnaires, Galbraith railed against what he perceived as widespread indifference to the plight of disabled veterans. Much of this attitude he chalked up to postwar ennui, but Galbraith also faulted his own organization for failing to grab the attention of a war-weary public. "We've got to bring [the disabled veteran issue] to life," he once declared in a fit of frustration. "We've got to get it into the newspapers."[30]

As a solution, Legion publicists turned to representational strategies of sensationalism, a literary and visual mode that arose as a product of (and response to) the hyperstimulating environment of early-twentieth-century urban America.[31] Galbraith believed that spreading gruesome, shocking, and heartrending portraits of disabled veterans' suffering would not only capture the public's imagination but also cement the Legion's reputation as the nation's foremost defender of veterans' interests. As Galbraith explained to his frequent collaborator, Legion muckraker and Pulitzer Prize–winning biographer Marquis James:

> We'll be striking, as you call it, and we'll be sensational. We'll put this disabled problem out of the pigeon-holes of three Washington bureaus and put it on the front page of every newspaper in America. We'll go the limit to do it, but we won't go outside the facts. . . . The facts are bad enough; they are a disgrace to the country, and I'm going to parade that disgrace before one hundred million people. Then what will be the repercussion? Why, the people will be shocked. They will say, "These conditions are terrible. We never dreamed such things could be. What can we do to set them right?"[32]

During his short tenure, Galbraith pressed the Legion's publicity arm to "Never pass up a bet to link the name of the Legion with revelation of the disgraceful conditions which surround our disabled." Once the public was suitably outraged, Galbraith argued, the Legion would "step forward and say, 'Do this, and this, and that, and that.' And it will be done."[33]

Under Galbraith's direction, the Legion launched a national media campaign to shock the American public out of its complacence. Legion publicity agents inundated news editors with photographs of disabled veterans abandoned in state asylums or locked up in squalid prison cells. The *American Legion Weekly* published damning exposés of cruelty and incompetence at the Federal Board for Vocational Education. Meanwhile, Galbraith barnstormed the country, delivering speeches, collecting press clippings, and personally lobbying on disabled veterans' behalf. As Marquis James would later admit, some Legion publicists (himself included) resorted to "journalistic audacity" in order to ratchet up the urgency of their stories. One highly publicized report centered on a group of 450 tubercular veterans found squatting in an Arizona amusement park. It soon became clear that the severity of the veterans' plight was highly exaggerated (most of the men, it seemed, were under the care of local charity groups). Nevertheless, Legion publicists continued to cite it as a true picture of disabled veterans' suffering.[34]

As Carolyn Cox has shown, Legionnaires took a special interest in giving voice to veterans affected by shell shock and other "invisible wounds." At a time when many Americans continued to associate war neuroses with malingering, cowardice, or worse, the American Legion portrayed shell-shocked vets as "men of honor to whom the nation had an equally honorable obligation."[35] The group's Rehabilitation Committee considered the care of psychologically damaged veterans to be the most pressing postwar problem facing the United States, a conviction reflected in much of the Legion's early activism.[36] Led by the eminent psychiatrist Thomas Salmon, Legionnaires testified before Congress, organized medical conferences, and published popular articles calling for the humane treatment of mentally traumatized vets. While such efforts were undoubtedly sincere, they also reinforced what would become a common theme in the Legion's early lobbying campaigns: disabled veterans' lack of political agency. As Legionnaires saw it, war-disabled vets—particularly men with war-related mental disorders—were almost wholly dependent upon their nondisabled counterparts to speak on their behalf. In the words of A. A. Sprague, head of the Legion's Rehabilitation Committee, "The man who has been deprived of his mind has made the greatest sacrifice of all. . . . Imprisoned within himself, he cannot call for help. Only his comrades can demand that every human agency be used to provide for his recovery."[37]

The DAV's media operations overlapped with (and diverged from) the American Legion's in several important ways. Shortly after its founding, the DAV established a small press bureau to keep both members and nonmembers abreast of the latest changes in veterans' legislation. The group's weekly (later semimonthly) newspaper carried inspirational stories of DAV fund-raising drives and relief efforts to thousands of readers. However, because of its smaller size and limited budget, DAV publicists often had to rely upon volunteers or free advertising to reach a national audience. As a result, the DAV's early propaganda work tended to focus on only a handful of messages. First, the DAV wanted Americans to know that the DAV existed, and that it was committed to winning fair treatment for all Great War disabled veterans. Second, like the Legion, it was eager to draw attention to the abuse and neglect endured by disabled veterans at the hands of the federal government. At the heart of the DAV's early mission was a belief in disabled veterans' capacity—as a group—to voice their own interests, without the filter of their able-bodied comrades.

The DAV had to make tough choices when projecting its image—and the image of disabled veterans in general—in the public arena. Drawing too much attention to disabled veterans' bodily traumas risked dehumanizing their fellow disabled vets, reducing them to congeries of diseases, incapacities, and scars. The Legion's strategy of sensationalizing disabled veterans' struggles posed similar hazards. Although the Legion proclaimed admiration for disabled veterans, the group frequently presented them as abject figures, emasculated by dependency and neglect. Worse still, oversentimentalizing disabled veterans threatened to turn them into charity cases or objects of pity. Throughout the Great War era, disabled veterans were frequently imagined along with war widows and orphans as part of a "trinity of relief," an image the DAV was keen to change.[38]

Indeed, cultural expectations of veterans' behavior seemed to place disabled veterans in a no-win situation. On the one hand, the DAV hoped to convey the material hardships faced by many disabled veterans. On the other hand, traditional codes of masculinity associated political and economic dependency with weakness and feminization. "Real men" did not complain when things turned bad, and they certainly did not badger the government for handouts. Not surprisingly, in its media campaigns, the DAV was often torn between highlighting a legitimate need for assistance and assuming the stigma of helplessness, even if doing so brought the promise of relief. Although this tension could never fully be resolved, DAV officials made a conscious effort to project a nuanced public image of disabled veterans, one that both celebrated the heroic virtues of war-produced disability and stressed the need for cooperative self-help.

In a typical recruiting article from 1928, for example, Minnesota state commander Lloyd Ruth characterized DAV members as "Men who, having FOUGHT THE FIGHT, having KEPT THE FAITH, returned home again with broken bodies, sightless eyes, ears held by silence, minus arms or legs or lungs seared by poisonous gas, to take up the ways of peace." He emphasized that DAV members were not inspired by mercenary values. Rather, they sought justice "for those who, through long suffering and despair, have become inarticulate." Like countless DAV-sponsored speeches, publications, and publicity posters, Ruth's recruiting ad cast disabled veterans in the role of selfless patriots, driven only by a desire to help their less fortunate "WOUNDED COLLEAGUES."[39]

For many veterans, it was this final message that mattered most. As much as they emphasized the suffering of disabled vets, DAV and American Legion publicity campaigns held up the disabled veteran as a model citizen. In the eyes of their fellow veterans, America's war-disabled were living reminders of a spirit of voluntary sacrifice and service that reached back to the founding of the republic. Ultimately, Legionnaires and DAV comrades hoped to convince both government officials and the public that disabled veterans were not like other men—and never would be. By giving their bodies and minds in wartime, they had earned a privileged place in US society. The view of Otis R. Hess, a DAV chapter commander in Cincinnati, was common among both Legionnaires and comrades: "It cannot be denied that the man who offered his life for the preservation of his country and who was wounded, gassed, shell-shocked, or otherwise disabled while in the military service of his country is justly entitled to be assured that the remainder of his life will not be that of poverty, dejectment, and discouragement."[40] Through their propaganda and public relations campaigns, the DAV and American Legion sent a clear message to the American public: disabled veterans deserved lives of dignity and material comfort, and it was veterans' collective duty to make sure they received them.

Speaking to the State

To this end, Great War veterans viewed the state as the primary lever for improving the lives of disabled vets. The state has always played a powerful role in the institutional lives of veterans' organizations. Before the first shot is fired, the state provides war's ideological architecture and material support. It is responsible for calling men to arms, putting them in uniform, carrying them into battle, and—in the case of the sick or wounded—treating their injuries. At war's end, veterans look to the state to provide the monetary and symbolic benefits they need to rebuild their lives. This is especially true for disabled veterans, whose bodies and lives are marked by service to their country. However, disabled veterans' relations with the state are often fraught with adversity and mistrust. While many vets rely upon the state for health care, pensions, and rehabilitation services, they tend to bristle at governmental interference in their daily lives. Moreover, as historian David Gerber points out, depending too heavily upon state assistance is often considered "inimical to the independence and self-confidence, and hence the manhood, of the disabled man."[41]

Still, Great War veterans' organizations pursued aggressive lobbying and administrative campaigns on behalf of disabled veterans. Unlike more militant groups, including the League of the Physically Handicapped, which formed to protest disability discrimination in the New Deal, the American Legion and DAV typically eschewed the "rhetoric and tactics of labor radicalism."[42] Instead, they preferred to use their political connections and broad institutional networks to work the system from the inside out. The two groups scored an early victory in 1921, when they helped pressure the federal government to consolidate its veterans' operations into a single agency, the US Veterans' Bureau.[43] The American Legion and DAV also set up in-house advocacy programs to expedite disabled veterans' claims for monetary compensation and other benefits. As many vets would discover, it was not enough to bear the scars of battle. In order to win government recognition, former soldiers needed well-documented case histories connecting their disabilities to wartime service. To this end, American Legion and DAV caseworkers helped veterans fill out paperwork, locate official records, and secure diagnoses from sympathetic physicians. Legion posts circulated handouts and questionnaires to help ex-servicemen determine their eligibility for government relief. For many years, the *American Legion Weekly* even published a missing-persons column to track down witnesses whose statements could validate veterans' claims.[44]

Beyond assisting vets with their pension files, the DAV and American Legion helped disabled veterans negotiate the pitfalls of government rehabilitation. In many respects, rehabilitation's aims contrasted sharply with the "Let's Stick Together!" spirit that animated Great War veterans' groups. After all, one of the primary goals of rehabilitation was to prompt former soldiers to shed their military identities; successfully rehabilitated men were expected to put the war behind them and reassimilate as civilians, a process sometimes called "deveteranization." In addition, rehabilitationists strove to "reconstruct public attitudes" toward war-disabled vets, eliminating hero-worship and special treatment.[45] The American Legion and the DAV, in contrast, had little interest in relinquishing their collective identities and claims upon public sentiment. Both groups expressed deep skepticism that even rehabilitated vets would ever be accepted as normal in able-bodied society.[46] More troubling still, they worried that the government's emphasis on rehabilitation would obscure the permanent need for more traditional forms of veterans' relief, such as pensions or institutional care.

Despite such concerns, veterans' groups largely embraced physical reconstruction and vocational training as just recompense for the financial setbacks endured by disabled vets. At the DAV's first national convention, Robert Marx publicly endorsed the "reclamation" of war-injured vets. In their efforts to return to the workforce, Marx told the crowd, "Wounded and disabled men of American today are winning a greater victory over the Kaiser than did the army of Pershing, for they are conquering the disability inflicted by the Hun."[47] During the early 1920s, the two groups' rehabilitation divisions worked closely with the Red Cross, the Federal Bureau of Vocational Education, and eventually the Veterans' Bureau to ensure that disabled veterans took full advantage of government-sponsored vocational education. When the Bureau of War Risk Insurance launched a national "Clean Up" campaign in 1921, the government enlisted the American Legion to track down thousands of disabled vets who had failed to enter rehabilitation. (The Legion also used the drive to "Clean Up" panhandlers, war neurotics, and others who might cast disabled veterans in a bad light.)[48] Long after the rehabilitation movement had waned, moreover, both the American Legion and the DAV employed salaried rehabilitation officers to visit hospitalized veterans and ghostwrite their appeals for further training or medical care.[49]

When it came to legislation, the Legion and DAV focused much of their energy on lobbying Congress for higher compensation rates and more generous civil service preferences. In addition, both groups worked to expand the definition of "service-connected disability" so that greater numbers of veterans became eligible for federal programs. On this front, the American Legion and the DAV urged lawmakers to redress the legal status of so-called presumptive cases, veterans whose disabilities were presumed to have originated in wartime but whose service records reflected no sign of injury or illness. The two groups succeeded in 1921, when Congress declared a presumptive service connection for cases of tuberculosis or neuropsychiatric disease developed within two years of veterans' discharge. The World War Veterans Act of 1924 liberalized disability benefits even further. Drafted by a pair of Legionnaires, senator David Reed (R-PA) and representative Royal Johnson (R-SD), the law granted hospitalization rights to all World War I veterans, whether they could claim a service-connected disability or not. It further declared that tuberculosis and neuropsychiatric cases reported prior to January 1, 1925, were presumed to have a service origin, unless the government could prove otherwise. With the stroke of the pen, tens of thousands of men became eligible for state benefits. Over the next four years, 78,000 more would join the ranks of the "war disabled," including men suffering the aftereffects of amoebic dysentery and venereal disease.[50]

Lobbyists for disabled veterans faced one of their toughest battles during the first hundred days of Franklin Roosevelt's New Deal. On March 20, 1933, Congress passed the Economy Act, a belt-tightening measure designed to reduce federal spending. Strongly supported by fiscal conservatives and probusiness groups, the act effectively scrapped the existing structure of veterans' benefits and empowered FDR to erect a new one in its place. Roosevelt's first set of veterans' regulations cut the pension rolls by half, eliminated service-connected presumptions for late-developing diseases, and slashed disability benefits across the board.[51] In retrospect, FDR's willingness to dismantle veterans' programs seems at odds with his political and personal commitments. His service as assistant secretary of the navy during World War I left him with a lifelong affinity for veterans. More significant, FDR knew the hardships of disability firsthand. In 1921, while vacationing on Campobello Island, the future president contracted a life-threatening bout of polio, leaving him paralyzed from the waist down. Throughout his subsequent career, FDR used his political celebrity to support disability research and therapy, even as he publicly downplayed the full extent of his own physical impairments.[52] Yet Roosevelt did not believe veterans belonged in a "special class of beneficiaries, over and above all other citizens," a sentiment he reiterated to a packed audience of Legionnaires at their October 1933 national convention.[53] In tough times, all Americans—including war's wounded survivors—were expected to sacrifice.

Some prominent veterans, including Legion commander Louis A. Johnson, initially supported the administration and urged the rank-and-file to follow suit, but outraged Legionnaires and DAV comrades quickly mounted a campaign to win back what they had lost. Rather than attacking the new president personally—a favorite tactic of the more militant VFW—Legionnaires and DAV comrades took their case to Congress and the American people, publicizing sensational stories of disabled veterans in desperate need of assistance.[54] Less than a year after the Economy Act was signed, Congress (over presidential veto) returned service-connected disability compensation rates to pre–Economy Act levels, reinstated partial compensation to 29,258 presumptive cases, and restored hospitalization privileges to all vets. It was only a partial victory (veterans' expenditures ultimately decreased by $150 million over FDR's first term).[55] Nevertheless, the battle over the Economy Act confirmed disabled veterans' status as a political category with no equal. Great Depression or not, they had sacrificed enough.

"Let's Stick Together, Buddy!"

For all of their legislative successes, the American Legion and DAV had few illusions about nonveterans' commitment to disabled vets. Although both groups worked closely with the Veterans' Bureau and private charities, they were reluctant to trust the government to solve America's Disabled Veteran Problem on its own. Political winds shifted quickly, and hard-won benefits could deteriorate in tough times. For this reason, both the Legion and DAV stressed the importance of sticking together with their fellow vets. For Great War veterans, "sticking together" was more than a group slogan; it was a source of political power, their only buffer against public indifference and government abuse. Vets who stuck together didn't just swap stories at yearly war reunions. They mobilized their collective resources—their bodies and wounds, money and votes, ideas and public reputations—toward a common cause.[56]

The American Legion and DAV were not shy about advertising the benefits that sticking together could yield. Throughout the 1920s, the Legion held large annual membership drives, with many local posts offering special-interest appeals (such as free movie tickets or accident insurance policies) to induce would-be Legionnaires to join.[57] DAV recruiters followed a similar tack, highlighting the material advantages of membership. Comrades in the Minneapolis chapter of the DAV, the nation's largest during the mid-1920s, were entitled to free notary service, a weekly newspaper, access to a nearby campground, weekly theater tickets, unpaid legal aid, and much more—all for the modest sum of $5 a year.[58] With the onset of the Great Depression, the DAV lowered its annual dues and held prize giveaways in order to attract new members. Some jobless comrades even found work selling DAV-licensed "forget-me-not" ice cream bars on the streets of Milwaukee.[59]

In many Depression-era communities, membership in a veterans' organization meant the difference between mere hardship and soul-crushing poverty. Throughout the 1930s, the American Legion and DAV knitted together an expansive social safety net, distributing food, blankets, rudimentary shelter, and heating fuel to down-and-out vets. With national jobless rates reaching 25 percent, the American Legion and DAV employment campaigns found work for tens of thousands of former doughboys.[60]

Much of the hands-on work of caring for "unfortunate" veterans—a description that encompassed unemployed, indigent, and permanently disabled vets—was performed by women: namely, members of the American Legion's and DAV's women's auxiliaries. Founded in February 1920, the American Legion Auxiliary was open to female relatives of Legionnaires or of men who had died in the Great War (women veterans could join the auxiliary, the Legion's main body, or both). Within the group, female Legionnaires devoted much of their time to family welfare, fund-raising, and social hygiene. Over time, the Legion Auxiliary developed a specifically political role, working to counter pacifist groups—traditionally dominated by women—and to promote a vision of patriotic American womanhood.[61]

Unlike its Legion counterpart, the DAV Women's Auxiliary tended to shy away from political controversy. Formed in 1922, it was comprised of the wives, mothers, sisters, and daughters of disabled veterans, along with Gold Star relatives and women with service-connected disabilities. The auxiliary's guiding philosophy was couched in the language of maternal obligation: "Any and everything which we may do should be in answer to the urge, 'this will be of service to the disabled men.'" Following this "urge," female comrades (as they were also called) engaged in a range of service activities. They sold Christmas cards, designed Armistice Day parade floats, ran hotdog stands at DAV conventions, and hosted war-themed "cootie" parties for hospitalized vets. One of the largest groups of DAV women was Kansas City's Ernestine Schumann-Heink Auxiliary, named after the Czech opera star and veterans' advocate who lost two sons in World War I. Meeting every two weeks, the group organized holiday celebrations for disabled veterans and distributed money, cigarettes, and Eskimo Pies to families in need. On the first Wednesday of every month, it sponsored performances by professional theater troops, musicians, and vaudeville acts at the local veterans' hospital (canine celebrity Rin Tin Tin was once the star attraction). Part charity group, part social club, DAV auxiliaries provided tangible relief to countless disabled men; in doing so, they integrated thousands of women into the community and culture of Great War vets.[62]

Ultimately, Great War veterans' societies promised their members a sense of comradeship and purpose, a feeling of masculine fraternity only to be found among other vets. In this respect, the American Legion and DAV were hardly unique. To some degree or another, all veterans' organizations are grounded in shared ideals of camaraderie, cooperation, and personal sacrifice. However, the content and contours of veterans' culture tend to be historically specific, reflecting the unique needs and desires of each generation of ex-servicemen. Following World War I, the American Legion and DAV promoted a decidedly upbeat (and euphemistic) culture of veteran solidarity, best described as *buddyhood*. Buddyhood was the social glue that held veterans' groups together, and its unspoken code pervaded all aspects of Legion and DAV life. Buddies spoke the same language, held the same values, and shared a common devotion to both their country and each other. Buddies did not put on airs, no matter who they were before the war or after. As former AEF commander John Pershing told a cheering crowd at the 1921 Legion convention, "Today, I am an ordinary buddy of the rear rank."[63] Above all else, buddies were not like other men. Tested by war, united in peace, they represented a separate class of citizens, bound together in a spirit of mutual defense.

References to buddies—alive or dead, old and young—saturated Legion speeches and public statements. At social gatherings, Legionnaires addressed each other as buddies, and Legion publicists made the buddy—almost always pictured as white, middle-class, and healthy—a key part of the group's public image. To some outside observers, the constant affirmation of Legion buddyhood was a cheap ploy to construct an illusion of martial fraternity among men with widely different military experiences.[64] Indeed, buddyhood often found its gaudiest expression at the group's annual conventions, which promised veterans a chance to escape their ordinary lives and recapture—if only for a few days—the excitement of the war years (fig. 21). Yet buddyhood was more than just a marketing tool (or an excuse to cut loose). It served as a kind of affective economy, meting out sympathy and a sense of belonging to all who joined its ranks.

In the DAV (whose members also addressed each other as "buddies"), buddyhood took on a quasi-religious status. In addition to the usual affinities born of military service, disabled vets were "bound together by the sacred ties of comradeship and strengthened by a common bond of suffering, of wound, injury, and disability," according to one DAV commander.[65] Disabled veterans believed the experience of impairment left them with a profound sense of mutual empathy. Percy Heron, a delegate at the DAV national convention in 1932, articulated a typical view of DAV buddyhood: "As disabled veterans we are drawn together closer in friendship and with more understanding and sympathy than the usual patriotic orders."[66] In fact, disabled veterans were widely considered— both by themselves and their nondisabled counterparts—as an elite caste of Great War buddies, their brotherly affections strengthened by their daily struggles to "carry on" in war's wake.

Not surprisingly, DAV buddies went to great lengths to police the boundaries of their exclusive fraternity. Disabled vets rarely aligned

FIG. 21. Members of the Philadelphia American Legion travel in boxcars to the 1920 national convention in Cleveland. At a time when vets were encouraged to return to "normalcy," veterans' conventions played an important role in helping Great War vets maintain their wartime allegiances and identities. They also helped foster the buddyhood that came to dominate post–World War I veterans' culture. Library of Congress, Prints & Photographs Division, LC-USZ62-94860.

themselves with disabled civilians, whose physical impairments lacked (in their minds) the connotations of patriotic sacrifice. Similarly, veterans disabled after World War I were viewed as second-tier buddies at best. In 1931, Robert Ragan, a DAV liaison officer from Tampa, Florida, submitted a resolution to admit veterans with non-service-connected disabilities as "associate members"—only to see it soundly defeated.[67] Over the next few years, as federal veterans' expenditures declined, more and more war-disabled veterans felt compelled to differentiate themselves from their postwar counterparts. DAV members worried that veterans with after-war disabilities would tarnish their sterling reputation, and they often portrayed such men's injuries as the product of poor judgment or faulty character. "We don't want to let in a fellow who is on a party every night, gets liquored up and then gets a leg cut off and gets

$40 a month," proclaimed Paul Kelly, a DAV buddy from California, in 1932. "We are not interested in him. We are interested in our comrades that served their flag during the war and suffered disabilities."[68]

Like the American Legion, the DAV made a conscious effort to celebrate the virtues of veterans' fraternity, using its national conventions, parades, and other events to foster a feeling of solidarity and mutual identification among its members. The DAV's second annual convention, held in San Francisco in 1922, was an especially festive affair. The Pullman Company offered disabled veterans a roundtrip fare of twenty-five dollars per person from anywhere in the country, and Henry Ford provided a caravan of fifty Model Ts to transport comrades to the event. Once there, the men were treated to a naval review, a "monster military parade," a concert by Rudolph Valentino (at a dollar a head), and a "Living Hall of Fame" consisting of the "greatest heroes" of each state. The DAV even organized sightseeing trips to Chinatown and nearby military hospitals where comrades could meet and commune with their fellow disabled vets.[69]

For all of their extravagance, veterans' reunions reflected a genuine longing for companionship and understanding. In a climate deeply hostile to physical difference of any kind, many disabled vets actively sought the company of buddies whose experiences of disability mirrored their own. Responding to such desires, veterans' groups, city and state governments, and private welfare organizations sponsored recreational facilities and campgrounds specifically for disabled veterans and their families. Some consisted of little more than a couple of rooms where disabled vets could relax with their buddies and relive memories of battles past. More elaborate sites featured sleeping facilities, game rooms, reading parlors, and beds for veterans passing through town. In 1923, the New York State American Legion opened the 1,275-acre Veterans' Mountain Camp at Big Tupper Lake as a sanctuary for tubercular and convalescent vets.[70] The next year, wealthy New Yorkers funded Camp Bluefields, a summer retreat for ex-servicemen undergoing rehabilitation at Columbia University. Located in the lush countryside of Rockland County, the former POW camp boasted an extensive lodge house (complete with a library and dance pavilion), individual bungalows for campers, a swimming pool, a baseball diamond, and two "Japanese chefs," according to a published report.[71] Among the best-known disabled veterans' rest

FIG. 22. Disabled veterans at Big Island Veterans Camp on Lake Minnetonka outside Minneapolis, Minnesota. Designed to provide disabled vets with a chance for inexpensive recreation, the rest camp featured thirty-six cabins, a large food-service building, and a dormitory that could house thirty people. Big Island and similar camps testified to some disabled veterans' willingness, even desire, to segregate themselves from their nondisabled peers. Courtesy of the Minnesota Historical Society.

camps was Big Island Veterans Camp. The camp was built on the site of a former amusement park just west of Minneapolis. Open to "sick, ailing, or unfortunate ex-servicemen," Big Island offered disabled veterans from the Midwest a chance to swim, fish, and socialize—away from the prying eyes of the nondisabled public (fig. 22).[72]

The nation's most famous clubhouse for disabled World War I veterans was located on East 66th Street in Manhattan. Founded in November 1920 by the National League for Women's Services, a charity organization that operated veterans' canteens throughout New York City, the Dug Out was originally intended to serve as a combination workshop-hostel for disabled veterans undergoing rehabilitation. It housed a small handicrafts shop, where men made toys and metal ornaments for sale, along with a cafeteria-style canteen open to all veterans, disabled or not. Early on, the Dug Out rented thirty small rooms for five dollars a week apiece and promoted itself as a "meeting place and social center by men who like to continue and renew the acquaintances formed during the War." Over time, however, it became something of an old soldier's home, a refuge for indigent, disabled vets unable or unwilling to strike out on their own.[73] Like similar facilities run by the DAV and American Legion, the Dug Out eventually came to symbolize both the benefits and drawbacks of Great War buddyhood. Within its walls, disabled veterans could find fraternal sympathy and shelter from a harsh, uncaring world. At the same time, the Dug Out further reinforced the division between disabled vets and the rest of American society.

The Veteran Racket

Whether building disabled veterans' clubhouses, sponsoring disability-related legislation, or exposing Veterans' Bureau mismanagement, the American Legion and DAV enjoyed great acclaim for their work on behalf of America's disabled buddies. During the economic boom years of the mid-1920s, the two groups' campaigns to expand federal benefits for disabled veterans attracted little public scrutiny. Eager to show their patriotic spirit, lawmakers were prone to support veterans' programs, even if groups like the American Legion sometimes reached too far. With the coming of the Great Depression, however, Americans took a closer look at the high costs—in both dollars and broken bodies—of the United States' intervention in the Great War. More than a decade after rehabilitationists had promised a solution to America's Disabled Soldier Problem, World War I veterans' benefits alone constituted the federal government's largest expenditure, rising from $225 million in 1919 to $581 million in 1932.[74] Critics from across the political spectrum raised alarms about a growing "veteran racket." Indeed, as economic conditions soured, long-simmering concerns about veterans' politics, preferential treatment, and manipulation of patriotic sentiment boiled over onto the front pages of the national press.[75]

As the largest and most powerful ex-servicemen's association, the American Legion attracted the lion's share of the criticism. Fiscal conservatives complained about the Legion's tight grip on the nation's pocketbook. Throughout the Depression, groups like the National Economy

League and the US Chamber of Commerce excoriated the Legion for raiding the US Treasury and, in one journalist's words, "browbeat[ing] the Congress into appropriating millions and millions of dollars for their own fat selves."[76] Civil libertarians saw the Legionnaires as a reactionary political force and a threat to all Americans' freedoms. According to the ACLU, perhaps the Legion's most vocal critic, the Legion promoted a hateful, militaristic ideology, lashing out against conscientious objectors, atheists, and all things German—all under the guise of 100% Americanism.[77] During the 1930s, many of the Legion's opponents likened the group to the militaristic, veteran-dominated fascist parties of Europe, drawing explicit parallels between Italian Blackshirts, German Brownshirts, and American Legionnaires.[78] No less disturbing—at least to contemporary observers—were the Legion's annual conventions. In a typical report, the Harvard *Crimson* described the Legion's 1930 convention as "merely an excuse for a wholesale brawl exceeding in its disgusting completeness any similar spectacle which the United States has to offer. Even Boston . . . has seen fit to allow a total relaxation of law and order during the stay in the Hub of the 'buddies' of the Legion, those glorious Americans who fought, the slogan says, to make the world safe for democracy, and who have come back to raise hell annually so no one can forget it."[79]

Some of the harshest anti-Legion sentiment focused on the rising tide of *peace veterans*, men who had left the war seemingly healthy but because of liberalized disability ratings now enjoyed the same benefits as soldiers wounded on the battlefield.[80] Backlash against peace veterans exploded in 1930, when Congress voted to extend federal disability benefits to ex-servicemen injured in civilian life. A compromise to forestall an even more radical measure, the Disability Allowance Act of 1930 departed from the accepted policy of compensating veterans for disabilities incurred during service. Instead, it granted disability allowances to all permanently disabled veterans, whether their disabilities were service-connected or not.[81] As one writer scathingly explained, "A man who was injured in 1932 in a taxicab accident would be entitled to a pension just as though his physical difficulties had resulted from a hand-to-hand fight in a German trench."[82] During its first year, more than half a million veterans applied for disability allowances, of which 239,073 were granted.[83] Although the Legion had initially lobbied against the bill, it soon threw its weight behind the measure, unleashing cries of hypocrisy in the popular press.

Among the Legion's fiercest critics were veterans themselves, including a number of dues-paying Legionnaires. Like all large organizations, the American Legion of the 1930s was rarely as unified as its public image implied. Rank-and-file members clashed with leadership over priorities and values, while some Legionnaires jumped ship entirely. Roger Burlingame, a former AEF lieutenant and author of *Peace Veterans: The Story of a Racket and a Plea for Economy* (1932), was so disgusted by the Legion's support of what he considered self-indulgent legislation that he formed his own veterans' group. Ten thousand members strong, the American Veterans' Association was governed by the motto "Justice to the war wounded, justice to the war dead, justice to the American people."[84] Ernest Angell, commander of the Legion's Willard Straight Post in New York City, criticized the Legion for ousting liberals from its ranks and stifling internal debate.[85] Writing in the *Nation* in 1933, Angell also derided the large number of veterans—400,000 by his count—receiving checks for disabilities unrelated to the war. At that time, the United States was spending more than $600 million a year on World War veterans and their dependents. "And still the Legion is not content," he raged.[86]

But where Angell saw a "half-billion-dollar swindle," other observers saw something even more insidious. Anti-Legion writer Marcus Duffield characterized the group as a bloated corporate bureaucracy that cynically invoked veteran "comradeship" to expand its political empire.[87] Author Katherine Mayo went further, accusing Legionnaires of "shamelessly trading on [the] merit and good name" of veterans disabled in service. In *Soldiers, What Next!* (1934), she portrayed the Legion's campaign to liberalize disability benefits as a classic bait-and-switch, exploiting the suffering of disabled veterans to secure a favored status for all ex-servicemen: "All this we had seen done under cover of a sleight-of-hand man's din—a hocus-pocus about 'the disabled buddy' too palpable, too thin, too cheap to have deceived the slightest study by an honest eye—a trick as false and cruel and harmful to the War-disabled man as it was shameless toward the Nation." The Great War's disabled heroes had been "used by unscrupulous gangs as certain other types of mobs use women—pushing them to the front to serve as shields behind which mischief may be more easily accomplished." As a result, the line between "disabled War Comrades" and "War-disabled Comrades" had become so blurred the distinction had lost all meaning.[88]

The American Legion's responses to such charges were uncompromising. Individual Legionnaires denounced the group's critics as subversives, Soviet propagandists, witless fools, and enemies of veterans everywhere.[89] Writer H. L. Mencken earned the nickname "Little Cootie" after daring to buck the Legion in print.[90] Ernest Angell's Legion post was suspended for publicly dissenting from official policy, and the American Legion used its considerable publicity apparatus to smear politicians and other public figures—including wayward Legionnaires—who failed to toe the Legion line. During the depths of the Depression, the American Legion attacked the National Economy League (and its supporters in big business) as shameless "war profiteers" more concerned with lining their own pockets than attending to veterans' welfare.[91] All the while, Legionnaires continued to reiterate their sacred duty to protect their "disabled buddies."

And the DAV? Although they enjoyed a lower profile than their "King Legion" counterparts, DAV comrades were not immune to public sniping. In the early 1920s, Stanley Frost, a well-known critic of Veterans' Bureau dysfunction, condemned the "beggar attitude" epitomized by the DAV's lobbying campaign, urging "Congress and public opinion to react promptly, but without discrimination, to stories of injustice or hardship."[92] Later writers raised questions about DAV "patrioteering" or made little effort to differentiate war-disabled DAV comrades from peace veterans, suspicious presumptive cases, and other beneficiaries of the veteran racket.[93] For the most part, however, the DAV escaped charges of debauchery and disabled buddy exploitation. Given its more limited agenda, the DAV won a reputation for putting the needs of America's war-disabled before anything else. Moreover, when faced with controversy, it was able to take shelter beneath the Legion's expansive umbrella. In 1933, journalist Talcott Powell offered a typically uncritical assessment. Unlike the Legion, Powell argued, the DAV had "no interest whatever in providing pensions for able-bodied men and malingers." Eschewing "professional flag-waving," DAV comrades worked "steadily in the interest of the disabled veterans whose welfare has been relegated to second place by the larger organizations which [were] seeking subsidies for undeserving members."[94]

The Disabled Bonus Army of 1932

But were disabled veterans the only ones who "deserved" federal subsidies? What about the men who managed to return from the Great War unscathed? What were the government's obligations to them?

No episode better illustrated veterans' unresolved feelings about the Great War's social contract than the Bonus March of 1932. The Bonus March was the best known of a series of veterans' protests demanding the immediate disbursement of "adjusted universal compensation," a cash "bonus" intended to offset the financial hardships of military service during World War I. Historians have traditionally used the Bonus March (and its bloody aftermath) to illustrate the social turmoil and fractured politics of Depression-era America.[95] More recently, scholars like Jennifer Keene and Stephen Ortiz have begun to reevaluate the Bonus March as a milestone in the history of veterans' activism, one that would eventually lead to such measures as the GI Bill.[96] Often overlooked in such analyses, however, are the ways Bonus Marchers relied upon increasingly expansive definitions of war disability to frame their demands. In this sense, the Bonus March (and the bonus issue in general) both challenged and ultimately reaffirmed disabled veterans' privileged status between the world wars.

Dating back to the early days of the Armistice, the bonus represented a radical shift in veterans' understanding of military service. Instead of viewing participation in war as a matter of civic duty, bonus supporters portrayed it as a social disability, one that left all veterans severely handicapped upon their return to civilian life. Their reasoning went something like this: While conscripted doughboys were busy setting aside their individual ambitions in service to the state, men at home were starting families, building careers, and flexing their capitalist muscles. By the Great War's end, veterans had fallen so far behind their civilian counterparts it was nearly impossible for them to catch up on their own. In effect, pro-bonus forces viewed the bonus as a kind of economic prosthesis, supplementing veterans' lost income and allowing them to "start even" with those who stayed behind. Within this conceptual framework, the category of "war disabled"—with its numerous rights and privileges—applied to all Great War vets. As Frederic Galbraith explained to American Legion readers in 1921, able-bodied vets were just "another class of disabled who have waited patiently until their physically incapacitated buddies should be cared for. Our next great legislative effort will be for them."[97]

Critics charged that bonus payouts would not only turn veterans into "mercenaries" but also siphon away precious resources from the men who needed them most.[98] In 1922, a *New York Times* editorial urged veterans to rethink their priorities: "This no time to demand, to insist upon, adjusted compensation—the afflicted, the defectives, the incapacitated must come first!"[99] The American Legion and DAV were initially conflicted about whether to support bonus legislation. Calls for the bonus threatened to undercut their arguments about the privileged status of disabled veterans. Then again, members of both groups believed the federal government had an obligation to "square up matters" for Great War vets, many of whom had been left in a financial "hole" because of their military service.[100] Although a number of prominent veterans tried to quell bonus demands, rank-and-file buddies overwhelmingly supported some form of monetary compensation. By the early 1920s, the three largest Great War veterans' groups were squarely behind the bonus bill. In 1924, Congress finally succumbed to veterans' pressure, granting monetary payments to all World War veterans ($1 per day for domestic service, $1.25 for service overseas). Vets who were owed $50 or less received their money immediately; the rest were issued certificates redeemable in 1945.

With the onset of the Great Depression, however, thousands of veterans began to lose patience. Unlike the VFW and DAV, both of which strongly supported the immediate payment of veterans' bonuses, American Legion leaders resisted.[101] After a direct appeal from Herbert Hoover, delegates at the 1931 Legion national convention voted 902–507 against the immediate demand for the bonus, calling upon "the able-bodied men of America, rich and poor, veteran, civilian, and statesmen, to refrain from placing unnecessary financial burdens upon Nation, State, or municipal governments."[102] But such admonitions did little to stem the pro-bonus tide, even among Legionnaires. In early 1932, veterans from across the United States decided to present their demands to Congress in person. By May, more than 20,000 Great War veterans had converged upon the nation's capital, setting up camp in a sprawling shantytown near the Anacostia River. Over the next three months, the self-styled Bonus Expeditionary Forces (BEF) waged a relentless campaign to win the support of lawmakers and the American people.

From the moment they arrived in Washington, Bonus Marchers made disability—physical, economic, and social—a dominant part of their collective image and public rhetoric. Blind, maimed, and otherwise disabled vets were prominently featured in BEF parades and publications, and veterans' spokesmen seemed eager to blur the lines between able-bodied Bonus Marchers and their war-disabled comrades. Harold B. Foulkrod, the self-described "chairman of the legislative committee of the BEF," offered a typical announcement at a hearing with District of Columbia officials: "We are the men who fought in France, and we are the men who gave everything we had—our bodies."[103] Outside observers similarly made sure to publicize the presence of war-disabled veterans in the BEF's ranks. Newspaper correspondent Floyd Gibbons, who himself had been seriously wounded at Belleau Wood, took special note of one group of disabled Bonus Marchers in particular:

> Four abreast they marched—
> five thousand strong . . .
> All were down at the heel.
> All were slim and gaunt and their eyes had a light in them.
> They were empty sleeves and limping men with canes. . . .
> They did not march in the light of day. They marched in darkness.[104]

Gibbon's "empty sleeves" were participants in the notorious Death March of July 12–17, 1932. The Death March was not so much an organized parade as a five-day silent vigil, with shifts of ragged vets trudging back and forth along the sidewalks of the Capitol grounds. The picketers' "crippled leader," Royal W. Robertson, was a minor film actor and rabble-rouser who had led a contingent of 450 veterans from Southern California. As a sailor in World War I, Robertson had suffered a severe neck injury after falling from his hammock. He wore a heavy steel neck brace attached to his head by a leather strap, which he thumped with his skull to punctuate his arguments.[105] On the day the Death March began, Robertson split ranks with other BEF leaders, personally petitioning vice president Charles Curtis to provide bonus payments to "needy" veterans—and needy veterans alone. The rationale for such an approach, Robertson argued, was pragmatic:

> If these men continue as they have been for the last two years, without money, food and clothing . . . they could [under the current disability law], be granted disability compensation if their health should

break down. . . . I am asking you and the Senate and the House to look at it from a business standpoint so the health of these men can be safeguarded and they can be kept from applying for their disability compensation.[106]

In Robertson's mind, "needy" and "disabled" veterans were virtually one and the same. A Bonus Marcher's disabled status was as much a product of government inactivity during the Great Depression as it was the result of wartime injury and disease.

The distinction between needy and disabled veterans collapsed even further during the Death March itself. As Congress deliberated the bonus's fate, Robertson's Death Marchers shuffled back and forth around the Capitol. One bandaged man, guilty of "transparent faking," collected coins and cigarettes; other Death Marchers collapsed on the sidewalk in fits of exhaustion and war-related stress. Robertson would claim that two-thirds of the men were disabled veterans, but the veracity of such pronouncements mattered little to sympathetic spectators.[107] When large crowds appeared early in the Death March, Robertson's brigade wrapped their heads in bandages and began to mimic "other stage properties of wartime disabilities." According to Talcott Powell, an eyewitness to the event, "Men began to hobble painfully and by the second day, the group looked like a retreat from a battlefield. No one seemed to question the authenticity of these sudden physical disabilities. It made a good show."[108]

In the end, the Death Marchers' theatrics were for naught. The Senate rejected the revised bonus bill, and on the afternoon of July 28, federal troops armed with bayonets and tanks drove the 9,000 remaining Bonus Marchers from the city. In the ensuing riot, mounted cavalrymen corralled the ragged veterans like cattle, while soldiers in gas masks hurled canisters of tear gas into the crowds of onlookers. By midnight, the BEF's campsite was engulfed in flames, lighting up the entire Washington skyline. For much of the American public, the "Battle of the Anacostia Flats" became a symbol of Republican insensitivity to needs of the Depression-era "Forgotten Man," and the episode helped catapult FDR into the White House less than eight months later. However, Great War veterans would have to wait another three years to receive their bonus checks, and then only over several presidential vetoes. Like his

Republican predecessors, Roosevelt refused to grant disability status to all veterans. Announcing his final veto in a nationally broadcast speech on May 22, 1935, FDR maintained that able-bodied vets should have to bear the brunt of hard times just like everyone else: "The veteran who is disabled owes his condition to the war. The healthy veteran who is unemployed owes his troubles to the depression. Each represents a separate and different problem."[109]

Conclusion

On the tenth anniversary of the Armistice, John Thomas Taylor, a prominent Legion lobbyist, reflected, "In all our history this is the first time that a veterans' organization has not only taken a part in but has actually solved many of the great problems, both economic and social, that come as the aftermath of war."[110] When it came to the Problem of the Disabled Veteran, veterans' groups had reason to bask in their accomplishments. Faced with public indifference, economic depression, and a cultural imperative of "normalcy," the American Legion and the DAV improved the welfare of countless disabled veterans. Through their legislative campaigns, Legionnaires and comrades carved out a privileged legal status for war-disabled vets, one that accorded them monetary and institutional benefits superseding those of all other US citizens. The groups forced the Veterans' Bureau to expand the definition of disabled veteran to include men whose ailments and infirmities had previously gone unrecognized by federal pension boards. Just as important, Legion and DAV rituals, reunions, and conventions offered disabled veterans access to a fraternal culture of buddyhood that promised to ward off social alienation.

But veterans' activism left behind troubling legacies as well. Following the bloodiest war in world history, veterans' groups largely reaffirmed the myth of war experience, glorifying the disabled veteran as a symbol of patriotic sacrifice and martial Americanism. Rather than bucking racial trends, the American Legion and DAV allowed local chapters to determine inclusion policies, a practice that further relegated veterans of color to a second-class status. Similarly, instead of trying to build coalitions with disabled civilians or veterans disabled in peacetime, the DAV helped widen the gap between war-disabled veterans and other disability groups. In many respects, such legacies were a direct consequence of veterans' efforts to elevate disabled veterans as model citizens—above not only their Great War buddies but also their civilian counterparts. Yet the American Legion and DAV had little confidence that interwar Americans would ever appreciate disabled veterans' bodily sacrifices. In fact, more than any legislative setback, Great War veterans were terrified that disabled vets—and the martial values they embodied—would be forgotten.

Forget-Me-Not Day

On the morning of Saturday, December 17, 1921, an army of high school girls, society women, and recently disabled veterans assembled for one of the largest fund-raising campaigns since the end of World War I. The group's mission was to sell millions of handcrafted, crepe-paper forget-me-nots to be worn in remembrance of disabled veterans. Where the artificial blooms were unavailable, volunteers peddled sketches of the pale blue flowers or cardboard tags with the phrase "I Did Not Forget" printed on the front. The sales drive was the brainchild of the Disabled American Veterans of the World War (DAV), and proceeds went toward funding assorted relief programs for permanently injured doughboys. Event supporters hoped high turnout would put to rest any doubt about the nation's appreciation of disabled veterans and their families. As governor Albert C. Ritchie told his Maryland residents on the eve of the flower drive: "Let us organize our gratitude so that in a year's time there will not be a single disabled soldier who can point an accusing finger at us."[1]

Over the next decade, National Forget-Me-Not Day became a minor holiday in the United States. In 1922, patients from Washington, DC, hospitals presented a bouquet of forget-me-nots to first lady Florence Kling Harding, at the time recovering from a major illness. Her husband wore one of the little flowers pinned to his lapel, as did the entire White House staff.[2] That same year, Broadway impresario George M. Cohan orchestrated massive Forget-Me-Not Day concerts in New York City. As bands played patriotic tunes, stage actresses worked the crowds, smiling, flirting, and raking in coins by the bucketful.[3] According to press reports at the time, the flower sales were meant to perform a double duty for disabled vets. Pinned to a suit jacket or dress, a forget-me-not bloom provided a "visible tribute" to the bodily sacrifices of the nation's fighting men.[4] As the manufacture of remembrance flowers evolved into a cottage industry for indigent vets, the sales drive acquired an additional motive: to turn a "community liability" into a "community asset."[5]

Although press accounts of Forget-Me-Not Day reassured readers that "Americans Never Forget," many disabled veterans remained skeptical.[6]

From the holiday's inception, the DAV tended to frame Forget-Me-Not Day in antagonistic terms, using the occasion to vent its frustration with the federal government, critics of veterans' policies, and a forgetful public. Posters from the first sales drive featured an anonymous amputee on crutches, coupled with the accusation "Did you call it charity when they gave their legs, arms and eyes?" As triumphal memories of the Great War waned, moreover, Forget-Me-Not Day slogans turned increasingly hostile. "They can't believe the nation is grateful if they are allowed to go hungry," sneered one DAV slogan, two years before the start of the Great Depression. Another characterized the relationship between civilians and disabled vets as one of perpetual indebtedness: "You can never give them as much as they gave you."[7]

6

"FOR THE MEM'RY OF WARRIORS WRACKED WITH PAIN"
Disabled Doughboys and American Memory

Little pale blossom of tint sky blue,
Why are you worn today?
Why is everyone buying you?
What do you stand for, pray! . . .

For the mem'ry of warriors wracked with pain,
Mangled while facing the foe;
Belgian soil bears a crimson stain
Where they offered their all, unthinking of gain,
(They know NOW their sacrifice was not in vain!)
in their Hospital Beds in a row!
— William Ellis Resister (c. 1930)[1]

In the aftermath of World War I, disabled veterans and their political allies came to see "memory" as an important part of their social contract with the American people. Having suffered on the nation's behalf, they believed their fellow citizens were duty-bound to remember their sacrifices in both symbolic and material form. Yet, despite a memory boom in the decades following World War I, many vets feared that the Great War's legacy of broken bodies and shattered minds would soon be forgotten, casualties of an amnesiac culture that preferred looking forward to looking back.

In recent decades, numerous scholars have examined how memory structures the identities and experiences of survivors of war and other traumas.[2] Much of this work focuses on the realm of cultural memory, a form of mass remembrance produced through public rituals, mass media representations, and popular culture.[3] Cultural memory is neither arbitrary nor permanent. As historian Jay Winter points out, societies "remember" only inasmuch as specific groups of people actively participate in processes of memorialization; when they "lose interest, or time, or for another other reason cease to act," memories fade away, perhaps to be remembered (or reproduced) at some later date.[4] Put simply, the terrain of memory is invariably contested, with competing factions vying to determine not only how the past is remembered but to what end.

Following World War I, veterans' groups like the DAV, the American Legion, and the Veterans of Foreign Wars (VFW) attempted to establish themselves as the primary arbiters of disabled veterans' remembrance. Unsatisfied by the symbolic gestures offered up by civic leaders, disabled veterans in particular demanded alternative forms of memorialization, ones that not only honored their military service, but also addressed the long-term physical, economic, and social consequences of war-produced disability. Animating much of their memorial work was a desire to construct what was described as a *purposeful* memory of disabled vets—a voluntary and productive model of public remembrance that paid tangible dividends to disabled veterans and their families.

Maintaining such a memory was more difficult than setting up a few monuments, however. The cultural idioms that dominated postwar memorial culture were better suited to remembering the Great War's dead than its traumatized survivors. More important, vets' impulses toward memorialization clashed with the messages of rehabilitation, which seemed to celebrate forgetting as a cultural ideal. It was against this backdrop that one of the most iconic figures of early twentieth American culture would take shape: the forgotten disabled doughboy. Rooted in the experiences of countless men, the forgotten disabled doughboy quickly hardened into stereotype, a constellation of images and histories that veterans and their cultural allies would use to bludgeon a forgetful public. Ultimately, battles over the memory of disabled veterans reflected deep anxieties about the human legacies of modern warfare and the incorporation of the disabled body into postwar life. They also set the stage for the appropriation of the disabled veteran as a symbol of government indifference in the wake of national trauma.

Memory Boom

Even as disabled veterans began their memorial campaigns, the United States was already in the midst of a national memory boom.[5] Long before the Armistice was signed, soldiers, ambulance drivers, nurses, and physicians flooded American bookstores with hastily written memoirs and diaries seeking to document—and posthumously memorialize—all aspects of life "over there." Fictional accounts of the Great War were not far behind, with Edith Wharton's *The Marne* (1918), John Dos Passos's *One Man's Initiation* (1920) and *Three Soldiers* (1921), Willa Cather's *One of Ours* (1922), E. E. Cummings's *The Enormous Room* (1922), Thomas Boyd's *Through the Wheat* (1923), and countless others published in the first half decade of the ceasefire. Cinematic memorials of the Great War were fewer and further between, but they included some of the most celebrated films of the 1920s and 1930s.

Of the literally thousands of war-related memoirs, novels, documentaries, and feature films produced in the decades following World War I, the vast majority disappeared from public consciousness almost as soon as they appeared. The exceptions—including Erich Maria Remarque's *All Quiet on the Western Front*, both the novel (1929) and its film version (1930)—were *soldiers' tales*, intimate narratives of male combatants under fire. Soldiers' tales condense the vast panorama of war into simple human dramas about an individual's (or a small group's) experiences in wartime. According to literary scholar Samuel Hynes, the popularity of soldiers' tales stems from their claims of authenticity, their promise of the "real" war as told by the men who fought it.[6] Unlike elite memorial productions of the state, soldiers' tales of the Great War era tended to focus on the singular horrors of the battlefront, the brutality of life in the service, and the destructive power (and strange beauty) of modern weaponry. Collectively, they bore retrospective witness to the Great War's rapacious appetite for male bodies and the human detritus the fighting left behind. With few exceptions, however, American soldiers' tales did not address the lives of veterans, disabled or otherwise, upon leaving the military. Consequently, the soldiers' tale failed to produce a cultural memory that disabled veterans might claim as their own.

Few films better illustrate the limitations of the soldiers' tale as a vehicle of disabled veterans' memory than King Vidor's *The Big Parade* (1925), one of the biggest hits of the silent film era. Based partly on amputee-author Laurence Stallings's *Plumes*, it follows the journey of Jim Apperson, an idle rich youth who enlists on a whim and is severely wounded while fighting in France. In a particularly devastating scene,

FIG. 23. King Vidor's *The Big Parade* (1925) shocked audiences with its horrific portrait of trench warfare. In this scene, the film's hero Jim Apperson (played by John Gilbert) is crawling through no man's land after he has been wounded in the leg, an injury that eventually requires its amputation. However, like most Great War soldiers' tales, *The Big Parade* does not address the long-term legacies of war disability. Instead, it concludes shortly after Apperson's tearful reunion with his wartime lover.

the camera holds on the shocked and ashamed faces of his family when they discover he has returned home missing part of his leg. Praised for its verisimilitude, *The Big Parade* offered movie audiences one of the first "realistic" visions of the chaos and mechanized carnage of trench warfare (fig. 23). But unlike Stallings's source novel, Vidor's war epic does not linger on disabled veterans' postwar struggles. Instead, it ends on a sentimental note, with Apperson returning to Europe and rushing into the arms of the French farm girl he loves. As with so many soldiers' tales, *The Big Parade* is far more adept at showing how combatants become disabled than what their lives are like in the wake of traumatic injury.

Objects of Great War memory were not limited to bookstores and the big screen. Spared the devastation of the actual fighting, American cityscapes were soon festooned with statues, remembrance gardens, and other permanent monuments to the Great War. Architectural memorials to the United States' participation in World War I ranged from modest grave markers and decorative tablets to gleaming white marble temples erected at the taxpayer's expense. The nation's largest war monument was built in downtown Indianapolis, just outside the American Legion's national headquarters. Covering five city blocks, Indiana's War Memorial Plaza included not one but three massive memorials: Cenotaph Square, a sunken garden surrounding an empty tomb; Obelisk Square, an open-air plaza centered around a fountain and a magnificent obelisk; and the Memorial Shrine, an opulent stone fortress complete with Ionic columns, classical statuary, and a four-story shrine room. Like other monuments of its kind, Indiana's War Memorial Plaza was funded by the state in lieu of veterans' bonuses, a decision that angered many former soldiers who would have preferred cash payments to statues and shrines.[7]

Although some cities adopted similar designs, many eschewed traditional monuments in favor of what became known as *living memorials*, commemorative structures and spaces more easily incorporated into everyday life.[8] Throughout the 1920s and 1930s, Americans dedicated thousands of swimming pools, drinking fountains, "liberty buildings," arboretums, and civic auditoriums to the memory of the Great War. (Birmingham's Legion Field and the University of Nebraska's Memorial Stadium both date from this era.) By May 1936, California alone boasted over one hundred memorial buildings, including Los Angeles' Patriotic Hall, home to more than thirty local posts of the American Legion.[9] Over time, several states passed laws dictating how and where Great War memory should be inscribed into the built environment. Florida required all state bridges be named after a fatal war casualty; the Pennsylvania state legislature went further, authorizing its counties, cities, and boroughs to plant memorial trees, decorate soldiers' graves on Memorial Day, and erect battle monuments both at home and overseas.[10] Within a few years of the ceasefire, it would have been difficult to travel to any part of the United States, no matter how remote, without encountering some reminder of the Great War.[11]

In his study of US war memory, G. Kurt Piehler argues that the proliferation of Great War monuments reflected a shared desire to "camouflage the division caused by the war." National leaders and patriotic groups in particular had a vested interest in remembering the nation's first European land war as an "idealistic struggle for liberty and democracy waged by a united people."[12] Racial and class divisions, inter-Allied rivalries, the war's ambiguous outcome, the mechanized slaughter on the modern battlefield—these had little place in the monumental memory of the Great War sanctified in city squares and Legion halls across the country. Where readers of Thomas Boyd or John Dos Passos might expect blood-and-guts realism, visitors to War Memorial Plaza would have been hard-pressed to imagine the random carnage of a World War I battlefield. For all their claim to historical truth, the nation's built memorials offered little insight into that most common of Great War dramas: the meeting of chemically propelled metal and human flesh.

American architects and politicians did not ignore the Great War's vast legacies of injury and death altogether. Like the Tomb of the Unknown Soldier, which was dedicated in Arlington Cemetery in 1921, the vast majority of American built memorials were decidedly funereal in tone, constructed to pay homage to US servicemen in "eternal bivouac." America's war dead came to occupy a privileged place in the nation's memory of the Great War, as was the case in all of the belligerent countries.[13] For the friends and relatives of fatal casualties, memorials to "fallen" doughboys served as important sites of emotional refuge and spiritual reaffirmation. In the early 1920s, the aptly named Bring Home the Soldier Dead League successfully lobbied the War Department to repatriate thousands of corpses to US cemeteries (eventually 70 percent of American servicemen buried in France were disinterred and reburied in the States).[14] While the nation's cult of the fallen dissipated over time, it never disappeared entirely. During the 1930s, after much of the public had become disillusioned with the "war to end all wars," communities across the United States continued to erect statues and monuments to local doughboys killed in action. Ultimately it did not matter whether US citizens viewed the Great War as a glorious crusade or a tragic mistake. All agreed, at least publicly, that the nation's dead deserved to be remembered.

But what about the memory of America's living casualties? How would disabled doughboys be "remembered" in the public imagination? And to what end would their memory be put? In many respects, the traditional modes of war memory—the soldiers' tales, the marble shrines, the "living" memorials—were inadequate to memorialize the experiences of disabled veterans.

Disabled Veterans and the Embodiment of Memory

To understand why, we need to step back from the Great War generation and consider disabled veterans' complex relationship to cultural memory in general. To begin with, there is the obvious, albeit deeply complicating, fact that disabled veterans are *survivors* of warfare. Unlike the dead, who rely upon others for commemoration, disabled vets have the capacity, at least in theory, to memorialize themselves. This is not to say that disabled veterans, even when collectively organized, have access to the economic capital or political clout necessary to cultivate remembrance on a mass scale. Nor is it to suggest that disabled veterans have always played a dominant role in determining how they are remembered in American culture. Still, disabled veterans can—and often do—serve as agents of their own remembrance, shaping the way their individual and collective experiences are perceived in the broader culture. In this respect alone, disabled veterans pose a far more unsettling threat to idealized commemorations of war than their dead comrades. While the dead "rest" in silence, mute witnesses of past conflicts, disabled veterans invariably "carry on"—their voices, their stories, even their bodies, all reminders of the lasting effects of war's violence.

In addition, when it comes to public remembrance, the stakes are much higher for disabled veterans than soldiers who die in battle. Public platitudes aside, even the most elaborate remembrance rituals offer nothing to those killed in combat. Dead soldiers are corpses, putrefying matter, carbon. It does not matter whether they are remembered as heroes, vilified as monsters, or forgotten altogether—the dead remain dead, and no amount of flag-waving can bring them back. For disabled veterans, on the other hand, memory's benefits are much more tangible. Most memorial practices are aimed at either raising money for disabled veterans or publicizing their poor treatment at the hands of government agencies. Others fulfill a more therapeutic role: they remind disabled veterans that they are appreciated, that their bodily injuries have meaning and value to someone besides themselves. Disabled veterans' own remembrance practices typically serve a third purpose as well, binding disabled vets together in a shared social identity. In short, disabled veterans have much to gain when they are remembered and much to lose when they are forgotten.

Even so, not all forms of war remembrance are equally advantageous to disabled vets. As historian Seth Koven has shown, traditional forms of memorialization, such as monuments or statuary, tend to inhibit public recognition of disabled veterans' ongoing struggles.[15] When relegated to a cenotaph or marble statue, war's memory might provide a sense of comfort to the families of the dead; it might even serve as a locus of community bereavement.[16] However, traditional war memorials provide little material benefit—no pension check, no summer camp, no disabled man's clubhouse—for war's disabled survivors. For this reason, disabled vets have historically eschewed monuments and memorials in favor of public legislation, veteran-themed holidays, and other modes of remembrance more likely to pay concrete dividends to themselves and their families.

Complicating matters further, many veterans struggle to come to terms with the memorial function of their own bodies. War amnesia is a luxury of noncombatants or the dead. Disabled veterans might learn to accept their injuries—they might even look upon them with pride—but they are not likely to forget them. With every twinge of pain, every glance into the mirror, war-injured veterans are reminded that they are different, that their lives will never be the same.[17] Moreover, because disabled veterans' bodies often serve as *public* repositories of war's violence, the memorial function of veterans' injuries is not limited to the psychic lives of individual vets. The blackened scar of a mustard gas burn, the wheeze of tubercular lungs, the bandaged stump of a missing leg—all, in media scholar Marita Sturken's words, "provide a perceptible site for a continual remembering of . . . war's effects."[18] More than any treaty or commemorative plaque, the damaged bodies of veterans preserve the record of war for future generations. Occupational therapists might rehabilitate a damaged limb; plastic surgeons might reconstruct a face mangled by shrapnel; but no scientific advancement can ever completely erase war's violent inscription in the flesh.

Even so, veterans' bodies represent an unruly terrain of war memorialization. Unlike marble or bronze, whose erosion is measured in decades if not centuries, the human body remains in a state of perpetual and visible change. Scars rupture, heal, and rupture again; old injuries are overlaid with new ones; diseases emerge and disappear. Moreover, veterans' injuries do not speak for themselves. Without narrative and context, a scar won on the field of battle looks the same as one received on the factory floor. Put another way: wounds might mark the occurrence of a war, but they offer no hint about what the conflict was about, whether it was worth fighting, or even how its survivors are coping in the present.[19]

More than anything else, though, the tension between disabled veterans and traditional modes of memorialization is a reflection of disabled vets' complex relationship to notions of historical closure. Beyond a tendency to venerate former combatants, most war memorials promote a linear or progressive model of history, drawing clear-cut distinctions between past and present. Often constructed years after a conflict's end, they are meant to provide a sense of resolution—a chance to mourn, reflect, heal, and move on. For many vets, however, closure of this sort is impossible. Among the psychologically traumatized, exposure to remembrance ceremonies and war-themed popular culture has been known to trigger disturbing flashbacks and mental breakdowns.[20] Memorials' inherent promise of closure is especially problematic for men and women in the grips of post-traumatic stress disorder (PTSD)—the "shell shock" of the Great War era—for whom the line between past and present, history and memory, breaks down. According to historian Jo Stanley, shell-shocked men are "helpless victims of their memory"; they are, quite literally, possessed—taken over in body and mind—by unassimilated images of the past.[21] Jay Winter has described shell shock as a "theater of memory out of control. The bodies of [traumatized] soldiers hold traces of memory; they are speaking to us, though not in a way we usually encounter."[22] In this sense, veterans with PTSD—and, to some degree, all disabled vets—pose a fundamental challenge to the linear models of history, memory, and temporality upon which traditional forms of war memorialization depend.

Returning to the Great War's aftermath, disabled doughboys' complex, and often antagonistic, relationship to war memory becomes easier to comprehend. On the one hand, disabled veterans and their allies actively embraced a memorial conception of the disabled body. On the other, they recognized that meaningful memory could not be based on scars alone. To the untrained eye, many disabled veterans, including men with severe physical impairments, appeared virtually normal. Moreover, the fierce demands of veteran masculinity seemed to promote a kind of self-imposed amnesia—at least, when it came to the ugly side of life "over there." Male veterans, then as now, were expected to downplay or mask the traumatic effects of military service—to keep quiet, forget the past, and move forward with their lives. This equation of masculinity with silence, of progress with willful forgetting, was echoed by advocates of the rehabilitation movement, who urged disabled veterans to put their war experience behind them. To be rehabilitated was to become "normal," unworthy of public memory. Laden with families, mortgages, and dreams of economic security, disabled vets required—and called for—a purposeful cultural memory, one that promised to make their lives better in tangible ways. In turn, they needed to cultivate a memory of war that resisted closure, forcing their fellow citizens to recognize war's lingering traumas.

Reassurances of Memory

What they got instead was mostly empty rhetoric. Throughout the 1920s and early 1930s, veterans' groups were inundated with letters and telegraphs—often published in the local and national press—promising to "always remember" or "never forget." Given the largely symbolic (and self-serving) nature of such efforts, reassurances of memory were especially prevalent around the winter holidays, a time when Americans were expected to reflect upon the less fortunate members of the body politic. Reprinted on the front page of the *New York Times*, Calvin Coolidge's 1925 Christmas greeting to the DAV offered a characteristic mixture of vacant promises and patriotic treacle:

> At this holiday season, on behalf of a grateful nation, I wish to extend to you best wishes for Christmas cheer and a full measure of happiness in the coming year.
>
> The heart of America will always beat the faster whenever the nation thinks of the sacrifices made by its veterans who fought to uphold its ideals.
>
> To those who, as a result of their devotion to their country, are fighting in hospitals for the restoration to health and for rehabilita-

tion I would say a world of special encouragement. Their bravery and fortitude now is no less than that shown on the field of battle.

This Government will not forget those who are disabled. It will afford the highest measure of relief possible to restore them to health and happiness.[23]

Any other day, the fiscally conservative Coolidge administration was deeply hostile toward the kinds of programs and benefits needed to "restore" disabled veterans to "health and happiness." But such niceties did not prevent Silent Cal and his Democratic counterparts from issuing similar proclamations. For many American leaders, remembrance was little more than a public speech-act: simply declaring one's intention to remember was all that mattered.

Reassurances of memory included more than the pontifications of politicians. Wealthy Americans engaged in a wide range of memorial work, from sponsoring yachting trips for disabled veterans (the choice of J. P. Morgan) to patronizing "Lest We Forget" evenings, upscale entertainments designed to raise money for veteran-related causes. During the early 1920s, the Knights of Columbus took tens of thousands of disabled veterans to professional baseball games and other sporting events, while charity-minded arts groups, such as the Stage Women's War Relief and the National Association for Music in Hospitals, entertained convalescing veterans with theater productions and musical revues. Ordinary Americans were asked to invite disabled veterans into their homes on holidays and to contribute gifts to disabled veterans' children at Christmas. In a 1921 published statement, the Lest We Forget Committee, a charitable organization devoted to the care of New York City's disabled veterans, offered the public a number of options for aiding the war-wounded. Interested citizens could take disabled vets on picnics, send them postcards in the hospital, or purchase magazine subscriptions for ex-servicemen's clubhouses. [24]

Over time, the federal government instituted its own memorial rituals for disabled veterans (though most helped Great War vets more in spirit than in the pocketbook). Among the most visible was a series of well-publicized garden parties held every spring on the White House lawn (fig. 24). The tradition of fêting disabled vets began with the Harding administration and soon became a de rigueur part of every president's

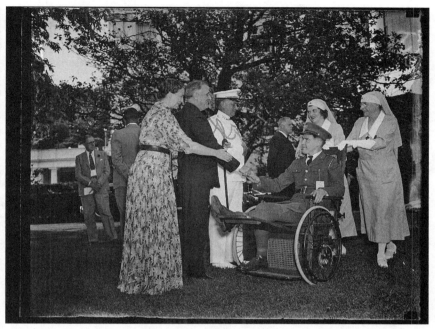

FIG. 24. Franklin and Eleanor Roosevelt at a White House garden party for disabled veterans on May 21, 1936. Although critical of disabled veterans' claims of preferential status, FDR nonetheless held up the annual spring tradition of entertaining disabled veterans from DC-area hospitals. Note how Roosevelt masks his own physical disability (standing upright and holding his cane in his hand) even as he greets the man in the wheelchair. Library of Congress, Prints & Photographs Division, LC-DIG-hec-47238.

social calendar. Typical of such affairs was a party hosted by the Hoover White House on June 11, 1931. That day's guests of honor included eight hundred World War I veterans from DC-area hospitals, along with a contingent of hospital attendants, Gold Star Mothers, and veterans of the Civil War. As the Marine Band belted out patriotic airs, Red Cross nurses and "pretty girls" from the Veterans' Bureau offices served ice cream, cake, and punch to the crowd. Individual doughboys could not expect much face time with the president. Pressed into a long receiving line upon their arrival, most disabled vets got little more than handshake from their commander-in-chief. By the time Hoover was free to mingle with his guests of honor (stopping first to chat with a group of "wheelchair cases" arranged in a semicircle on the south lawn), the affair was nearly over.[25]

Although portrayed as cozy get-togethers, White House garden parties were, at their heart, acts of political theater, photographed and filmed for audiences across the United States. Their primary purpose was to demonstrate the president's devotion to the nation's wounded warriors; to show that on this day, disabled vets came first. In addition, they functioned as a form of civic training, teaching both disabled veterans and the nondisabled public how, when, and why disabled vets should be honored. In this sense, the White House's tendency to treat war memorialization as a special event or media spectacle had a significant impact on the official memory of disabled veterans for years to come. Namely, it transformed all instances of remembrance into instances of *commemoration*. To remember disabled veterans was to celebrate their sacrifices, to honor their commitment to their nation—not to grapple with the long-term effects of war's destruction of soldiers' bodies. This tendency also meant that disabled vets were "remembered" intensely for short bursts of time (a day, a few hours, the length of a medal ceremony) before inevitably lapsing from public consciousness.

Veteran-related holidays encouraged a similarly intermittent pattern of commemoration. According to historian Matthew Dennis, Americans have used holidays to "define themselves and their place in a collective national past," particularly following times of social crisis.[26] In the decades after World War I, the United States saw an upsurge of holidays and festivals expressly dedicated to commemorating veterans and their service. Largely forgotten today, these "invented traditions" included Army Day (April 6), a tribute to the US entrance into World War I; Hospital Day (May 12), a holiday dedicated to disabled veterans' hospital experiences; and Argonne Day (September 24), a commemoration of the Great War's final—and, for Americans, bloodiest—campaign.[27] Backed by government leaders, conservative groups, and often veterans themselves, such holidays tended to promote a hyperpatriotic vision of martial masculinity and national valor, positioning disabled veterans as uncritical spokesmen for American military adventures, past and future. In 1930, for instance, the highlight of New York City's Army Day celebration was a long military parade on Fifth Avenue capped by busloads of disabled veterans (the message "Preparedness Is the Best Insurance against War" was affixed in large bunting to the buses' sides).[28] Like their predecessor Memorial Day, a product of the Civil War, Great War holidays served as occasions for disabled veterans to grab the national spotlight and insist upon their public remembrance.[29] (Indeed, the DAV typically scheduled Forget-Me-Not drives to overlap with Argonne Day, with the hope of generating extra publicity and boosting flower sales.) Nevertheless, the memory of disabled veterans generated by such events tended to be uncritical and backward-looking, more focused on the glories of sacrifices past than the pressing hardships of the present.

Poppy Day and the Gendered Economics of Remembrance

Not surprisingly, the Great War's best-known and most lucrative ritual of remembrance asked the least of its participants. Preceding its DAV counterpart (Forget-Me-Not Day) by several months, Poppy Day was observed by the sale of artificial "memorial poppies" to pay homage to US war casualties and raise money for disabled veterans' relief. The adoption of handcrafted poppies as emblems of World War I memory is often credited to Moina Belle Michael, a Georgia educator and self-described "old maid" who had volunteered briefly with the YMCA during the war.[30] According to her autobiography, Michael received her inspiration after reading Canadian physician John McCrae's poem "In Flanders Fields" in the November 1918 issue of *Ladies' Home Journal*. First published three years earlier, McCrae's pastoral elegy to the Allied dead was the "most popular poem of the war," and its message from beyond the grave—"We are the dead. Short days ago / We lived, felt dawn, saw sunset glow"—was made devastatingly poignant following the author's death in January 1918.[31] Today, the poem is best remembered for the haunting imagery of its opening lines—"In Flanders fields the poppies blow, / Between the crosses, row on row"—a reference to the bright scarlet flowers that spontaneously blossomed in the gore-slaked soil of southern Belgium and northern France.[32] Michael had read the poem several times before; yet on this day she was so moved by McCrae's words, she immediately jotted down her own poetic response on the back of a nearby envelope. From that moment on, she later wrote, Michael pledged "*always* to wear a red poppy of Flanders Fields as a sign of remembrance and the emblem of 'keeping the faith with all who died.'"[33]

Within days, Michael had launched a grassroots public relations campaign to spread the gospel of the poppy, "the second Holy Grail, which caught the sacrificial blood of millions."[34] Her hard work paid off in September 1920, when the American Legion voted to adopt the Flanders Field Memorial Poppy as its national emblem of remembrance, leading to the first memorial flower sales on a nationwide scale.[35] Other veterans' organizations and patriotic groups quickly followed suit, including the Veterans of Foreign Wars, which sold millions of its trademarked "Buddy Poppies" throughout the 1920s.[36] In 1924, the Legion alone sold more than four million poppies at its Memorial Day fund drives, and its Poppy Division provided interested parties with motion-picture trailers, sales plans, and a host of "exploitation ideas" to spur poppy sales. By the start of World War II, receipts from the sale of Great War memorial poppies topped $7 million a year. The "Poppy Lady" (as Michael came to be known) was a national celebrity, and the practice of wearing remembrance poppies had been adopted in more than fifty nations around the world.[37]

In her letters to women's clubs and veterans' groups, Moina Michael argued that tangible symbols like the Flanders Field Poppy were necessary if Americans hoped to keep veterans' sacrifices alive in public memory: "Out of every great event of the world has come an emblem. 'Lest we forget.' Into this war went many emblems: The flags of nations, the Red Cross, the Red Triangle, the service flag and pin. Now out of this war should come some symbol perpetually to remind us and unfailingly to teach coming generations the value of the light of liberty and our debt to those who so valiantly saved it for us."[38]

In Michael's mind, red poppies were ideal tokens of veterans' remembrance—not only because of their sanguine color, but also because of their geographical association with the Great War landscape. The significance was apparent when the American Legion, seeking a nationalist icon, briefly changed its remembrance flower to the all-American daisy in 1921. Still outraged twenty years later, Michael recalled, "I saw no meaning, no symbolism, no sentiment, no appropriateness in the DAISY as a Memorial symbol for my Buddies sleeping in Flanders Fields, nor for those returning to our American hospitals, whose wounds testified that their bloom crimsoned the Poppies of 'Flanders Fields' with a deeper and more brilliant red."[39] To Michael and her followers, blood-red poppies signified what traditional memorial practices obscured: the centrality of injury to modern warfare. No other flower would suffice.

In 1923, World War I memorial poppies generated controversy of a different kind. Finding native supplies exhausted, one Indiana flower wholesaler began importing poppies manufactured in Germany. When women Legionnaires in Cedar Rapids, Iowa, discovered that their poppies had been "tainted" by enemy hands, they burned 10,000 of the obnoxious blooms in a public bonfire. Other groups returned the flowers unsold, declaring them an "insult" to the memory of America's fighting men. Eventually, the Legion's national headquarters intervened, supplying the aggrieved posts with French- and Belgian-produced poppies, and warning the public against accepting German copycats.[40] At first glance, the incident might appear little more than a brief relapse of wartime nativism. Despite national overtures of reconciliation, anti-German sentiment still ran deep, particularly within Legion ranks.

But the indignation expressed in Cedar Rapids takes on even greater resonance if considered through the lens of gender and economics. While hardly the most profitable industry, the manufacture of poppies and other remembrance flowers provided a source of income to the Great War's most victimized populations. During the war's immediate aftermath, poppy production was largely the purview of Allied war widows and other impoverished women. In 1920, Anne E. Guerin, the wife of a French federal court judge, toured the United States promoting the sale of widow-produced poppies to raise money for French and Belgian war orphans. It was not long, however, before the industry came to monopolized by men—namely, disabled veterans. In many respects, the masculinization of remembrance flower production was typical of postwar American industry in general, which witnessed large-scale replacements of female workers with returning war veterans.[41] Disabled vets were especially eager to reestablish their masculinity and economic independence through productive work. Given the failures of government rehabilitation programs, niche operations like artificial poppy construction assumed greater significance, particularly for the most seriously impaired.

By the mid-1920s, America's war-wounded made nearly all of the Buddy Poppies, Flanders Fields Remembrance Poppies, and forget-me-nots sold in the United States. The American Legion, DAV, and VFW established workshops and factories across the country where disabled veterans churned out remembrance flowers year round. (Production was not limited to flowers; at the American Legion's Minneapolis Poppy Shop disabled vets manufactured commemorative trinkets, vases, plaques, "Protect Children" signs, and tire covers.) Veterans were typically paid "a penny a poppy" and could earn three or four dollars for an entire day's work. The most seriously disabled veterans sometimes formed partnerships (known as Poppy Corporations) when they could not complete the flowers on their own. To many observers, the money earned was less important than the gendered currency of self-esteem. "Three dollars a day—not much," observed one Ohio newspaper, "but for men who have lain for months feeling that they were useless incumbrances [*sic*] on the earth, three crisp one-dollar bills actually earned seem like a fortune."[42] With Poppy Day, Moina Michael and her Legionnaire allies established a model of disabled veterans' remembrance that melded memorialization and remasculinization. In the process, they created a template for purposeful memory that disabled veterans would emulate for generations to come.

"Remembrance as a Principle" and Armistice Day

Looking back, it's no surprise that organizations like the American Legion and the DAV played a major role in shaping and maintaining the cultural memory of Great War disabled vets. The cultivation of wartime memory is essential to all veterans' groups. Memories of warfare—whether genuine or borrowed, rooted in wartime experience or obscured by years of peace—lend veterans' groups an aura of shared experience, identity, and trauma. They are part of what unites veterans as a group and what differentiates them from others.. The American Legion considered its mission to safeguard veterans' collective memories so important that it was enshrined in the group's constitution.[43] Lest the nation forget about World War I, the Legion's National Memorials Committee sponsored Memorial Day parades and built playgrounds, parks, and other "practical memorials to victory and sacrifice."[44]

Although veterans' groups were deeply concerned about preserving the memory of war within their own ranks, much of their memorial effort was directed at noncombatants—civilians with the power to fund extensive recreational and relief projects for disabled vets. Many vets believed that the American public had a decidedly short memory when it came to military affairs. As "memory dims with the passage of time, and events of yesteryear merge with the blur of history," wrote one DAV comrade, "heroes of another day again become but the empty echoes of marching hosts."[45] Faced with such obstacles, veterans' groups increasingly used war remembrance as a weapon in the battle for the hearts and pocketbooks of the American people. Newton D. Baker, who served as US secretary of war during World War I, acknowledged as much in his address to the 1931 American Legion convention. According to Baker, all ex-servicemen's organizations pursued three common goals:

> first, that those who died for the cause may always be reverently and devotedly remembered; and second, that those who were disabled in the service may be constantly and adequately brought to the grateful remembrance of their country in order that their disabilities may be properly cared for; and, third ... to keep alive the memory of the devotion and faith which was the high point of their experience, and to impress upon those who come after them how great and good a country is and its institutions are for which men are willing to die in battle.[46]

In other words, veterans' groups did not simply remember the Great War for memory's sake. They fostered a dynamic culture of nostalgia aimed at winning devotion for the dead, securing medical benefits for the disabled, and "impressing" upon future generations the values of military service.

Perhaps the clearest articulation of veterans' commitment to purposeful remembrance can be found in a memorial address by Gill Robb Wilson, an American Legion chaplain, at the Legion's tenth annual convention in 1928. Wilson used the address not only to memorialize Legionnaires who had died since the last meeting but also to distinguish the mechanics of human memory from what he called "remembrance as a principle." While memory was a trait common to everyone, Wilson told the crowd, "Strong men remember and determine! The American Legion is founded not upon remembrance as a human attribute, but upon remembrance as a vessel in the temple of history, which has been brewed in the soul of the nation."[47] For veterans like Wilson, remembrance was an active force for political and social change. To remember the Great War and the men who fought it was the first step in redrawing US society along more patriotic and veteran-friendly lines.

For disabled veterans of World War I, the most important date on the remembrance calendar was November 11, the anniversary of the Great War's ceasefire. Long before Congress decreed it an official holiday in 1938, Americans adopted Armistice Day as a time to reflect upon the war's legacies. Across the country, cities marked the occasion with public pageantry, remembrance-themed banquets, and veterans' parades. Given the war's ambiguous outcome, the significance of Armistice Day remained highly contested throughout the postwar decades, both in the United States and around the world.[48] Many Americans viewed Armistice Day as a chance to rekindle the national ideals and martial spirit of the war years.[49] To this end, a cottage industry quickly emerged to outfit memory-hungry celebrants with miniature flags, patriotic chapbooks, and other Armistice Day paraphernalia. Among other observers, however, Armistice Day conjured up feelings of regret and opportunities lost. In his famous Armistice Day radio address of 1923, an ailing Woodrow Wilson characterized the anniversary as a tragic reminder of the United States' failed foreign policy, specifically the nation's withdrawal into "sullen and selfish isolation" in the wake of Allied victory.[50]

Beginning in 1919, the American Legion and other veterans' groups played a key role in transforming Armistice Day from a commemoration of the Great War's end into a *veterans'* day, a tribute to the men who fought.[51] Speaking in 1921, Ferdinand Foch, the former supreme commander of Allied forces in World War I, set the tone for future celebrations: "Armistice Day, the 11th of November, should be made sacred throughout the entire civilized world. It is a day when we think of the noble sacrifices made by the hero dead, of the brilliant records of duty performed left on the field of battle by the wounded, of the spirit of patriotism and bravery shown by those who, fortunately, escaped shot and shell."[52]

Legionnaires viewed Armistice Day as an occasion to spur membership drives, raise money for veteran-related charities, and remind the public of its obligations to the war's "less fortunate" survivors. In the weeks leading up to the big event, the American Legion's public relations department flooded national newspapers with ads asking readers to contribute funds "for those who suffered most" (that is, disabled veterans and war orphans). Like many Legion gatherings, the group's Armistice Day ceremonies mingled solemn reflection and martial bombast, with speakers alternating between lofty paeans to "carrying on" and calls for future military preparedness. Because the Legion strove to foster a unified cultural memory of the war, nothing was left to chance. Throughout the 1920s and 1930s, the Legion's National Americanism Commission circulated scripted programs for Armistice Day ceremonies, including suggested addresses for local commanders. One of the group's goals for Armistice Day was to solidify the American Legion's reputation as the principle guardian of disabled veterans' memory and well-being. It was not enough to guarantee that Americans remembered the plight of disabled vets. Legionnaires hoped to memorialize their own role in helping disabled veterans during times of need.[53]

Forgetting the Disabled Doughboy

Despite such efforts, many vets insisted that Americans had forgotten the Great War's wounded warriors, a charge that would be repeated with increasing vitriol throughout the interwar period. Given the tenuous nature of collective memory, veterans were right to be alarmed. As a number of scholars have shown, both individuals and groups rely heavily upon social processes of forgetting to construct stable identities and work through past traumas.[54] Matthew Dennis argues, "Purposeful remembering requires purposeful forgetting, as collective pasts are assembled through an editing process that leaves much on the cutting-room floor."[55] Writing about the post–Vietnam War era, Marita Sturken goes further, declaring: "All memories are 'created' in tandem with forgetting; to remember everything would amount to being overwhelmed by memory."[56] Following World War I, advocates of a "return to normalcy" endorsed the willful forgetting of large chunks of the nation's war experience—the misery of the battlefield, the long-term hardships of survivors, the conflict's legacies of disability and death—in the service of a smooth transition to peacetime life. For Great War veterans, however, forgetting was not the lubricant of postwar prosperity. It was a national pathology, a social contagion that threatened the very lives of disabled veterans and their families.

To read press reports, the guns of the Argonne were hardly cool before Americans began to forget about the Great War's disabled vets. As early as November 11, 1919, the American Legion insisted that the nation's "crippled soldiers" had been "not only forgotten but deluded and defrauded," setting the tone for things to come.[57] By the early 1920s, problems with government-sponsored rehabilitation, Veterans' Bureau bureaucracy, and postwar unemployment left many disabled vets feeling thoroughly abandoned. In 1921, Dr. Thomas W. Salmon, a renowned expert on war neuroses, reported that thousands of shell-shocked doughboys had been discarded in lunatic asylums or state prisons due to a lack of funds. Testifying before a congressional committee, Salmon explained, "Men so committed as a rule are never visited by Federal officials to see whether they are properly cared for or whether the institutions in which they are confined are even fireproof or fit for human beings."[58] Similar stories—many true, some embellished—circulated widely throughout the 1920s. By mid-decade, there was a common consensus—at least among veterans and their sympathizers—that the Great War's living casualties had been relegated to the human scrap heap: neglected, unwanted, and left to suffer in anonymity.

Of all the Great War's forgotten casualties, the most tragic were those "remembered" too late. Throughout the post–World War I decades, morbid tales detailing the discovery of malnourished, enfeebled, or deceased veterans were common. The story of Oscar Johnson, a highly decorated veteran from South Norwalk, Connecticut, typified the genre. Winner of both the Distinguished Service Cross and the Croix de Guerre, Johnson was severely gassed while serving in France, leaving him incapacitated on and off for years after his return home. "Too proud to beg and too ill to work," according to the *New York Times*, Johnson eventually took up refuge in a coal barn near the South Norwalk waterfront, where local authorities found him semi-conscious from starvation and exposure. Johnson died a few days later, after which the town honored its "outstanding hero of the World War" by staging an elaborate funeral and lowering all city flags to half mast—a noble gesture, but hardly the sort of purposeful remembrance that would have saved Johnson from an early grave.[59]

By the time of Oscar Johnson's death in February 1931, the forgotten disabled doughboy had become something of a stereotype in American popular culture. Although less flashy than other contemporary media caricatures (the gin-guzzling "jazz baby," the gun-toting gangster, etc.), the forgotten disabled doughboy had no less a hold on the public consciousness—popping up in countless films, illustrations, cartoons, and journalistic accounts between the world wars. When rendered in print or projected onto the big screen, he closely resembled his Civil War antecedent, the penniless Yankee amputee who stumped his way through countless GAR speeches and *Harper's Magazine* cartoons. Yet, unlike his nineteenth-century counterpart, he was characterized as much by his surroundings—his spatial and social dislocation from mainstream life—as by his bodily impairments. Sometimes he could be found languishing in a dingy hospital bed; at others, squatting in a deserted amusement park or exiled to a government soldiers' home. Ignored by those who once cheered him, the forgotten disabled doughboy emerged in the 1920s and 1930s as a powerful symbol of the United States' broken promises and unfulfilled obligations. In fact, his very "forgottenness" was the greatest injury of all. Wounds, physical hardship, loss of life and limb—such were to be expected of all military conflicts. But to forget about the nation's disabled warriors as well—for veterans and their allies, there was no greater crime.

In retrospect, few cultural figures better embodied the suspected miseries of the Great War's forgotten casualties than Donald Mahon, the living corpse at the center of William Faulkner's debut novel, *Soldiers' Pay* (1926). The book opens shortly after Mahon, a pilot, is shot down in combat, leaving him severely disfigured and mentally traumatized. Returning to his hometown in rural Georgia, he is initially greeted as both conquering hero and sideshow freak, his "withered" and war-scarred body a curiosity for all see:

> Donald Mahon's homecoming, poor fellow, was hardly a nine days' wonder even. Curious, kindly neighbors came in—men who stood or sat jovially respectable, cheerful: solid business men interested in the war only as a by-product of the rise and fall of Mr. Wilson, and interested in that only as a matter of dollars and cents, while their wives chatted about clothes to each other across Mahon's scarred, oblivious brow; a few of the rector's more casual acquaintances democratically uncravated, hushing their tobacco into a bulged cheek, diffidently but firmly refusing to surrender their hats; girls that he had known, had danced with or courted on summer nights, come now to look once upon his face, and then quickly aside in hushed nausea, not coming any more unless his face happened to be hidden on the first visit (upon which they finally found opportunity to see it).[60]

While the townspeople resume their normal lives, Mahon's war-wracked body remains an anachronism, a terrible "hang-over of warfare" that his former friends and neighbors are all too eager to forget. With the exception of an envious military cadet too young to experience combat for himself, no one is especially interested in contemplating war wounds and the men who bear them. "Once Society drank war, brought [boys] into manhood with a cultivated taste for war," observes Faulkner's narrator near the novel's end, "but now Society seemed to have found something else for a beverage."[61] Like so much Great War fiction, *Soldiers' Pay* did not dwell upon the banal, everyday realties faced by most disabled veterans, forgotten or otherwise. Rather, in Faulkner's hands, the forgotten disabled doughboy emerges as American memory's unbearable Other—an abject presence so hideous in appearance and terrifying in implication that it defies memorialization.[62]

The forgotten stereotype gained additional symbolic currency after 1932, when Franklin Delano Roosevelt made the Forgotten Man a central theme in his presidential campaign.[63] Introduced in a radio address on April 7, Roosevelt's Forgotten Man was initially conceived as a foot soldier in the "infantry of [the nation's] economic army." Industrious by nature, he longed only to pay his bills and keep the bank from taking his home—goals thwarted by unscrupulous businessmen, government bureaucrats, and the tyrannies of unregulated capitalism.[64] In an early campaign film, FDR's standard-bearer Boston mayor James M. Curley declared that four years of "industrial depression" had produced more than ten million Forgotten Men, among them thousands of veteran Bonus Marchers camped out "in the shadow of the National Capitol."[65]

As the Depression wore on, the term *Forgotten Man* evolved into a catch-all to describe any beleaguered person struggling to make ends meet. Forgotten Men (and Women) drifted through the Dust Bowl ballads of Woody Guthrie and the novels of John Steinbeck; they stalked the city streets of photographers Margaret Bourke-White and Lewis Hine; they rode the rails in films like Mervyn LeRoy's *I Am a Fugitive from a Chain Gang* (1932) and William Wellman's *Heroes for Sale* (1933). And there was the rub: at a time when large swaths of the American public were characterized as "forgotten," where did that leave disabled veterans? Did they constitute an elite cohort of Forgotten Men or were they, at long last, just like everyone else? The answers to such questions would be contested throughout the Great Depression—as they would be in periods of economic adversity to follow. While disabled veterans continued to insist that they deserved special consideration from the state, their struggles were increasingly subsumed within a national narrative of suffering, one that linked all Americans' hardships to the United States' failure to fulfill its wartime promises. Indeed, in popular media, wounded and disabled veterans were often used as stand-ins for the nation as a whole, their injured bodies symbols of failed economic policies and government neglect.

Nowhere was this metaphorical substitution used to greater effect than in Mervyn LeRoy's musical *Gold Diggers of 1933* (1933). Choreographed by Busby Berkeley, with music and lyrics Harry Warren and Al Dubin respectively, the film tells the story of a group out-of-work entertainers attempting to mount a Broadway show about the Great Depression. In the show's final number, "Remember My Forgotten Man," Berkeley and LeRoy artfully combine dance, mise-en-scène, and inventive camerawork to draw explicit links between national forgetfulness, World War I, and the hardships facing out-of-work vets. The sequence opens with what would have been a familiar sight in 1933: a homeless man picking up discarded cigarette butts and wandering the city streets. How did he (and millions like him) wind up in such straits? As if to answer this question, "Remember My Forgotten Man" flashes back to 1917, when happy doughboys marched off to war amidst public fanfare.

As the sequence unfolds, early exuberance turns to sorrow. American soldiers are shown slogging through the rain and limping wearily back from the front. Berkeley uses treadmills to keep the actor-soldiers in perpetual motion and to highlight the circuit of militarized bodies, from manly health to pitiful injury. At one point, two treadmills moving in opposite directions are positioned side by side, sharpening the contrast between the uniformed bodies that enter battle and the limping, bloodied, stretcher-born mass that returns. When the sequence jumps back to 1933, America's wounded warriors are now shivering in breadlines, waiting desperately for a bite to eat.

Accompanying the stage theatrics is a bluesy dirge sung by a cast of war widows, grieving mothers, and lost loves. In the first verse, Carol (Joan Blondell) implores the American public to make good on its social contract of remembrance:

Remember my forgotten man
You put a rifle in his hand
You sent him far away
You shouted hip-hurray
But look at him today

The urgency of her demand escalates as "Remember My Forgotten Man" builds to a dizzying crescendo. With silhouettes of soldiers circling overhead, a line of homeless vets trudges painfully (and futilely) toward the

FIG. 25. In the climax of Mervyn Leroy's *Gold Diggers of 1933*, actress Joan Blondell (*center*) exhorts the audience to remember the Great War soldiers who became the Forgotten Men of the Great Depression.

camera (fig. 25). As they begin to sing, what was once a call for remembrance becomes a desperate plea for survival:

Remember your forgotten man
You've got to help us live again
One day we march away
to fight for USA
but where are we today?

Through its merging of cinematic spectacle and social commentary, the sequence offered a powerful indictment of American forgetfulness in all its forms—social, economic, and political. Moreover, *Gold Diggers of 1933* provided audiences with a visual and narrative template for understanding what many Depression-era Americans had long suspected: that the United States' economic woes were directly tied to the nation's decision to enter World War I.

The Stakes of Memory

The battle over the cultural memory of disabled veterans did not end with the Great Depression, or even with the United States' entrance into World War II. In 1943, the American Legion returned to Congress with stories of the "Forgotten Battalion," the latest generation of war-injured men cast aside by federal bureaucracy. Describing the scene in *American Legion Magazine*, David Cameron complained, "It seems impossible to believe, now, that thousands of disabled men discharged during the war were forced to depend on charity for their very existence for months before the country they had fought to defend got around to caring for them."[66] For all of veterans' memory work—the holidays, the fund-raising drives, the exposés of institutional forgetfulness—many vets believed that Americans were falling back into old habits. Unless the United States acted quickly, it risked creating a new army of Forgotten Men—larger, angrier, and unwilling to settle for pageants and parades.

What was at stake in the public remembrance of disabled veterans? Why was it so important that Americans never forget the men "for whom there was no Armistice"? Despite wounded doughboys' well-known reputation for reticence, many commentators assumed that all veterans wanted to be remembered, whether they said so or not. From this perspective, public forgetfulness came to be viewed as a form of trauma in itself, a secondary wound that compounded veterans' already existing physical and mental anguish.[67] In addition, the American public's participation in memory-themed fund-raisers, holidays, and civic functions had a tangible effect on disabled veterans' lives, if only in a small way. Profits from forget-me-not and poppy sales helped fund summer camps, clubhouses, medical care, and rehabilitation projects for disabled vets.[68] More to the point, veterans' groups like the American Legion understood *purposeful* remembering and forgetting as a key part of their broader project of redrawing American society along more veteran-friendly lines. Indeed, for Great War veterans, the forgotten disabled doughboy fulfilled numerous roles simultaneously: he was a rhetorical sledgehammer for lobbying the state, a tangible symbol of social and governmental indifference, and a stark reminder of why nonveterans could not be trusted to keep the spirit of the war alive.

Ultimately, many interwar Americans believed there was a more significant reason to remember the Great War's disabled vets: future national security. Vets and their allies argued that America's failure to remember its disabled doughboys set a dangerous precedent for the future, when the United States once again called upon its citizen-soldiers to take up arms. In his 1922 Forget-Me-Not Day proclamation, New York governor Nathan Miller sounded what would become a common refrain among advocates of disabled veterans' remembrance: "A nation that forgets its defenders and withholds its active sympathy from the disabled soldiers invites similar forgetfulness in the day of its perils."[69] And yet, not everyone saw disabled veterans as icons of courage and national sacrifice. As Americans became increasingly disillusioned with the Great War, they came to view disabled veterans as evidence of why martial conflict should be abandoned altogether.

James M. Kirwin

On November 26, 1939, three months after the start of World War II in
Europe, James M. Kirwin, pastor of the St. James Catholic Church in
Port Arthur, Texas, devoted his weekly newspaper column to one of the
most haunting figures of the World War era: the "basket case." Originating as British army slang in World War I, the term referred to quadruple
amputees, men so horrifically mangled in combat they had to be carried
around in wicker baskets. Campfire stories about basket cases and other
"living corpses" had circulated widely during the Great War's immediate
aftermath. And Kirwin, a staunch isolationist fearful of US involvement
in World War II, was eager to revive them as object lessons in the perils
of military adventurism. "The basket case is helpless, but not useless,"
the preacher explained. "He can tell us what war is. He can tell us that if
the United States sends troops to Europe, your son, your brother, father,
husband, or sweetheart, may also be a basket case." In Kirwin's mind,
mutilated soldiers were not heroes to be venerated; they were monstros-
ities, hideous reminders of why the United States should avoid overseas
war-making at all costs. Facing an upsurge in pro-war sentiment, the
reverend implored his readers to take the lessons of the basket case to
heart: "We must not add to war's carnage and barbarity by drenching
foreign fields with American blood. . . . Looking at the basket case, we
know that for civilization's sake, we dare not, MUST NOT."[1]

"WHAT IS WRONG WITH THIS PICTURE?"
The Disabled Soldier in Interwar Peace Culture

In the aftermath of World War I, veterans' groups like the American Legion and the Disabled American Veterans (DAV) were not the only ones calling upon Americans to remember the Great War's disabled soldiers. Beginning in the early 1920s, members of the interwar peace movement routinely publicized the injuries of World War I veterans as well. A loose coalition of religious pacifists, feminists, social radicals, and conservative isolationists, the peace movement played a key role in reframing the national debate about the legacies of modern war on American life.[1] At their height in the Great Depression, antiwar groups mobilized millions of Americans behind policies of international cooperation, disarmament, and neutrality. The result was the most powerful campaign against militarism until the Vietnam War—and a model for peace activism ever since.

Unfortunately, the interwar peace movement remains little more than a footnote in most histories of the period.[2] Contemporary critics, including some veterans, accused peace activists of misguided sentimentality and "discomfort with the reality of power in world politics"—charges that continued to be echoed by consensus historians and politicians throughout the Cold War era.[3] The movement gained renewed currency during the 1960s, and over the past few decades a small coterie of peace historians and activists have amassed an impressive body of work on the movement's leaders, gender politics, and competing ideological factions.[4] However, scholars have failed to appreciate the importance of injury and disability within interwar peace propaganda. When it came to politics, strategies, and even long-term goals, antiwar activists were often bitterly divided. But nearly all peace groups agreed on one thing: the value of the disabled veteran as a rhetorical weapon for peace.

Indeed, the bodies of wounded, disabled, and mutilated combatants occupied a prominent place in the iconography and culture of the interwar peace movement. In their plays, drawings, parade floats, photo books, and political activism, peace forces bombarded the American public with descriptions and images of soldiers' bodies ripped apart by modern weaponry. Peace groups used representations of disabled soldiers to debunk romantic myths of war's glory, challenge government propaganda, and highlight the lingering traumas of military conflict. Convinced that looking at wounded bodies would demystify war's seductiveness, they distributed horrific photographs of mangled combatants and encouraged the American public to visit veterans' hospitals to bear witness to war's devastation in the flesh. Many injury-themed cultural productions were aimed at youth, America's future generation of war casualties, who themselves embraced the disabled veteran as evidence of the need for peace. Even veterans' groups incorporated wounded soldiers into their own peace work, drawing upon their cultural authority to reinforce the groups' status as the nation's foremost experts on matters of foreign policy.

Examining interwar peace propaganda reveals lingering anxieties about the presence of disabled veterans in American society. Equally important, it offers a window into the peace movement's mass politicization of disability, dependency, and bodily difference, a practice that would become commonplace among antiwar campaigns throughout the twentieth century. In the eyes of peace activists, disabled vets were not only living embodiments of war's horrors, but also abject figures against which the promises of peace—happiness and wholeness, safety and health—came into sharp relief. Decades before the Vietnam War, when disabled veterans reemerged as visible symbols of antiwar resistance, the interwar peace movement sought to undermine the valorization of military injury in American culture. Ultimately, interwar peace activists—like rehabilitationists and veterans' groups before them—saw in the Problem of the Disabled Veteran an opportunity to forge a better future. For some peace groups, that future centered on a permanent skepticism about the effectiveness of US military intervention in world affairs. Others, however, sought a more ambitious path for global modernity, one in which armed conflict between nations was abandoned altogether.

Postwar Disillusion and the Growth of American Peace Culture
The rise of disabled veterans as antiwar symbols can only be understood against the backdrop of Americans' growing disillusion with World

War I. At home, the Great War's immediate aftermath was marked by racial unrest, high unemployment, and a crackdown on civil liberties. Overseas, where a handful of imperialist powers continued to dominate much of the globe, the war had done little to make the world "safe for democracy," as Woodrow Wilson had promised. Revelations about trumped-up German atrocities, combined with best-selling attacks on the global arms industry, only added to Americans' sense of betrayal. By the late 1920s and early 1930s, many former war supporters felt they had been deceived by government propaganda, and that the United States had entered the Great War on false pretenses. Over time, millions of Americans came to believe that the Great War had served no redeeming purpose whatsoever—other than to remind them why future conflicts needed to be avoided.[5]

US foreign policy in the 1920s and 1930s manifested similar misgivings. Throughout the interwar years, the federal government took several steps—some substantive, others merely symbolic—to ease international tensions and reduce the likelihood of another Great War. At the Washington Naval Conference of 1921–1922, the United States—along with Japan, Great Britain, France, and others—signed multiple treaties halting naval expansion in the Pacific and limiting the total capital-ship tonnage of its navy. In 1926, after years of fierce debate, the United States entered the Permanent Court of International Justice. Two years later, it joined sixty-one other nations in signing the Kellogg-Briand Pact, an agreement outlawing war as "an instrument of foreign policy." Although largely toothless, the pact codified pacifist tendencies into international law, giving peace advocates around the world some measure of hope that the age of world wars was behind them.[6]

A driving force behind the government's antiwar resolve was one of the largest and most dynamic peace movements in US history. Its member organizations spanned the ideological spectrum, representing diverse political positions and operational strategies. On the political right were patriotic and veterans' groups, such as the American Legion, the National Security League, and the American Coalition of Patriotic, Civic, and Fraternal Societies, which emphasized military and naval preparedness as the best means of securing peace for the United States. Occupying the peace movement's political center were the Carnegie Endowment for International Peace, the American Peace Society, and the National Council for Prevention of War—establishment groups linked less by ideology and more by their shared commitment to international cooperation, education, and military disarmament. Groups of absolute pacifists and war resisters, such as the Fellowship of Reconciliation, the War Resisters League, and the Peace Patriots, placed a similar emphasis on international understanding, even as they reiterated their refusal to support any form of military conflict. The far left of the political peace spectrum was made up of socialist and radical groups, most prominently the League for Industrial Democracy, the American Student Union, and the American League Against War and Fascism, which believed that peace could never be achieved under a capitalist system.[7] An additional category of peace activists emerged in the late 1930s, when some peace advocates (including leftists) joined conservative nationalists, right-wing mothers, and outspoken anti-Semites under the banner of "America First" in a final effort to avoid US participation in World War II.[8]

In total, the number of organizations specifically devoted to the study of peace and "international questions" increased tenfold after the Armistice, jumping from 120 when World War I began to some 1,200 by 1926. At its peak in the mid-1930s, the interwar peace movement included, by some contemporary estimates, more than twelve million active participants, along with millions of sympathizers and fellow travelers.[9] Aside from veterans' organizations, nearly all interwar peace groups shared a common goal: to replace the nation's martial traditions with a culture of peace. Despite their opposition to US military adventurism, however, antiwar activists were not isolationists, as they have frequently been characterized. The vast majority of peace advocates championed international cooperation—in some form or another—as crucial to the maintenance of global peace.[10] For many peace groups, support for anti-interventionist foreign policy went hand-in-hand with efforts to strengthen the United States' ties to the rest of the world. Neutrality, explained feminist peace activist Florence Brewer Boeckel in 1938, was a "policy of isolation from war, not of isolation from world affairs."[11]

No interwar group did more to cultivate peace culture in the United States than World Peaceways. Founded in 1931 as a nonprofit "scientific agency for peace promotion," World Peaceways rejected the amateurism that plagued many antiwar groups of its time. Enlisting the services of advertising guru Bruce Barton, it aimed to spread antiwar sentiment on a "practical business-like basis," incorporating the latest methods of "advertising publicity and public communication." By the mid-1930s, the group's public relations machine rivaled those of the largest American corporations. Peaceways publicists blanketed American cities with posters, billboards, and exhibitions, and the group's "pulpit service" furnished topical sermons on international events to more than a thousand ministers. World Peaceways' weekly analysis of foreign affairs, *The World Observer*, appeared on one hundred forty radio stations in forty-seven states, while its sister program, *To Arms for Peace*, introduced CBS listeners to a virtual who's-who of peace-minded statesmen, educators, and celebrities. Recognizing that economic incentives often trumped humanitarian concerns, World Peaceways organized a "Peace Pays" campaign to convince US businesses that America's twenty million "peace advocates" were a "market worth cultivation." In September 1935, the group (with the cooperation of E. R. Squibb and Sons) even began distributing World Peaceways Pledges in drugstores throughout the United States, so that customers could affirm their commitment to ending "the destruction of human life by the merciless machinery of war."[12]

Not all Americans denounced military values during the 1920s and 1930s. Affirmative accounts of the Great War, including Willa Cather's Pulitzer Prize–winning *One of Ours* (1922) and Edith Wharton's *A Son at the Front* (1923), remained popular throughout the interwar decades. Hollywood epics such as George W. Hill's *Tell It to the Marines* (1926), Howard Hughes's *Hell's Angels* (1930), and Henry Hathaway's *The Lives of a Bengal Lancer* (1935) continued to portray war as a site of masculine adventure. What's more, many veterans were deeply committed to commemorating World War I and those who fought it. By the late 1930s, however, no arena of US culture was untouched by antiwar sentiment. Thanks to the efforts of groups like World Peaceways, the desire for world peace "came to be more talked about, more written about, more sincerely considered by the plain people, by leaders of opinion, and by the government itself" than at any previous point in US history.[13] As late as July 1941, five months before the Japanese bombing of Pearl Harbor, a Gallup Poll found 79 percent of US citizens opposed to military intervention in World War II.[14] Without a doubt, Americans' shared revulsion against war and military intervention played a decisive role in keeping the United States out of the conflict as long as it did. It was within this context that peace groups' appropriation of disabled veterans—as both tangible reminders of war's destruction and powerful symbols of anti-war resistance—must be appreciated.

"Hello, Sucker": The Disabled Soldier as Antipropaganda Icon

As antiwar icons, disabled soldiers had two primary appeals. First, peace groups believed that they would never win the battle for public opinion on "intellectual grounds alone." As World Peaceways president Theresa Mayer explained, "The same emotions that are utilized by a munitions maker" to stir up lust for war "must be recognized and utilized by" the forces of peace.[15] In the minds of many peace activists, graphic images and descriptions of war-wounded soldiers provided effective counterevidence to hoary platitudes about the virtues of wartime service. Second, wounded or disabled veterans were attractive antiwar symbols because of the persistent economic, social, and physical difficulties associated with their welfare. In their references to the Great War's wounded survivors, peace activists were eager to remind the American public about the high costs of veterans' pensions, the rising numbers of presumptive cases, and the "long-drawn-out misery" of countless former doughboys.[16] To punctuate their critiques, peace groups also drew upon familiar cultural stereotypes linking disability to helplessness, emasculation, and bodily corruption.

Although peace groups integrated injury-themed images and narratives into a variety of antiwar campaigns, they were most frequently used to ridicule the physical and spiritual benefits of military service. Unlike rehabilitationists and veterans' groups, peace advocates rejected the view that war could ever serve as a path to a better life. In cartoons like William Gropper's "Join the Morons," first published in the *New Masses* in 1927, antiwar artists juxtaposed familiar recruiting slogans with horrific portraits of war-mangled veterans, their specific disabilities providing ironic counterpoint to the decidedly upbeat rhetoric used to entice young men into uniform (fig. 26). Gropper's collection of disabled "morons" included a blinded veteran begging for public charity ("See the

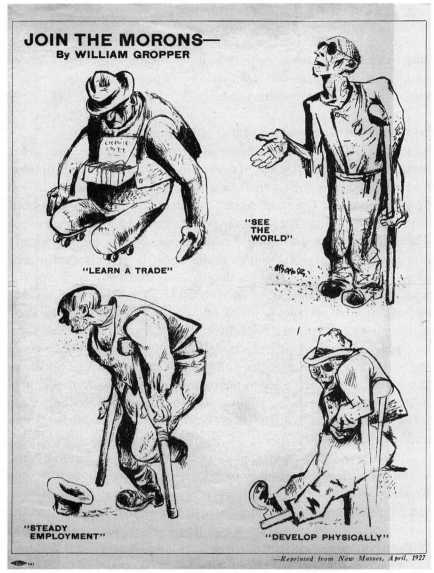

FIG. 26. By contrasting popular recruiting slogans with illustrations of indigent or grotesque disabled veterans, antiwar artists sought to debunk myths about the benefits of overseas soldiering. William Gropper, "Join the Morons," *New Masses*, April 1927. Courtesy of Craig Gropper.

FIG. 27. Cartoon images of amputees accompanied by the slogan "The Army Builds Men" were commonplace in interwar peace culture. This example is taken from a recruiting card of the Fellowship of Reconciliation, an interfaith peace organization founded during World War I. Fellowship of Reconciliation Records, Swarthmore College Peace Collection. Courtesy of the Fellowship of Reconciliation.

World"); a monstrous one-eyed figure with a withered arm, a wooden peg leg, and a face deformed by shrapnel ("Develop Physically"); and a stump-legged amputee selling pencils while pushing himself along on roller skates ("Learn a Trade").[17] Many interwar peace groups—from the Fellowship of Reconciliation, a Quaker peace assembly, to the Marxist-led League for Industrial Democracy—circulated similar images of leg-less, pauperized veterans to satirize government propaganda. In the eyes of war's critics, the Great War's production of sick, disabled, and dead bodies made one recruiting promise especially ripe for mockery: "The Army Builds Men" (fig. 27)[18]

Despite their derision, peace groups worried that large numbers of Americans could, once again, fall prey to patriotic sloganeering. In her 1936 mass recitation *Uncle Sam Wants You*, writer Susan M. Shepherd parodied the United States' best-known recruiting poster, telling would-be soldiers they would receive thirty dollars a month "for losing a leg, coughing up a lung . . . [f]or strewing your guts on the open field."[19] One particularly memorable flyer produced by World Peaceways went further, castigating Americans—including past generations of disabled vets—for failing to question wartime propaganda. Entitled "Hello, Sucker," it featured a colorful illustration of a wheelchair-bound veteran, his legs wrapped in a dingy blanket (fig. 28). As if anticipating the viewers' potential unease, the flyer's author explained: "Yes, we know it's cruel. *But let's look at the bitter truth.* Here is a man decent enough and honest enough so that he couldn't realize there were men *in*decent and *dis*honorable enough to promote war for purely selfish reasons. So he went to war. And behold his reward."[20] Whereas groups like the DAV regularly portrayed such men as dignified heroes, "Hello, Sucker" cast them as objects of ridicule—victims not only of war's senseless violence, but also of their own ignorance.

Beyond challenging militarist propaganda, antiwar forces used images like "Hello, Sucker" to underscore disabled veterans' status as Forgotten Men. Like their counterparts in the veterans' movement, peace activists believed that the government had thoroughly neglected the Great War's wounded warriors, leaving them underpensioned and underappreciated. As a result, peace groups felt that one of the best ways to curtail future enlistment was to publicize disabled veterans' privation and abandonment. An illustration on the cover of socialist cartoonist Art Young's 1922 quarterly, *The Soldier*, typified peace groups' sentiments. The image depicted a grinning, one-legged amputee watering a tree sapling that had sprouted from his unused boot. "Bonus or no bonus," the caption proclaimed, "Private McGinnis is going to have a wooden leg, if he has to grow one."[21] Ironically, men like Private McGinnis were often portrayed as among the luckier members of their war-disabled cohort. As antiwar groups frequently pointed out, many former doughboys, including men with neuro-psychiatric problems or facial wounds, were "condemned to living death," wasting away in asylums or soldiers' homes.[22] In his radio play *The God of War Presents His Bill*

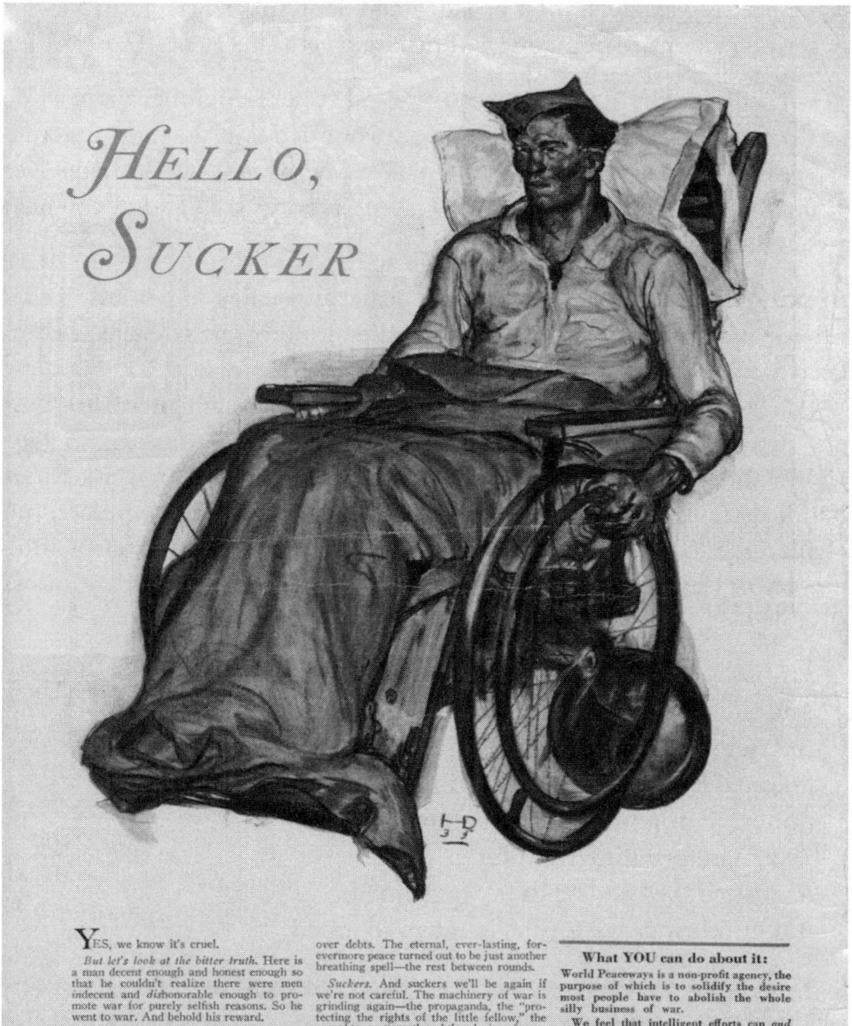

FIG. 28. World Peaceways, "Hello, Sucker." The publication of "Hello, Sucker" in the mid-1930s ignited a firestorm of debate in the popular media and beyond. Writing to the editor of *Time Magazine*, one disabled veteran called the "sucker" moniker a "low-down insult, a slap at all my buddies who went west, as well as those of us still carrying on." However, other vets defended the image, explaining: "We were suckers all right and if enough people know it may be they won't be suckers like us." (Letters to the Editor, *Time Magazine*, April 20, 1936.) The image was so memorable, author Sloan Wilson referenced it in his novel *The Man in the Gray Flannel Suit* nearly twenty years later. World Peaceways Collected Records, Swarthmore College Peace Collection.

"For Services Rendered," first broadcast in September 1937, John Nesbitt described an entire population of disabled vets

> carefully hidden away where no one will see or remember them when the next war comes . . . so hideously wounded that they no longer resemble men. Let them be spoken of only in whispers. Let their wives and children visit them only in darkened rooms so that they can hear only their voices.[23]

In bringing attention to such men, peace advocates hoped to remind Americans of the lingering pain and alienation of the Great War's forgotten combatants.

Peace groups were especially critical of government proclamations about former doughboys' smooth reintegration into postwar society. Unlike their counterparts in the rehabilitation movement, war's critics had little faith that disabled veterans could ever fully reassimilate into civilian life. As poet Edmund Vance Cooke observed on the tenth anniversary of the Great War's end, the conflict was not over for countless disabled vets:

> Armistice Day! when a new sun rose
> And the hate and the horror reached a close. . . .
> But here is the slave of a crawling crutch,
> Maimed by the shrapnel's devilish whim,
> And trinkets and tributes don't mean much
> To a man torn limb from limb.
> Armistice Day! and a peace proclaimed,
> But how is it peace for the halt and maimed?[24]

Along similar lines, peace-minded artists and activists used disabled veterans to skewer government claims about the miracles of reconstructive surgery and military medicine. For antiwar artists, surgeons' capacity to reconstruct war-mangled bodies was not a sign of technological progress—nor did it signal that the age of "safe" warfare was at hand. If anything, advances in wound treatment and orthopedics only reaffirmed peace advocates' deep suspicion that medical science was in league with the war-makers. In a ditty from 1922, Art Young offered a typical take on government reconstruction efforts: "Make em over as good as new / With wood and rivet, bolt and screw. /

Sodder [*sic*] them, tire them, ready to go / To another victory—say Mexico."[25]

There was an additional, if unstated, reason peace groups populated their antiwar propaganda with injured veterans: to deflect charges of naïveté and softheartedness. Opponents of the interwar peace movement often argued that antiwar activists knew nothing about the hard realities of modern warfare. In an attempt to discredit their opposition, pro-war forces pointed to the large numbers of women and religious pacifists who populated the movement's ranks—evidence, they claimed, of the fuzzy-headed idealism that undergirded calls for world peace.[26] War-injured soldiers, however, could not be dismissed so easily. When disabled veterans spoke, people listened—at least, peace groups hoped they did. Even in fictionalized form, veterans' claims of masculine experience helped shield antiwar arguments from the taint of feminine sentimentality. Indeed, many interwar peace texts functioned as acts of political ventriloquism, with disabled veterans giving voice to the author's own antiwar critique.

Consider, for example, children's author Charles Tazewell's *Three Who Were Soldiers*, first broadcast on World Peaceways' CBS radio show in the mid-1930s. Modeled on Charles Dickens's *A Christmas Carol*, Tazewell's drama was set in the office of Joel Cready, a prominent newspaper publisher, on New Year's Eve. Three patients are missing from a local veterans' hospital, but Cready pays the news little attention (he is too concerned with the Italian invasion of Ethiopia and talk of looming conflicts in China and Western Europe). After drifting off, the publisher is startled by the ghostly appearance of three war-mangled vets, who assail Cready and his media cohort for filling recruits' minds with martial glory.

1ST SOLDIER: You know many like us. You printed pictures of us marching down to the troop ships. You said our faces were of young crusaders—and the guns over our shoulders were shining lances.

2ND SOLDIER: You couldn't take pictures of us marching now. You see—I haven't any legs.

3RD SOLDIER: And you couldn't speak of our faces—mine was blown away in the Argonne.

1ST SOLDIER: And I can't carry a gun anymore. You see—I haven't any arms.

Little more than thinly fictionalized polemic, Tazewell's radio play none-theless delivered a powerful argument: the best time to stop war fever was before it started. The fact that disabled veterans delivered the mes-sage only added to its credibility.[27]

What Every Future (Disabled) Veteran Should Know

In their explicit references to lost legs, blinded eyes, and blown-away faces, productions like *Three Who Were Soldiers* amplified what would become a common theme in interwar peace culture: the devastation of the male soldier's body. Eager to debunk war's romance, peace groups believed that no sane young man would ever rush off to war if he truly grasped the mutilation and long-term suffering awaiting him. Among peace groups, it was vital to take would-be soldiers (along with their friends and family members) on a tour of war's carnage and brutality—from the front lines of the battlefield where American boys were blown to pieces; to the surgical posts and hospitals, where they were stitched back together; to the sanatoriums and veterans' homes, where thousands of ex-doughboys lived only to die. Peace advocates were convinced that gov-ernment censors continued to shield the Great War's bodily toll from the American public. Consequently, they were determined to set the record straight about war's ferocious consumption of lives and limbs before it was too late.

Perhaps the most widely read handbook on soldiers' disfigurement was Harold Shapiro's 1937 antiwar catechism, *What Every Young Man Should Know about War*. Composed as a series of questions and answers, Shapiro's book was a primer on what could—and most likely would—happen to American servicemen in the next armed conflict:

> Q. What would high explosives do to my face?
> A. They would probably produce extensive, highly repulsive, disfig-uring injuries. The resulting complications from high explosives may, however, be immediately (and perhaps thankfully) fatal.[28]

> Q. What may be my fate after being wounded?
> A. You may be buried alive in shelled trenches; you may be frozen to death or die of hunger and thirst; you may be burned or your fro-zen feet may drop off with your shoes; you may actually complete the amputation of your own mangled limbs; you may consort

with the dying, the dead, the decomposed. You may become ill, delirious, insane before you have reached the hospital train.[29]

Despite the dark humor evident in many of Shapiro's answers, his book was not meant for comic effect. Drawing heavily upon US medical reports and eyewitness accounts from World War I, the author promised his readers "the unvarnished, unsugar-coated truth—a postgraduate course" on what happened to soldiers' bodies before, during, and after battle.[30] As in many antiwar texts of its kind, *What Every Young Man Should Know about War* focused heavily upon injuries of emasculation and castration in an attempt to sever the link between military service and virile masculinity.[31] Shapiro's young male readers learned how long it would take mustard gas to burn their genitals, what to expect when their wounds attracted flies, and how best to determine if a bullet had passed through their intestines. Above all, they learned that—in the age of scientific slaughter—disfigurement and death were virtually inevitable for anyone who dared to enter the field of battle.

Two years later, Hollywood screenwriter Dalton Trumbo pressed a similar argument in his highly acclaimed novel *Johnny Got His Gun* (1939). A strident critic of US militarism, Trumbo wrote the book to halt the calls for American intervention in the escalating hostilities around the globe. It tells the story of Joe Bonham, an American infantryman whose limbs and face are blown away on the final day of World War I. Deaf, blind, and mute, Joe spends years lying helplessly in a hospital bed, a prisoner in the "cell of his own horrible body."[32] Eventually, Joe learns to communicate with the outside world by tapping Morse code with his head, and he concocts a plan to tour the country as an "educational exhibit," displaying his mutilated torso as an antidote to wartime euphemism.

> People wouldn't learn much about anatomy from him but they would learn all there was to know about war. That would be a great thing to concentrate war in one stump of a body and to show it to people so they could see the difference between a war that's in newspaper headlines and liberty loan drives and a war that is fought out lonesomely in the mud somewhere between a man and a high explosive shell.[33]

Joe dreams of visiting schools, war industries, shipyards, and small towns— any place he can show "all the little guys what would happen to them" in the next Great War.[34] Released at the height of anti-intervention fervor in the United States, *Johnny Got His Gun* became an instant best-seller, going through seven printings in its first year. Indeed, Trumbo's vision of a healthy male combatant reduced to a "piece of meat" was considered so timely that, in 1940, NBC adapted *Johnny* as a one-hour radio drama, with future *Yankee Doodle Dandy* star James Cagney cast in the lead role.[35]

A two-character sketch published by the New Theatre League, a federation of leftist theater groups based in New York City, took a more lighthearted approach to educating the public about the bodily fate awaiting American troops. Edward Mann's "Lecture Demonstration" (1939) opens with an anonymous man walking on stage and greeting the audience. Citing an uptick in fighting abroad, the man notes that although Americans regularly read about soldiers killed and injured in wartime, they often struggle to comprehend the magnitude of war's slaughter in human terms. "So this evening," he announces, "I am going to try to show you just what casualty figures might mean to us Americans in terms of human beings, in terms of Johnnie Jones, an average American boy." For the remainder of the sketch, the man teaches "Johnnie," an eighteen-year-old war skeptic, the corporeal cost of wartime service. At the man's instruction, Johnnie lies down on the stage imagining his future as a corpse, stumbles about as if blinded by mustard gas, and struggles to pick up objects without using his fingers (these, the man tells him, have been shot away). In one particularly comic moment, after kicking the youth in the shins, the man holds up an artificial leg and reassures him: "Well, it won't hurt when you have one of these." By the demonstration's end, both Johnnie and the audience have learned a valuable lesson: If average American boys do not want to end up corpses or cripples, they must stand up to the forces pushing the United States toward war.[36]

Envisioning War's Horrors

While peace advocates were committed to educating the American public about war's inevitable horrors, they recognized that productions like "Lecture Demonstration" were not always up to the task. Peace groups believed Americans would never fully understand why war needed to be avoided, if not abolished altogether, until they bore witness to the true extent of war's slaughter. In this regard, photography and documentary visual culture proved invaluable to the antiwar cause, both in the

United States and around the globe. Since the emergence of war photography in the Crimean War, pacifist and anti-imperialist groups in the United States and Western Europe had mobilized photographic images to contest romanticized visions of modern combat. In large part, the appeal of photography stemmed from its perceived truthfulness—the widespread consensus that photographs offered an unblemished window into historical reality.[37] For critics of mechanized warfare, as historian Berd Hüppauf has argued, "The impact of shocking and gruesome photographs on public memory and imagination could not be matched by paintings or drawings simply because of the perceived authenticity of photography."[38] Moreover, by the 1920s and 1930s, there was a rich tradition of mobilizing "realistic" images for progressive reform—from Jacob Riis' photo exposé of lower Manhattan tenements, *How the Other Half Lives* (1890), to New Deal photographers' campaign to document Depression-era rural poverty.[39]

Following World War I, pacifists and other critics of modern war began to distribute photographs of war's bodily horrors at an unprecedented pace. As early as 1920, former members of the American Field Service, a Quaker ambulance unit, assembled *The Absolute Truth*, a collection of thirty Signal Corps photographs taken near the front lines. The first image, titled *Where They Fell*, featured a tightly framed shot of two dead faces. One man's skin had been burned from his forehead to his lower jaw, leaving behind a ghoulish white mask; the other soldier, pictured in profile, was missing much of his left cheek, allowing viewers to peer into the empty cavity where his teeth had once been. While the dead dominated *The Absolute Truth*, the Great War's living casualties were prominently featured as well. *Fractured Bones*, a photograph that might well have appeared in a rehabilitation journal, revealed the cramped quarters of a World War I hospital ward, the patients' beds lined up only a few feet apart. The more provocatively titled *Have We Forgotten Them?* offered a parallel scene, showing scores of gassed men, their faces wrapped in bandages, waiting to be loaded into a Red Cross ambulance. Collectively, the images constituted an unassailable document of the Great War's human trauma. That said, compared to later productions, *The Absolute Truth* offered a somewhat amorphous antiwar critique, eschewing extensive commentary on war's causes and cures. Aside from the photographs' pithy (albeit mildly satirical) captions, the book relied solely on its documentary-style photographs to reveal the Great War's "absolute truth."[40]

In 1924, the anarchist pacifist Ernst Friedrich, founder of Berlin's International Anti-War Museum, assembled the most influential collection of antiwar photographs of the era, *Krieg dem Kriege!* (trans. *War against War!*). Originally published in four languages (German, English, French, and Dutch), it represented a new genre of antiwar polemic: the horror or "atrocity" photo album. Unlike its Quaker antecedent, Friedrich's collection made no effort to mask its intent. Its opening manifesto assailed nationalist politicians and religious leaders for provoking the "mass butchery" of the lower classes, urging readers to unite in a general strike against future militarism.[41] To make his case, Friedrich included nearly two hundred photographs—along with assorted propaganda posters, pro-war cartoons, and drawings of toy soldiers—documenting both the idealization and ugly realities of mechanized combat. Along the way, the book presented a visual compendium of war's horrors, its pages filled with mass graves, decimated forests, emaciated prisoners, and mutilated soldiers, some barely recognizable as human. Throughout *War against War!*, Friedrich employed a rhetorical strategy (hinted at in *The Absolute Truth*) that would become standard in all horror photo albums between the world wars, juxtaposing patriotic slogans and propaganda images with deliberately shocking images of war's carnage. The book's goal was not only to lay bare the ultimate consequences of militarist rhetoric, but also to provoke a visceral hatred of warfare, one that could be channeled into future political action.[42]

Like many peace activists to follow, Ernst Friedrich had little faith in language to illuminate the true horrors of industrial-age warfare. Proletarian critics had written in "glowing wrath against this mass murder," he observed:

> But all the treasury of words of all men of all lands suffices not, in the present and in the future, to paint correctly [war's] butchery of human beings.
>
> Here, however, in the present book,—partly by accident, partly intentionally—a picture of War objectively, true and faithful to nature, has been photographically recorded for all time.[43]

Upon its publication, Friedrich's ocularcentric critique was lauded by leftist intellectuals, proletarian writers, and antiwar activists throughout Europe, selling 35,000 copies within its first six months. By 1930, it had gone through ten editions in Germany alone, with translations printed, according to one estimate, in forty different languages. *Het Volk*, a social democratic newspaper published in Holland, raved about *War against War!*, urging its readers to "face the clutching terror that lies in wait for you in the pages of this book, and compel others to undergo the same experience." The International Federation of Trade Unions, a Marxist labor organization, agreed. "If such pictures were to be put in history-books, they might indeed frighten children on dark nights," it conceded. "But which is worst [*sic*], the fears of a nervous child, or the realities of the future, if the misled millions go out again to unspeakable torture, mutilation and death?"[44] Despite limited publicity in the United States, *War against War!* gained a small but influential audience among American activists and educators. In 1933, Edwin Leavitt Clarke even assigned *Krieg dem Kriege!* to his Sociology of International Conflict class at Rollins College, though he feared traumatizing his students. On the class syllabus, Clarke cautioned, "Look at the pictures as long as you wish, but no longer."[45]

The notoriety of *War against War!* soon inspired a number of copycat productions in the United States and around the world. The best known was *The Horror of It: Camera Records of War's Gruesome Glories*, a horror photo album published in New York City in 1932.[46] Its antiwar pedigree was impressive by any standards. Edited by Frederick A. Barber, author of the peace primer *"Halt!" Cry the Dead* (1935), the book contained introductions by two of the leading lights of the interwar peace movement: liberal theologian Harry Emerson Fosdick, and feminist Carrie Chapman Catt, founding president of the National Committee on the Cause and Cure of War.[47] Drawn from military archives in France, Germany, Great Britain, and the United States, the album's ninety-one photographs assaulted viewers with nightmarish scenes of human suffering and mechanized death: corpses stacked like cordwood, mountains of human skulls, executed prisoners swinging from nooses. Fosdick believed such images would "stop the mouths of those who think war a moral tonic, or a glorious tradition, or an inspiration to useful patriotism, or a way of advancing human progress." Beyond that, Fosdick hoped the pictures would finally dispel the charge that "peacemakers" were "soft-headed idealists" untutored in the harsh realities of international conflict.[48]

In addition to its format, *The Horror of It* shared much in common with *War against War!*, upon which it was undoubtedly modeled. Like its German antecedent, Barber's collection used ironic photo captions to mock the "glories" of modern combat. *The Horror of It* also held up mutilated soldiers, both dead and alive, as the ultimate confirmation of war's horrors. A number of the photographs showed combatants in various states of decomposition, their rotting corpses infested with maggots or ground into the earth like human waste. Others highlighted soldiers' transformation from bodily health to grotesque disfigurement. A series of photographs near the book's end, for example, featured haunting close-ups of men with severely disfiguring injuries to the eyes, mouth, and face. In perhaps the most jarring of the bunch, the acerbically titled *Reconstruction*, seven men stared vacantly at the camera, their monstrous faces twisted and scarred. One of the men wore a crude prosthetic mask that reached from just below his eyes to his chin; another man's mouth (or what remained of it) was so swollen and protruding, it looked like that of a sucker-fish (fig. 29).[49] Who were these pathetic figures? To Barber, their identities were not important. As emblems of war's dehumanization, they were best left anonymous—hideous remnants of a conflict many Americans longed to forget.

Like Friedrich, contributors to *The Horror of It* placed great faith in the power of photography to lay bare "war's plain, stark, ugly meaning."[50] Carrie Chapman Catt proclaimed that, in an age of technologically produced images, warring nations could no longer disguise war's cruelty behind a patina of false consciousness. "Blessings on the camera," she beamed, "which now for the first time in the history of the world, provides the means of teaching youth the terrible, undeniable facts of war. The camera tells the truth, speaks all languages and can cross all frontiers."[51] Contemporary readers of *The Horror of It* seemed to agree with Catt's sentiments, praising the book for its myth-shattering honesty. Writing in the Columbia University newspaper, student-editor Reed Harris declared,

> The book tells the story [of war] simply and powerfully. Dismembered bodies draped grotesquely over a wire fence, a sniper dangling from a limb of a tree, long lines of rotting corpses lying in ditches,

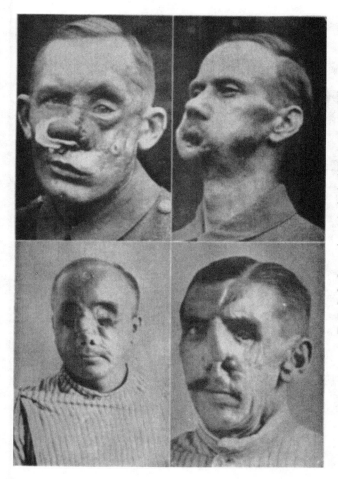

FIG. 29. Images of injured faces were a prominent feature of antiwar photo albums of the 1920s and 1930s. Included primarily to shock and disgust, such photographs challenged rehabilitationists' faith in technology to reconstruct the victims of wartime violence. Untitled image from Frederick A. Barber, *The Horror of It: Camera Records of War's Gruesome Glories* (New York: Brewer, Warren, and Putnam, 1932).

dead men being shoveled like manure into carts, faceless and formless remnants of the bloody carnival—these are the things you will see.[52]

Interwar peace advocates generally looked upon technology with distrust, associating modernist technophilia with the Great War's mass production of disability and death. However, they had a special place in their hearts for photography, without which war's "gruesome glories" might never see the light of day.

In fact, Barber and company believed it was the horror photographs' reproducibility that made them such potent instruments for peace.

What Is Wrong With This Picture?

Everything is wrong.

The young man in the picture is a terrible sight to look at. He had half of his face shot away in the last World War.

War gives the great masses of people death, agony and destruction. It gives the millionaires more millions of dollars in profits. War is fought only in the interests of the profit-makers.

The roots of war must be removed. The economic life of America must be reorganized to remove the hunt for private profit—the greatest cause of war.

Young People's Socialist League of America

549 Randolph Street
Chicago, Ill.

(Read the other side)

FIG. 30. This recruiting flyer for the Young People's Socialist League of America features one of the most commonly reproduced injury-themed photographs of the post–World War I era. "What Is Wrong with This Picture?," Young People's Socialist League of America Records, Swarthmore College Peace Collection.

Rather than seeking out new images, antiwar photo editors recycled the same photographs in multiple albums or displays, a practice that largely elided the national identities of their subjects. One of the most iconic (and widely reproduced) antiwar photographs of the 1920s and 1930s, for example, featured the left profile of an unidentified soldier. His nose, lips, teeth, and upper palate had been sheared away (most likely by a piece of shrapnel or a shell fragment), the remains of his face producing a jarring chiaroscuro against the dark backdrop (fig. 30). The image first appeared in *War against War!*, where it was published with the caption:

"The 'health resort' of the proletarian. Almost the whole face blown away" (this in reference to German field marshal Paul von Hindenburg's infamous boast, "War agrees with me like a stay at a health resort"). In 1930, the Young People's Socialist League of America reprinted the photograph on one of its handbills, coupled with the question: "What Is Wrong with This Picture?"[53] In Frederick Barber's collection, the image bore the title *Living Death* and was printed opposite a similar photograph simply called *Torture*. Two years later, it showed up yet again in *No More War*, an antiwar photo album published in Paris by the International Federation of Trade Unions, this time with the commentary "Alive, but what has life for him?"[54] In each case, the image provided viewers with indisputable evidence of war's power to transform healthy young men into grotesque caricatures of their former selves. More important, it served to counter rehabilitationist and nationalist visual culture, which tended to portray disabled veterans as medical marvels or heroes to be admired. Answering its own question, the Young People's Socialist League of America proclaimed of the photograph: "Everything is wrong. The young man in the picture is a terrible sight to look at."

Of course, it was precisely because the man was such a "terrible sight" that Americans needed to look at him. For antiwar groups, the act of looking at war casualties was imbued with profound moral and political significance—it was a necessary step on the path to peace consciousness. Peace activists encouraged Americans to stare at the war-disabled, to grow angry and disgusted at the sight of former soldiers' injuries, and to imagine their own bodies similarly mutilated. Within the peace movement, photographs of injured or dead soldiers served as both links to the past (what had happened in the last Great War) and glimpses of the future (what would happen in the next one). Besides promoting collections like *War against War!* and *The Horror of It*, prominent peace groups circulated their own images of diseased, mutilated, and war-disabled men. At the same time, antiwar filmmakers (along with B-movie hacks hoping to tap America's growing peace market) began to re-edit old war footage in order to highlight the bodily horrors of modern combat. Although virtually unknown today, agit-prop "documentaries" such as *The Big Drive* (1933), *The Death Parade* (1934), and *Forgotten Men: The War as It Was* (1934) assailed movie audiences with big-screen images of corpse-strewn trenches and pitiful amputees. In the words of Edward Gallner, publicity director of a 1933 antiwar doc (also named *Forgotten Men*), such films served one purpose above all others: to remind audiences that "unbalanced minds, broken and torn limbs, misshapen bodies and distorted outlooks are still with us . . . to demand that there shall be no more wars."[55]

Beyond looking at images, peace activists encouraged Americans to seek out the dead and wounded for themselves. Photographs and moving pictures were powerful testaments to war's needless violence, but in the eyes of war's critics, they were no match for firsthand encounters with actual casualties. According to some antiwar writers, the sensory experience of meeting disabled veterans in the flesh—viewing men's mangled bodies, smelling the hospital stench of antiseptics, listening to the tubercular coughs of the gassed—was the only surefire way to appreciate war's human toll. In her poem "God's Challengers," which was written after a visit to a veterans' hospital, Marion Perham Gale proclaimed of the men she had seen:

> These are the mother's sons
> Who fought
> "To make the world
> Safe for Democracy,"
> These are the men
> Who, silent, tread
> The stony road
> To Calvary.
>
> Go look at them,
> I say,
> To you, and you, and you!
> The truth is known
> By, oh, so few![56]

Other writers made similar demands of the American public. In their visits to veterans' hospitals, Arthur Derounian urged his readers, "Ask to see the blinded; the neurasthenic and psychaesthenic. . . . Visit the forbidden 'machine shop.' A maze of wires and pulleys support a thigh, a chest, a pelvis that was pounded by flying steel twenty years ago."[57]

Major general Smedley Butler was an especially vocal proponent of visiting war-disabled veterans. Twice honored with the Medal of Honor, the "Fighting Quaker" was the most celebrated marine of his era, a veteran of US campaigns in the Caribbean, Mexico, and China (where he was wounded helping to suppress the Boxer Rebellion). But following World War I, Butler's faith in US foreign policy began to wane, and by the 1930s, he had become a fierce critic of American imperialism and military adventurism.[58] In his best-selling attack on the armament industry, *War Is a Racket* (1935), Butler recounted how, during a tour of eighteen VA hospitals, he met thousands of disabled veterans—once the "pick of the nation" now reduced to the "living dead."[59] Writing four years later, as the world teetered on the brink of global holocaust, Butler was even more adamant about the need to visit World War I–era disabled veterans. Addressing the mothers of America's future casualties, Butler asked,

> Have you ever been in one of those huge Veterans Hospitals it has been necessary to build to take care of the thousands of helpless and maimed cripples still with us from the LAST war? If you have, you will not need a reminder of what war can do to your boy, how it can render his life useless and broken at twenty, and yet keep him cruelly alive for the whole span of it. If you have not, I advise you to go and see one of them, for nothing could bring home to you more clearly or tragically the fact that in the last analysis it is your boy who is going to pay the piper. . . . Those withered, elderly, spiritless men who lie and sit so patiently in their wards day after day in those hospitals, waiting for the end, as they have waited since they got there twenty years ago, were the flower of our boys in their time.[60]

For Butler, Americans had an obligation to visit such men, to see for themselves the terrible destruction and suffering wrought by war. That was the only way the public could truly understand why the United States needed to avoid another foreign conflict at all costs.[61]

A Challenge to Youth

Very often, the main audience of disability-themed peace propaganda was young people, especially high school and college students. Looking back on their parents' experiences in World War I, American students of the late 1920s and 1930s were primed to embrace the cause of peace. Economic hardships at home and rising fascism abroad soured many youth on the notion that military intervention—no matter how noble in principle—could ever serve the interests of US prosperity and world progress. Inundated with stories about trumped-up German atrocities, the booming "armaments racket," and the lingering Problem of the Disabled Veteran, vast numbers of American youth viewed the United States' decision to enter World War I as a tragic mistake—one their generation was determined not to repeat. The gore-filled pages of revisionist history, Great War literature, and antiwar popular culture only added to students' antiwar resolve. An undergraduate at the University of Minnesota during the 1930s, future journalist Eric Sevareid noted of his classmates: "We read *Three Soldiers*, and *All Quiet on the Western Front*, and *Death of a Hero* with compassion and a sick feeling in our stomachs. We were young, and to those just beginning to taste the wonderful flavors of life the idea of death is a stark tragedy of unutterable horror."[62]

Although not all American youth joined in, high school and college students provided the lifeblood of the interwar peace movement. Working alongside their adult counterparts, student peace activists fought to "demilitarize" school textbooks, promote peace-themed curricula, and rid their campuses of the Reserve Officers' Training Corps (ROTC). Student newspapers attacked munitions makers and voiced their opposition to US intervention in "foreign wars." Thousands of American college students signed oaths pledging to refuse military service except in case of homeland invasion; countless more boycotted "militaristic" films and rallied community support to the antiwar cause. Seeking to form a "united front" against war, loose coalitions of Marxist, pacifist, liberal, and religious student activists assembled at antiwar congresses throughout the 1930s. The largest peace-oriented youth group, the 20,000-member American Student Union, sponsored student strikes across the nation. In 1936 alone, roughly 500,000 college students left their classrooms in support of military disarmament and world peace.[63]

When targeting teen audiences, peace activists frequently articulated an injury-centric vision of modern warfare, drawing explicit links between military service and bodily mutilation. According to antiwar artists and organizers, war was not a gateway to adulthood; it was a machine for transforming the flower of American youth into corpses and cripples. The appeal of this message—exemplified in countless antiwar pamphlets, photo albums, and youth-oriented illustrations—was that it struck at young people's most precious possessions: their physical appearance and bodily health. Peace groups believed that American youth (far more than adults) did not adequately respond to economic or social analyses, and that they required visceral proof of war's bodily horrors to withstand its promises of adventure. Ultimately, peace proponents wanted students to view debates about military intervention, neutrality, and preparedness in bodily terms. Their primary message: if students failed to prevent war (or secure their own right to nonparticipation), they would pay the price in injury, disability, disfigurement, and death.

To this end, peace groups served up an assortment of casualty-themed youth propaganda, from picture books and stereographs to puzzles and games. Much of this material was deliberately playful in design, intended both to educate and to entertain. In 1938, Philadelphia businessman Warren Bowman earned over $1 million selling antiwar trading cards, each one-cent pack containing a stick of gum and a colorful portrait of war's horrors.[64] Other peace advocates sought to integrate antiwar messages into the classroom. Between the late 1920s and the start of World War II, peace groups actively targeted public schools and universities, distributing lesson plans and teaching materials to educators across the United States. By the early 1930s, antiwar pedagogy was so commonplace that *Scholastic* devoted an entire issue of its weekly high school reader to the bodily dangers of modern warfare. The magazine's front cover featured a gruesome illustration of no man's land, strewn with barbed wire and studded with rotting corpses. Inside, students found an antiwar reading list; excerpts from William March's combat novel, *Company K* (1932); shocking photographs from Laurence Stallings's best-selling photohistory, *The First World War* (1931); and articles detailing the latest advances in body-rending technologies. On the issue's back cover, a World Peaceways advertisement issued a "ringing challenge to youth" to "Save the World from War's Insane Slaughter." As if students needed another reminder of what awaited them, the ad was topped with a photograph, taken from *The Horror of It*, of a row of listless amputees. The caption? "The Army Builds Men."[65]

Not surprisingly, many students adopted images of dead, wounded, and disabled soldiers to lend symbolic weight to their own antiwar productions. During the mid-1930s, members of the Princeton-based youth group the Veterans of Future Wars led protest marches dressed as disabled veterans, twirling crutches over their heads like batons.[66] Antiwar students seized upon amputees with particular intensity (they were easy to draw, easy to recognize, and easy to understand). In 1934, a group of New York City high school students designed cartoon illustrations of legless veterans as visual analogues of war's needless destruction, a motif that permeated antiwar youth culture.[67]

Nowhere was students' appropriation of disability iconography more pronounced than in their contributions to the National Circulating Library of Students' Peace Poster Contest (NCLSPPC). Held annually between 1935 and 1951, the contest was the brainchild of Nancy Babb, a teacher and tenement inspector from Southampton, Virginia, who spent World War I performing relief work in Eastern Russia. Unwilling to "return to normalcy," Babb was determined to keep the memory of war's horrors alive in the public imagination.[68] Still, by the mid-1930s, she worried that much of the peace-themed visual culture then in circulation lacked the aesthetic punch to attract the attention of American youth. Babb founded the NCLSPPC partly out of a desire to replenish the supply of cheap, mass-produced posters available to peace groups. More important, she viewed the contest as an ideal opportunity to win a new generation of young people to the cause of international cooperation and world peace.[69]

The antiwar messages articulated in the winning entries ran the gamut of interwar peace ideology. Students called for world friendship and international cooperation, stressed the economic costs of the military conflict, and drew upon Christian iconography and teachings to make the case for peace. However, few topics attracted more attention than the bodily consequences of modern warfare. The stamp sheets and propaganda leaflets published by the National Circulating Library of Students' Peace Poster Contest catalogued war's casualties in grisly detail: torsos draped over barbed wire, skeletons and decapitated heads, wounded soldiers in the throes of death, and blind men masked by gauze. A number of posters attempted to capture the immediate effects of modern weaponry on soldiers' bodies. One of the most arresting images, "Oh God—For What!," designed by Albert Maestro, a student at Eton College, depicted the impact of a bullet piercing a soldier's eye, a fountain of blood and gore spurting from the wound (fig. 31).

FIG. 31. Albert Maestro, "Oh God—For What!" National Circulating Library of Students' Peace Posters Collected Records, Swarthmore College Peace Collection.

Other designs focused on the long-term effects of physical and mental trauma. In "The Results of War, Crippled for Life," an illustration of two amputees (a sailor and an infantryman) resting on their crutches, William Pantelakis of Salt Lake City reminded viewers that not all war casualties die on the battlefield; many return home to face social alienation, poverty, and disabling pain. Vera B. Rodolf, a high school student from El Paso, sent a similar message in her award-winning entry, "The Spoils of War." This nightmarish image featured a pair of war-disabled men—an amputee with his entire head covered in bandages and a wheelchair-bound veteran frozen in a perpetual look of horror. To a generation of future cannon fodder, the poster's tagline expressed an indisputable truth: "War seeks its victims in the young."[70]

FIG. 32. Typical of much interwar peace culture, Walker Brunsch's "For Some the War Will Never End: Why Start Again?" uses the amputee as a stand-in for all disabled veterans. Moreover, it affirms the notion—promoted by both veterans and peace groups—that war never ends for disabled vets. National Circulating Library of Students' Peace Posters Collected Records, Swarthmore College Peace Collection.

As with so much antiwar propaganda, the students' posters tended to recycle the most iconic and sensational incarnations of Great War disability—amputees, blind veterans, or pitiful combinations of the two—despite the relative rarity of such figures on US casualty rolls. Nevertheless, the images' reliance upon visual stereotypes detracted little from their rhetorical power. As far as student artists were concerned, Americans had a clear choice when it came to military intervention (fig. 32). They could pursue a path of international cooperation and peace, saving their youth from the miseries of their Great War–era counterparts. Or they could relearn the mistakes of their forefathers, in the process sentencing their sons to infirmity, mutilation, and death.

Experts in Suffering

Young people were not the only targets of interwar peace propaganda. Antiwar activists also tried to enlist ex-servicemen into the battle for peace. Although by no means as strident as student peace activists, Great War veterans attempted to shape national debates about the physical, psychological, and economic costs of US military intervention abroad. Through their efforts to assist the Great War's disabled vets, the American Legion, the Disabled American Veterans, and other veterans' groups focused public attention on the hardships and social alienation of earlier generations of combatants, providing peace groups with fertile ground for sowing unease about future conflicts. Emboldened by their legislative successes, veterans cultivated a public image as the nation's preeminent experts on matters of war and peace—a privileged status often afforded them by government officials and civilian peace groups. At a 1930 congressional hearing to "promote peace" and equalize war's burdens, Thomas Kirby, the DAV national legislative chairman, promoted military preparedness and "universal conscription" as deterrence against enemy attack. Equally significant, Kirby reiterated what would become a commonplace among former soldiers: that "no cross section of Americans has had a greater opportunity to appreciate the horrors of war" than the Great War's disabled vets.[71]

Of all Great War–era veterans' groups, none boasted more about its commitment to peace promotion than the American Legion. In its 1936 *Handbook on Peace and Foreign Relations*, the Legion proclaimed it was "best equipped of all civic organizations to discourage the opinion that war is inevitable," appealing to Americans to support its platform of military preparedness and national defense.[72] Fiercely isolationist, Legionnaires had little faith that international arbitration and collective security could stem the tide of war forever. Consequently, the group encouraged the US government to invest in preventive measures at home, including a strong military to ward off future invasion.[73] Although Legion leaders frequently espoused the same antiwar rhetoric as their nonveteran counterparts, the group seldom cooperated with civilian peace advocates, many of whom viewed the organization's motives with suspicion. The Legion considered pacifism "un-American," and its members openly ridiculed supporters of international disarmament as dangerously naïve. Moreover, even at the height of peace culture in the United States, prominent Legionnaires were reluctant to abandon the wounded soldier as a heroic ideal. "I should rather *my* sons were dead on the field of battle than to know that they would not respond, gladly, eagerly, to their country's call in time of war, and *live*," declared J. Ray Murphy, chairman of the group's Americanism Commission, in 1935.[74] Hissed at a 1938 appearance at Columbia University, a campus well known for antimilitarist student activism, Legion national commander Daniel Doherty told the assembled undergrads that "the reason you have an opportunity to be here tonight is due in large measure to the fact that young men in 1917 and 1918 interposed their bodies between you and shrapnel."[75]

Yet Legionnaires were not the bloodthirsty warmongers their critics made them out to be. The American Legion waged public campaigns against "war profiteers" and, despite its notorious phobia of international treaties, formally endorsed the Kellogg-Briand Pact outlawing war as an instrument of foreign policy. Even more telling, on July 4, 1920, Legionnaires joined ex-soldiers from Great Britain, France, Belgium, Yugoslavia, Greece, and Italy to form the Fédération Interalliée des Anciens Combattants (FIDAC), an international confederation of Allied war veterans.[76] The group was organized with the dual mission to "promote peace" and to preserve "the links which bound the Allied and Associated ex-service men during the War of 1914–1918, fought in common for a common cause." From its Paris headquarters, FIDAC published its own magazine, the *FIDAC Review*, and organized thousands of exchange visits between veterans and schoolchildren of the Allied countries. FIDAC officers helped war-wounded vets track down paperwork, locate former comrades, and file for pension benefits—actions designed not only to benefit individual veterans, but also to unite all ex-combatants under the banner of cooperation and mutual understanding.[77]

In fact, many Legionnaires understood peace promotion—even if combined with military preparedness—as an extension of their work on behalf of disabled vets. In his 1924 article "What Our Neglected Veterans

Want," Legion writer Robert M. Field cited veterans' injuries as evidence of the need for international harmony:

> America's immediate duty is to care for the disabled, her veterans say. But to stop with that would be treason to our dead. For there is a graver duty.
>
> Deeper and more significant is the growing, if inarticulate, demand that honest and direct effort be made to organize against the recurrence of war. Had there been no war there would be no disabled veterans. Were there no disabled veterans today politics would be compelled to seek other fields for the spoils system. War and suffering: The first cannot exist without the second.[78]

Like many Legionnaires, Field believed that the disabled veteran was less a problem in his own right than a symptom of broader pathology: modern war. In his mind, the only way to prevent the existence of future disabled veterans was to ensure that US soldiers never reached the line of fire.

There is little evidence to suggest that the majority of disabled veterans—or veterans in general—were active participants in the more radical wings of the interwar peace movement. However, that did not stop some militant peace groups, above all the American League Against War and Fascism (ALAWF), from trying to recruit disgruntled doughboys. Following a call by writers Theodore Dreiser, Sherwood Anderson, and Upton Sinclair to unify all "opponents of war" beneath a common banner, the ALAWF was established at the three-day US Congress Against War in September 1933. It brought together a coalition of farm-labor, youth, leftist, and veterans' organizations, including the Workers' Ex-Servicemen's League and the Bonus Expeditionary Forces. Speaking at the group's first Congress, one veteran told the cheering crowd that Great War vets were ready to take up the battle for peace: "We no longer look forward to war with the adventurous, active interest of the soldiers of yesterday—we know that war means death and suffering for most of us, as well as for millions of other workers." In later years, Smedley Butler became one of the ALAWF's most respected spokesmen, and the group's annual meetings offered former soldiers—including members of the Jewish War Veterans and wayward Legionnaires—a chance to voice their concerns about the militaristic and fascistic tendencies of mainstream veterans' groups.[79]

Similarly, war-injured veterans were conspicuously present at many antiwar protests of the interwar era. The French novelist Henri Barbusse, author of the Great War classic *Under Fire* (1916), served as chairman of the ALAWF and traveled the United States speaking out against the dangers of militarism. Lesser-known war casualties sold remembrance poppies at peace conferences, delivered speeches at antiwar rallies, and testified about their personal struggles since the Armistice. At some peace events, activists hobbled on canes and wrapped their heads in bandages to remind crowds about the persistent suffering of disabled vets. In preparation for 1935's "No More War Parade" in New York City, the Green International, a radical pacifist organization, urged ex-soldiers to march together in rows, clearly identifying their veteran status. The group also instructed participants to construct parade floats showing legless veterans pushing themselves along the sidewalk. Accompanying them was that most ironic of recruiting slogans, "The Army Builds Men."[80]

As peace groups were quick to point out, some World War veterans made remarkable contributions to the antiwar effort. In the midst of the Depression, Frederic S. Hale, a World War I veteran from Greenwich, Connecticut, pledged his entire Bonus check to World Peaceways, urging his former comrades to follow his lead.[81] Harold R. Peat, the Canadian infantryman, autobiographer, and film actor who had once wowed American audiences with his wartime adventures, had an especially dramatic change of heart. After revisiting Europe in the early 1920s, "Private Peat" not only repudiated his earlier statements on war's glories, but made something of a career lecturing North American audiences about the need for peace.[82] Nevertheless, one was far more likely to encounter a disabled veteran cowering on an antiwar poster than organizing a peace rally. Peace groups publicized the specter of war-produced injury with abandon; yet outside of veterans' organizations, World War casualties rarely made it into the top ranks of interwar peace groups. With notable exceptions, moreover, many of the most gruesome displays of disabled soldiers' bodies—including *War against War!* and *The Horror of It*—were produced not by disabled veterans themselves but by civilians who had escaped war's violence unscathed. Ultimately, disabled veterans were far more useful to the interwar peace movement as symbols—iconic representatives of war's horrors—than as generals in the battle for peace.

Problems with the Pictures

Although the injury-themed poetry, posters, and photographs produced in connection with the interwar peace movement inspired later generations of antiwar activists, troubling questions remain about the overall effectiveness of peace groups' propaganda strategies. Did images of disabled combatants produce the desired effect on their audiences? Was constantly reminding the American public about the bodily traumas of World War I a successful way of cultivating peace? Obviously, some peace advocates thought so; otherwise, they would not have circulated stories, photographs, stage plays, and other cultural productions about war-produced disability as widely as they did. Indeed, the fact that certain images or narrative tropes appeared so frequently in interwar peace culture suggests a high degree of consensus about their usefulness in the rhetorical war against war.

However, at least some observers, both inside the peace movement and looking on from afar, questioned whether exhibiting war's "ugly truth" was the best means of debunking the romance of martial service. In his landmark essay "The Moral Equivalent of War" (1910), published four years prior to World War I, William James argued that talk of war's horrors only added to the allure of combat.[83] Later writers suggested that peace propaganda focusing on war's misery was counterproductive, stirring up passions without providing audiences with the analytical tools to make sense of what they were seeing. In a report to the National Committee on the Cause and Cure of War, Marion H. Barbour expressed grave doubts about the effects of gruesome "counter-propaganda" on potential peace converts:

> Peace novels depicting the horror of war, peace films showing the evils of war, peace drama, collections of would-be peace pictures, best known of which is probably "The Horror of It." Unless they do more than stir the emotions through associations, unless they prompt an effort to penetrate the situation out of which war arises, they will only intensify the responses of fear and hate already there.[84]

Salvador de Madariaga, the chief of the Disarmament Section of the League of Nations, arrived at a similar conclusion. In an article reprinted in *Reader's Digest*, he argued that the success of gruesome "war books" was not a sign of antiwar hegemony; rather, it was a reflection of people's fascination with the grotesque. "Often our eyes will come back again and again, not to the most beautiful, but the most overwhelmingly ugly person in a room," de Madariaga noted. "And so with war and horrors."[85]

In 1923, Major Sherman Miles, a future chief of Army Intelligence and US congressman, raised additional concerns about peace groups' emphasis on disability and death. Writing in the *North American Review*, Miles scolded peace groups for focusing on war's ugliness while failing to understand the roots of international conflict. In his mind, "peace societies" were so fascinated by the "horrors of war . . . they [had] no curiosity about its causes and functions." Miles's dismissal of the "negative campaign of pacifism" represented more than a disagreement about tactics. Instead, he rejected the assumption underpinning almost all disability-themed peace propaganda: that repeated exposure to representations of injury and destruction produced a lasting "abhorrence of war." Despite peace groups' best efforts, Miles believed that "the next generation, like all preceding generations reared in peace, [would] be influenced by the excitement, the adventure and the glory of war." Over time, war's devastation would fade from memory and the romance of battle would win the day.[86]

Although Miles underestimated the peace movement's efforts to examine the roots of military conflict, it would be a mistake to dismiss his criticisms out of hand. In retrospect, the gratuitous, even pornographic, character of some interwar peace productions is undeniable. In works like Arthur Derounian's *They Shall Not Die in Europe*, an antiwar pamphlet first published in 1935, one can almost sense the author's giddy pleasure in recounting war's horrors. No face is too mangled, no wound too gruesome, that it could not be shared with the American public. (In fact, the more mangled, the more gruesome, the better.)

Equally disturbing was peace groups' willingness to engage in the very sort of mythologizing they decried in government propagandists. Consider, for example, their treatment of "basket cases," the limbless veterans James Kirwin and others adopted as the ultimate symbols of war's destruction. In 1919, Merritte Weber Ireland, surgeon general of the US Army, along with several newspapers, responded to a public outcry by launching an investigation into the fate of America's quadruple amputees. At the end of their search, they had found nothing, and the basket case should have been discarded as just another wartime exaggeration.[87] Yet basket case sightings persisted well after the Great War's end—at military reunions, in the dark recesses of government asylums, and in the pages of antiwar fiction.[88] To what extent did Americans believe in basket cases, "men with legs and arms amputated who must be wheeled and fed and humored"?[89] Perhaps we will never know. What is clear, however, is that in their pursuit of a world without war, peace activists were willing to perpetuate a mass hallucination on the American people.

In the end, the interwar peace movement failed in its effort to cultivate a permanent peace culture in the United States and around the globe. In November 1939, when James Kirwin published his news column on the lessons of the basket case, the movement was already beginning to unravel. By 1940, the United States was actively rebuilding its military arsenal, and with the Japanese bombing of Pearl Harbor on December 7, 1941, debates about US military intervention were effectively silenced. Nevertheless, this movement's arguments and cultural contributions have never disappeared altogether. In their novels, stage plays, photo albums, and films, antiwar activists highlighted the physical suffering and social alienation of Great War–era disabled veterans, transforming the disabled veteran from an icon of national sacrifice into a symbol of war's cruelty. War's critics routinely turned to the mangled, blinded, and maimed bodies of soldiers to contest the rationales for modern combat and, more important perhaps, show the human cost of the United States' military ventures abroad.

Unfortunately, when it came to disabled veterans, the 1930s peace movement left behind another legacy as well: a tendency to stigmatize disability and bodily difference, with seemingly little consideration for the men whose bodies and lives they exploited. In their posters, photographs, and visual displays, peace groups reduced disabled veterans to flat caricatures: emasculated, helpless, and grotesque, living embodiments of war's horrors. With few exceptions, peace artists made little attempt to address disabled veterans as complex individuals, men whose injuries represented just one facet of their identity. Did disabled veterans really want curious hospital visitors to stare at them? Should peace groups seek permission before disseminating disabled veterans' stories of pain and suffering? Was it possible that some vets might view their injuries with pride? To begin to answer such questions would have required a degree of human empathy—an awareness of disabled veterans as more than just political symbols—that is regrettably absent in much of the interwar peace culture. Instead, peace advocates tended to dehumanize the very sort of men they hoped to save, publicizing disabled veterans as "cautionary tales" for future generations.[90]

IV

OLD BATTLES, NEW WARS

Harold Russell

The most famous disabled veteran of the "Good War" era never saw action overseas. On June 6, 1944, Harold Russell was serving as an Army instructor at Camp Mackall, North Carolina, when a defective explosive blew off both of his hands. Sent to Walter Reed Medical Center, Russell despaired the thought of spending the rest of his days a cripple. As he recounted in his 1981 autobiography, *The Best Years of My Life*, "For a disabled veteran in 1944, 'rehabilitation' was not a realistic prospect. For all I knew, I was better off dead, and I had plenty of time to figure out if I was right." Not long after his arrival, his mood brightened after watching *Meet Charlie McGonegal*, an Army documentary about a rehabilitated veteran of World War I. Inspired by McGonegal's example—"I watched the film in awe," he recalled—Russell went on to star in his own Army rehabilitation film, and was eventually tapped by director William Wyler to act alongside Fredric March and Dana Andrews in *The Best Years of Our Lives* (1946), a Hollywood melodrama about three veterans attempting to pick up their lives after World War II.[1]

Russell played Homer Parrish, a former high school quarterback turned sailor who lost his hands during an attack at sea. Much of Russell's section of the film follows Homer's anxieties about burdening his family—and especially his fiancée, Wilma—with his disability. In the film's most poignant scene, Homer engages in a form of striptease, removing his articulated metal hooks and baring his naked stumps to Wilma—and, it turns out, to the largest ticket-buying audience since the release of *Gone with the Wind*. Even as Homer decries his own helplessness—"I'm as dependent as a baby," he protests—Wilma tucks him into bed and pledges her everlasting love and fidelity. In the film's finale, the young couple is married; however, there is little to suggest that Homer's struggles are over.

Though Russell worried what disabled veterans would make of the film, *The Best Years of the Our Lives* was a critical and box-office smash. For his portrayal of Homer Parrish, Russell would win not one but two Academy Awards (one for Best Supporting Actor and the other for "bringing aid and comfort to disabled veterans"). He would spend the next few decades working with American Veterans (AMVETS) and other veterans' groups to change public perceptions of disabled veterans. "Tragically, if somebody said 'physically disabled' in 1951," he later observed, "too many Americans thought only of street beggars. We DAV's were determined to change that." In 1961, he was appointed as vice chairman of the president's Committee on Employment of the Handicapped, succeeding to the chairman's role three years later.[2]

A decade before his death in 2002, Russell returned to the public spotlight when he was forced to sell one of his Oscars to pay for his wife's medical bills.[3]

8

"THE SHINY PLATING OF PRESTIGE"
Disabled Veterans in the American Century

> After the last war the shiny plating of prestige quickly rubbed off the status
> of a veteran, and the glamour of a wound honorably received on a far-off
> field of battle proved to have little staying power. I doubt if human nature
> has changed much in a quarter of a century.
> — Keith Wheeler, *We Are the Wounded* (1945)[1]

> It is a safe forecast that from 1945 to 1972 the United States will go up and
> down the same road, in care of its disabled, which it traveled from 1918
> to 1948. There will be variations, but the same set of problems must be
> dealt with.
> — Richard Seelye Jones, *A History of the American Legion* (1946)[2]

When Americans opened their newspapers in early 1941, the nightmarish stories of overseas combat seemed eerily familiar. The weapons
were larger and more powerful, and some of the belligerent nations had
switched sides, but the bloodshed and destruction appeared much the
same. Equally familiar were the debates playing out in kitchens, work-
places, and legislatures across the country. Should the United States
try to remain neutral? Would this latest world war have the same result
as the first? And if the United States did enter the fight, what would be
the cost? For the previous two decades, American peace activists and
isolationists had waged a powerful campaign against US involvement in
armed conflict. The war of 1917–1918 had not "made the world safe for
democracy," as Woodrow Wilson had claimed. If anything, it had made
things worse. Still, Americans wondered: What if this war was different?
What if this war was worth the risk?

That February, *Life* magazine publisher Henry Luce penned a five-
page manifesto he hoped would push US leaders out of their martial

complacency. "The American Century" was both a call to arms and an ideological blueprint for global hegemony. Luce challenged readers to abandon 1930s-era isolationism and embrace the nation's manifest destiny to "exert upon the world full impact of our influence for such purposes as we see fit and by such means as we see fit." According to the author, a longtime supporter of Great Britain and a vocal advocate of US military intervention in Europe, the United States had squandered its "golden opportunity" to assume world leadership after World War I. In the ensuing decades, American leaders had only "bungled" it further, allowing war and tyranny to spread across globe. But the time for hesitation had passed, he insisted. As the "most powerful and vital nation in the world," the United States had a sacred responsibility to seize the reins of global leadership and spread its "great American ideals" across the earth.[3] Strikingly absent in Luce's essay—and in the knockoffs that followed—was any mention of the injured bodies this doctrine of martial internationalism would inevitably produce.

Within the next year, Luce's readers began to find out. As the launching pad for the American Century, World War II was the nation's deadliest conflict since the Civil War. By the time it was over in August 1945, more than 400,000 US military personnel were dead, and the number of nonfatal casualties was even higher.[4] Initial reports suggested the rise of a new disability veterans' crisis, much like the one that had accompanied the Great War's end. Yet it never developed, at least not to the degree it had twenty-five years earlier. Though disabled veterans confronted many of the same obstacles (social prejudice, bureaucratic neglect, etc.) as their World War I predecessors, the social and political context in which they did so was significantly different. Rehabilitation, considered a novel experiment following World War I, was now standard practice, thoroughly institutionalized throughout the Veterans Administration (VA) system. In addition, disabled GIs returned to a nation soon to be flush with economic prosperity, where self-styled "experts" and the latest consumer technology promised a quick fix to any problem. Most important of all, postwar "victory culture," coupled with the onset of the Cold War, discouraged Americans from questioning the legitimacy of US foreign policy—even if they wanted to.[5] In a culture that heralded the start of World War II as a necessary step for global peace and progress, the powerful discourse eulogizing the moral righteousness of the "Good

War" undermined the possibility of a deeper critique's acquiring widespread resonance. Despite lingering doubts about the war's long-term consequences, most Americans resigned themselves to the notion that winning World War II had been worth the sacrifice.

But that does not mean they felt the same way about *all* wars or about the American Century as a whole. From Korea to Vietnam to the Persian Gulf, the Problem of the Disabled Veteran would remain the American Century's dark shadow, reemerging in those moments when the bodily toll of US militarism seemed to outweigh the necessity of overseas intervention. The return of the Disabled Veteran Problem in the decades following World War II reveals a lingering undercurrent of anxiety about the United States' newfound role as a global military power. What emerges is a portrait of a nation deeply ambivalent about its military commitments and the bodily price they exact.

The Good War's "Raw Chunks"

By most measures, World War II was the most destructive conflict in history. Across the globe, more than sixty million people were killed, with millions more suffering the effects of injury, social dislocation, and disease. In the age of total war, nothing—and no one—was off limits. Nazi Germany pursued a campaign of mass genocide, systematically murdering upward of six million Jews, homosexuals, and people with disabilities. During the six-week "Rape of Nanking" of 1937–38, Japanese troops massacred 260,000 Chinese civilians, in some cases burying their victims alive or nailing them to telephone poles. Tens of thousands of girls, many as young as a few months old, were raped and killed, often while family members were forced to watch. For their part, the Allies (like their Axis foes) embraced the terror bombing of civilians as a legitimate military tactic. On March 9, 1945, less than six years after president Franklin D. Roosevelt decried so-called strategic bombing as "inhuman barbarism," three hundred US B-29s firebombed Tokyo, creating an inferno of 1,800 degrees and incinerating 85,000 people. Less than five months later, the world got a glimpse of Armageddon. The combined death toll from the atomic attacks on August 6–9, 1945, topped 205,000. Whatever vestige of moderation remained among US warmakers, writes historian Michael Glover, "perished in the fireball above Hiroshima."[6]

And yet, in the United States, this most brutalizing of military conflicts was quickly (if incompletely) transformed into what Studs Terkel would deem the "The Good War."[7] The Good War is not so much a fabrication as a cultural myth. It's the version of World War II Americans like to remember—a triumphant, morally righteous crusade shorn of its ugliness and moral complexity.[8] The Good War cannot be traced to a single author or historical event. In 1975, novelist James Jones, a veteran of both Pearl Harbor and the invasion of Guadalcanal, blamed the passage of time for the Good War's existence:

> The truth is, thirty-five years has glossed it all over and given World War II a polish and a glow that it did not have at the time. The process of history always makes me think of the way that Navahos polish their turquoise. They put the raw chunks in a barrel half filled with birdshot, and then turn the barrel and keep turning it until the rough edges come out smooth and shining. Time, I think, does the same thing with history, and especially with wars.[9]

Today, critics are more likely to point the finger at other culprits: wartime propaganda factories and Hollywood filmmakers; schoolteachers and memorial makers; video game artists and popular documentarians; contemporary politicians eager to tap a well of nostalgia.[10] Whatever the causes, two things are clear: the myth of the Good War has served to inhibit historical understanding of World War II and the men and women who fought it. What is worse, Good War mythmaking has worked to legitimize other military conflicts. As Gene LaRocque, a retired navy admiral who survived the Japanese attack on Pearl Harbor, once put it, "World War Two has warped our view of how we look at things today. . . . The twisted memory of it encourages the men of my generation to be willing, almost eager, to use military force anywhere in the world."[11]

From the start, few of the Good War's raw chunks were more carefully sanitized than the bodily destruction of American "GIs," the nickname for US Army troops in World War II. For much of the conflict, images of wounded or dead combatants were strictly censored, and the most disturbing photo evidence of American casualties was either destroyed or locked away in classified government files, only to be seen at war's end.[12] The generation that grew up in the Good War's shadow was spared the worst of the slaughter as well. Before the 1960s, Hollywood depicted

World War II as a virtually bloodless conflict. Nonfatal wounds were antiseptic and clean; fatal casualties either died quickly—like John Wayne's Sergeant Stryker in *Sands of Iwo Jima* (1949)—or slumped to the ground with little visual evidence of bodily trauma. Unromantic forms of war injury (wounds from training camp accidents, psychoneurotic disorders, etc.) rarely made it into American theaters, nor did socially stigmatizing wounds to the face, brain, spine, or genitals.

To this day, official memories of World War II tend to gloss over veterans' injuries and postwar struggles. The recently constructed National World War II Memorial in Washington, DC, for example, makes only brief allusion to US war casualties and leaves visitors with no sense of the hardships endured by disabled GIs at combat's end. At the memorial's dedication in 2004, TV news anchor Tom Brokaw (who had deemed World War II–era Americans the "Greatest Generation" a few years earlier) seemed to reduce the war's psychological toll to a bad night's sleep. "Those of you who returned with unshakable nightmares of war," he told the crowd, "were held through long nights by your uncomplaining wives, and when daybreak came you went off together to resume your lives without whining or whimpering."[13] However, many vets found the war described in such comments to be unrecognizable. As Edward W. Wood, Jr. wrote in his 1991 autobiography, "Those who called World War II a good war did not experience the one in which I fought. Most of all, they did not know what it was to come back to the United States from the land of the wounded."[14]

On the battlefield (which by then, thanks to long-range bombers and ballistic rockets, spanned entire continents), the threat of injury and death was a pervasive presence. World War II–era drill instructors continued to tout the relevance of hand-to-hand combat, but many soldiers died anonymously from weapons designed to kill en masse. Historian Michael C. C. Adams notes, "About 85 percent of physical casualties were caused by shells, bombs, and grenades; only 10 percent or less by bullets."[15] Men were killed by "friendly fire" or blown completely to bits, only a finger or a dog tag to be found. Although there was no good place to fight, combat was especially savage in the Pacific, where fear and racial hatred fueled slaughter on both sides. During the eighty-two-day Battle of Okinawa (April–June 1945), more than 12,500 US soldiers, marines, and sailors were killed; the entrenched Japanese forces literally fought to the death, losing roughly 100,000 men to combat injuries or suicide (by some estimates, civilian deaths were even higher).[16] When the battle was over, a young E. B. Sledge recalled, the island was "the most ghastly corner of hell I had ever witnessed. . . . The whole area was pocked with shell craters and churned up by explosions. Every crater was half full of water, and many of them held a Marine corpse. The bodies lay pathetically just as they had been killed, half submerged in muck and water, rusting weapons still in hand. Swarms of big flies hovered about them."[17]

To deal with the pain, soldiers smoked, brewed homemade liquor, and popped pills, but it was not enough. According to a study conducted by the Surgeon General's Office, the average World War II infantryman could only spend about two hundred days in combat before he started to "break down."[18] The US military had attempted to curb psychological problems by weeding out those considered most likely to collapse under fire. Of the eighteen million men examined for military service during World War II, 970,000 were rejected for "neuropsychiatric disorders and emotional problems." However, as Richard A. Gabriel points out, "In four years of war, no more than about 800,000 US ground soldiers saw direct combat. Of these, 37.5 percent became such serious psychiatric cases that they were lost to the military effort for the duration of the war. . . . Another 596,000, or about 74 percent, were admitted to medical facilities for psychiatric problems for a length of time ranging from weeks to months."[19]

J. Glenn Gray, author of the classic *The Warriors: Reflections on Men in Battle* (1959), recalled that most of his fellow soldiers fought the war with a "dazed consciousness"; having witnessed so many "gaping wounds" and heard so many "agonized cries" of pain, they could not "consciously endure the thought of the same thing happening to them."[20] Those who did break down were often characterized as "malingerers" or "mommies' boys" who lacked the manly backbone of their fellow comrades.[21]

As was the case in World War I, government propagandists went to great lengths to manage public knowledge of US casualties. On top of its censorship efforts, the newly formed Office of War Information (OWI) flooded wartime newspapers and magazines with upbeat stories about medical miracles taking place on faraway battlefields. In addition, the OWI recycled the Committee on Public Information's practice of incorporating disabled GIs (and other disabled people) into its poster campaigns. Typically, images of the disabled were used to communicate one of two messages. The first concerned disabled people's value as war workers. With millions of able-bodied men in uniform, war industries were urged to consider segments of the population (women, people of color, the elderly) previously thought unsuitable for industrial labor. "HIRE THE HANDICAPPED," exhorted one poster in all caps, because "American Needs *All* of US." The OWI also used images of disabled GIs to check public overconfidence in the inevitability of US victory. By 1943, the tide of the war had turned, and government officials worried that too much "good news" would lead to complacency on the home front. Showing disabled (and dead) soldiers was meant to remind the American public of the dangers US soldiers continued to face in the field. In particular, the OWI was eager to dispel racist assumptions (many of which it had already fostered) about the incompetence of the United States' Pacific rival. One especially memorable poster centered on the face of a recently blinded GI wearing dark sunglasses and carrying a cane; its accusatory tone was unmistakable: "So the Jap's a Snap? I Can't See It" (fig. 33).[22]

Although Americans at home did not spend much time looking at disabled soldiers, a growing cohort of social scientists and military planners began to sketch the outline of a new disabled veteran crisis, one that threatened to dwarf anything that emerged after World War I.[23] Given the size and severity of US casualty rolls, they were right to be concerned. Rapid advancements in emergency transportation, military medicine, and pharmacology (especially sulfa drugs and penicillin) lowered the hospital mortality rate of World War II casualties to one half of the Great War level (from 8 percent to less than 4 percent). By June 1944, there were already 208,519 World War II veterans drawing disability pensions, roughly 7 percent of whom were categorized as "totally disabled."[24] Over the course of the war, 678,000 US servicemen sustained nonfatal injuries, including 300,000 whose injuries required extensive hospitalization and convalescent care. A million more men suffered debilitating psychiatric symptoms, while countless others were haunted by traumatic memories for the rest of their lives.[25] Although Americans longed to welcome their wounded warriors home as heroes, they expressed deep concerns about the reintegration of disabled veterans into

FIG. 33. During World War II, the Office of War Information deployed images of disabled veterans to curb home-front complacency and shame viewers into purchasing war bonds. This 1944 poster was one of several produced by Revere Copper and Brass Incorporated that featured disabled veterans. The casual racism of the poster's title was typical of American propaganda during World War II, which often relied upon physiological stereotypes ("cross-eyed") and racist language ("Japs") to mock and dehumanize the nation's Japanese enemies. Revere Copper and Brass Inc., "The Japs Aren't as Cross-Eyed as You Think" (1944), Ad*Access Online Project, Ad# W0182, John W. Hartman Center for Sales, Advertising and Marketing History, Duke University David M. Rubenstein Rare Book and Manuscript Library.

civilian life. In May 1945, the Office of the Surgeon General proclaimed, "The physically disabled veterans represent one of the most serious problems confronting the Nation today."[26]

Postwar Readjustments

Despite such warnings, the Problem of the Disabled Veteran after World War II did not inspire the decades of introspection and policy critique that had followed World War I. One reason was the widespread acceptance of rehabilitation as both an ideological program and technical practice. Considered something of an experiment in the 1920s, by World War II rehabilitationist thinking—about returning men to "normalcy," eliminating "hero worship," and remasculinizing disabled veterans— permeated all levels of veterans' treatment.[27] As two prominent rehabilitationists, Wilma T. Donahue and Clark Tibbetts, explained in 1945: "The measures developed for the care of veterans of the First World War were largely palliative and experimental in nature. Today's provisions are based on the experiences and modifications of the twenty-five intervening years."[28] World War II–era orthopedists, physical therapists, and vocational experts were confident that the vast majority of disabled veterans could successfully readjust to postwar society as productive citizens. Not only that, they believed that many, if not most, Americans were ready to accept disabled veterans without prejudice. In their 1945 book, *Normal Lives for the Disabled*, Edna Yost and Lillian Gilbreth sounded an optimistic note: "As a nation, we are more awake to the rights and capacities of the able-disabled for productive places in the economic system" than ever before.[29]

To ensure rehabilitation's success, the Veterans Administration and health workers produced hundreds of pamphlets, magazine articles, flyers, and newsreels designed to reintroduce the gospel of rehabilitation to the American public (fig. 34). As was the case following World War I, much of this material was aimed at male veterans' wives and families.[30] Because one goal of rehabilitation was to reestablish traditional gender roles, women were told not to flaunt their physical strength or independence in front of their newly disabled husbands. Rehab experts also advised patience, particularly in the first few days or weeks of disabled veterans' homecoming. According to psychiatrist Alexander Dumas and science writer Grace Keen, authors of *A Psychiatric Primer for the Vet-*

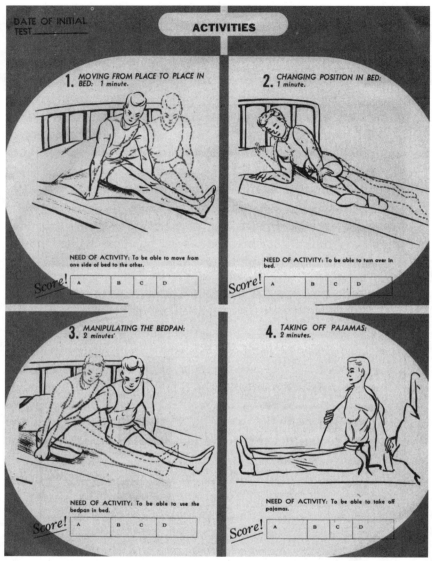

FIG. 34. The rehabilitation of disabled veterans of World War II was as much an exercise in confidence-building as physical reconstruction. This image was taken from a workbook for veterans with spinal cord injuries. Vets were instructed to score their ability to perform everyday tasks like putting on pajamas or going to the bathroom and to track their improvement over time. Although the workbook stressed the importance of physical independence, it indicated that full body mobility was not needed to make a good living. "Once seated behind your desk or at your workbench," it told readers, "your good head and hands MAKE YOU THE EQUAL OF ANY MAN!" Veterans' Administration, *What's My Score?* [VA Pamphlet 10:10], 1946.

eran's Family and Friends (1945), some vets "may be nervous, explosive and impatient, chain-smokers, seekers after stimulants and diversions." Without the rigid structure of military life, others "will react so violently against regimentation that they will resent the slightest advice or suggestion as to what they should do." Still others, having been trained as killers, will struggle to readjust their "attitude toward human life." These behaviors were normal, even expected. The best thing wives and families could do, Dumas and Keen counseled, was encourage vets to put the war behind them: "Once he has talked it out, he should try to forget it. Do not encourage him to go on reliving again and again the horrors of it all. He may be too much inclined, as many neurotics are, to linger in the past, to mull over failures and dwell on might-have-beens. He must try to learn that these things that trouble him are past and gone. He cannot undo them, but he can make the present and the future what he will."[31]

Government specialists warned that soldiers who failed to "deveteranize" would never assimilate into peacetime society. A few would become "professional veterans," spending the rest of their lives trying to exploit their military injuries for personal gain. Most would wind up like Joe Macarthy, the fictional disabled vet profiled in the VA instructional film *The Road to Decision* (1947).[32] One of many pro-rehabilitation films produced in the late 1940s, *The Road to Decision* was staged as a conversion narrative, in which the film's protagonist comes to align his own values (attaining economic independence) with those of the state (rebuilding a national workforce and reducing postwar disillusion).[33] When the audience first meets Joe, he is drinking alone at a bar. He has both "dame trouble and job trouble" because he can't find work and can't afford to get married on his government pension. Things begin to turn around after he meets Edgar, a veteran of the Battle of Anzio and now a double amputee. Before the war, he was a "tool room stooge," but thanks to the VA, he is now training to become an architectural draftsman. The film flashes back to Edgar's time in the hospital, allowing viewers to follow him through every step of the rehabilitation process. In the final sequence, a still skeptical Joe calls the Veterans Administration to begin his own vocational training.

Although government-sponsored rehabilitation would prove far more successful in the late 1940s than it did in the early 1920s, its expansion and refinement cannot fully explain Americans' diminished anxieties about disabled vets. Other factors also played a part, including the best-known piece of veterans' legislation of the twentieth century: the Servicemen's Readjustment Act of 1944.[34] Better known as the GI Bill, it extended many of rehabilitation's benefits—job training, university education, health care—to all honorably discharged service personnel. More than that, it helped transform the American social landscape, swelling the ranks of the middle class and sending more than seven million veterans to college.

Nostalgia has glossed over many of the GI Bill's own "raw chunks." As journalist Michael Bennett points out, "The road to the passage of the GI Bill had to be built over the broken bodies, and sometimes broken minds, of thousands of early casualties of the war."[35] Likewise, not all of the "Greatest Generation" were considered equally deserving. African Americans, especially in the South, faced intimidation and were less likely to take advantage of the benefits owed them. The same was true of women, many of whom were redefined as "civilian contractors," making them ineligible for veterans' programs. Gays and lesbians faced hostility as well; large numbers were railroaded out of the service midwar, and in 1945 VA director Frank T. Hines (the man who had replaced Charles Forbes twenty years earlier) barred military personnel discharged for "homosexual acts or *tendencies*" from receiving veterans' benefits.[36] In retrospect, the highly exclusionary nature of the GI Bill is undeniable, boosting (largely) white men's economic opportunities even as the United States' architecture of discrimination began to be dismantled. (President Harry Truman officially ordered the desegregation of the US armed forces in 1948.) But at the time, the bulk of the bill's beneficiaries were not inclined to protest on others' behalf. Most were too busy using their military service as a "stepping stone to a better life."[37]

There were additional reasons disabled GIs failed to provoke the collective handwringing of their Great War counterparts. For one thing, World War II shifted public attention away from military casualties to civilian ones. This tendency would continue in the decades that followed, and despite the high military casualties in Vietnam, it has only intensified in recent years, especially since the terrorist attacks of September 11, 2001. Even as the war was being fought, some Americans saw World War II as the dawn of a new age in human destruction. As Rufus E.

Clement observed in the *Journal of Negro Education*, "In this day of mechanized blitzkrieg, of unrestricted submarine sinkings and of saturation bombing, the list of civilian dead and injured may at times approach, and occasionally exceed, the list of casualties in the armed forces. This is a condition which we have come to recognize and to accept as one of the added horrors of modern warfare."[38] Throughout the war, Franklin D. Roosevelt spoke openly about the need to prevent war's carnage from spilling over onto US shores, concerns that would be magnified during the Cold War, when civil defense planners imagined "hypothetical Hiroshimas" across the United States.[39] Between 1945 and the mid-1960s, US military casualties *over there* often seemed a small price to pay to prevent nuclear holocaust at home. In turn, the disabled soldier's resonance as an emblem of war's destruction diminished in comparison to that of World War II's civilian casualties. When imagining the worst horrors of the modern age, Americans were far more likely to think of irradiated Japanese children or Holocaust victims than war-wounded vets.

Optimism about veterans' futures was further fueled by the material abundance World War II left in its wake. Although many Americans were initially anxious about what the postwar world would bring (Would there be another economic depression? Was World War III on the horizon? How long before the United States was "nuked"?), such concerns were partly tempered by promises of television sets and suburban bliss.[40] Between 1945 and 1960, the US economy surged to unprecedented levels of wealth and productivity; America's gross national product rose by 250 percent, with unemployment rates never exceeding 7 percent. By 1950, few would have believed that disabled veterans represented a serious threat to the American economy—at least not now. Popular magazine stories with titles like "They May Be Disabled—But Man! Can They Work!" (1951) and "They Call *Him* Disabled?" (1953) sent the message that disability was no longer an obstacle to economic independence.[41] Beyond that, notions of a lingering Disabled Veteran Problem ran counter to what historian Alan Brinkley calls the "almost religious faith in technological progress that came to characterize" postwar American society.[42] In this so-called Age of Experts, no problem was beyond the reach of American technical know-how. The human body was considered especially ripe for reengineering. As a result, the decades following World War II witnessed a sharp rise in "medical consumerism" as growing

FIG. 35. By the 1950s, public images of disabled veterans often mirrored the broader culture of consumerism and economic prosperity. Many companies advertized their products as remedies to the physical dependency long associated with war disability. In this ad, Pete Muzelak, a paralyzed World War II infantryman, testifies to the easy handling of his plywood Cruis Along boat, which he is able to captain alone for six days at a time. Author's collection.

numbers of Americans sought elective surgery to bring their inner and outer selves into alignment (fig. 35).[43]

No factor did more to dampen public outcry about the human cost of World War II than the unequivocal nature of the US military victory and the veneer of "patriotic orthodoxy" that came to characterize its official memory.[44] After a brief period of national self-reflection, when the meaning of the war was still up for grabs, the constraints of the liberal consensus ideology at home—and communist containment abroad—made it politically risky to express even the slightest doubt about World War II and its long-term effects. The continued legitimacy of the Good War—as both a governing faith of postwar America and a means of binding citizens to the state—depended upon a subtle elision of the Disabled Veteran Problem. Simply put: World War II could not be the Good War unless the Problem of the Disabled Veteran disappeared from the culture at large. Psychiatrist Franklin Fearing recognized as much in an article published in the October 1945 issue of *Hollywood Quarterly*. Fearing theorized that one's awareness of war disability as a *problem* was largely a matter of ideological perspective:

> If you see the war as the organized commitment to destructive aggression, during which individuals were subjected to terrified stress, you will probably believe that its consequences for the survivors will be the more or less permanent impairment of the human mind and body. If you see the war as the organized commitment to the achievement of a high and worthy goal, you may not be unaware of its destructive effects, but you will be able to detect compensating values.[45]

After World War II, Americans were encouraged, even required, to look past war's "destructive effects" and focus instead on its "compensating values." Indeed, the grand bargain of the Good War, as sold to families at home, service personnel overseas, and the generation that came of age in the 1950s and 1960s, was that Americans' postwar rewards of freedom and economic prosperity were only possible *because* of the nation's willingness to accept injury as a price worth paying.

Carrying On in an Age of Militarization

Despite the prevailing victory culture, concerns about the bodily cost of US participation in World War II were not entirely stifled by the Good War myth. Although most vets slowly, if painfully, readjusted to civilian life, the gap between pro-rehabilitation propaganda and the actual experiences of disabled veterans was hard to ignore. Disabled veterans' organizations—including the newly formed Paralyzed Veterans of America and the Blinded Veterans Association—led vocal campaigns to protest the scandalous conditions in which many disabled veterans lived. As had been the case following World War I, congressional investigations found disabled vets languishing in run-down hospitals and treatment centers, waiting weeks, even months, before their claims for compensation were heard.[46] Unable to find permanent employment, some disabled veterans made a living touring on charity sports teams—or worse, in circus sideshows—that crisscrossed the country throughout the late 1940s and 1950s. Old stigmas about the social impropriety of damaged bodies had not disappeared either. In Pasadena, California, residents wrote angry letters to the local newspaper demanding that disfigured veterans from the local hospital be kept off the streets.[47]

For a while, veterans' postwar struggles even became a prominent theme in popular culture. Award-winning films such as William Wyler's *The Best Years of Our Lives* (1946), Delmer Daves's *Pride of the Marines* (1945), and Fred Zinnemann's *The Men* (1950) cast a sympathetic spotlight on the emotional and physical hardships of World War II vets. As antidotes to Good War mythology, these films had their limitations. Rather than investigating the social and economic contexts that produce disability, they tended to frame it as an individual problem—a final battle to be won. Moreover, as media scholars Leonard Quart and Albert Auster point out, they "remained tied to the old Hollywood formulas, particularly that of the good woman leading her man to social and psychological adjustment."[48] These drawbacks notwithstanding, post–World War II disability dramas exposed a social reality that was to be largely erased from Good War mythology: that despite years of government-sponsored vocational training, many disabled veterans would never fully readjust. They would remain outsiders, physically and psychologically cut off from the domestic abundance of America life (fig. 36).

In the early 1950s, fears about the bodily toll of the American Century intensified. In large part, they were driven by what Michael S. Sherry has described as the militarization of American society. Even as the glow of victory persisted, Sherry writes, US political leaders decided to make "permanent many of the militarized features of American life and politics improvised during the 1930s and World War II. War—as deed or state of mind or model, as horror to be contemplated, deterred, or waged—moved to the center of American political culture in a more lasting way."[49] Militarization was dangerous business, particularly for those tasked with elevating the United States' status as a global military superpower. The United States' first cohort of disabled veterans after World War II were casualties of the military's rapid efforts to beef up its nuclear arsenal. As Robert J. Topmiller and T. Kerby Neill point out, "Up to 380,000 American service personnel were exposed to varying levels of radiation" between the end of World War II and the signing of the Nuclear Test Ban Treaty in 1963.[50]

In the immediate aftermath of their exposure, many "atomic veterans" (as they came to be called) complained of headaches, diarrhea, and

FIG. 36. Critical of the militarization of American culture after World War II, the National Council Against Conscription returned to a favorite motif of prewar peace groups—the juxtaposition of amputees and the recruiting slogan, "The Army Builds Men." Cover of the National Council Against Conscription, "The Army Says" (c. 1947), copy in Peace Pamphlets, Library of Congress.

skin abrasions. In later years, they suffered permanent pain and high rates of cancer. However, because the Department of Defense was eager to downplay the dangers of radiation poisoning, atomic veterans were routinely denied the compensation afforded other veteran cohorts. In 1950, they even took their case to the Supreme Court, only to be told, "We know of no American law which ever has permitted a soldier to recover for negligence, against either his superior officers or the Government he is serving." It would take another thirty years before the Veterans Administration began to recognize their claims—though even then, atomic veterans were often met with stiff resistance.[51]

When the Cold War finally turned hot, Americans' begrudging acceptance of high casualties in World War II proved more an aberration than a new norm. Sometimes deemed the "Forgotten War," the Korean War (1950–53) left more than 54,000 Americans dead and 103,000 severely wounded.[52] Although public support for US intervention in Korea was initially high, the bloody stalemate that followed robbed the conflict of what little Good War appeal it had. As months passed and casualties mounted, more and more Americans viewed the war with ambivalence, if not outright hostility. According to historian Paul M. Edwards, "Political sensitivity at home was increasingly attuned to [rising] casualty reports," which many newspapers published on a weekly basis.[53]

Caught off guard by the war's sudden start, the US Army Medical Department was unprepared for the conditions US troops would be facing, including the dangers of Korea's frigid winters. Frostbite and dysentery were widespread, and by early 1951, nearly one-tenth of US troops were suffering from battlefield fatigue.[54] Clarence Mosley, a twenty-two-year-old aerial gunner from Paterson, New Jersey, became the Air Force's first quadruple amputee. After bailing out of his plane, he was exposed to frostbite for five days before he was found.[55] The military attempted to censor graphic images of mutilated GIs, but it could not fully shield the American public from the war's devastation of bodies and minds. In her dispatches home, war correspondent Marguerite Higgins painted a desperate picture of US aid stations overflowing with wounded soldiers and marines, and Edward R. Murrow's *See It Now* spread images of injured Korean War vets to television sets across the nation.[56]

Adding to the growing unease, the war's ambivalent ending left a cloud of suspicion over the men who fought it. In the popular media, Korean War veterans were often characterized as "soft" or "weak-willed," and they received little of the fanfare that had greeted their World War II counterparts. This was the especially the case of disabled former prisoners of war (POWs), who carried the added stigma of potential brainwashing.[57] Not surprisingly, many disabled Korean War veterans had a difficult time transitioning back to civilian life. Although the federal government authorized a new GI Bill, it was not as generous or expansive as the version passed during World War II, and only 77,000 disabled veterans took part in federal rehabilitation programs.[58] To a public already uneasy about the United States' commitment to militarization at home and war abroad, Korean War veterans symbolized a national failure. Summarizing popular attitudes in September 1953, *New York Times* reporter Howard A. Rusk declared, "We do not have the same high interest in veterans' affairs that we had at the end of the last war despite the fact that we have 2,200,000 veterans of the Korean conflict."[59]

"New" Veterans on the March

If the Korean War sparked mass concerns about the bodily legacies of the American Century, the Problem of the Disabled Veteran returned in full force in the decades surrounding the Vietnam War. The United States' longest war to that time (c. 1962–77), the Vietnam War would prove a turning point in American attitudes toward disabled veterans and their significance for US foreign policy. Over the course of the war, more than 51,000 Americans were killed and 270,000 wounded, including 21,000 who would be listed as permanently disabled.[60] Besides those who suffered physical injuries, between 500,000 and 1.5 million Vietnam veterans experienced symptoms of post-traumatic stress disorder, including debilitating flashbacks, rage, and social withdrawal.[61] Because of improved antibiotics, better-equipped hospitals, and faster means of evacuating injured troops, casualty survival rates were higher than ever before. As brigadier general Thomas J. Whelan testified before a Senate subcommittee in November 1969, "In World War II, the average time from wounded to treatment was 10.5 hours for abdominal wounds. . . . In the Korean war it was 6.3 hours. In Vietnam, because of the extensive use of the helicopter ambulance, the average time is 2.8 hours. . . . Some cases have arrived at the hospital within 20 minutes from the time of wounding on the battlefield."[62]

But such advances often appeared hollow. In the field, fighting conditions were brutal, and many soldiers had a hard time connecting their personal combat experiences to any kind of broad strategy for "winning" the war. Back at home, television networks broadcast a conflict that bore little resemblance to TV-friendly World War II (with its bloodless wounds, evil enemies, and predictable happy ending). Although journalists had a much freer hand in shaping the public image of the war—Richard Nixon once sneered, "This was the first war in our history during which our media were more friendly to our enemies than to our allies"—Vietnam was not the blood-soaked "living-room war" of popular memory.[63] Before the Tet Offensive (January–February 1968), less than a quarter of film reports contained scenes of fighting or of combat casualties (and even then, shots tended to be brief, accounting for only a few seconds of screen time). In *The "Uncensored War,"* David Hallin notes that television executives toned down the bloodshed because they were worried about "offending the families of killed or wounded soldiers if coverage was too graphic."[64] Even so, most TV watchers did not like what they saw: a daily newsreel of advances, retreats, and aerial bombings with little perceptible purpose (other than killing as many Vietnamese as possible) and no end in sight.

Revelations about the abuse of hospitalized soldiers only added to Americans' wartime ennui. For a nation in a state of perpetual (cold) war for more than two decades, the United States both entered and exited Vietnam grossly ill-prepared to treat the conflict's inevitable casualties. In early 1970, members of the Paralyzed Veterans of America helped sneak famed *Life* photographer Co Rentmeester into a VA hospital in the Bronx. What he discovered shocked the nation—though given what was by now a lengthy history of such abuses, it should not have. Over-crowded and understaffed, the facility was, in journalist Charles Child's words, a "medical slum."[65] Water dripped from holes on the roof, and the entire hospital reeked of garbage and human waste. Crammed into filthy wards, spinal injury patients waited hours for even the most ru-dimentary care, their untended urine bags leaking onto the floor. And then there were the rats. One patient recalled awaking in the middle of the night to discover a rodent crawling across his paralyzed body. When he screamed for help, the orderly accused him of being drunk. Eventu-ally, some men took to rigging makeshift traps, but they did little to halt the infestation. Nor did they ease the patients' state of mind. If anything, the rats' presence only fueled the men's sense of betrayal—their belief that the "half dead" veterans of Vietnam had "fought for nothing."[66]

In the minds of some federal officials, soldiers returning from Viet-nam represented a "new" type of veteran, one that was fundamentally different from those who fought in World War II.[67] Coming of age amidst the civil rights movement and the cultural revolutions of the 1960s, this new veteran was poorer, blacker, more skeptical of authority. As de-scribed by Cecil P. Peck, a prominent VA psychologist, the Vietnam vet was characterized by

alienation from his own feelings and from other persons; a lack of vocational or social goals; a refusal to identify with persons working in the "establishment"; a shaky personal identity; a kind of diffuse paranoia which involves dimensions of suspicion, honesty, trust, "uptightness"; anger which is frequently intense; latent suicidal tendencies which are related to guilt; and doubt about one's ability to love other persons. In other words, many persons would interpret the above attributes as an asocial and antisocial mess which achieves tension reduction by way of alcohol, drugs, rock music and sex.[68]

In retrospect, these sorts of complaints were hardly new. In fact, Great War–era physicians and social commentators voiced nearly identical concerns (the rock music notwithstanding) about the men who returned home in 1918. Nevertheless, the sense of confusion and fear that often accompanied such claims was palpable. In the eyes of the Veterans Administration, along with many other state and cultural institutions, the millions of men who fought in Vietnam were a *problem* generation even before they put on their uniforms.

As the war dragged on, the ideological assertion at the heart of the Good War narrative—that sacrifice was a tolerable and necessary price to pay for freedom and progress—was thrown into stark relief, and disabled veterans reemerged as powerful symbols of personal outrage and national guilt. Like their counterparts during the 1920s and 1930s, Vietnam War–era peace groups hoped that viewers would look upon the disabled veteran as evidence of war's needless destruction. But this time around, disabled veterans were not relegated to photographs or "Hello, Sucker"-style illustrations (fig. 37). A number of disabled vets took up prominent positions in the antiwar movement. Never before had organized groups of disabled veterans actively protested a US conflict while it was still taking place.

The most visible veteran-led peace group was the Vietnam Veterans Against the War (VVAW), which was founded by six ex-soldiers in 1967. The VVAW sponsored the Winter Soldier Investigation into US war crimes and, borrowing techniques from guerrilla theater, staged protest marches and occupations at historical monuments across the country—often while enduring verbal taunts and physical assaults. At war's end, the VVAW fought to expose abuses within the VA system and advocate on behalf of Agent Orange victims. Although their numbers were never large—historian Andrew E. Hunt estimates that VVAW enrollment peaked at around 30,000—their influence was nonetheless profound, offering up a model for other, activist-minded veterans' groups to come. The Problem of the Disabled Veteran, largely neutralized for

"When Johnny comes marching home again hurrah, hurrah."

John Diakoyani
Hoboken, N.J.

Stop the crippling. Stop the killing. Stop the war.
Write, wire or call your congressman today.
Help Unsell The War, Box 903, F.D.R. Station, New York, N.Y. 10022

FIG. 37. During the Vietnam War, disabled veterans reemerged as powerful visual icons within the antiwar movement. This particular vet, John Diakoyani of Hoboken, New Jersey, had his leg amputated after a rifle-cleaning accident eleven days before he was scheduled to leave Vietnam. (Barbara Barnes and Rachel Cowan, "Twice Victims of the War," *Village Voice*, June 17, 1971, 66.) The Committee to Help Unsell the War, "When Johnny Comes Marching Home Again Hurrah, Hurrah," Library of Congress, Prints & Photographs Division, LC-USZ62-102948.

two decades by the discourse of *acceptable sacrifice*, was back—and more dangerous than ever. Tossing away their Silver Stars and Purple Hearts, the VVAW were a living portrait of the American Century coming apart at the seams.[69]

The career of one of the Vietnam War's best-known disabled veterans illustrates how fragile the Good War myth had become—and perhaps always had been. Born on the fourth of July 1946, and raised on a steady diet of Audie Murphy and John Wayne, Ron Kovic joined the Marines Corps at age seventeen. In his second tour of duty in Vietnam, he was shot through the right shoulder, an injury that damaged his spinal cord and left him functionally impotent and paralyzed from the waist down. As he recounted in his best-selling memoir *Born on the Fourth of July* (1976), Kovic's early innocence quickly turned to anger and betrayal. He raged against his perceived emasculation: "I have given my dead swinging dick for America. I have given my numb young dick for democracy. . . . Oh God oh God I want it back! . . . Nobody ever told me I was going to come back from this war without a penis." Just as disturbing was the treatment he received once home. While recovering at a VA hospital for a broken leg, Kovic was kept in a filthy room and, at one point, was left to wallow in his own excrement for nearly an hour. After the shootings at Kent State in 1970, he began to attend antiwar rallies, joined the VVAW, and became a popular speaker on television and at rallies (fig. 38). Kovic was the "Hello, Sucker" poster come to life. "I'm the example of war," he would declare. "Look at me. Do you want your sons to look like this? Do you want to put on the uniform and come home like me?"[70]

The highpoint of Kovic's wartime protest came at the 1972 Republican Convention in Miami, when after working his way onto the convention floor, he attracted the attention of CBS reporter Roger Mudd. "I am a Vietnam veteran," he spoke into the camera. "I gave America my all and the leaders of this government threw me and the others away to rot in their VA hospitals. What's happening in Vietnam is a crime against humanity. . . . If you can't believe the veteran who fought the war and was wounded in the war, who can you believe?" It was a powerful and familiar argument, one that disabled veterans had been using for centuries. They *knew* war. When it came to war's destruction, they were both experts and evidence. And this war, Kovic argued, was a bad war.[71]

The United States' withdrawal from Vietnam in 1973 did not dampen Kovic's activist fire. The next year, he joined fellow wheelchair vets in a hunger strike to protest conditions in VA hospitals, and he would spend the next forty years (at this point) agitating against militarization at home and militarism abroad. Other disabled veterans carried out similar activities, working alongside psychiatrists and social workers

FIG. 38. Members of the Vietnam Veterans Against the War during the "Last Patrol" protest at the August 1972 Republican Convention in Miami, Florida. During the Vietnam War, disabled veterans moved to the forefront of the antiwar movement, a significant shift from the World War I era when they were deployed mainly in the form of symbolic images. Ron Kovic (*right*) is holding an upside-down American flag as a symbol of distress. Copyright Associated Press.

to raise public awareness of PTSD. Some disabled Vietnam veterans even joined the ranks of the burgeoning disability rights movement, an activist coalition that transformed social policy toward disabled people in the United States. Unfortunately, in the years following the war, the achievements of disabled Vietnam veterans were often overshadowed by distorting myth. Even as thousands of disabled veterans, including future Republican presidential nominee John McCain and Democratic senator Max Cleland, achieved remarkable political and economic success, the specter of the mentally unhinged Vietnam vet—from *Taxi Driver* (1976) and *The Deer Hunter* (1978) to *First Blood* (1982) and beyond— would haunt the American imaginary for decades to come.

Kicking the Disabled Soldier Syndrome
In the nineteenth century, progressive militarists believed that the mass slaughter of the Civil War was an aberration and that future wars— fought with "safe" weapons and against "primitive" opponents—would bear little danger. During World War I, military leaders and social scientists argued that government-sponsored rehabilitation would eliminate the Problem of the Disabled Veteran from American life by allowing disabled veterans to return to economic independence. In the 1940s, rehabilitationists knew they had not fully succeeded; nevertheless, they remained hopeful that technology and social planning would soon eliminate all of the problems associated with war injury. However, in the wake of the social and political upheaval of Vietnam, US leaders began to pursue new strategies for minimizing the social impact of wartime disability and death without compromising war-making capabilities.

One strategy harkened back to the "safe war" technological discourse of the Progressive era; only instead of making weapons safer, now the goal was to remove soldiers' bodies from the battlefield altogether. By the early 1980s, rapid developments in computer technologies, imaging systems, and light aircraft allowed military planners to imagine a new American way of war (for a new American Century). In future conflict, machines (rather than humans) would be the primary instruments and targets of combat, and soldiers' bodies would only come into limited contact with enemy fire.[72] By the same token, military practice shifted toward an emphasis on "force protection" and "risk aversion." According to Andrew Bacevich, by the 1990s, the United States "spared nothing in its efforts to avoid casualties." Using proxy fighters and relying increasingly on air power, the armed forces were able to chip away at "any residual inhibitions that Americans entertained about the use of force."[73]

A second—and ultimately more radical—strategy involved redefining military service, from an obligation to a choice. Believing that internal dissent and public aversion to casualties—a phenomenon sometimes known as *body bag syndrome*—had cost the United States in Vietnam, politicians and military planners sought to remove politically unwilling and economically mobile Americans from wartime service. The first step in this direction came in 1973, when Congress authorized the creation of the All-Volunteer Force (AVF), a move that simultaneously professionalized the US armed forces and fundamentally altered the concept of citizen-soldier. By adopting a "limited liability model of citizenship" (a move that inevitably shifted the burden of the nation's defense to the most economically vulnerable), the armed forces virtually assured that mass protests against the bodily costs of war would be low, even if casualty rates were high.[74] In the future, war would be fought by *other* people's sons (and increasingly daughters). The military had never been truly representative, of course. Class, race, gender, sexuality, and other factors had always affected who served where, when, and in what capacity. Cultural critic Leslie Fiedler admitted he had "never known a single family that had lost a son in Vietnam, or indeed, one with a son wounded, missing in action, or held prisoner of war . . . despite the fact that American casualties in Vietnam are already equal to those of World War I."[75] When he wrote his 1980 essay "What Did You Do in the Class War, Daddy?" James Fallows noted that the postdraft military was less representative than it was during Vietnam (when it was already disproportionately black, poor, and uneducated).[76] In the post-Vietnam, postdraft era, war would be a job left to the professionals—and volunteers would know the risks going in.[77]

The initial trial run of these two interrelated strategies took place in the deserts of Kuwait and Iraq in 1991. At the end of little more than a month of fighting, the war was over—and the United States had won. Surrounded by cheering troops, George H. W. Bush, the last US president to serve in World War II and himself a wounded vet, triumphantly announced, "By God, we've kicked the Vietnam syndrome once and for all!" And, at first, the military's efforts seemed to have paid off. Out of a total US troop deployment of nearly 700,000, only 148 Americans were killed in action, and fewer than 500 members of the armed forces were wounded. Wartime boosters attributed the United States' low casualty rates to advancements in emergency wound treatment, medical evacuation, and post-traumatic care. They also pointed to the United States' increasing capacity to inflict war-winning military power—via long-range aerial bombardment, unmanned drones, and computerized "smart" weapons—without putting American troops in harm's way.[78] Finally, it seemed, the United States had perfected a model for carrying out Henry Luce's vision of the American Century by military means.

However, Americans' early optimism about the possibilities of casualty-free combat—at least among US forces—soon gave way to disappointment. In the years following the ceasefire, the Kuwait War left a widespread legacy of disability and ill health among thousands of US service personnel, including those associated with what has come to be called Gulf War Syndrome. A decade after the war's end, nearly 160,000 Gulf War veterans were receiving government benefits for service-connected disabilities.[79] As the American Century drew to a close, survival rates among wounded soldiers were at an all time high. But the more significant dream—the dream of war without casualties, of the nation imposing its will unimpeded across the globe—remained as distant as it had one hundred years earlier.

Tammy Duckworth

At first glance, Ladda Tammy Duckworth bears little resemblance to the popular stereotype of a wounded hero. The daughter of a Thai immigrant and an ex-Marine, the "self-described girlie girl" joined the ROTC in the early 1990s. Earning a master's degree in international affairs at George Washington University, she enlisted in the Illinois National Guard with the sole purpose of becoming a helicopter pilot, one of the few combat careers open to women at the time.[1] Life in uniform was far from easy. Dubbed "mommy platoon leader," she endured routine verbal abuse from her male cohort. As she recalled to reporter Adam Weinstein, the men in her unit "knew that I was hypersensitive about wanting to be one of the guys, that I wanted to be—pardon my language—a swinging dick, just like everyone else, so they just poked. And I let them, that's the dumb thing."[2] She persisted all the same, eventually coming to command more than forty troops.

On November 12, 2004, the thirty-six-year-old Duckworth was copiloting a Black Hawk helicopter in the skies above Iraq when a rocket-propelled grenade exploded just below her feet. The blast tore off her lower legs and she lost consciousness as her copilot struggled to guide the chopper to the ground. Duckworth awoke in a Baghdad field hospital, her right arm shattered and her body dangerously low on blood. Once stabilized, she followed the aerial trajectory of thousands of severely injured Iraq War soldiers—first to Germany and then on to Walter Reed Medical Center (in her words, the "amputee petting zoo"), where she became an instant celebrity and a prized photo-companion for visiting politicians.

Duckworth has since devoted her career to public service and veterans' advocacy. Narrowly defeated in her bid for Congress in 2006, she headed the Illinois Veterans Bureau from 2006 to 2009 and later went on to serve in the Obama administration as assistant secretary of the Department of Veterans Affairs. At the VA, she "boosted services for homeless vets and created an Office of Online Communications, staffing it with respected military bloggers to help with troops' day-to-day questions."[3] Yet politics was never far from her heart, and in November 2012, Duckworth defeated Tea Party incumbent Joe Walsh to become the first female disabled veteran to serve in the House of Representatives.

Balanced atop her high-tech prostheses (one colored red, white, and blue; the other, a camouflage green), Duckworth might easily be caricatured as a *supercrip*, a term disability scholars use to describe inspirational figures who by sheer force of will manage to "triumph" over their disabilities and achieve extraordinary success. Indeed, it's easy to be awed by her remarkable determination, both before and after her injury. However, as just one of tens of thousands of disabled veterans of Afghanistan and Iraq, Duckworth is far less remarkable than many of us would like to believe. Nearly a century after Great War evangelists predicted the end of war-produced disability, she is a public reminder that the goal of safe, let alone disability-free, combat remains as illusive as ever.

Toward a New Veteranology

At its heart, this has been a book about fantasies and two in particular: the fantasy that the United States can remain a global military power without incurring the social, economic, and physical consequences associated with veterans' disabilities; and the fantasy that Americans will permanently reject war because of the risks to soldiers' bodies and minds.

Both fantasies have been proven false—in World War I, in World War II, in Korea, in Vietnam, in the Persian Gulf. And yet, both continue to seduce and inspire Americans to believe that the Problem of the Disabled Veteran is nearing its end.

Postdisability Dreams in the Age of Terror

On December 18, 2009, James Cameron's long-awaited sci-fi epic *Avatar* debuted in American theaters. Set on a distant moon named Pandora more than a hundred years in the future, the film depicts a conflict between an American mining expedition, protected by a Blackwater-style security force, and the Na'vi, a tribe of ten-foot tall, blue-skinned, ecofriendly primitives. Because Pandora's biosphere is poisonous to humans, expedition scientists travel in the form of "avatars," genetically modified human-Na'vi hybrids that they control remotely from the safety of a lab. The plot accelerates when one company employee, Jake Sully, a paraplegic former Marine, is tasked with infiltrating the indigenous population and driving them off their sacred homelands (fig. 39). If successful, he is promised the restoration of the use of his legs, a prize for which—the audience is made to understand—he would do just about anything. Predictably, the battle-hardened soldier has a change of heart and, still passing as alien and nondisabled, leads the Na'vi in a successful rebellion against his former employers. In the film's final sequence, Sully permanently merges with the avatar body, his political and physical transformation now complete.

Avatar went on to be the highest-grossing film of all time, topping $2.7 billion at the global box office. In the torrent of media coverage that

FIG. 39. In James Cameron's *Avatar* (2009), Sam Worthington plays Jake Sully, a paraplegic ex-marine who eventually transcends his bodily impairments using a remote controlled avatar. Nearly a century after World War I, pop culture imagery of disabled veterans continues to focus on the bodies of white heterosexual men with outwardly visible physical disabilities.

followed its release, critics tended to focus on the film's eye-popping 3-D visuals, its blunt critique of American militarism, and its dubious racial politics. Largely overlooked in the industry hype, however, was *Avatar*'s message about disability: namely, its faith in the power of advanced technology to curtail, if not eliminate, the functional limitations of bodily impairment. James Cameron was by no means the first to speculate on the possibilities of a technologically augmented, postdisability world. Even as World War I still raged, essayist Herbert Kaufman wondered in the pages of *Carry On* magazine, "How much of a body does a man need to earn a living in this year of wheels and wires? . . . What with telephones, elevators, motor cars and like couriers and carriers, a respectable remnant of the human frame can overcome most of the handicaps of mutilation."[1] Since that time, postdisability narratives—from *The Empire Strikes Back* (1980) to *RoboCop* (1987/2014) to *Iron Man* (2008)—have become a staple of American culture, feeding popular fantasies (and fears) about humans' ability to enhance and transcend their corporeal existence. Soon, some futurists predict, not even death will be immune to the unrelenting march of technoprogress. According to acclaimed inventor and author Ray Kurzweil, the "human body version 1.0" is on the precipice of a new stage in biotechnological evolution. Our organs replaced with artificial implants, our cells patrolled by nanotech robots, our minds uploaded into vast computer networks: in the future, death and disability as we know them will be obsolete.[2]

Although by no means the leading factor in *Avatar*'s success, Cameron's vision of biotechnological transcendence undoubtedly struck a special chord with US audiences. At the time of the film's release, the American-led "Global War on Terror" (GWOT) had just entered its eighth year, and the war-weary public was eager for any sign of optimism. Launched in response to the terrorist attacks of September 11, 2001, phase 1 of the GWOT targeted al-Qaeda and Taliban strongholds in Afghanistan, a nation still recovering from the decade-long Soviet invasion of the 1980s. In March 2003, after spending months—falsely it turns out—accusing Iraqi dictator Saddam Hussein of harboring weapons of mass destruction, the Bush administration opened a second front in Iraq. Confident of the United States' technological superiority, Ken Adelman, aide to then secretary of defense Donald Rumsfeld, predicted that the Iraq campaign would be a "cakewalk."[3] Vice president Dick Cheney was similarly upbeat. Asked if the public was "prepared for a long, costly, and bloody battle with significant American casualties," Cheney reassured MSNBC's Tim Russert that American troops would be "greeted as liberators."[4] Indeed, television coverage of the opening hours of the US invasion seemed to suggest that the Iraq War would be a largely bloodless affair, at least as far as American forces were concerned. As "Shock and Awe" missile attacks lit up the Baghdad skyline, many in Washington were confident that the promise of clean, safe, virtual warfare had finally been realized.

However, even in an age of surveillance satellites and computer-guided smart bombs, the fog of war remained as thick as ever. Much to the surprise of US war planners, both Operation Enduring Freedom (Afghanistan) and Operation Iraqi Freedom (Iraq) devolved into grinding anti-guerrilla campaigns, characterized by brutal fighting on all sides. To be sure, America's proclaimed enemies, military or otherwise, bore the brunt of the violence. According to a 2006 *Lancet* study, more than 600,000 Iraqis were killed in the first three years of the US invasion alone.[5] Yet Afghan and Iraqi insurgents did not give up without a fight. Unable to compete with American high-tech weaponry, they quickly turned to homemade bombs and other improvised explosive devices (IEDs in military jargon) to combat US forces in the field. The resulting injuries rivaled the most damaging in the annals of American warfare. Lacking adequate body armor, many IED victims were killed instantly, their flesh ripped apart in showers of flying shrapnel. Those who survived were routinely evacuated with mangled extremities, internal bleeding, fourth-degree burns, and traumatic brain injury (TBI), sometimes billed as the "signature wound" of the Global War on Terror. Exhibited by 50 percent of all IED casualties, symptoms of TBI range from memory loss and blurred vision to depression and impaired brain function.[6] TBI casualties have become so common that, in August 2012, the US Army teamed up with the National Football League to study the long-term effects of head trauma. At a ceremony to mark the joint initiative, NFL commissioner Roger Goodell explained to an audience of retired athletes and West Point cadets, "Together, we can make a big difference, sharing medical research, and helping players and fighters and bringing a greater awareness to society as well."[7]

It is too early to determine the final American casualty roll for the Global War on Terror. Imagined as a permanent war against a permanent enemy, the United States' current campaign will likely produce a steady stream of casualties well into the future. Writing in *Foreign Policy* in early 2008, Harvard business analyst Linda J. Bilmes noted that, by the fifth anniversary of the Iraq invasion, upward of 70,000 US troops had been "wounded in combat, injured in accidents, or airlifted out of the region for emergency medical care." Of the 750,000 Iraq War troops discharged from service, more than a third received "treatment at medical facilities, including at least 100,000 with mental health conditions and 52,000 with post-traumatic stress disorder." One army study calculated that "as many as 20 percent of returning soldiers have suffered mild brain injuries, such as concussions," while tens of thousands came home suffering the effects of severe bodily trauma, including amputations and neurospinal injuries. Over the next century, Bilmes predicted, the United States would spend between $500 and $700 billion on veterans' care—or roughly the same amount that had been spent on military operations to that point. (As for the total cost of the war, she and her coauthor, the Nobel Prize–winning economist Joseph Stiglitz, projected a

$3 trillion price tag, only to later admit that their estimate was too low.)[8] Nearly a century after pension critics grumbled about the high cost of veterans' care, the United States is no closer to lowering the monetary toll of its military adventures.

New Wars, Familiar Stories

In many respects, the disabled soldiers of Iraq and Afghanistan return home to a nation markedly different from the one that greeted their doughboy counterparts nearly a century earlier. Thanks to the disability rights movement, American culture is more accepting of disabled people than it was in 1919. Today's disabled veterans are guaranteed legal protection, within limits, under the Americans with Disabilities Act (1990), and courses in disability studies and history are taught at colleges across the United States. The fragmentation of the mass media has allowed for a diversity of cultural representations of disabled veterans, beyond the old archetypes of pitiful amputee and deranged killer. Even as mainstream news outlets turned away from the Iraq War, images of disabled veterans circulated widely on TV talk shows, prime-time scripted dramas, and serial melodramas, many of which, according to television scholar Stacy Takacs, "open up questions about the conduct, costs, and consequences of imperial warfare."[9] At the same time, disabled vets have been able to use new media technologies, especially online video-sharing and blog sites, to construct their own cultural representations, beyond the confines of traditional veterans' groups.

The veterans themselves are different too. One of the most significant changes from 1917–18 is the rising number of female combatants. As of 2009, more than 160,000 female soldiers had been sent to Afghanistan and Iraq, up from 7,500 in Vietnam and 41,000 in the first Gulf War.[10] Today's military is not a land of equality. Sexism and sexual harassment continue to run rampant, and women in uniform are routinely the targets of misogynistic slurs, sexual degradation, and violent assault.[11] According to Robert J. Topmiller and T. Kerby Neill, "Over 70 percent of women vets seeking counseling report being raped while in the military."[12] Even so, the widening acceptance of female combatants, as well as the recent repeal of "Don't Ask, Don't Tell," suggests that the military is taking slow, often begrudging steps, toward meeting the basic standards of civil rights.

However, I'm struck by how much has stayed the same. Despite rising numbers of female vets, official representations of disabled veterans, including those enshrined at the American Veterans Disabled for Life Memorial on the National Mall, remain almost universally focused on the bodies of men. Issues of masculinity—particularly the need to help disabled male veterans return to a state of economic productivity and sexual virility—continue to dominate media coverage of wounded soldiers. Moreover, even as the conflicts in Iraq and Afghanistan have demonstrated the destructive capacity of seemingly dated weapons (IEDs, AK-47s), much of the popular journalism around disabled veterans remains saturated with a gross technophilia, waxing poetically about the latest high-tech solution to disabled veterans' problems.

Likewise, the disabled soldier remains a popular symbol among critics of American militarism and government indifference. In April 2004, BD, the football coach turned soldier in Garry Trudeau's comic strip *Doonesbury*, lost a leg in a rocket-propelled grenade attack near Fallujah, leading some newspapers to pull the strip. Two years later, Pulitzer Prize–winning cartoonist Tom Toles resurrected the semimythical "basket case" as an antidote to the euphemistic proclamations of former secretary of defense Donald Rumsfeld. General Peter Pace, then chairman of the Joint Chiefs of Staff, along with its five members, criticized the cartoonist's "callous depiction of those who have volunteered to defend this nation, and as a result, have suffered traumatic and life-altering wounds." Toles defended his cartoon, as did Dave Autry, deputy communications director for the Disabled American Veterans. "It was graphic, no doubt about it," Autry admitted. "But it drove home a point, that there are critically ill patients that certainly need to be attended to."[13] That said, much antiwar art continues to stigmatize disabled people, reducing them to horror-objects designed to fascinate and shock (fig. 40).

There are other similarities between the Great War era and the War on Terror years. Veterans and their families continue to encounter numerous problems negotiating the vast VA bureaucracy, even with the help of government-appointed counselors. Disability claims routinely take months to process, and the typical wounded combatant has to fill out more than twenty forms to receive disability benefits. Furthermore, many veterans believe that the VA disability ratings schedule is too rigid, and that the armed forces have been slow to recognize the long-term

FIG. 40. A century after soldiers and antiwar groups began to publicize the existance of "basket cases," artists from across the political spectrum continue to use quadruple amputees to criticize the architects of US foreign policy and the global projection of American militarism. The first image is an editorial cartoon produced by Tom Toles for the *Washington Post*; the second was posted on the website of White Aryan Resistance, a white supremacy group based in California. Despite their ideological differences, both images draw sharp distinctions between the material reality of the veteran's mangled body—held up as a source of authenticity—and the mystifying nature of military discourse (e.g., the euphemistic language of "Dr. Rumsfeld," the "crummy medal" received by the disabled skinhead). Tom Toles, "I'm Listing Your Condition as 'Battle Hardened,'" Toles © 2006 The Washington Post. Reprinted with permission of Universal Uclick. All rights reserved. White Aryan Resistance, "George Bush Sent Me to Iraq to Fight a War for Israel and All I Got Was This Crummy Medal."

effects of TBI on combat casualties returning from overseas. One official with the Department of Defense even suggested that the cost of caring for disabled veterans was "taking away from the nation's ability to defend itself," a charge that has been repeated by critics of the United States' pension system since the Civil War.[14]

Worst of all, scandals at some of the nation's top military hospitals reveal familiar patterns of negligence and neglect. In February 2007, *Washington Post* reporters Dana Priest and Anne Hull published a headline-grabbing exposé of the conditions at Walter Reed Medical Center, the nation's premier treatment facility for disabled combatants. Their two-month investigation found disabled Iraq War veterans living in squalid, cockroach-infested rooms, where black mold dotted the walls and mouse feces stained the floors. Men with disabling memory and cognitive issues were forced to navigate the large campus on their own, and many patients described a general attitude of indifference among hospital staff.[15] Similar reports poured in from across the country, and Walter Reed's commander, major general George Weightman, was quickly fired, as was secretary of the army Francis Harvey.[16]

In the wake of the scandal, the army attempted to reform its tarnished image by establishing a series of warrior transition units (WTUs) designed to "provide closely managed care" for recent veterans with severe physical or psychological trauma. As of April 2012, there were some 7,200 soldiers stationed at warrior transition units across the United States. But, as the *New York Times* and other sources reported, WTUs did little to transform the culture of neglect that continues to pervade sectors of today's military. Consigned to these "warehouses of despair," sometimes for days on end, patients complained of harsh treatment and an over-reliance upon narcotics and psychotropic drugs to treat their symptoms. A study at one unit found that a majority of the noncommissioned officers in charge of patient discipline "believed that soldiers were faking post-traumatic stress or exaggerating their symptoms."[17] Nearly a century after the Great War's end, disabled veterans remain a suspect class, marginalized even by those charged with their care.[18]

To an outside observer, the fact that today's veterans face many of the same obstacles as those encountered in 1918 prompts the question of why Americans have failed to learn from their mistakes. Why is it, after every war, journalists and veterans themselves report the same old stories of abuse, indifference, and neglect? Why, despite our promises to "never forget," do disabled veterans remain vulnerable to the vicissitudes of collective memory and public policy? Why do we conclude that paying with bodies and minds is worth the price of global influence and power?

In his recent book, *The War Comes Home: Washington's Battle against America's Veterans* (2009), journalist Aaron Glantz, who has spent years documenting the plight of disabled veterans, provides some compelling answers. He points to the fact that "Washington officials, like Americans in general, prefer to see war as a series of lines and arrows on a map rather than something with consequences for human beings." In the abstract, war can be glorious, manly, even mundane—but "when the American public comes face-to-face with the true cost of war, war itself becomes less popular." He also notes the economic vulnerability and political fragmentation of veterans themselves. Drawn largely from the ranks of the rural and urban poor, today's disabled veterans rarely vote as a class and often lack the deep pockets and lobbying muscle of other interest groups. Most damningly, Glantz ascribes the nation's policy failures to a concerted effort to disguise the bodily toll of American militarism. "The sorry state of care for Iraq and Afghanistan war veterans is not an accident," he argues. "It's on purpose. After the invasion of Iraq in 2003, the Bush administration fought every effort to improve care for wounded and disabled veterans. At the root of that fight was its desire to hide the true costs of the war in order to boost public support."[19]

Another factor impeding Americans' ability to recognize the bodily cost of war is the ideology of individualism that has been a core part of the nation's social imagination since its founding. Despite the rise of the welfare state, many Americans continue to view *social* problems as *individual* problems and thus are unwilling (or unable) to recognize the ways in which broader structures of meaning and power can circumscribe people's lives. If disabled veterans somehow fall behind the rest of us, the logic goes, it is not because of the social environment or even discrimination; it is because as individuals they lack the will and determination to succeed. In the 1910s and 1920s, this viewpoint was at the heart of the rehabilitation movement, which sought to "deveteranize" disabled veterans: that is, transform veterans (as a class) into a group of civilians who would rise and fall by their own merits. Such goals have been particularly resonant over the last three decades, as the New Right has systematically dismantled New Deal and Great Society social safety nets across the board. Indeed, the fact that disabled veterans—unlike other socially vulnerable populations—have been able to hang onto many of their state benefits is a testament to their willingness to fight as a class to demand an exceptional status among US citizens.

Since Vietnam, an additional factor has made it even easier for disabled veterans to slip between the cracks in American society: the professionalization of the military itself. Throughout much of the twentieth century, the viability of American war-making has depended upon public recognition of veterans' sacrifices to help fuel mass enlistment and win consent for future military endeavors. Following World War I, advocates of rehabilitation charged that reconstructing wounded doughboys was a matter of national security, arguing that it would affect later generations' willingness to serve. The need to recognize—and reward—

veterans' collective sacrifices continued throughout the 1940s and 1950s, as "Good War" veterans, including John F. Kennedy, George H. W. Bush, and Bob Dole, sought to leverage their war-wounded status to gain high political office. In fact, in the mid-1940s, veterans' experts confidently asserted that every family in the country was directly affected by the conflict's legacy of injury. Not so today. In a nation of more than 300 million people, veterans represent but a small fraction of the population, disabled veterans a smaller fraction still. Ten years into a permanent War on Terror, it is likely that many, perhaps even most, Americans do not encounter disabled veterans on a regular basis. But even if they did, there's little to suggest it would either translate into heightened social visibility for disabled veterans or slow down the military machine. In an age where military budgets have become sacrosanct and war itself has been ceded to the "professionals," public support of the sort required in the world wars, Korea, and even Vietnam is not necessary. If today's disabled soldiers are no longer recognized as a Problem (with a capital P), it is not because their numbers are decreasing—they aren't—or because they are receiving more generous care—far from it. They aren't recognized as a Problem because, when it comes to waging permanent war, the fate of disabled veterans is no longer a complicating factor.

Ultimately, Americans' repeated failure to confront the Problem of the Disabled Veteran stems from the impossibility of reconciling the United States' global military ambitions with the risk inherent in all military conflict. In recent years, the United States' solution seems to be to replace human flesh with machine and to improve the speed of post-injury care, all the while continuing to sacrifice the bodies of the nation's enemies instead of its own. But this approach rests on a faulty logic: that somehow injury can be eliminated from warfare; that with enough scientific management and technological know-how, with the combined minds of government and the private sector thrown at the problem, the United States will be able to eliminate war's effect on the men and women who fight. This is the same self-deluding ambition that captivated the ballistics experts of the late nineteenth century, the atomic scientists of World War II, and the body armor manufacturers of the present. And, as it has in the past, it is doomed to fail. That is because injury is not an error in warfare; it is not a mistake to be fixed. It is the *purpose* of warfare.

Looking toward the future, I believe only three strategies can help curb America's Disabled Veteran Problem in the twenty-first century: adopt a "kill-them-all" military mentality (preemptively slaughtering the nation's enemies from a distance), work to eliminate prejudice toward all manifestations of bodily difference in American society, or abandon war as we know it. I would suggest the latter two paths. I fear we have set our sights on the first one.

Inspiration from the Past

For those of us concerned about the social consequences of the United States' seemingly endless wars, it is easy to be despondent. A decade after the start of the Global War on Terror, the gap between patriotic rhetoric and painful reality seems to widen every year. A few monuments notwithstanding, there's little evidence that disabled vets will remain in the public eye for long. The high rates of homelessness and substance abuse among Iraq and Afghanistan War veterans suggests that many are in danger of disappearing altogether, swallowed up in the permanent underclass that has come to define large segments of twenty-first-century American society. Disabled veterans do enjoy a privileged status when compared to other vulnerable constituencies, including disabled civilians. Across the nation, patriotic volunteers have raised tens of millions of dollars on disabled veterans' behalf. But without sustained and organized political pressure, who's to say that expansive veterans' programs can survive the rapid dismantling of the welfare state?

Perhaps the peace warriors of the 1920s and 1930s were right: *Wars happen, soldiers get hurt, people forget. There's nothing we can do about it, short of eliminating war altogether.* This is an unlikely prospect for a nation that remains addicted to armed solutions to political problems. But an inspiration from the past gives me reason for hope.

At the end of his book, *The Veteran Comes Back* (1944), sociologist and former Great War soldier Willard Waller called for the development of an interdisciplinary body of research on disabled veterans and their problems. This new field of study, which Waller deemed *veteranology*, was aimed at helping disabled veterans readjust to peacetime society as healthy and productive citizens. Flush with the heady optimism that would come to characterize much of post–World War II American life, Waller envisioned a great center of veteran research in which cooperative studies of the veteran problem could be carried on. . . . In such a center doctors and psychiatrists could invent new methods to heal the minds and bodies of veterans, social workers could work out the best practices for veterans' relief and try to put the psychoneurotic veteran back on his feet, historians could inquire into the fate of veterans in the past, and economists, psychologists, sociologists, criminologists, and experts in government could carry on their appropriate researches.

Waller's model veteranology facility included laboratories, libraries, planning bureaus, and a "division of propaganda to disseminate its findings to the public."[20] Like his Progressive-era forebears, Waller was confident that comprehensive research and education would save the United States billions of dollars in pensions and hospital care. Equally important, it would enable countless disabled veterans, past and present, to make the hard transition back to civilian life.

More than sixty years later, Waller's vision of a nationally funded center of veteranology remains little more than a pipedream. Yet the need to think critically and comprehensibly about disabled veterans is as pressing as ever. Thus, I want to close by issuing a call for a New Veteranology, one that seeks not only to improve the lives of disabled veterans but also to ask tough questions about the cultural values underlying so much of the work on veterans' behalf. What does it mean to readjust in the wake of traumatic impairment, and by whose standards should veterans' readjustment be measured? To what extent do current rehabilitation practices reinforce socially limiting categories of gender, sexuality, and health? What role should veterans' groups play in directing future research on veterans' relief? And, as the US military increasingly outsources its functions to private contractors, how will the social contract between disabled veterans and the federal government evolve? Answering such questions will require the cooperation of a wide array of researchers, activists, and interest groups.

As its starting point, the New Veteranology should be rooted in the ideals and activism of the disability rights movement. On a conceptual level, this means discarding the medical model of disability in favor a more nuanced understanding of the ways disability functions as an "elastic social category shaped and reshaped by cultural values, societal arrangements, public policies, and professional practices."[21] Furthermore, in keeping with the disability rights mantra, "Nothing about Us without Us," the New Veteranology needs to draw heavily upon the insights, activism, and life struggles of disabled veterans themselves. In the past, physicians, psychiatrists, and social workers have devalued the voices and experiences of disabled veterans in order to assert their professional authority and expertise. In today's veteranology, all parties must formally recognize disabled veterans' agency, both individual and collective, to determine their treatment, rehabilitation, and future endeavors.

Indeed, a New Veteranology would have to cultivate honest dialogues between all of the parties—disabled veterans and military officials, academics and activists, policy makers and publicists, doctors and social workers—engaged in disabled veterans' relief. Such dialogues should include people whose disabilities cannot be traced to military service. All too often, disabled veterans have leveraged their wounded-warrior status to win benefits that are off-limits to the civilian disabled. However, as the All-Volunteer Force shrinks and the gap between civilian and military culture widens, disabled veterans risk falling into obscurity. If twenty-first-century disabled veterans hope to win social justice, humane treatment, and equal opportunity (for themselves and others), they will have to reach out to their civilian counterparts.

Beyond that, disabled veterans would be well served by considering their experiences from a transnational perspective, as members of a larger population of marginalized subjects victimized by the violence of globalization. To be sure, when it comes to the social consequences of physical and mental impairment, the world—to misparaphrase the *New York Times* columnist Thomas Friedman—is far from flat. Nevertheless, contemporary populations of disabled veterans from the United States to the Sudan are products of the same global system, their traumas visible markers of a new era of perpetual and largely taken-for-granted warfare. For globalization, whether defined as neoimperial expansion or international interconnectedness, is a violent process. It disrupts communities, transforms economies, spurs mass migrations—factors that increasingly lead marginalized populations to view military service as their only viable opportunity for a better life. Because globalization frequently, if not always, is accompanied by military conflict, the mangling of bodies remains one of its key features. Indeed, disabled veterans can be grouped—alongside political refugees, migrant workers, and slaves—among globalization's most victimized yet fastest-growing populations.

Finally, and most importantly, a New Veteranology must be grounded in healthy skepticism about the narratives and mythologies that continue to perpetuate America's culture of war. Writing in 2005, Andrew Bacevich observed, "Today as never before in their history Americans are enthralled with military power. . . . More than America's matchless material abundance or even the effusions of its pop culture, the nation's arsenal of high-tech weaponry and the soldiers who employ that arsenal have come to signify who we are and what we stand for."[22] At a time when the US military uses slick advertising campaigns and video games to win new recruits, veteranologists must pressure government officials to be more honest about war's legacies of disability and death. In turn, students of the New Veteranology must seek to educate the public about the social, psychological, and physical consequences of war—and its aftermath—without resorting to stigmatization and sentimentality.

None of this will be easy. Despite the US military's history of failures, stalemates, and catastrophes over the past half century, Americans remain seduced by war—as a proving ground for masculinity, a vehicle for progressive change, and a stage upon which to exhibit national power. Even so, it is imperative that Americans take a hard look at the cultural fantasies that continue to spur the United States into battle. Until Americans tackle this final project head on—until they are willing to reexamine their own complicity in war's devastation of bodies and minds—the disabled veteran will remain an ever pervasive Problem.

ACKNOWLEDGMENTS

I'll let you in on a little secret. For decades, one of the cheapest lunches in Washington, DC, could be found at the Walter Reed Army Medical Center. Its cafeteria menu was subsidized, a tacit acknowledgment (I can only hope) of the economic hardships facing many military families. I made this discovery in the fall of 2004 when conducting research at the National Museum of Health and Medicine, a morbid archive of medical paraphernalia, tissue samples, and surgical photographs tucked into a quiet corner of Walter Reed's sprawling 113-acre campus. I was in graduate school at the time, and the cafeteria's discount prices were a pleasant relief from the exorbitant sums I'd been paying elsewhere in my travels. Still, as I gobbled my veggie burger, salad, and hot apple pie—all for less than five bucks—I couldn't help but reflect upon my surroundings. Most of all, I was struck by how little I knew about my fellow diners: the teenagers in bathrobes, walking stiffly on canes like old men; the amputees in wheelchairs, trays balanced upon their knees, gliding to a halt beneath an open table. Who were these men and women? How did they come to this place?

In retrospect, my ignorance is understandable—and worthy of acknowledgment. I never served in the armed forces, and though my father was a National Guardsman in the late 1960s, he rarely spoke of his time in uniform. What's more, mainstream American culture hasn't exactly raised me to think about what happens when men and women are injured in warfare. When I started my research, I wasn't even sure where Walter Reed was located (I was hoping California) or whether it was still in operation.

Nearly a decade later, I'm not certain I have any definitive answers, only a nagging belief that—despite all of our technological advances and optimistic rhetoric—the most recent generation of war-wounded vets will face many of same problems as their twentieth-century forebears. Still, if this book can shed even a little light on the hidden histories of disabled veterans in America, it will be worth the effort.

To that end, I have benefited from the friendship, generosity, and intellectual support of a host of people. The following have my special thanks:

Jenny Gowen: She married me, is smart and strong, and is my best friend. It's hard to imagine my life (or this book) without her. And I don't want to.

David Gray: His fingerprints are on every page. If this book has any lasting value, it's because of him.

David Monteyne: My writing partner from graduate school, he taught me that readers don't need five or six examples to prove a point. Two often suffice. Sadly, it's a lesson I still haven't learned.

Peter Kizilos-Clift: My inspiration to look beyond an academic audience. I continue to look. Write on.

Andrew Rosa: On those long drives to Stillwater, he was my ear and I was his.

Matt Smith: Always interested, always interesting. My best pal, he reminds me that good writing is work—and takes work.

Kris Horvath: Long ago, Kris convinced me to take World War I seriously. I pick up where he leaves off.

My colleagues at Oklahoma State University in the History Department and the American Studies Program, especially Laura Belmonte and Stacy Takacs, who supported me at every turn.

All of the mentors and fellow travelers who provided feedback, writing opportunities, and professional advice along the way: Stephen Ortiz, Pearl James, David Gerber, among many others.

Michael Sherry, Susan Burch, and Lewis Erenberg, whose constructive and encouraging reviews of my manuscript showed me a vision of what this book could become.

All of the good people at the University of Chicago Press. Special thanks are reserved for Carol Fisher Saller (whose copyediting saved me countless embarrassments), Tim McGovern (always quick to answer the most tedious of emails), and my incomparably patient editor Doug Mitchell. For some reason, Doug never gave up on me and never scolded (despite my procrastination). It's not his style. I pay a mortgage (not rent) because of Doug.

Librarians and archivists in general, and the librarians and archivists of these institutions in particular: the Minnesota Historical Society, the Library of Congress, the National Archives (DC and College Park), the Swarthmore College Peace Collection, the Margaret Herrick Library, the Wilson Library and the Wangensteen Historical Library of Biology and Medicine at the University of Minnesota, the National Museum of Health and Medicine, the Dakota County Historical Society (Lakeville, Minnesota), the UCLA Film & Television Archive, the Edmon Low Library at Oklahoma State University.

The Mays' writing group at the University of Minnesota, especially Matt Becker, Megan Feeney, Scott Laderman, Melissa Williams, Jennifer Beckham, Sharon Leon, and Stephen Young. I also want to thank Keith Richotte for showing me how to live with my wife, and Joseph Bauerkemper for allowing me to act like a "mentor" (at least, for a year or so).

The American Studies Department at the University of Minnesota, where this project first took shape. I am especially indebted to Thomas C. Wolfe (in whose office I first began to think seriously about disabled soldiers); Jani Scandura (who once assured me that I would be working on this book for five more years; I laughed—that was seven years ago); and Elaine Tyler May (the most generous, encouraging, and persistently relevant scholar I know). I reserve particular thanks for Lary L. May, a model teacher and an even better mentor. If I've learned anything from Lary, it's that one should never shy away from the big argument, even if it means exposing the ugly side of something that people love. I hope this book spins his mind.

And finally my family, especially my mom and my sister, who believed me when I said I was writing a book even when I wasn't.

This book is dedicated to Prudence, Simon, Charlie, "los Hogg," and the Bear.

NOTES

INTRODUCTION

1. Richard Seelye Jones, *A History of the American Legion* (Indianapolis: Bobbs-Merrill, 1946), 3.
2. White House Press Office, "President Bush Goes on Run with Staff Sergeant Christian Bagge," June 27, 2006 (available at http://www.whitehouse.gov/news/releases/2006/06/20060627-5.html).
3. Bagge expresses this sentiment in a video on the website of Homes for Our Troops, a nonprofit dedicated to building specially adapted domiciles for severely injured war veterans. At the time, Bagge, his wife, and his young child were living in a two-story home with only limited wheelchair access. Available at http://www.homesforourtroops.org/site/PageServer?pagename=ChristianBagge.
4. Mike Francis, "Ore. Soldier Deals with Loss of Legs in Iraq," September 17, 2005 (available at http://www.kgw.com/iraq/stories/kgw_091705_life_soldier%27s_loss.5e76a869.html). In his subsequent public statements, Bagge continued to express misgivings about the US mission in Iraq. When interviewed by CNN on the eve of the 2007 "surge" of some 20,000 additional troops in Iraq, Bagge declared: "I've always supported the president. I've always wanted to believe that it's going to work and this time, I just—I don't think it's going to work. We have 21,000 troops to come in and secure that part of the country, right? Now what happens when we pull out? The same thing that's happening now. We know that the solution lies in the Iraqi people to secure their own country, not in the number of troops that we put there." *CNN Live Event Special*, aired January 11, 2007 (transcript available at http://transcripts.cnn.com/TRANSCRIPTS/0701/11/se.01.html).
5. The mission of the Wounded Warrior Project can be found on the group's website: http://www.woundedwarriorproject.org/mission.aspx (accessed October 24, 2012).
6. Historically, Americans' fears about the social and political consequences of war-produced disability have gone by other names as well, including the "problem of the disabled soldier," the "problem of the war cripple," the "problem of the returning veteran," and the "problem of the wounded soldier." In this book, I have chosen to capitalize the Problem of the Disabled Veteran (i.e., the social crisis and moral panic) in order to distinguish it from the problems experienced by disabled veterans themselves.
7. Not surprisingly, disabled World War I veterans from European and Commonwealth nations have attracted far more scholarly attention than their American counterparts. Key studies include Robert Whalen, *Bitter Wounds: German Victims of the Great War, 1914–1939* (Ithaca: Cornell University Press, 1984); Joanna Bourke, *Dismembering the Male: Men's Bodies, Britain, and the Great War* (Chicago: University of Chicago Press, 1996); Deborah Cohen, *The War Come Home: Disabled Veterans in Great Britain and Germany, 1914–1939* (Berkeley: University of California Press, 2001); Marina Larsson, *Shattered Anzacs: Living with the Scars of War* (Sydney: University of New South Wales Press, 2009).

8. For statistics about American casualties, see Allan R. Millet and Peter Maslowski, *For the Common Defense: A Military History of the United States*, rev. ed. (New York: Free Press, 1994), 653.

9. John Maurice Clark, *The Costs of the World War to the American People* (New Haven: Yale University Press, 1931), 188; K. Walter Hickel, "Medicine, Bureaucracy, and Social Welfare: The Politics of Disability Compensation for American Veterans of World War I," in *The New Disability History: American Perspectives*, ed. Paul K. Longmore and Lauri Umansky (New York: New York University Press, 2001), 238.

10. David A. Gerber, "Introduction: Finding Disabled Veterans in History," in *Disabled Veterans in History*, ed. David A. Gerber (Ann Arbor: University of Michigan Press, 2000), 19.

11. On the social construction of disability, see Susan Burch and Ian Sutherland, "Who's Not Yet Here? American Disability History," *Radical History Review* 94 (Winter 2006): 127–47.

12. Paul K. Longmore, *Why I Burned My Book and Other Essays on Disability* (Philadelphia: Temple University Press, 2003), 56.

13. On the "inexpressibility" of pain, see Elaine Scarry, *The Body in Pain: The Making and Unmaking of the World* (New York: Oxford University Press, 1985).

14. Daniel Pick, *War Machine: The Rationalisation of Slaughter in the Modern Age* (New Haven: Yale University Press, 1993), 16.

15. According to a report by the American Legion, as of June 30, 1928, 2,247 female Great War veterans had service-connected disabilities. Of the 192 women hospitalized for their injuries, 77 suffered from tuberculosis, 54 from mental disease, and 61 from general medical or surgical ailments. "Proceedings of the Tenth National Convention of the American Legion" [1928], 70th Cong., 2nd sess. (1929), H. Doc. 388, 129.

16. Cf. Jennifer D. Keene, "The Long Journey Home: African American World War I Veterans and Veterans' Policies," in *Veterans' Policies, Veterans' Politics: New Perspectives on Veterans in the Modern United States*, ed. Stephen R. Ortiz (Gainesville: University Press of Florida, 2012), 146–70; Adriane Lentz-Smith, *Freedom Struggles: African Americans and World War I* (Cambridge: Harvard University Press, 2009).

17. On the structural nature of whiteness in American society, see George Lipsitz, *The Possessive Investment in Whiteness: How White People Profit from Identity Politics*, rev. ed. (Philadelphia: Temple University Press, 2006); and Steve Martinot, *The Machinery of Whiteness: Studies in the Structures of Racialization* (Philadelphia: Temple University Press, 2010).

18. No longer in fashion with historians, the myth of the "lost generation" continues to resonate within popular culture and some literary circles, providing a simplistic (and ultimately distorting) framework for understanding the diversity of responses to World War I. Classic critiques of the "Lost Generation" include Roderick Nash, *The Nervous Generation: American Thought, 1917–1930* (Chicago: Rand McNally, 1970), and the essays in Lawrence R. Broer and John D. Walther, eds., *Dancing Fools and Weary Blues: The Great Escape of The Twenties* (Bowling Green, OH: Bowling Green State University Popular Press, 1990).

19. Even the best scholars of military history have an unfortunate habit of pushing the wounded and disabled to the margins of the national war story. In her otherwise

brilliant and highly critical synthesis, *The Vietnam Wars, 1945–1990,* for example, Marilyn B. Young devotes less than three pages (out of nearly four hundred) to post-traumatic stress disorder. See *The Vietnam Wars, 1945–1990* (New York: Harper-Perennial, 1991), 321–22, 323.

20. Linda J. Bilmes, "Iraq's 100-Year Mortgage," *Foreign Policy Magazine* (March-April 2008): 85.

THOMAS H. GRAHAM

1. The story of Thomas H. Graham is taken from Office of the Surgeon General of the United States, *The Medical and Surgical History of the War of the Rebellion, 1861–1865,* pt. 2, vol. 2 (Washington, GPO, 1883), 96. Hereafter abbreviated as *MSHWR.*
2. Richard H. Shyrock, "A Medical Perspective on the Civil War," *American Quarterly* 14:2 (Summer 1962): 162.

CHAPTER ONE

1. Theda Skocpol, *Protecting Soldiers and Mothers: The Political Origins of Social Policy in the United States* (Cambridge: Harvard University Press, 1992), 151.
2. Julia Cresswell, *The Oxford Dictionary of Word Origins,* 2nd ed. (New York: Oxford University Press, 2009); *Oxford Dictionary of English* (Oxford: Oxford University Press, 2010).
3. Martha Edwards, "Philoctetes in Historical Context," in *Disabled Veterans in History,* ed. David A. Gerber (Ann Arbor: University of Michigan Press, 2000), 65.
4. Quoted in Bernard Rostker, *Providing for the Casualties of War: The American Experience through World War II* (Santa Monica, CA: RAND Corporation, 2013), 11.
5. Edwards, 64.
6. Matthew Leigh, "Wounding and Popular Rhetoric at Rome," *BICS* 40 (1995): 195–216; Douglas C. McMurtrie, *The Disabled Soldier* (New York: Macmillan, 1919), 13.
7. Rostker, 14–15.
8. Sharon Romm, "Arms by Design: From Antiquity to the Renaissance," *Plastic and Reconstructive Surgery* 84:1 (July 1989): 158.
9. Geoffrey L. Hudson, "Disabled Veterans and the State in Early Modern England," in Gerber, *Disabled Veterans in History,* 119.
10. McMurtrie, 13–14.
11. Hudson, 117, 119.
12. For more on the concept of "martial citizenship," see Patrick J. Kelly, *Creating a National Home: Building the Veterans' Welfare State, 1860–1900* (Cambridge: Harvard University Press, 1997).
13. Hudson, 117.
14. Henri-Jacques Stiker, *A History of Disability,* trans. William Sayers (Ann Arbor: University of Michigan Press, 1999), 101.
15. McMurtrie, 20.
16. Ibid., 22–23; "American Has Rewarded Veterans of All Wars," *New York Times,* March 15, 1931, 141.
17. Dixon Wecter, *When Johnny Comes Marching Home* (Cambridge, MA: Riverside Press, 1944), 52–53. On the history of disabled Revolutionary War veterans, see Daniel Blackie, "Disabled Revolutionary War Veterans and the Construction of

Disability in the Early United States, c. 1776–1840" (PhD diss., University of Helsinki, 2010).

18. David A. Gerber, "Veterans," in *Encyclopedia of American Disability History*, ed. Susan Burch (New York: Facts on File, 2009), 3:928.

19. Millet and Maslowski, 163.

20. John Ellis, *The Social History of the Machine Gun* (Baltimore: Johns Hopkins University Press, 1986), 25.

21. Richard H. Shryock, "A Medical Perspective on the Civil War," *American Quarterly* 14:2 (Summer 1962): 164–65.

22. Ira M. Rutkow, *Bleeding Blue and Gray: The Untold Story of Civil War Medicine* (New York: Random House, 2005), 40.

23. Quoted in Shryock, 162.

24. Laurann Figg and Jane Farrell-Beck, "Amputation in the Civil War: Physical and Social Dimensions," *Journal of the History of Medicine and Allied Sciences* 48:4 (1993): 454.

25. Richard A. Gabriel, *The Painful Field: The Psychiatric Dimension of Modern War* (New York: Greenwood Press, 1988), 15, 18, 124–25.

26. On drug and alcohol use among Civil War veterans, see James Marten, "Nomads in Blue: Disabled Veterans and Alcohol at the National Home," in Gerber, *Disabled Veterans in History*, 275–94.

27. Eric T. Dean, Jr., *Shook over Hell: Post-Traumatic Stress, Vietnam, and the Civil War* (Cambridge: Harvard University Press, 1997), 151–53.

28. Kelly, 3.

29. Wecter, 187, 183.

30. Ibid., 211.

31. William Pyrle Dillingham, *Federal Aid to Veterans, 1917–1941* (Gainesville: University of Florida Press, 1952), 185.

32. Kelly, 26.

33. Figg and Farrell-Beck, 462.

34. Jaylynn Olsen Padilla, "Army of 'Cripples': North Civil War Amputees, Disability, and Manhood in Victorian America" (PhD diss., University of Delaware, 2007), 85.

35. Wecter, 213.

36. Padilla, 88, 89.

37. Ibid., 99–100; Kim E. Nielsen, *A Disability History of the United States* (Boston: Beacon Press, 2012), 83.

38. E.g., *MSHWR* 9:309, 366.

39. Robert I. Goler and Michael G. Rhode, "From Individual Trauma to National Policy: Tracking the Uses of Civil War Medical Records," in Gerber, *Disabled Veterans in History*, 171.

40. Skocpol, 151, 128.

41. William Pyrle Dillingham, *Federal Aid to Veterans, 1917–1941* (Gainesville: University of Florida Press, 1952), 212. Disabled Union troops were not the only veterans receiving pensions during the late nineteenth and early twentieth centuries. Veterans of the War of 1812, the Mexican War, the Transcontinental Indian Wars, the Spanish-American War, and the United States' intervention in the Boxer Rebellion, as well as veterans of the regular armed forces, were also eligible for various forms of monetary compensation.

42. Disabled Confederate veterans had no access to federal soldiers' homes. See R. B. Rosenburg, *Living Monuments: Confederate Soldiers' Homes in the New South* (Chapel Hill: University of North Carolina Press, 1995).
43. Kelly, 2, 188, 50, 108, 105.
44. Abraham Lincoln, "Lincoln's Second Inaugural Address," in *Lincoln's Gettysburg Oration and First and Second Inaugural Addresses* (New York: Duffield and Co., 1907), 46.
45. Ibid., 3.
46. Quoted in "The Pension List," *Harper's Weekly*, February 19, 1898, 171.
47. On the pension examiner's efforts to weed out undeserving vets, see Padilla, 87–94. On widespread suspicions about Civil War pensioners, see Peter Blanck, "Civil War Pensions and Disability," *Ohio State Law Journal* 62 (2001): 109–238.
48. Padilla, 50–54.
49. Quoted in Wecter, 209.
50. Stephen Crane, *The Red Badge of Courage*, ed. Donald Pizer (New York: W. W. Norton, 1994).
51. Figg and Farrell-Beck, 474.
52. Robert I. Goler, "The Symbol of the Veteran Amputee in American Culture" (PhD diss., George Mason University, 2009), 16; on postwar reconciliation, also see David W. Blight, *Race and Reunion: The Civil War in American Memory* (Cambridge: Belknap Press of Harvard University Press, 2002).
53. Cf. Nielsen, 78–99; Sarah Rose, "No Right to Be Idle: The Invention of Disability, 1850–1930" (PhD diss., University of Illinois at Chicago, 2008).
54. On the emergence of the normal body, see Lennard J. Davis, *Enforcing Normalcy: Disability, Deafness, and the Body* (London: Verso, 1995).
55. John F. Kasson, *Houdini, Tarzan, and the Perfect Man: The White Male Body and the Challenge of Modernity in America* (New York: Hill and Wang, 2001), 41; D. A. Sargent, "Physical Characteristics of the Athlete," in D. A. Sargent et al., *Athletic Sports* (New York: Charles Scribner's Sons, 1897), 100.
56. Douglas C. Baynton, "Disability and the Justification of Inequality in American History," in *The New Disability History: American Perspectives*, ed. Paul K. Longmore and Lauri Umansky (New York: New York University Press, 2001), 36.
57. On the importance of "wholeness" to Victorian notions of total health, see Bruce Haley, *The Healthy Body and Victorian Culture* (Cambridge: Harvard University Press, 1978).
58. Quoted in Erin O'Connor, "'Fractions of Men': Engendering Amputation in Victorian Culture," *Comparative Studies in Society and History* 39:4 (October 1997): 749.
59. *MSHWR* 8:368.
60. On the legal segregation and institutionalization of disabled and "unsightly" people in the United States, see Philip M. Ferguson, "The Legacy of the Almshouse," in *Mental Retardation in America: A Historical Reader*, ed. Steven Noll and James W. Trent, Jr. (New York: New York University Press, 2004), 40–64; Susan Schweik, *The Ugly Laws: Disability in Public* (New York: New York University Press, 2009).
61. Stephen Mihm, "'A Limb Which Shall Be Presentable in Polite Society': Prosthetic Technologies in the Nineteenth Century," in *Artificial Parts, Practical Lives: Modern Histories of Prosthetics*, ed. Katherine Ott, David H. Serlin, and Stephen Mihm (New York: New York University Press, 2002), 287.

62. A. A. Marks, *Manual of Artificial Limbs: An Exhaustive Exposition of Prosthesis* (New York: A. A. Marks, 1906), 183.
63. Oliver Wendell Holmes, "The Human Wheel, Its Spokes and Felloes," *Atlantic Monthly*, May 1863, 578, 574 (emphasis in the original).
64. Nancy Fraser and Linda Gordon, "A Genealogy of *Dependency*: Tracing a Keyword of the US Welfare State," *Signs: Journal of Women in Culture and Society* 19:2 (Winter 1994): 314, 325.
65. See Michael S. Kimmel, *Manhood in America: A Cultural History*, 2nd ed. (New York: Oxford University Press, 2006).
66. Fraser and Gordon, 320.
67. My use of the term *rationalist* is indebted to sociologist Max Weber, who viewed rationalization—or the application of principles of scientific rationality, technical invention, and mathematical calculability to all aspects of human intercourse—as a central characteristic of modern industrial society. Max Weber, *The Protestant Ethic and the Spirit of Capitalism*, trans. Talcott Parsons (London: Routledge, 1992).
68. A. Scott Earle, "The Germ Theory in America: Antisepsis and Asepsis," *Surgery* 65:3 (March 1969): 508–22.
69. Figg and Farrell-Beck, 460.
70. Quoted in ibid., 461. For similar sentiments, see Padilla, 118–64.
71. O'Connor, 767; Lisa Herschbach, "Prosthetic Reconstructions: Making the Industry, Re-Making the Body, Modelling the Nation," *History Workshop Journal* 44 (1997): 23–57.
72. On more recent experiments in wound ballistics, see Susan Lindee, "Experimental Injury: Wound Ballistics and Aviation Medicine in Mid-Century America," in *Dark Medicine: Rationalizing Unethical Medical Research, ed.* William R. LaFleur, Gernot Böhme, and Susumu Shimazono (Bloomington: Indiana University Press, 2007), 121–37.
73. For descriptions of late nineteenth-century experiments in wound ballistics, see Victor Horsley, "The Destructive Effect of Small Projectiles," *Nature* 50 (1894): 104–8; "Deadly Long-Range Rifles," *Lafayette Advertiser* [LA], April 28, 1894, 1; William Flack Stevenson, *Wounds in War: The Mechanism of Their Production and Their Treatment* (New York: William Wood and Co., 1898); "Modern Warfare," *Galveston Daily News*, May 16, 1899, 8.
74. Stevenson, 59.
75. For testimonials to the inevitable "decline" of industrialized warfare between Western nations, see Alexander Sutherland, "The Natural Decline of Warfare," *Nineteenth Century* 45 (April 1899): 570–78; Emile Zola, "War," *North American Review* 170 (April 1900): 449–63; "The Passing of Great Wars," *Harper's Weekly* 46 (August 30, 1902): 1193; Havelock Ellis, "The War against War," *Atlantic Monthly* 107 (June 1911): 751–61.
76. Quoted in Stevenson, 41.
77. On the history and influence of the Army Medical Museum, see Rutkow, 247–53; Goler and Rhode, 163–84.
78. Although ostensibly devoted to the study of military medicine, the museum's collection extended well beyond the battlefield. The broken bones of the Civil War dead and wounded mingled with shriveled Native American papooses, bison ribs

pierced with arrowheads, and bodily specimens derived from railroad collisions. One case contained the preserved heads of three Maori tribesmen; another, a plaster cast of a fifty-one-and-a-half-pound tumor removed from the scrotum of a young African American man from Georgia. Although museum officials claimed such items were kept for "ethnological study," it is difficult to imagine any scientific value behind one of the museum's most popular displays: a fragment of the spinal cord and the third, fourth, and fifth vertebrae of presidential assassin John Wilkes Booth. J. J. Woodward, "The Army Medical Museum at Washington," *Lippincott's Magazine*, March 1871, 242, 238; Louis Bagger, "The Army Medical Museum in Washington," *Appleton's Journal*, March 1, 1873, 295.

79. Goler and Rhode, 166–67.
80. Charles Reginald Shrader, ed., *Reference Guide to United States Military History, 1865–1919* (New York: Facts on File, 1993), 1–5.
81. John Whiteclay Chambers II, "The American Debate over Modern War, 1871–1914," in *Anticipating Modern War: The German and American Experiences, 1871–1914*, ed. Manfred F. Boemeke, Roger Chickering, and Stig Förster (Cambridge: Cambridge University Press, 1999), 243.
82. On the development of militarism, see Volker R. Berghahn, *Militarism: The History of an International Debate, 1861–1979* (Cambridge: Cambridge University Press, 1984); Daniel Pick, *War Machine: The Rationalisation of Slaughter in the Modern Age* (New Haven: Yale University Press, 1993).
83. For conflicting interpretations of the "antimodern" tendencies of Progressive-era militarism, see T. J. Jackson Lears, *No Place of Grace: Antimodernism and the Transformation of American Culture 1880–1920* (New York: Pantheon, 1981); and David Axeen, "'Heroes of the Engine Room': American 'Civilization' and the War with Spain," *American Quarterly* 36 (Fall 1984): 481–502.
84. Teunis S. Hamlin, "The Place of War in the Civilization of the Twentieth Century," *Independent*, March 1, 1900, 532. For similar arguments, see Charles Morris, "War as a Factor in Civilization," *Popular Science Monthly* 47 (October 1895): 823–34; Harriet B. Bradbury, "War as a Necessity of Evolution," *Arena* 21:1 (January 1899): 94–96.
85. John P. Mallan, "Roosevelt, Brooks Adams, and Lea: The Warrior Critique of the Business Civilization," *American Quarterly* 8 (Fall 1956): 218.
86. Stephen B. Luce, "The Benefits of War," *North American Review*, December 1891, 673, 672.
87. See T. C. Taylor, "The Study of War," *North American Review*, February 1896, 181–89; H. F. Wyatt, "War as the Supreme Test of National Value," *Nineteenth Century*, February 1899, 216–25; Homer Lea, *The Valor of Ignorance* (New York: Harper and Brothers, 1909).
88. Horace Porter, "The Philosophy of Courage," *Century Illustrated*, May-October 1888, 251.
89. John S. Billings, "The Health of the Survivors of the War," *Forum*, January 1892, 654.
90. Chambers II, 247–48; C. Roland Marchand, *The American Peace Movement and Social Reform, 1898–1918* (Princeton: Princeton University Press, 1973).
91. Charles J. Bullock, "The Cost of War," *Atlantic Monthly* 95 (April 1905), 433–45; Piero Gleijeses, "1898: The Opposition to the Spanish-American War," *Journal of Latin American Studies* 35 (November 2003): 684.

92. "Bishop Potter on Expansion," in *The Anti-Imperialist Reader: A Documentary History of Anti-Imperialism in the United States*, ed. Philip S. Foner and Richard C. Winchester (New York: Holmes & Meier, 1984), 1:259.

93. William Restelle, "The Costliness of War," *Arena* 36 (October 1906): 343.

94. Only one volume was translated from the original Russian (1898) into English (1899). All references are taken from I. S. Bloch, *Is War Now Impossible? The Future of War in Its Technical, Economic, and Political Relations*, trans. R. C. Long (New York: Doubleday and McClure Co., 1899).

95. Ibid., lxi, 147–51.

96. For a similar statement on the impossibility of war between industrialized nations, see Jack London, "The Impossibility of War," *Overland Monthly* 35 (March 1900): 278–82.

97. Quoted in Edwin D. Mead, "Jean de Bloch and 'The Future of War,'" *New England Magazine*, May 28, 1903, 308.

98. Bloch, ix–x.

99. Gerald Linderman, *The Mirror of War: American Society and the Spanish-American War* (Ann Arbor: University of Michigan Press, 1974), 29.

100. Shrader, 24. A more recent medical history of the Spanish-American War suggests an even higher survival rate—95 percent—for wounded soldiers. Vincent J. Cirillo, *Bullets and Bacilli: The Spanish-American War and Military Medicine* (New Brunswick: Rutgers University Press, 2004), 30.

101. *War Articles* 73:5 (July 30, 1898): 136–37.

102. Ibid., 30, 9.

103. Henry I. Raymond, "The Morbidity of the United States Forces for the First Calendar Month in the Field at Tampa, FLA," *Medical News*, July 9, 1898, 44.

104. Michael Golay, "The Spanish-American War," in *Facts about the American Wars*, ed. John S. Bowman (New York: H. W. Wilson Co., 1998), 34–37.

105. Kristin L. Hoganson, *Fighting for American Manhood: How Gender Politics Provoked the Spanish-American and Philippine-American Wars* (New Haven: Yale University Press, 1998), 7.

106. Cirillo, 19, 16, 160.

107. "The Spanish Bullets," *Medical News*, July 9, 1898, 49.

108. Robert J. Topmiller and T. Kerby Neill, *Binding Their Wounds: America's Assault on Its Veterans* (Boulder, CO: Paradigm, 2011), 25.

109. For a nuanced discussion of cultural attitudes toward Spanish-American War casualties, see Bonnie M. Miller, *From Liberation to Conquest: The Visual and Popular Culture of the Spanish-American War of 1898* (Amherst: University of Massachusetts Press, 2011), 166–77.

110. Quoted in Kathleen Dalton, *Theodore Roosevelt: A Strenuous Life* (New York: Vintage, 2002), 176.

111. Theodore Roosevelt, *The Rough Riders* (New York: Charles Scribner's Sons, 1925), 232–33.

112. Dalton, 175.

113. Theodore Roosevelt, "The Men Who Pay with Their Bodies for Their Souls' Desire," in *The Great Adventure: Present-Day Studies in American Nationalism* (New York: Scribner's, 1919), 18, 29.

ARTHUR GUY EMPEY

1. A smash hit upon its release, *"Over the Top"* sold 350,000 copies in 1917 alone and soon became a popular Vitagraph film, with Empey starring in the lead role. Arthur Guy Empey, *"Over the Top," by an American Soldier Who Went* (New York: G. P. Putnam's Sons, 1917).
2. Ibid., 279–80.
3. Ibid., 255–60.
4. Ibid., 277.

CHAPTER TWO

1. Quoted in Louis J. F. Moore, "Win the War: The Poster as Power," *Philadelphia Record*, January 27, 1918.
2. John Keegan, *The First World War* (New York: Alfred A. Knopf, 1999), 135–36.
3. On the belief that World War I would never end, see Paul Fussell, *The Great War and Modern Memory* (London: Oxford University Press, 1975), 71–74.
4. George W. Norris, quoted in *Congressional Record*, 65th Cong., 1st sess., vol. 15 (1917), 213.
5. Page Smith, *America Enters the World: A People's History of the Progressive Era and World War I* (New York: McGraw-Hill, 1985), 456. For similar arguments, see Thomas C. Leonard, *Above the Battle: War-Making in America from Appomattox to Versailles* (New York: Oxford University Press, 1978), 92; Susan D. Moeller, *Shooting War: Photography and the American Experience of Combat* (New York: Basic Books, 1989), 99; Evan Andrew Huelfer, *The 'Casualty Issue' in American Military Practice: The Impact of World War I* (Westport, CN: Praeger, 2003), 39.
6. Margaret R. Higonnet, introduction to *Nurses at the Front: Writing the Wounds of the Great War*, edited by Margaret R. Higonnet (Boston: Northeastern University Press, 2001), viii.
7. Quoted in Leonard, 132.
8. Isolationism has always functioned more as a cultural myth than an accurate description of US foreign affairs. Since the nation's founding, the United States has pursued an almost relentless campaign of economic and territorial expansion, relying upon military force to extend its sphere of influence from the Caribbean to the Philippines. On American expansion before World War I, see David Ryan, *US Foreign Policy in World History* (New York: Routledge, 2000), 55–69.
9. On isolationism during the Great War era, see John Milton Cooper, *The Vanity of Power: American Isolationism and the First World War, 1914–1917* (Westport, CN: Greenwood, 1969).
10. Quoted in *Congressional Record*, 65th Cong., 1st sess. (1917), 137.
11. According to literary scholar Trudi Tate, "Perhaps the most enduring image of the Great War is the male body in fragments." *Modernism, History, and the First World War* (Manchester: Manchester University Press, 1998), 78.
12. George R. Kirkpatrick, *War—What For?* (West La Fayette, OH: Author, 1914).
13. Henry T. Schnittkind, *Shambles: A Sketch of the Present War* (New York: n.p., 1915), 15.
14. Larry Wayne Ward, *The Motion Picture Goes to War: The US Government Film Effort during World War I* (Ann Arbor, MI: UMI Research Press, 1985), 17–18.
15. Ellen N. La Motte, *The Backwash of War: The Human Wreckage of the Battlefield as Witnessed by an American Hospital Nurse*, in Higonnet, 5, 16.

16. On the myth of the war experience, see George L. Mosse, *Fallen Soldiers: Reshaping the Memory of the World Wars* (New York: Oxford University Press, 1990), 15–33.

17. Owen Wister, introduction to *The Aftermath of Battle: With the Red Cross in France*, by E. D. Toland (London: Macmillan, 1916), ix.

18. Theodore Roosevelt, "The Men Who Pay with Their Bodies for Their Souls' Desire," in *The Great Adventure: Present-Day Studies in American Nationalism* (New York: Scribner's, 1919), 17.

19. Quoted in Donald J. Murphy, *America's Entry into World War I* (San Diego: Greenhaven Press, 2004), 99.

20. *Congressional Record*, 65th Cong., 1st sess. (1917), 214.

21. Ibid., 317, 371, 337.

22. Ibid., 208, 237, 381.

23. Ibid., 379–80.

24. Geoffrey R. Stone, *Perilous Times: Free Speech in Wartime from the Sedition Act of 1798 to the War on Terrorism* (New York: W. W. Norton, 2004).

25. Ronald Schaffer, *America in the Great War: The Rise of the War Welfare State* (New York: Oxford University Press, 1991), 109–26; also see Alan Dawley, *Changing the World: American Progressives in War and Revolution* (Princeton: Princeton University Press, 2003).

26. David M. Kennedy, *Over Here: The First World War and American Society* (New York: Oxford University Press, 1980), 42.

27. William L. Langer, *Gas and Flame in World War I* (New York: Alfred A. Knopf, 1965), xix.

28. Kennedy, 180.

29. See Michael S. Kimmel, *Manhood in America: A Cultural History*, 2nd ed. (New York: Oxford University Press, 2006).

30. Quoted in Moeller, 92.

31. Quoted in Mary B. Mullet, "The Chances of Getting Killed or Hurt in This War," *American Magazine* 85:3 (March 1918): 117.

32. Private Peat, "Why We Come Smiling Out of Hell," *American Magazine* 85:3 (March 1918): 8, 7. Peat describes his wounding in detail in Harold R. Peat, *Private Peat* (New York: Grosset and Dunlap, 1917).

33. Private Peat, "Why We Come Smiling Out of Hell," 58, 60.

34. Leonard, 92.

35. For similar proclamations, see "A Bullet That Heals Every Wound It Makes," *American Magazine* (April 11, 1915): 2; Laura S. Portor, "The Bright Side of War," *North American Review* 103 (June 1916): 883–94.

36. "General Impressions of Heavy Losses Not Borne Out by Authoritative Figures," *Minnesota in the War (September 1917–February 1919), the Official Bulletin of the Minnesota Commission of Public Safety* 1:2 (September 15, 1917).

37. C. L. Gibson, "Caring for American Wounded in France," *Scribner's Magazine* 63:5 (May 1918): 597; John R. McDill, *Lessons from the Enemy: How Germany Cares for Her War Disabled* (Philadelphia: Lea and Febiger, 1918).

38. "Just Think: Without Hands—Without Feet," *Ladies Home Journal*, June 1918, 107. On the magazine's role in World War I, see Joanne L. Karetsky, *The Mustering of Support for World War I by The Ladies' Home Journal* (New York: Edwin Mellen Press, 1997).

39. Gorgas quoted in Mullet, 41, 43.
40. Ibid., 41, 117; Judson D. Stuart, "A Soldier Has a Better Chance Than a Baby," *Illustrated World* 29:5 (July 1918): 728.
41. "General Impressions of Heavy Losses Not Borne Out by Authoritative Figures."
42. "A Man's Chances in War," *Outlook* 116 (August 22, 1917): 604.
43. Stuart, 728.
44. Thomas B. Love, "The Social Significance of War Risk Insurance," *Annals of the American Academy of Political and Social Science* 79 (September 1918): 46. For a broader discussion of war risk insurance, see William Pyrle Dillingham, *Federal Aid to Veterans, 1917–1941* (Gainesville: University of Florida Press, 1952), 10–30.
45. Roger Daniels, *The Bonus March: An Episode of the Great Depression* (Westport, CN: Greenwood, 1971), 16–17.
46. Love, 47.
47. Dillingham, 27; Love, 49.
48. Dillingham, 27.
49. Daniels, 16–18.
50. Dillingham, 30.
51. A copy of *His Best Gift* can be found at RG 111H-1542, National Archives at College Park—Motion Pictures, National Archives, College Park, MD (hereafter NACP).
52. United States Surgeon-General's Office, *The Medical Department of the United States Army in the World War* (Washington: GPO, 1927), 6:533. Hereafter all references to this text will appear as *MDUSAWW*.
53. These included the eponymous "trench foot," "trench fever," and "trench mouth." Ibid., 536–37; 534.
54. *MDUSAWW* 12:407; John Ellis, *The Social History of the Machine Gun* (Baltimore: Johns Hopkins University Press, 1986), 42–59.
55. Jack L. Snyder, *The Ideology of the Offensive: Military Decision Making and the Disasters of 1914* (Ithaca: Cornell University Press, 1989).
56. Exploding shells were responsible for 17,439 nonfatal US casualties; shrapnel for 33,787; and unspecified gunshots for 74,883. *MDUSAWW* 15:2, 15:1019.
57. The United States' relatively short time in combat is also responsible for this relatively low figure. Great Britain, for example, had 42,000 war amputees, although this figure does not include the many men who had body parts amputated in the war's aftermath because of lingering injuries, chronic pain, or infection. Ibid., 15:71.
58. Ibid., 15:2, 15:1017, 15:1023.
59. Ellis, *The Social History of the Machine Gun*, 66.
60. For a detailed description of the medical aspects of gas warfare in World War I, see *MDUSAWW* 14.
61. Ibid., 34.
62. *MDUSAWW* 10:1.
63. C. S. Read, *Military Psychiatry in Peace and War* (London: Lewis, 1920), 143. On World War I–era debates about the etiology of war neuroses, see Ben Shephard, *A War of Nerves: Soldiers and Psychiatrists in the Twentieth Century* (Cambridge, MA: Harvard University Press, 2001).
64. John M. Kinder, "Military Psychiatry," in *Encyclopedia of War and American Society*, ed. Peter Karsten (New York: Sage, 2005).

65. Robert H. Zieger, *America's Great War: World War I and the American Experience* (Lanham, MD: Rowman and Littlefield, 2000), 111.

66. Ibid., 166, 170, 178, 182.

67. Nonbattle fatalities abounded during World War I. By the OSG's own count, 621 men died as a result of plane crashes, 302 in auto accidents, and 476 from rifle wounds. Eighty-two men drowned when their ships sank en route to Europe, while 745 soldiers were accidentally crushed to death. In addition, more than one hundred American soldiers were murdered while in uniform; nearly six hundred others committed suicide (many no doubt because of psychological stress). Ibid., 146.

68. Ibid., 182.

69. Harry Iverson File, box 11, Regional Office Training Case Files, 1918–1928, NM 30, RG 15, National Archives, Washington, DC (hereafter NAB); Roy Moore File, box 15, Regional Office Training Case Files, 1918–1928, NM 30, RG 15, NAB; Joseph Evans, box 19, Regional Office Training Case Files, 1918–1928, NM 30, RG 15, NAB.

70. Reprinted as Charles Hanson Towne, "Ruins," *Carry On* 1:1 (June 1918): 10.

71. Theodore Roosevelt, "For Their Souls' Desire," *Carry On* 1:2 (August 1918): 5.

72. Huelfer, 5.

73. *MDUSAWW* 15:2, 15:230.

74. Huelfer, 6.

75. Harvey Cushing, *From a Surgeon's Journal, 1915–1918* (Boston: Little, Brown, 1936).

76. Fussell, 170.

77. John L. Golob, *Buck Private: The Wartime Letters of John L. Golob, 1918–1919*, edited by Martin Golob (Miami: M. Golob, 1997), 8–9.

78. Guy Emerson Bowerman, Jr., *The Compensations of War: The Diary of an Ambulance Driver during the Great War*, edited by Mark C. Carnes (Austin: University of Texas Press, 1983), 161.

79. Cf. William Brown, *The Adventures of an American Doughboy* (Tacoma: Smith-Kinney, 1919), 27.

80. L. H., "On Being Wounded," *Living Age* 294 (September 8, 1917): 618.

81. Mark Meigs, *Optimism at Armageddon: Voices of American Participants in the First World War* (New York: New York University Press, 1997), 65.

82. Golob, 12.

83. J. Breckinridge Bayne, *Bugs and Bullets* (New York: Richard R. Smith, 1944), 84, 12–13.

84. On the link between being wounded and escaping the war, see James Norman Hall, *Kitchener's Mob: The Adventures of an American in the British Army* (Boston: Houghton Mifflin, 1916), 182–83; Ellis, *The Social History of the Machine Gun*, 112; Arthur Guy Empey, *"Over the Top," by an American Soldier Who Went* (New York: G. P. Putnam's Sons, 1917), 109, 249.

85. Quoted in Schaffer, 169.

86. Hall, 121.

87. "What About the Tuberculosis?" *Carry On* 1:8 (May 1919): 22–23.

88. Arthur H. Samuels, "Invisible Wounds," *Carry On* 1:2 (September 1918): 13.

89. Quoted in Nancy K. Bristow, *Making Men Moral: Social Engineering during the Great War* (New York: New York University Press, 1996), 32.

90. Stuart McGuire, *History of US Army Base Hospital No. 45 in the Great War* (Richmond: William Byrd, 1924), 174.

91. On the history of the CPI, see Stewart Halsey Ross, *Propaganda for War: How the United States Was Conditioned to Fight the Great War of 1914–1918* (Jefferson, NC: McFarland, 1996).

92. Moeller, 151.

93. Quoted in Smith, 451–52.

94. Quoted in ibid., 136.

95. Alfred E. Cornebise, *The Stars and Stripes: Doughboy Journalism in World War I* (Westport, CN: Greenwood Press, 1984), 87.

96. *War Cyclopedia: A Handbook for Ready Reference on the Great War* (Washington: GPO, 1918), 295.

97. Craig V. Campbell, *Reel America and World War I: A Comprehensive Filmography and History of Motion Pictures in the United States, 1914–1920* (Jefferson, NC: McFarland and Co., 1985), 101; Lawrence H. Suit, *Guts and Glory: The Making of the American Military Image in Film*, rev. ed. (Lexington: University of Kentucky Press, 2002), 19.

98. Bennett E. Tousley to Arthur E. Bestor (December 3, 1917), folder A-3-1/A-3-6, box 1, entry 75: General Correspondence of the Speaking Division, Sept. 1917–Aug. 1918, RG 63, NACP.

99. C. W. R. Bowlby, folder Walsh-Watt, entry 68: Correspondence with and concerning special speakers serving under the speaking division and speakers' bureau (Oct. 1917–Nov. 1918), RG 63, NACP; Lieutenant Roberto de Violini, folder Correspondence, Special Speakers (Vaughn-Walsh), entry 68: Correspondence with and concerning special speakers serving under the speaking division and speakers' bureau (Oct. 1917–Nov. 1918), RG 63, NACP; Captain Leslie Vickers, *Life in the Trenches and Other Aspects of the Great War*, copy found in folder B-2-15, box 3, entry 75: General Correspondence of the Speaking Division, Sept. 1917–Aug. 1918, RG 63, NACP.

100. Charles S. Wyckoff to George Creel (September 21, 1917), folder A-4-10/A-4/12, box 1, General Correspondence of the Speaking Division, Sept. 1917–Aug. 1918, RG 63, NACP.

101. Rosemarie Garland Thomson, "Seeing the Disabled: Visual Rhetorics of Disability in Popular Photography," in *The New Disability History: American Perspectives*, ed. Paul K. Longmore and Lauri Umansky (New York: New York University Press, 2001), 341.

102. I explore this topic further in "Iconography of Injury: Encountering the Wounded Soldier's Body in American Poster Art and Photography of World War I," in *Picture This! World War I Posters and Visual Culture*, ed. Pearl James (Lincoln: University of Nebraska Press, 2009), 340–68.

103. *Bulletin for Cartoonists* no. 5, Bureau of Cartoons, Committee on Public Information, July 6, 1918.

104. *Bulletin for Cartoonists* no. 16, Bureau of Cartoons, Committee on Public Information, December 28, 1918.

105. Christina S. Jarvis, *The Male Body at War: American Masculinity during World War II* (DeKalb: Northern Illinois University Press, 2010), 88.

106. Red Cross Week Campaign, *Bulletin* no. 5 (Washington: GPO, 1917), 4.

107. The Third Liberty Loan, *Bulletin* no. 29 (Washington: GPO, 1918), 2.

108. Keegan, 6–7.

109. "Disabled Men Cheer Message of Wilson," *New York Times*, February 4, 1922, 4.

110. "Wounded Veterans Appeal for League," *New York Times*, November 2, 1920, 6.

ELSIE FERGUSON

1. Elsie Ferguson, "Helping Our Heroes Thru the Red Cross: A Visit to Hero Land," *Motion Picture Magazine* 17:5 (June 1919): 28–29.

CHAPTER THREE

1. Elizabeth R. Stoner "The Crutches' Tune," *Everybody's Magazine* 49 (April 1919): 90.
2. Quoted in "'Shameful Neglect' of our Disabled Dough-Boys," *Literary Digest* 58:4 (January 22, 1921): 7.
3. Banner headline of the *New York Times*, November 11, 1918, 1.
4. "News of Armistice Flashed to City," *New York Times*, November 11, 1918, 2. On the immediate aftermath of World War I, see David M. Kennedy, *Over Here: The First World War and American Society* (Oxford: Oxford University Press, 1980), 231–95.
5. For general overviews of the demobilization of US troops following World War I, see Benedict Crowell and Robert Forrest Wilson, *Demobilization: Our Industrial and Military Demobilization after the Armistice, 1918–1920* (New Haven: Yale University Press, 1921); James Mock and Evangeline Thurber, *Report on Demobilization* (Norman: University of Oklahoma Press, 1944).
6. Crowell and Wilson, 48–50.
7. E. Jay Howenstine, Jr., "Demobilization after the First World War," *Quarterly Journal of Economics* 58:1 (1943): 91–105.
8. Dixon Wecter, *When Johnny Comes Marching Home* (Cambridge, MA: Riverside Press, 1944), 304–10; Mock and Thurber, 135.
9. As additional rewards for their service, Great War veterans were allowed to keep their uniforms, coats, toilet kits, and shoes, and, if they had served abroad, their gas masks and helmets. Crowell and Wilson, 48–57; Wecter, 297–301, 310–14.
10. Crowell and Wilson, 63.
11. Wecter, 298–99.
12. Roger Burlingame, *Peace Veterans: The Story of a Racket and a Plea for Economy* (New York: Minton, Balch, and Co., 1932), 14.
13. "A Welcome They Would Appreciate," *Chicago News*, May 29, 1919, clipping in folder for Chicago, box 1, NM-84, RG 165, National Archives, College Park, MD (hereafter NACP).
14. John L. Golob, *Buck Private: The Wartime Letters of John L. Golob, 1918–1919*, edited by Martin Golob (Miami: M. Golob, 1997), 38.
15. E.g., Wecter, 302.
16. Harold Hersey, *When the Boys Come Home* (New York: Britton, 1919), 12–13.
17. Mary Ryan, "The American Parade: Representations of the Nineteenth-Century Social Order," in *The New Cultural History*, ed. Lynn Hunt (Berkeley: University of California Press, 1989), 138.
18. Craig V. Campbell, *Reel America and World War I: A Comprehensive Filmography and History of Motion Pictures in the United States, 1914–1920* (Jefferson, NC: McFarland and Co., 1985), 130.
19. Wecter, 302.
20. In order to receive a gold wound chevron, a man had to receive a wound in action with the enemy, or as the result of an enemy act (including disablement by gas) that required treatment from a medical officer. See "Here's the Dope on the

Wound Stripe," *Fort Sheridan Reveille,* May 26, 1919, 4, clipping in Otis Historical Archives (hereafter OHA), 162, National Museum of Health and Medicine, Walter Reed Medical Center, Washington, DC (hereafter NMHM).

21. "Chicago Will Pay Homage to Heroes on Honor Day," *Fort Sheridan Recall,* c. September 27, 1919, clipping in OHA 162, NMHM.

22. Quoted in James Louis Small, ed., *Home—Then What? The Mind of the Doughboy, A.E.F.* (New York: George H. Doran, 1920), 35, 171.

23. John Kendrick Bangs, forward to ibid., xix.

24. The historiography of the social and political changes of the early years of the Armistice is vast. Useful overviews include Thomas J. Knock, *To End All Wars: Woodrow Wilson and the Quest for a New World Order* (New York: Oxford University Press, 1992); Michael E. Parrish, *Anxious Decades: America in Prosperity and Depression, 1920–1941* (New York: Norton, 1992); and Richard Slotkin, *Lost Battalions: The Great War and the Crisis of American Nationality* (New York: Henry Holt, 2005). On the flu pandemic, see Gina Kolata, *Flu: The Story of the Great Influenza Pandemic of 1918 and the Search for the Virus That Caused It* (New York: Touchstone, 2001).

25. Nancy Gentile Ford, "'Put Fighting Blood in Your Business': The US War Department and the Reemployment of World War I Soldiers," in *Veterans' Policies, Veterans' Politics: New Perspectives on Veterans in the Modern United States*, ed. Stephen R. Ortiz (Gainesville: University Press of Florida, 2012), 121.

26. "Men in Service and Discharged—Minneapolis Gratefully Opens Its Gates," Minneapolis Citizens Welcome Committee (c. 1919), folder for Minnesota, box 2, NM-84, RG 165, NACP.

27. "Beneficial Soldier Legislation as Enacted by Various States: Special Aid and Assistance" (c. 1919), folder for Bulletins, box 1, entry 352, NM-84, RG 165, NACP; Talcott Powell, *Tattered Banners* (New York: Harcourt, Brace, 1933), 212–13.

28. Quoted in Ford, 123.

29. Quoted in Frederick Lewis Allen, *Only Yesterday* (New York: Bantam, 1946), 75.

30. See boxes 1–5, entry: Correspondence on Behalf of Veterans without Jobs, March–April 1919, NM-84, RG 165, Records of the War Department and Special Staffs, NACP.

31. Quoted in Ford, 130.

32. Ralph V. Anderson file, box 13, entry 15: Regional Office Training Case Files, 1918–1928, NM 30, RG 15, National Archives Building, Washington, DC (hereafter NAB).

33. Francis Burke file, box 15, entry 15: Regional Office Training Case Files, 1918–1928, NM 30, RG 15, NAB.

34. Such suspicions were encouraged by a number of comedic films about fake war cripples that played to great success both before and after World War I. See Martin F. Norden, *The Cinema of Isolation: A History of Physical Disability in the Movies* (New Brunswick: Rutgers University Press, 1994).

35. Newton D. Baker to Arthur Woods (August 28, 1919), reprinted in Arthur Woods, War Department News Release (1919), folder for Bulletins, box 1, NM-84, entry 352, RG 165, NACP.

36. "Peddling by Soldiers Must Stop, Says US," *Rocky Mountain News*, May 25, 1919, clipping in folder for Denver, box 1, NM 84, entry 353, RG 165, NACP.

37. "Declare War on Peddlers in Uniform," *Kansas City Journal*, May 14, 1919, clipping in folder for Missouri, box 2, NM 84, entry 353, RG 165, NACP.

38. Benjamin Malzberg, "Demobilization and the Crime Rate," *Journal of Delinquency* 4 (1919): 152–57; Clarence Darrow, *Crime: Its Cause and Treatment* (New York: Thomas Y. Crowell, 1922). For a summary of similar studies, see Betty R. Rosenbaum, "Relationship between War and Crime in the United States," *Journal of Crime Law and Criminology* 30:5 (January–February 1940): 722–40.

39. Philip Gibbs, *Now It Can Be Told* (Garden City, NY: Garden City Publishing, 1920), 552, 554.

40. Wecter, 413–18. In 1940, Betty Rosenbaum cited "the development of the high-power motor car and the automatic gun, together with prohibition and its machine-gun gang warfare" as "causative factors" in the 1920s crime wave (733).

41. On popular perceptions of shell shock after World War I, see Anthony Babington, *Shell-Shock: A History of the Changing Attitudes to War Neurosis* (London: Leo Cooper, 1997); Norman Fenton, *Shell Shock and Its Aftermath* (St. Louis: C. V. Mosby, 1926).

42. Examples include "Reports on War Disabled: Treasure Office Says 40% are Mentally Deranged," *New York Times*, January 1, 1921; "70,000 Insane Soldiers Uncared For," *New York Times*, April 4, 1921; "Crazed Man Scares Red Cross Workers," *New York Times*, May 30, 1922.

43. Annessa C. Stagner, "Healing the Soldier, Restoring the Nation: Representations of Shell Shock in the USA during and after the First World War," *Journal of Contemporary History* 49:2 (2014): 255–74.

44. Judge Florence E. Allen, "Because Wars Unleash Demoralizing Instincts," in *Why Wars Must Cease*, ed. Rose E. Young (New York: Macmillan, 1935), 109. General F. P. Crozier *quoted in Allen*, 109.

45. Maude Radford Warren, "Backwash," *Everybody's Magazine* 41:3 (September 1919): 13.

46. Quoted in Willard Waller, *The Veteran Comes Back* (New York: Dryden Press, 1944), 178.

47. Frederic J. Haskin, "Shopping Bureau for Soldiers," *Bridgeport [NY] Standard Telegram*, September 22, 1919, 8.

48. Warren G. Harding, "Back to Normal: Address before Home Market Club," *Rededicating America: Life and Recent Speeches of Warren G. Harding*, ed. Frederick E. Schortemeier (Indianapolis: Bobbs-Merrill: 1920), 223.

49. "Elks Make Harding a 'Surprise' Visit, *New York Times*, July 21, 1920, Special ed., 7.

50. Michael A. Cohen, *Live from the Campaign Trial: The Greatest Presidential Campaign Speeches of the Twentieth Century and How They Shaped Modern America* (New York: Walker & Co., 2008), 65–72.

51. Warren G. Harding, "Speech of Acceptance: Address at Formal Notification of His Nomination for the Presidency, at Marion, Ohio, July 22, 1920," in Schortemeier, 59.

52. Harold Littledale, "Thousands of Disabled Men Untrained in This District," *New York Evening Post*, February 18, 1920, 1; "Our Debt of Honor," *The Nation* (November 24, 1920).

53. Quoted in "'Shameful Neglect' of Our Disabled Doughboys," *Literary Digest* 68:4 (January 22, 1921): 5

54. Waller, 239.

55. Quoted in ibid., 5.

56. "70,000 Insane Soldiers Uncared For, He Says," *New York Times*, April 4, 1921, 32.

57. Helen Ledyard Birch, "Plea for War Cripples," *New York Times*, July 24, 1921, 64.

58. Quoted in "'Shameful Neglect' of Our Disabled Doughboys," *Literary Digest* 68:4 (January 22, 1921): 7. Similar assessments can be found in "Miller Hits Ingratitude," *New York Times*, April 2, 1921, 9; Helen Ledyard Birch, "Plea for War Cripples," *New York Times*, July 24, 1921, 64; "Gross Neglect and Profiteering in Caring for Disabled Veterans," *Literary Digest* (February 4, 1922): 46.
59. "Gold Mothers Weep at Inquiry," *New York Times*, April 6, 1921, 17; "War Maimed Tell of Federal Neglect," *New York Times*, March 4, 1921, 15.
60. "Pershing Demands Justice for Heroes," *New York Times*, April 5, 1921, 8.
61. On the Gold Star Mothers, see G. Kurt Piehler, *Remembering War the American Way* (Washington, DC: Smithsonian Institution Press, 1995), 101–7.
62. "Gold Mothers Weep at Inquiry," 17.
63. On the creation and early institutional culture of the Veterans' Bureau, see Rosemary A. Stevens, "The Invention, Stumbling, and Reinvention of the Modern US Veterans Health Care System, 1918," in Ortiz, *Veterans' Policies, Veterans' Politics*, 38–62.
64. Richard Severo and Lewis Milford, *The Wages of War: When America's Soldiers Came Home—From Valley Forge to Vietnam* (New York: Simon and Schuster, 1989), 247–59; "Million a Day for Our Wounded," *Literary Digest* (February 18, 1922): 14–15; "Gross Neglect and Profiteering in Caring for Disabled Veterans," *Literary Digest* (February 4, 1922): 46.
65. Severo and Milford, 255.
66. For more on the Minnesota veterans' farm colonies, see John M. Kinder, "Architecture of Injury: Disabled Veterans, Federal Policy, and the Built Environment in the Early Twentieth Century," in Ortiz, *Veterans' Policies, Veterans' Politics*, 65–93.
67. Severo and Milford, 259–60.
68. Ray Robinson, *Matty: An American Hero; Christy Mathewson of the New York Giants* (New York: Oxford University Press, 1993), 193.
69. "Disabled War Hero Victim of Red Tape," *New York Times*, December 7, 1923, 23. See also "The Plight of a Veteran," *New York Times*, November 26, 1929, 30.
70. Zane Grey, *The Call of the Canyon* (New York: Harper and Brothers, 1921), 4.
71. Laurence Stallings, *Plumes* (New York: Grosset and Dunlap, 1924).
72. Joan T. Brittain, *Laurence Stallings* (Boston: Twayne, 1975), 17–29.
73. Stallings, *Plumes*, 4.
74. Ibid., 79.
75. Ibid., 100, 105.
76. Ibid., 347.
77. Ibid., 90.
78. Ibid., 182, 169.
79. Ibid., 92.
80. Ibid., 291.
81. Liberty Bonds advertisement, *Kansas City Times*, October 1, 1918, 5; "Across the Seas They Call," *Placerville [CA] Mountain Democrat*, May 18, 1919, n.p.
82. "The Carry On Club Opens," *New York Times*, April 6, 1919, 5; "To Carry On," *Sandusky [OH] Register*, February 7, 1920, 4.
83. Mary L. Dudziak, *War Time: An Idea, Its History, Its Consequences* (New York: Oxford University Press, 2012), 15.

84. Joseph Conrad Fehr, "The Ultimate Casualties," *Commonweal* (May 27, 1931): 97.

85. Fehr, 97. According to Katherine Mayo, by 1927, roughly half of all patients receiving treatment at Veterans' Bureau hospitals were suffering from "neuropsychiatric disabilities" such as shell shock or dementia praecox. Katherine Mayo, *Soldiers, What Next!* (Boston: Houghton Mifflin, 1934), 62.

86. John Maurice Clark, *The Costs of the World War to the American People* (New Haven: Yale University Press, 1931), 196, 180. Tragically, Clark's ballpark figure of $25 billion would turn out to be low, given his failure to anticipate future wars against Germany and Japan, Korea, and Vietnam over the next fifty years.

SUNDAY AT THE HIPPODROME

1. On the conference, see John Culbert Faries, *Three Years of Work for Handicapped Men: A Report of the Activities of the Institute for Crippled and Disabled Men* (New York: Institute for Crippled and Disabled Men, 1920); "Pity Maimed Fighters? Yes, But How About Jobs?" *New York World*, March 24, 1919, 4; "Hughes Reassures Disabled Soldiers," *New York Times*, March 24, 1919, sec. 9, 1.

2. Quoted in "Pity Maimed Fighters? Yes, But How About Jobs?" 4.

CHAPTER FOUR

1. Curtis E. Lakeman, *Home Service and the Disabled Soldier or Sailor* (N.p.: American Red Cross, 1918), 5.

2. Gelett Burgess, "Victim *versus* Victor," *Carry On* 1:1 (June 1918): 20.

3. Although most historical studies of Great War–era rehabilitation have focused on Western Europe, there has been a recent growth in scholarship on American rehabilitation programs. See Scott Gelber, "'Hard-Boiled Order': The Reeducation of Disabled WWI Veterans in New York City," *Journal of Social History* 39:1 (2005): 161–80; Ana Carden-Coyne, "Ungrateful Bodies: Rehabilitation, Resistance, and Disabled American Veterans of the First World War," *European Review of History* 14:4 (2007): 543–65; Michael J. Lansing, "'Salvaging the Man Power of America': Conservation, Manhood, and Disabled Veterans during World War I," *Environmental History* 141 (January 2009): 32–56; Beth Linker, *War's Waste: Rehabilitation in World War I America* (Chicago: University of Chicago Press, 2011).

4. "The Passing of the Cripple," *Outlook* 117 (October 3, 1917): 166.

5. See Frank B. Gilbreth, *Motion Study: A Method for Increasing the Efficiency of the Workman* (New York: Van Nostrand, 1911); and Gilbreth, *Bricklaying System* (Easton: Hive, 1974 [1909]).

6. Elsbeth Brown, "The Prosthetics of Management: Motion Study, Photography, and the Industrialized Body in World War I America," in *Artificial Parts, Practical Lives: Modern Histories of Prosthetics*, ed. Katherine Ott, David H. Serlin, and Stephen Mihm (New York: New York University Press, 2002), 260–63.

7. Frank B. Gilbreth, "The Problem of the Crippled Soldier: What Shall Be Done with Him after the War?" *Scientific American Supplement* 80 (December 25, 1915): 402.

8. Maurice Bourrillon, "Functional Readaptation and Professional Re-education of the Disabled Victims of the War," in *The Provision of Employment for Members of the Canadian Expeditionary Force on Their Return to Canada* (Ottawa: J. de L. Tache, 1915), 30.

9. For similar views, see Robert Blanchard, "Physical Reconstruction and What It Means to the Wounded," in *USA General Hospital No. 28*, edited by Edward O. Harrs and Sydney B. Flower (Fort Sheridan, IL: 1919), 30; "The Problem of the Disabled," *Recalled to Life* 1:3 (April 1918): 367; Edward T. Devine, *Disabled Soldiers and Sailors: Pensions and Training*, no. 12 in the Preliminary Economic Studies of the War, edited by David Kinley (New York: Oxford University Press, 1919), 9.

10. Thomas Gregory, "Restoring Crippled Soldiers to a Useful Life," *World's Work* 36 (August 1918): 428.

11. T. B. Kidner, "Guiding the Disabled to a New Job," *Carry On* 1:3 (September 1918): 18. Similar critiques can be found in Douglas C. McMurtrie, "The High Road to Self-Support," *Carry On* 1:1 (July 1918): 17–21; Major John L. Todd, "The Meaning of Rehabilitation," *Annals of the American Academy of Political and Social Science* 80 (November 1918): 7.

12. Barbara Spofford Morgan, "Problem of the Returning Soldier," *North American Review* 208 (October 1918): 524.

13. War Department Office of the Surgeon General (hereafter OSG), "Introductory," in *Abstracts, Translations, and Reviews of Recent Literature on the Subject of the Reconstruction and Reeducation of the Disabled Soldier and Sailor, Bulletin 4* (May 25, 1918): I.

14. Garrard Harris, "The Returned Disabled Soldier: What of Our Attitude Toward Him?" *Outlook* 120 (December 11, 1918): 594.

15. Theodore Roosevelt, "For Their Souls' Desire," *Carry On* 1:2 (August 1918): 5.

16. On American Progressivism, see Alan Dawley, *Changing the World: American Progressives in War and Revolution* (Princeton, NJ: Princeton University Press, 2003).

17. Samuel Gompers, "Labor Stands Ready," *Carry On* 1:3 (September 1918): 3.

18. See Glenn Gritzer and Arnold Arluke, *The Making of Rehabilitation: A Political Economy of Medical Specialization, 1890–1980* (Berkeley: University of California Press, 1985).

19. Much of this biographical information can be found in Herbert A. Kellar, "Douglas Crawford McMurtrie: Historian of Printing and Bibliographer," in *Douglas C. McMurtrie: Bibliographer and Historian of Printing*, by Scott Bruntjen and Melissa L. Young (Metuchen, NJ: Scarecrow Press, 1979), 1–5.

20. Blanchard, 30.

21. William C. Gorgas, "A Message from the Surgeon General," *Carry On* 1:1 (July 1918): 3.

22. My use of the term *remasculinization* is indebted to Susan Jeffords, *The Remasculinization of America: Gender and the Vietnam War* (Bloomington: Indiana University Press, 1989).

23. "The Creed of the Disabled Soldier," *Carry On* 1:9 (June 1919): front inside cover.

24. Charles A. Lauffer, "The Injured in Industry," *Carry On* 1:9 (June 1919): 11.

25. Paul L. Benjamin, "Winning Back," *Carry On* 1:8 (May 1919): 9.

26. Burgess, 20.

27. Samuel Hopkins Adams, "You and Our Maimed Soldiers," *Red Cross Magazine* 14:6 (1919): 66.

28. Gregory, 428.

29. On Progressives' fear of "waste," see Cecilia Tichi, *Shifting Gears: Technology, Literature, Culture in Modernist America* (Chapel Hill: University of North Carolina Press, 1987).

30. War Department Office of the Surgeon General, "Introductory," I.
31. Mary W. Standlee, *Borden's Dream: The Walter Reed Army Medical Center, Washington, DC,* 150, unpublished manuscript, box 1, RG 112, National Archives, College Park, MD (hereafter NACP).
32. OSG, "The Fundamentals of Physical and Vocational Reconstruction of the Disabled Soldier," *Abstracts, Bulletin* 4 (May 25, 1918), v, ix.
33. OSG, *Abstracts, Bulletin* 4 (May 25, 1918), 131.
34. Herbert Kaufman, "The Only Hopeless Cripple," *Carry On* 1:4 (October–November 1918): 22.
35. See A. J. Dekker to Assistant Director, Rehabilitation Division, USVB (April 26, 1922), folder for San Antonio, TX, box 11, RG 15, NAB.
36. C. R. Forbes to District Managers 1, 2, 3, 4, and 7 (January 26, 1922), box 3, RG 15, NAB.
37. Douglas C. McMurtrie, "War Cripple Axioms and Fundamentals," in OSG, *Abstracts, Bulletin* 4 (May 25, 1918): 3.
38. This emphasis on standardized trades was characteristic of what was sometimes referred to as the "American" approach to rehabilitation. By contrast, European rehabilitationists often stressed the importance of developing specialized workshops with equipment specially designed for disabled veterans, particularly amputees.
39. McMurtrie, "The War Cripple," *Columbia War Papers* 1:17 (1917): 14–15.
40. William Hughes Mearns, "Memorandum on the High Lights of Reconstruction Literature" (c. 1919), p. 2, folder for Vocational and Industrial Training April–June 1919, box 232, RG 112, NACP.
41. OSG, "The Need of a 'Cheer-Up' Official in Our Base Hospitals and Hospital Ships," *Abstracts, Bulletin* 2 (March 15, 1918): 14.
42. Quoted in ibid., 16.
43. Dixon Wecter, *When Johnny Comes Marching Home* (New York: Riverside Press, 1944), 395.
44. John Aaron file, box 11, NM 30, RG 15, NAB; Fred Doucette file, box 6, NM 30, RG 15, NAB; Charles Rushford file, box 4, NM 30, RG 15, NAB.
45. Louis Jones file, box 22, NM 30, RG 15, NAB.
46. Sylvester Howland file, box 10, NM 30, RG 15, NAB.
47. Ibid. Additional details were drawn from Sarah F. Rose's discussion of Howland's case history in "No Right to Be Idle: The Invention of Disability, 1850–1930" (PhD diss., University of Illinois at Chicago, 2008), 307–9.
48. "Crippled Soldiers Disheartened by Delays," *New York Times,* August 24, 1919, 43.
49. "The Vocational Rehabilitation Program and Its Administration," 6–11; Wecter, 394–95. Historians Richard Severo and Lewis Milford approximate that 30 percent of soldiers approved for FBVE training dropped out due to extensive delays and red tape. *The Wages of War: When America's Soldiers Came Home—From Valley Forge to Vietnam* (New York: Simon and Schuster, 1989), 249.
50. Although we cannot be certain to what extent race was a factor in Joseph Ray's case, his white instructors denied the charge of racism, and Ray was refused further training. In the end, Ray was dismissed from the school shortly before his rehabilitation date. "Decision of the Rehabilitation Committee Chicago Sub-District Office" (June 4, 1924); "Memo" (June 11, 1924); "Report to the Chief Inspection Division Control Service" (June 12, 1924); all in folder for U.S Veterans' Bureau Vocational School, Federal Board School of Music, Chicago, IL, box 4, RG 15, NAB.

51. See Robert H. Zieger, *America's Great War: World War I and the American Experience* (Lanham, MD: Rowman and Littlefield, 2000), 126–35.

52. Frank Billings to Emmett J. Scott (April 24, 1919), box 232, RG 112, NACP.

53. For a broader discussion of federal policies toward African American veterans following World War I, see Jennifer D. Keene, "The Long Journey Home: African American World War I Veterans and Veterans' Policies," in *Veterans' Policies, Veterans' Politics: New Perspectives on Veterans in the Modern United States*, ed. Stephen R. Ortiz (Gainesville: University Press of Florida, 2012), 146–70; Chad L. Williams, *Torchbearers of Democracy: African American Soldiers in the World War I Era* (Chapel Hill: University of North Carolina Press, 2010).

54. "Organization of USVB Vocational School, Silver Spring, MD," folder for Silver Spring, MD, box 11, RG 15, NAB.

55. E. W. Beatty to Clinton J. Wallace (August 14, 1923), box 1, 15 PC-15 63, RG 15, NAB.

56. "Letter from Fort McHenry," box 1, 15 PC-15 63, RG 15, NAB.

57. P. H. Roney to J. R. A. Crossland, "Report on A&M School, Normal, AL," box 1, 15 PC-15 63, RG 15, NAB.

58. J. R. A. Crossland, "Report on Inspection of A&M State Normal School, Prairie View, TX" (June 2, 1922), box 1, 15 PC-15 63, RG 15, NAB.

59. C. A. Greer to J. R. A. Crossland (July 26, 1922), box 1, 15 PC-15 63, RG 15, NAB.

60. Statement of Buster Sunter (August 7, 1922), enclosed in P. H. Roney to J. R. A. Crossland, "Report on A&M School, Normal, AL," box 1, 15 PC-15 63, RG 15, NAB.

61. James E. Sanford to J. R. A. Crossland (November 10, 1921), box 1, 15 PC-15 63, RG 15, NAB.

62. E. G. Dexter to the Director of the US Veterans' Bureau (July 5, 1924), folder for Camp Sherman, Chillicothe, OH, box 2, RG 15, NAB.

63. George R. Kelton to Frank T. Hines (May 19, 1924), folder for Waynesville, NC, box 13, RG 15, NAB.

64. "Remarks of E. H. Hale Delivered before the Assembled Trainees at Pascagoula," folder Pascagoula, Mississippi, box 8, Rehabilitation Historical File, RG 15, NAB.

65. Zieger, 87.

66. E. H. Hale to the Director USVB (October 20, 1921), folder for Pascagoula, Mississippi, box 8, Rehabilitation Historical File, RG 15, NAB.

67. Keene, 153.

68. On anxieties related to women in the rehabilitation process, see Linker, 61–78.

69. E. P. Chester to F. O. Smith (February 22, 1922), folder for Baltimore, MD, Fort McHenry, box 1, RG 15, NAB.

70. Reprinted in Surgeon General of the Army to Commanding Officer, General Hospital no. 2 (September 19, 1919), box 231, RG 112, NACP.

71. William N. Bisphan to the Surgeon General of the Army (September 23, 1919), box 231, RG 112, NACP.

72. James E. Baylis to Chief of Morale Branch (October 15, 1919), box 231, RG 112, NACP.

73. Douglas C. McMurtrie, *The Disabled Soldier* (New York: Macmillan, 1919), 104.

74. W. Frank Persons, "Looking After the Soldier's Family," *Carry On* 1:1 (July 1918): 20.

75. Arthur H. Samuels, "Reconstructing the Public," *Carry On* 1:1 (June 1918): 16.

76. Ibid., 15. For more on the need to spread the message of rehabilitation, see John Culbert Faries, *Three Years of Work for Handicapped Men: A Report of the Activities*

of the Institute for Crippled and Disabled Men (New York: Institute for Crippled and Disabled Men, 1920), 68.

77. McMurtrie, *The Disabled Soldier*, 109–10.

78. Ibid., 110.

79. See Stephen C. Mason, "The Manufacturers' Message to Our Disabled Fighting Men," *Ladies' Home Journal* 35 (October 1918): 76.

80. Ford Motor Company, *Disabled Veterans Working in Industry*, 200FC-34d, National Archives at College Park—Motion Pictures, NACP.

81. Ford Motor Company, *The Reawakening*, 200FC-2478, National Archives at College Park—Motion Pictures, NACP.

82. Douglas C. McMurtrie, introduction to Faries, *Three Years of Work*, 5.

83. Faries, 3–4, 65–68.

84. Ibid., 70–75. For a reprint of Douglas C. McMurtrie's flyer, *Your Duty to the War Cripple*, see the *American Journal of Care for Cripples* 7:1 (September 1918): 82.

85. Adams, 62.

86. Federal Board for Vocational Education, *What the Employers of America Can Do for the Disabled Soldiers and Sailors* (Washington, DC, 1918), 7; Charles M. Schwab, "Launching Men Anew," *Carry On* 1:2 (August 1918): 6–8.

87. Herbert Kaufman, "Do Not Dare Pity Them" (1917), folder for April–June 1918, box 233, RG 112, NACP.

88. For examples of publicity materials aimed at family members, see Frank Parker Stockbridge, "If He Comes Home Disabled, What Can We Do for Him?" *Ladies' Home Journal* 35 (October 1918): 76; Edith Day Robinson, "As Our Wounded Come Home" *The Independent* 96 (December 14, 1918): 362–63, 379; Federal Board for Vocational Education, *To the Household of the Disabled Soldier and Sailor* (Washington, DC, 1918).

89. Julian W. Mack, "A Chance—With a Running Start," *Carry On* 1:2 (August 1918): 11.

90. Maurice Bourrillon, "To Disabled Soldiers," *Carry On* 1:7 (April 1919): 3.

91. Mack, 13.

92. Gertrude Atherton, "Beggars No More," *Carry On* 1:4 (November 1918): 17, 19.

93. See Douglas C. McMurtrie, "War Cripple Axioms and Fundamentals," in OSG, *Abstracts, Bulletin* 4 (May 25, 1918): 17; "Bright Chances for Older Men and Disabled Soldiers," *Current Opinion* 66 (June 1919): 403–4.

94. Todd, 3.

95. "Remarks of Dean Burris at the opening of a Preliminary Conference on Training Teachers of Occupational Therapy, held at the University of Cincinnati, November 4, 1918," p. 2, box 235, entry 29, RG 112, NACP.

96. "The Passing of the Cripple," 166.

97. Atherton, 20.

98. H. M. Kahler, quoted in "Human Salvage," *Literary Digest* 52 (January 8, 1916): 63.

99. This argument corresponds with that of cultural anthropologist Henri-Jacques Stiker, who contends that rehabilitationists' failures to address the root causes of disability in the "dangers of technological society (work, wars, speed, etc.)" were due to the influence of liberalism, an ideology that "consists in seeing all forms of impairment as accidents." Henri-Jacques Stiker, *A History of Disability*, trans. William Sayers (Ann Arbor: University of Michigan Press 2000), 175, 174.

100. Frank T. Hines, "Ten Years of Caring for Our Maimed Heroes," *New York Times*, November 11, 1928, 159. On the numbers of Great War veterans who were eligible for, entered, and completed government rehabilitation programs, see John Maurice Clark, *The Costs of the World War to the American People* (New Haven: Yale University Press, 1931), 189–90.

101. Stanley Frost, "Grab-Bag Training for Veterans," *The Outlook* 135 (September 26, 1923): 142–44.

102. Clark, 190.

103. Richard Lee Strout, "Veterans and the High Cost of War," *The Independent* 121 (October 13, 1928): 342; Clark, 181.

104. Hines, 159.

THE SWEET BILL

1. "Legion Will Carry Fight to Congress," *Fort Wayne Journal-Gazette*, December 16, 1919, 7.

2. "Disabled Yank Bill Sent to the Senate with the 'Do Pass' Sign," *Woodland [CA] Daily Democrat*, December 23, 1919, 8.

3. Marquis James, *A History of the American Legion* (New York: William Green, 1923), 99–101; "Wilson Signs Bill for War Cripples," *New York Times*, December 25, 1919, 13.

4. House, *Proceedings of the 10th National Convention of the Disabled American Veterans of the World War*, 71st Cong., 2nd sess. (1930), H. Doc. 494, 4. See also Rodney G. Minott, *Peerless Patriots: Organized Veterans and the Spirit of Americanism* (Washington: Public Affairs Press, 1962), 50.

CHAPTER FIVE

1. John Lax and William Pencak, "Creating the American Legion," *South Atlantic Quarterly* 81:1 (Winter 1982): 49.

2. Stuart McConnell, *Glorious Contentment: The Grand Army of the Republic, 1865–1900* (Chapel Hill: University of North Carolina Press, 1992).

3. House, *Proceedings of the 12th National Convention, Disabled American Veterans of the World War* (hereafter *DAV 1932*), 72nd Cong., 2nd sess. (1932), H. Doc. 450, 11.

4. David A. Gerber, "Disabled Veterans, the State, and the Experience of Disability in Western Societies, 1914–1950," *Journal of Social History* 36:4 (Summer 2003): 902.

5. Stephen R. Ortiz, "The New and Great War of American Citizenship: Overseas Veterans, Masculinity, and Citizenship in the Great Depression," paper presented at the American Studies Association Annual Meeting, November 2003. See also Stephen R. Ortiz, *Beyond the Bonus March and GI Bill: How Veteran Politics Shaped the New Deal Era* (New York: New York University Press, 2010).

6. Davis R. B. Ross, *Preparing for Ulysses: Politics and Veterans during World War II* (New York: Columbia University Press, 1969), 9.

7. Although Legion bylaws waived all consideration of rank within the order, many enlisted men remained suspicious of the Legion's close ties to military brass. In turn, the Legion headquarters adhered to a rigid state's-rights policy, permitting Southern whites to deny the applications of all but a small number of African American posts. See William Pencak, *For God and Country: The American Legion, 1919–1941* (Boston: Northeastern University Press, 1989), 68–69; Jennifer D. Keene, *World War I* (Westport, CT: Greenwood Press, 2006), 187.

8. George S. Wheat, *The Story of the American Legion* (New York: G. P. Putnam's Sons, 1919), 186.
9. Quoted in Marcus Duffield, *King Legion* (New York: Jonathan Cape and Harrison Smith, 1931), 1. On the early history of the American Legion, see Pencak, *For God and Country*; Richard Seelye Jones, *A History of the American Legion* (Indianapolis: Bobbs-Merrill, 1946).
10. Quoted in American Legion National Rehabilitation Committee, *The American Legion at Work for the Sick and Disabled* (1922), 157.
11. Louis Johnson quoted in William Gellermann, *The American Legion as Educator* (New York: Teacher's College, Columbia University, 1938), 72.
12. This sketch of the DAV's founding and early leadership draws heavily upon the group's official history, *Wars & Scars: A Diamond Anniversary History of the Disabled American Veterans* (Cold Spring, KY: Disabled American Veterans, 1995). Insights and details are also drawn from Rodney G. Minott, *Peerless Patriots: Organized Veterans and the Spirit of Americanism* (Washington: Public Affairs Press, 1962), 50–53; "Living Hall of Fame," *Overland Monthly* 79 (March 1922): 11–13; *DAV 1932*.
13. This quote was frequently repeated. See House, *Proceedings of the 11th National Convention, Disabled American Veterans of the World War* (hereafter *DAV 1931*), 72nd Cong., 1st sess. (1931), H. Doc. 50, 11.
14. The name was shortened to the Disabled American Veterans in January 1941.
15. *DAV 1931,* 52; *Wars & Scars.*
16. *DAV 1931*, 119.
17. See *Minnesota DAV Annual* 9:1 (1928): 46.
18. House, *Incorporating the Disabled American Veterans*, 67th Cong., 1st sess. (1921), H. Rept. 263, 2.
19. *DAV 1931*, 6.
20. Roger Daniels, *The Bonus March: An Episode of the Great Depression* (Westport, CN: Greenwood Press, 1971), 24.
21. Marquis James, *A History of the American Legion* (New York: William Green, 1923), 135.
22. *Wars & Scars*, 12.
23. Steven Trout, *On the Battlefield of Memory: The First World War and American Remembrance, 1919–1941* (Tuscaloosa: University of Alabama Press, 2010), 30.
24. *DAV 1931*, 22.
25. Minott, 52.
26. American Legion National Rehabilitation Committee, 27.
27. Pencak, 64.
28. Duffield, 298–309.
29. American Legion National Rehabilitation Committee, 27.
30. Quoted in James, 162.
31. Ben Singer, "Modernity, Hyperstimulus, and the Rise of Popular Sensationalism," in *Cinema and the Invention of Modern Life*, ed. Leo Charney and Vanessa R. Schwartz (Berkeley: University of California Press, 1995), 72–99.
32. Quoted in James, 163.
33. Quoted in ibid., 164, 163.
34. Ibid., 95, 165–67; Jones, 131.

35. Caroline Cox, "Invisible Wounds: The American Legion, Shell-Shocked Veterans, and American Society, 1919–1924," in *Traumatic Pasts: History, Psychiatry, and Trauma in the Modern Age*, ed. Mark S. Micale and Paul Lerner (Cambridge: Cambridge University Press: 2001), 305.

36. American Legion National Rehabilitation Committee, 51, 16.

37. Ibid., 64.

38. Senator James J. Davis quoted in *DAV 1931*, 47.

39. Lloyd Ruth, "The Disabled Veterans Are—," *Minnesota DAV Annual* 9:1 (1928): 5.

40. Quoted in House, *Proceedings of the 13th National Convention of the Disabled American Veterans of the World War* (hereafter *DAV 1933*), 73rd Cong., 2nd sess. (1933), H. Doc. 153, 2.

41. Gerber, "Disabled Veterans," 901.

42. Paul K. Longmore, "The League of the Physically Handicapped and the Great Depression: A Case Study in the New Disability History," in *Why I Burned My Book and Other Essays on Disability* (Philadelphia: Temple University Press, 2003), 71.

43. Ross, 10–11; Pencak, 176; Francis-Arrington-Jones Post of the American Legion to F. B. Forbes, American Legion file, August 1918–June 1925, RG 15, (National Archives, Washington, DC (hereafter NAB).

44. American Legion Service Division, "Form A-1" and "Know Your Rights as an Ex-Service Man" in *Outline of Suggested Activities for Service Officers and American Legion Local Posts*, American Legion file, August 1918–June 1925, RG 15, NAB; *Wars & Scars*.

45. Arthur H. Samuels, "Reconstructing the Public," *Carry On* 1:1 (June 1918): 16.

46. See Dewitt Law, *Soldiers of the DAV: A History of Disabled War Veterans and the American Pension System* (Pasadena, CA, 1929).

47. "Disabled Veterans Must Be Fully Reclaimed," *Fort Wayne News-Sentinel*, June 28, 1921, 8.

48. Memorandum from Charles F. Sheridan, National War Risk Officer, to All Local Posts of the American Legion (c. 1921), American Legion file: August 1918–June 1925, RG 15, NAB; "Outline of Suggested Activities for Service Officers of American Legion Local Posts" (July 28, 1921), American Legion file: August 1918–June 1925, RG 15, NAB.

49. *DAV 1932*, 87–96.

50. Jones, 137–38.

51. Pencak, 193; William Pyrle Dillingham, *Federal Aid to Veterans, 1917–1941* (Gainesville: University of Florida Press), 76.

52. On FDR's disability, see Hugh Gregory Gallagher, *FDR's Splendid Deception*, rev. ed. (Arlington, VA: Vandamere Press, 1994).

53. Quoted in Pencak, 194.

54. Pencak, 193, 196. Stephen R. Ortiz contrasts the VFW's and the American Legion's responses to the Economy Act in "The 'New Deal' for Veterans: The Economy Act, the Veterans of Foreign Wars, and the Origins of New Deal Dissent," *Journal of Military History* 70 (April 2006): 415–38.

55. Dillingham, 79, 81.

56. "You Need Us," *Minnesota DAV Annual* 9:1 (1928): 46.

57. Duffield, 19–21.

58. "You Need Us," 46.

59. *DAV 1933*, 235, 227.

60. Pencak, 188; *Wars & Scars*.

61. Jones, 328–33.

62. House, *Proceedings of the 10th National Convention of the Disabled American Veterans of the World War*, 71st Cong., 2nd sess. (1930), H. Doc. 494, 167–90.

63. Quoted in James, 230.

64. Duffield, 18.

65. William E. Tate quoted in *DAV 1932*, 11.

66. Quoted in ibid., 3.

67. *DAV 1931*, 129–30.

68. *DAV 1932*, 180.

69. "Disabled Veterans Are Given Meeting," *Nevada State Journal*, June 23, 1922, 3; "Living Hall of Fame," 11–13.

70. "Singers to Help Disabled Veterans Get Funds for Their Mountain Camp," *New York Times*, June 3, 1923, X10.

71. "Come Back Club Gives Military Ball," *New York Times*, February 27, 1926, X10; "The Come Back Club Dance," May 3, 1924, 15.

72. Big Island Veterans Camp file, Excelsior Historical Society, Excelsior, Minnesota; "Report on the Operation of Big Island Veterans' Camp," file: Big Island Veterans Camp, Minnesota Historical Society, St. Paul, Minnesota.

73. "The Gang's All Here," Otis Historical Archives 245, National Museum of Health and Medicine, Washington, DC. See also "The Work of the 'Dug-Out,'" *New York Times*, June 12, 1921, 74; "Aid Disabled Veterans of Dug Out," *New York Times*, May 20, 1930, 35; "Teas to Aid the Dug Out," *New York Times*, May 11, 1931, 23.

74. Dillingham, 223.

75. On public outcry against the "veteran racket," see J. Pendleton Herring, "Scotching the Veterans' Lobby," *North American Review* 23 (1933): 48–54; Dillingham, 73–74.

76. Quoted in Pencak, 171.

77. Ibid., 14–16.

78. On the "fascistic tendencies" of the American Legion, see Duffield, 168–69; Gellermann, 46–47, 264–66; Milton S. Mayer, "The American Legion Takes Orders," *American Mercury* (1935): 146–57; Pencak, 20–23.

79. Duffield, 34; see also Pencak, 94–95.

80. Katherine Mayo, *Soldiers What Next!* (Boston: Houghton Mifflin, 1934), 101.

81. In order to receive an allowance, veterans with permanent disabilities deemed 25 percent or higher had to meet two conditions: first, they had to have been exempt from income tax the previous year (evidence of their "need"); and second, their disabilities could not be a result of "willful misconduct." These two conditions were immediately challenged by Legion-friendly congressmen.

82. Talcott Powell, *Tattered Banners* (New York: Harcourt, Brace, and Co., 1933), 194.

83. Dillingham, 52–53.

84. On the American Veterans' Association, see Dixon Wecter, *When Johnny Comes Marching Home* (Cambridge, MA: Riverside Press, 1944), 48–49.

85. Gellermann, 39; Ernest Angell, "The Legion Expels Its Liberals," *New Republic* 75 (June 7, 1933): 93–94.

86. Ernest Angell, "American Legion Versus America," *The Nation* 136 (March 15, 1933): 287.

87. Duffield, 13–24, 18.

88. Mayo, 124, 136, 125, 169, 193.

89. Duffield, 205–22.

90. Frederick Palmer, "A Personal View—Little 'Cootie' Mencken," *American Legion Monthly* (August 1927): 41.

91. Pencak, 174–75.

92. Stanley Frost, "Salvaging the Veterans' Bureau," *The Outlook* 135 (October 3, 1923): 179.

93. Walter Millis, "Bewildered Doughboys," *The Nation* 141 (September 25, 1935): 363.

94. Powell, 253.

95. See Frederick Lewis Allen, *Since Yesterday: The 1930s in America, September 3, 1929–September 3, 1939* (New York: Perennial, 1986); Howard Zinn, *A People's History of the United States* (New York: HarperPerennial, 1990).

96. See Jennifer D. Keene, *Doughboys, the Great War, and the Remaking of America* (Baltimore: Johns Hopkins University Press, 2001); Ortiz, *Beyond the Bonus March and GI Bill*; Paul Dickson and Thomas B. Allen, *The Bonus Army: An American Epic* (New York: Walker and Co., 2004).

97. Quoted in Jacob Armstrong Swisher, *The American Legion in Iowa, 1919–1929* (Iowa City: State Historical Society of Iowa, 1929), 137.

98. Daniels, 36.

99. "They Should Come First," *New York Times*, January 23, 1922, 8.

100. James, 126.

101. Ortiz, "Rethinking the Bonus March: Federal Bonus Policy, the Veterans of Foreign Wars, and the Origins of a Protest Movement," *Journal of Policy History* 18:3 (2006): 276.

102. Quoted in ibid., 286.

103. Quoted in Dickson and Allen, 86.

104. Quoted in ibid., 131.

105. Daniels, 85; "Robertson Promises to Picket Mayflower Hotel," *Olean [NY] Times Herald*, July 21, 1932, 1.

106. Quoted in Jack Douglas, *Veterans on the March* (New York: Workers Library, 1934), 194.

107. Dickson and Allen ,146; Douglas, 197.

108. Powell, 234.

109. Franklin D. Roosevelt, "The President Vetoes the Bonus Bill, May 22, 1935," in *The Public Papers and Addresses of Franklin D. Roosevelt* (New York: Random House, 1938–50), 4:293.

110. John Thomas Taylor, "There Ought to Be a Law—And There Is," *American Legion Monthly* (November 1928): 72.

FORGET-ME-NOT DAY

1. Quoted in "Forget-Me-Not Day," *Frederick [MD] Daily News*, December 16, 1921, n.p.; "Plan US Tag Day for Wounded Vets," *Appleton [WI] Post-Crescent*, December 10, 1921, 12; "Forget-Me-Not Day," *Iowa City Press-Citizen*, December 9, 1921, 4; "Legion Post Plans to Help Disabled," *Oakland Tribune*, December 8, 1921, 13.

2. "'Forget-Me-Not Day' to Aid Wounded Veterans," *Fort Wayne [IN] News Sentinel*, November 4, 1922, 21; "Wins Harding's Approval," *New York Times*, November 3, 1922, 23.

3. "Forget-Me-Not Day Aids Soldier Fund," *New York Times*, November 5, 1922, 9.
4. "Forget Me Not Day," *Walnut Grove [MN] Tribune*, September 19, 1929, 1.
5. Clipping of "Forget-Me-Not Sale Saturday," *Dakota County [MN] Tribune*, September 23, 1927, in Argonne Farms file, Dakota County Historical Society, Lakeville, MN.
6. Frances Montgomery, "Little Blue Flower Flourishes as City Shows Remembrance," *Oakland [CA] Tribune* November 6, 1922, A9.
7. "Many Disabled Veterans Ask Aid of Public," *Oakland [CA] Tribune*, December 2, 1927, A7.

CHAPTER SIX

1. "A Forget-Me-Not Answers," reprinted in "Forget-Me-Not to Again Speak for the Dead," *Albert Lea [MN] Evening Tribune*, September 25, 1930, 5.
2. Edward T. Linenthal, *The Unfinished Bombing: Oklahoma City in American Memory* (New York: Oxford University Press, 2001); Theo Farrell, *The Norms of War: Cultural Beliefs and Modern Conflict* (Boulder, CO: Lynne Rienner, 2005); Jay Winter, *Remembering War: The Great War between Memory and History in the Twentieth Century* (New Haven: Yale University Press, 2006); Erika Doss, *Memorial Mania: Public Feeling in America* (Chicago: University of Chicago Press, 2012).
3. Marita Sturken, *Tangled Memories: The Vietnam War, the AIDS Epidemic, and the Politics of Remembering* (Berkeley: University of California Press, 1997); Alison Landsberg, *Prosthetic Memory: The Transformation of American Remembrance in the Age of Mass Culture* (New York: Columbia University Press, 2004); E. Ann Kaplan, *Trauma Culture: The Politics of Terror and Loss in Media and Literature* (New Brunswick, NJ: Rutgers University Press, 2005).
4. Winter, 3. Because remembering is an active practice, Winter prefers the term "remembrance" to "memory." In his words, "To privilege 'remembrance' is to insist on specifying agency, on answering the question who remembers, when, where, and how?" Memory, on the other hand, is best understood in both narrative and economic terms—as a way of structuring collective stories about the past, and as a kind of social resource, a commodity produced through representation and ritual (4). In this chapter, I have tried to use "remembrance" when describing the active process and "memory" to describe the result.
5. On the concept of a "memory boom," see Winter; and Jeffrey K. Olick, Vered Vinitzky-Seroussi, and Daniel Levy, introduction to *The Collective Memory Reader*, ed. Olick, Vinitzky-Seroussi, and Levy (Oxford: Oxford University Press, 2011), 3–62.
6. Samuel Hynes, *A Soldier's Tale: Bearing Witness to Modern War* (New York: Penguin, 1998).
7. James M. Mayo, *War Memorials as Political Landscape: The American Experience and Beyond* (New York: Praeger, 1988), 80–86.
8. On the international debate between supporters of traditional memorial practices and advocates of utilitarian designs, see G. Kurt Piehler, *Remembering War the American Way* (Washington, DC: Smithsonian Institution Press, 1995), 105–13.
9. Thomas M. Owen, Jr., "American World War Memorials," *FIDAC: Interallied Review of the Five Continents* 12:5 (May 1936): 6.
10. "Proceedings of the Tenth National Convention of the American Legion" [1928] (hereafter *American Legion 1929*), 70th Cong., 2nd sess. (1929), H. Doc. 388, 195, 225.

11. Not all state-sponsored memorials were made of metal or stone. Vermont appropriated $25,000 for the publication of an official history of the state's participation in the war, providing each Vermont veteran with a bound copy in 1928. Likewise, the Iowa state legislature appropriated $1,000 per year to archive the lives of Iowans in wartime. By 1936, the state's collection included more than 4,000 photographs, war posters, and other wartime artifacts. Owen, Jr., 8, 6.

12. Piehler, 96.

13. On the cult of the "fallen" in European memory, see George L. Mosse, *Fallen Soldiers: Reshaping the Memory of the World Wars* (New York: Oxford University Press, 1990).

14. Piehler, 96–97.

15. Seth Koven, "Remembering and Dismemberment: Crippled Children, Wounded Soldiers, and the Great War in Great Britain," *American Historical Review* 99:4 (October 1994): 1169.

16. On the relationship of war memorials to postwar bereavement, see Jay Winter, *Sites of Memory, Sites of Mourning: The Great War in European Cultural History* (Cambridge: Cambridge University Press, 1995).

17. On disabled veterans' inability to forget, see Bob Herbert, "Forget the War? Many Can't," *New York Times*, August 4, 2005, A23.

18. Sturken, 73.

19. Elaine Scarry, *The Body in Pain: The Making and Unmaking of the World* (New York: Oxford University Press, 1985), 113–18.

20. See Jo Stanley, "Involuntary Commemorations: Post-Traumatic Stress Disorder and Its Relationship to War Commemoration," in *The Politics of War Memory and Commemoration*, ed. T. G. Ashplant, Graham Dawson, and Michal Roper (London: Routledge, 2000), 240–62.

21. Stanley, 240.

22. Winter, *Remembering War*, 57.

23. "Coolidge Sends a Greeting to All Disabled Veterans," *New York Times*, December 21, 1925, 1.

24. "Disabled Soldiers on Morgan's Yacht," *New York Times*, August 14, 1921, 25; "To Give Dialect Recital," *New York Times*, June 25, 1931, 23.

25. "Disabled Veterans Guests of Hoovers," *New York Times*, June 11, 1931, 27.

26. Matthew Dennis, *Red, White, and Blue Letter Days: An American Calendar* (Ithaca: Cornell University Press, 2002), 1.

27. My use of the term "invented tradition" is, of course, borrowed from Eric Hobsbawm. See "Introduction: Inventing Tradition," in *The Invention of Tradition*, ed. Eric Hobsbawm and Terence Ranger (Cambridge: Cambridge University Press, 1983), 1–14.

28. "10,000 Parade 5th Ave. in Military Display," *New York Times*, April 6, 1930, 3.

29. On the founding and evolution of Memorial Day, see Ellen M. Litwicki, *American Public Holidays, 1865–1920* (Washington, DC: Smithsonian Institution Press, 2000).

30. The following account of Michael's life is drawn largely from Moina Michael, *The Miracle Flower: The Story of the Flanders Fields Memorial Poppy* (Philadelphia: Dorrance, 1941).

31. Paul Fussell, *The Great War and Modern Memory* (New York: Oxford University Press, 1975), 248; John McCrae, "In Flanders Fields," in *In Flanders Fields and Other Poems* (New York: G. P. Putnam's Sons, 1919), 3.

32. McCrae, 3.

33. Michael, 47.

34. Ibid., 65.

35. There is some degree of irony in the fact that Poppy Day sales were not always conducted on a Great War–themed holiday. While the VFW routinely sold its Buddy Poppies on Armistice Day, the American Legion preferred Memorial Day (May 30), a holiday whose observance predated World War I by decades.

36. Bill Bottoms, *The VFW: An Illustrative History of the Veterans of Foreign Wars of the United States* (Rockville, MD: Woodbine House, 1991), 65–66.

37. Michael, 87–88. Other veterans' and charity groups also sold war remembrance flowers. The Jewish War Veterans, the Veterans of Belleau Wood, and the US Marine Brigade mainly participated in Legion-led flower sales. The Children of the American Loyalty League, on the other hand, peddled paper "No-Man's-Land" roses—manufactured by disabled veterans—to fund a mountain home for American war orphans. "Coolidge Gets a Paper Rose," *New York Times*, December 12, 1924, 19; "First Day Poppy Sale Breaks Old Records," *New York Times*, May 26, 1925, 21.

38. Elmo Scott Watson, "The Red Poppy—Symbol of Armistice Day," *Indiana Weekly Messenger*, October 30, 1930, 7.

39. Michael, 84.

40. "Tainted 'Poppies' Will Feed Fire; Legion Hurt at Slur," *Indianapolis Star*, May 23, 1923, 2.

41. It is also notable that flower selling, which promised volunteers no monetary return for their efforts, continued to be dominated by women.

42. "The Story of Poppies," *[Elyria, OH]Chronicle-Telegram*, May 22, 1929, 2.

43. Douglas I. McKay described memory preservation as "the fourth of the fundamental principles of the American Legion." Quoted in *American Legion 1929*, 61.

44. Richard Seelye Jones, *A History of the American Legion* (Indianapolis: Bobbs-Merrill, 1946), 242–43.

45. J. L. Monnahan, "What of the War Disabled," *Minnesota DAV Annual* 9:1 (1929): 17.

46. Newton D. Baker quoted in "Proceedings of the Thirteenth National Convention of the American Legion" [1931], 72nd Cong., 1st sess. (1932), H. Doc. 48, 9.

47. Quoted in *American Legion 1929*, 19.

48. On the contested meaning of Armistice Day in Great Britain, see Adrian Gregory, *The Silence of Memory: Armistice Day, 1919–1946* (Oxford: Berg, 1994).

49. See A. P. Sanford and Robert Haven Schauffler, eds., *Armistice Day* (New York: Dodd, Mead, 1927).

50. Arthur S. Link, ed., *The Papers of Woodrow Wilson* (Princeton: Princeton University Press, 1993), 68:466–7.

51. Litwicki, 240.

52. "Foch Sees Ingots Rolled into Plates," *New York Times*, November 11, 1921, 3.

53. American Legion, "Suggested Address for Use by Legion Speaker on Armistice Day," in *Armistice Day*, 160.

54. See Adrian Forty and Susanne Kuchler, eds., *The Art of Forgetting* (London: Berg, 2001).

55. Dennis, 7.

56. Sturken, 7.

57. "Has American Abandoned Her Crippled Soldiers?" *The Outlook* 123 (November 12, 1919): 289.

58. Quoted in "'Shameful Neglect' of our Disabled Dough-boys," *Literary Digest* 68:4 (January 22, 1921): 1.

59. "Norwalk Hero of War Dies of Starvation," *New York Times*, February 26, 1931, reprinted in *Disarm!* 1 (Autumn 1931): 16–17.

60. William Faulkner, *Soldiers' Pay* (New York: Liveright, 1997), 145.

61. Faulkner, 194–95.

62. On the theory of the abject, see Julia Kristeva, *Powers of Horror: An Essay on Abjection*, trans. Leon S. Roudiez (New York: Columbia University Press, 1982).

63. Although henceforth associated with the Great Depression, the term *Forgotten Man* did not originate with FDR or his speechwriters, but with a pair of Progressive era intellectuals, William Graham Sumner and Walter H. Page. See William Graham Sumner, "The Forgotten Man," *The Forgotten Man and Other Essays*, ed. Albert Galloway Kellner (New Haven: Yale University Press, 1919), 494–95; Walter H. Page, "The Forgotten Man," *The Rebuilding of Old Commonwealths: Being Essays Towards the Training of the Forgotten Man in the Southern States* (New York: Doubleday, Page, 1902), 22, 31.

64. Franklin D. Roosevelt, "The Forgotten Man," in *The Public Papers and Addresses of Franklin D. Roosevelt*, vol. 1, *1928–1932* (New York: Random House, 1938), 624.

65. Quoted in James H. Guilfoyle, *On the Trail of the Forgotten Man* (Boston: Peabody Masters, 1933), 180–81.

66. Quoted in Aaron Glantz, *The War Comes Home: Washington's Battle against America's Veterans* (Berkeley: University of California Press, 2009), 71.

67. Nearly a century a later, this sentiment is echoed in the motto of the Wounded Warrior Project, a disabled veterans' service organization founded in 2003: "The greatest casualty is being forgotten." See http://www.woundedwarriorproject.org/.

68. "Disabled American Vets to Have Day," *Fitchburg [MA] Sentinel*, November 7, 1922, 11.

69. Quoted in "Forget-Me-Not Day Proclamation Out," *Syracuse Herald*, November 4, 1922. For similar sentiments, see "Hails 'Forget-Me-Not Day,'" *New York Times*, November 2, 1922, 17.

JAMES M. KIRWIN

1. J. M. Kirwin, "Religious Musings," *Port Arthur News*, November 26, 1939, Sunday editorial page.

CHAPTER SEVEN

1. My use of terms like "peace movement," "peace groups," and "peace activists" is intentionally broad, incorporating individuals and organizations sympathetic to such policies and philosophies as US neutrality, nonintervention, the arbitration of international conflicts, anti-militarism, and anti-imperialism.

2. Typical of this trend is Howard Jones's widely adopted survey *Crucible of Power: A History of US Foreign Relations since 1897* (Lanham, MD: SR Books, 2001), which contains only a few fleeting references to the interwar peace movement.

3. Robert Woito, "Between the Wars," *Wilson Quarterly* 11:1 (1987): 109.

4. On the renewed currency of the interwar peace movement (and the rise of academic peace history) during the Vietnam War era, see Peter van den Dungen and Lawrence S. Wittner, "Peace History: An Introduction," *Journal of Peace Research* 40:4 (July 2003): 363–67; and Charles F. Howlett, "Studying America's Struggle against War: An Historical Perspective," *History Teacher* 36:3 (March 2003): 297–330. For general introductions to interwar peace activism, see Charles F. Howlett and Glen Zeitzer, *The American Peace Movement: History and Historiography* (Washington, DC: American Historical Association, 1985); Charles Chatfield, ed., *Peace Movements in America* (New York: Schocken, 1973); Harriet Hyman Alonso, *The Women's Peace Union and the Outlawry of War, 1921–1942* (Knoxville: University of Tennessee Press, 1989).

5. On Americans' disillusion with World War I, see Rose E. Young, ed., *Why Wars Must Cease* (New York: Macmillan, 1935); Thomas Leonard, *Above the Battle: War-Making in America from Appomattox to Versailles* (New York: Oxford University Press, 1978); Neil A. Wynn, *From Progressivism to Prosperity* (New York: Holmes and Meier, 1986); Erika G. King, "Exposing the 'Age of Lies': The Propaganda Menace as Portrayed in American Magazines in the Aftermath of World War I," *Journal of American Culture* 12:1 (March 1989): 35–40; David J. Goldberg, *Discontented America: The United States in the 1920s* (Baltimore: Johns Hopkins University Press, 1999).

6. The United States did not abandon the use of military force between the world wars. Even as isolationist politicians decried "foreign entanglements," American troops occupied the Dominican Republic (1916–1924), Haiti (1915–1934), and Nicaragua (1926–1933), among other places. See Mary A. Renda, *Taking Haiti: Military Occupation and the Culture of US Imperialism, 1915–1940* (Chapel Hill: University of North Carolina Press, 2001).

7. See Elton Atwater, *Organized Efforts in the United States toward Peace* (NY: National Committee on the Cause and Cure of War, 1936).

8. John Whiteclay Chambers II, "The American Debate over Modern War, 1871–1914," in *Anticipating Modern War: The German and American Experiences, 1871–1914*, ed. Manfred F. Boemeke, Roger Chickering, and Stig Förster (Cambridge: Cambridge University Press, 1999), 44, 50; Glen Jeansonne, *Women of the Far Right: The Mothers' Movement and World War II* (Chicago: University of Chicago Press, 1997).

9. Merle Curti, *Peace or War: The American Struggle, 1636–1936* (Boston: J. S. Canner, 1959), 273.

10. See Lawrence Wittner, *Rebels against War: The American Peace Movement, 1933–1983*, rev. ed. (Philadelphia: Temple University Press, 1984).

11. Quoted in ibid., 27.

12. This summery of World Peaceways' activities is taken from a number of documents contained in World Peaceways, boxes 1–2, CDGA, Swarthmore College Peace Collection (hereafter SCPC).

13. Curti, 268.

14. George H. Gallup, *The Gallup Poll: Public Opinion, 1935–1948* (New York: Random House, 1972), 290.

15. "Minutes of the Annual Meeting" (March 27, 1934), folder program work and corr. 1934, box 1, World Peaceways, CDGA, SCPC.

16. Mary E. Woolley, "Because Wars Waste Human Life," in Young, *Why Wars Must Cease*, 38.

17. William Gropper, "Join the Morons," reprinted from *New Masses*, April 1927, copy in folder 1922–29, box 3, subject file 1, Art in War and Peace: Graphics, SCPC.

18. "The Army Builds Men," a Fellowship of Reconciliation's recruiting card in folder misc. graphics, 1930–34, box 3, subject file 1, Art in War and Peace: Graphics, SCPC.

19. Susan M. Shepherd, *Uncle Sam Wants You (A Mass Recitation)* (Brookwood, NY: Labor Publications, 1936).

20. "Hello, Sucker," folder Advertisements (color), box 1, CDGA, World Peaceways, SCPC.

21. Art Young, *"The Soldier," Art Young Quarterly* 1:1 (1922): 7.

22. Edward Anton Gallner, *The Tragedy and Horror of War: Forgotten Men ed[ition]; An Exposé of the War Racket* (New York: Independent Book Corporation, 1933), 3.

23. John Nesbitt, *The God of War Presents His Bill "For Services Rendered"* (World Peaceways, 1937), folder 1936–37, box 1, CDGA, World Peaceways, SCPC.

24. Edmund Vance Cooke, "Armistice Day," in *Selected Poems for Armistice Day*, ed. C. B. McAllister (New York: Dean, 1928), 35–36.

25. Art Young, 7.

26. On the perceived feminization of the antiwar movement, see Harriet Hyman Alonso, *Peace as a Women's Issue: A History of the US Movement for World Peace and Women's Rights* (Syracuse: Syracuse University Press, 1993).

27. Charles Tazewell, *Three Who Were Soldiers*, in folder scripts of radio plays, dramas, box 1, Literature re: Peace, subject file 1, SCPC.

28. Harold Shapiro, *What Every Young Man Should Know about War . . .* (New York: Knight Publishers, 1937), 70.

29. Ibid., 82–83.

30. Ibid., preface.

31. For a similar analysis of the emasculating effects of war wounds, see Arthur Derounian, *They Shall Not Die in Europe* (1939), Peace Pamphlets part 3, Library of Congress, Washington, DC.

32. Dalton Trumbo, *Johnny Got His Gun* (1939; repr., New York: Bantam Books, 1959), 63, 184.

33. Ibid., 224.

34. Ibid., 225.

35. Ibid., 63; Martin F. Norden, *"Johnny Got His Gun*: Evolution of an Antiwar Statement," in *Hollywood's World War I: Motion Picture Images*, ed. Peter C. Rollins and John E. O'Conner (Bowling Green, OH: Bowling Green State University Popular Press, 1997), 161.

36. Edward Mann, "Lecture Demonstration," in *Peace in Our Time* (New York: New Theatre League, 1939), 2–6, copy in folder 1939, box 3, subject file 1, Literature re: Peace (Scripts, etc.), SCPC.

37. For a critique of the notion that photography can offer a phenomenological guarantee of "reality," see John Tagg, *The Burden of Representation: Essays on Photographies and Histories* (Minneapolis: University of Minnesota Press, 1993).

38. Bernd Hüppauf, "The Emergence of Modern War Imagery in Early Photography," *History and Memory* 5:1 (1993): 134.

39. Terry Smith, *Making the Modern: Industry, Art, and Design in America* (Chicago: University of Chicago Press, 1993), 283–328.

40. A copy of *The Absolute Truth* can be found at the First Division Museum at Cantigny in Wheaton, Illinois.

41. Ernst Friedrich, *War against War!* (1924; repr., with an introduction by Douglas Kellner, Seattle: Real Comet Press, 1987), 21–28.

42. For an illuminating discussion of Ernst Friedrich's rhetorical strategy in *War against War!*, as well as his philosophy of pacifistic anarchism, see Douglas Kellner, introduction to Friedrich, 9–18.

43. Friedrich, 21.

44. These reviews, as well as the statistic about the book's six-month sales figures, are taken from a British advertising booklet for Ernst Friedrich's *The War in Pictures* (*Krieg dem Krieg!*). A copy is found in folder undated, box 4, subject file 1, Art in War and Peace: Graphics, SCPC.

45. Edwin Leavitt Clarke, Syllabus for "Sociology of International Conflict" (1933) at Rollins College, folder 1930–4, subject file 1, Psychological Aspects of War and Peace, SCPC.

46. Frederick A. Barber, ed., *The Horror of It: Camera Records of War's Gruesome Glories* (New York: Brewer, Warren, and Putnam, 1932).

47. Christine A. Lunardini, *The ABC-CLIO Companion to the American Peace Movement in the Twentieth Century* (Santa Barbara, CA: ABC-CLIO, 1994), 43–44, 86.

48. Harry Emerson Fosdick, foreword to Barber, 8, 7.

49. Barber, 103.

50. Fosdick, 7.

51. Carrie Chapman Catt, foreword to Barber, 11.

52. Reed Harris, "Carnage for $1.35," *Columbia Spectator*, March 31, 1932. Quoted in Eileen Eagan, *Class, Culture, and the Classroom: The Student Peace Movement of the 1930s* (Philadelphia: Temple University Press, 1981), 29.

53. Young People's Socialist League of America, "What Is Wrong with This Picture?," folder undated, box 4, subject file 1, Art in War and Peace: Graphics, SCPC.

54. Friedrich, 233; Barber, 105; *No More War* (Paris: Imprimerie Coopérative Lucifer, 1934), 54.

55. Gallner, 73.

56. Marion Perham Gale, "God's Challengers," excerpted in Barber, 100.

57. Derounian, 7.

58. On the political evolution of Smedley D. Butler, see Hans Schmidt, *Maverick Marine: General Smedley D. Butler and the Contradictions of American Military History* (Lexington: University Press of Kentucky, 1998).

59. Smedley D. Butler, *War Is a Racket* (1935; repr., with an introduction by Adam Parfrey, Los Angeles: Feral House, 2003), 33.

60. Smedley D. Butler, "Common Sense Neutrality," in Butler, 56.

61. Ibid., 57.

62. Quoted in Eagan, 31.

63. On student peace activities between the world wars, see Eagan; Robert Cohen, *When the Old Left Was Young: Student Radicals and America's First Mass Student Movement, 1929–1941* (New York: Oxford University Press, 1993).

64. John Dinan, "Collecting the Horrors of War," *MHQ* 20:1 (2007): 44–47.

65. *Scholastic* 23:7 (November 11, 1933), copy in subject file 1, Cost of war: noneconomic (human) costs of war, SCPC.

66. For more on the Veterans of Future Wars, see Eagan 186–87; "Veterans of Future Wars," *March of Time* newsreel, vol. 2, episode 4 (April 17, 1936), Record 200, National Archives, College Park, MD.

67. See "The Student Looks at War" (New York: Fieldston School, 1934), copy in Peace Pamphlets, pt. 2, Library of Congress.

68. On Babb's life, see "New Century Club Sponsors Prize Peace Poster Exhibit" (May 19, 1941), clipping in folder press coverage of poster contests, box 1: General Correspondence, 1935–51, National circulation Library of Peace Posters, CDGA, SCPC; Nancy Bon, "Native of Southampton Had Lead Role in Relief Work in 1921 Russian Famine" (October 18, 1949), and clipping from the *Friend's Intelligencer* (June 30, 1951), in folder biographical info, Babb, Nancy, CDGA, SCPC.

69. The contest asked students to design original pieces of antiwar art. Posters were judged on originality, the strength of their slogans, and technique, with juries awarding prizes according to students' educational background. Winning artists received small monetary prizes, yearly subscriptions to pacifist magazines, and one-year college scholarships, and their designs were reprinted and sold in poster sets, photosets, and large sheets of stickers and stamps. In 1935, the year the first contest was held, Babb's call to "Promote Peace through Graphic Art" attracted fewer than one hundred entries; within a few years, several thousand students were participating in the contest annually. See Collection Introduction, "Peace Poster Contest Report and Plans for 1937–38," "Fifth Annual Report" (1940), and assorted press clippings, in folder General 1935, box 1, CDGA, SPCA; "National Circulating Library of Students' Peace Posters" (1939), in box 4, Art in War and Peace: Graphics, SCPC.

70. Facsimiles and some originals of the student peace posters discussed above and below can be found in Student Posters (facsimiles), box 2, National Circulating Library of Students' Peace Posters, CDGA, SCPC.

71. House, *Joint Resolution to Promote Peace and to Equalize the Burdens and to Minimize the Profits of War*, 72nd Cong., 1st sess. (1930), H. Doc. 163, 2.

72. *A Handbook on Peace and Foreign Relations* (Indianapolis: American Legion, 1936), 39.

73. William Gellermann, *The American Legion as Educator* (New York: Bureau of Publications, Teachers College, Columbia University, 1938), 169–99.

74. Quoted in Gellermann, 177.

75. Quoted in William Pencak, *For God and Country: The American Legion, 1919–1941* (Boston: Northeastern University Press, 1989), 6.

76. Rupert Hughes, "The War We Lost by Pacifism," *American Legion Monthly* (September 1931): 22.

77. On the founding, activities, and philosophies of FIDAC, see *A Handbook on Peace and Foreign Relations*, 12–19.

78. Robert M. Field, "What Our Neglected Veterans Want," *Our World* (May 1924): 95, 101.

79. "We Call You to a Conference against War," "Proceedings of US Congress Against War" and "US Congress Against War" (pamphlet), file: US Congress Against War, New York City (September 29–October 1, 1933), box 6: US, 1894–1959, subject file: Events re: peace: individual events, SCPC; "Proceedings 3rd US Congress Against War and Fascism," January 3–5, 1936, folder 1936, box 1: American League Against War and Fascism, 1933–37, CDGA American League for Peace and Democracy, SCPC.

80. Frank Olmsteed, "The No More War Parade," folder No More War Parade (May 19, 1934), subject file 1, Events re: Peace Parades and Rallies, SCPC; Green International, "No More War Parade, May 18th, 1935," folder No More War Parade (May 18, 1935, 1:30 pm), subject file 1, Events re: Peace Parades and Rallies, SCPC.

81. World Peaceways press release (May 25, 1936), "Connecticut Veteran Allots Bonus to Peace," file: Program and Correspondence 1936–37, box 1, CDGA World Peaceways, SCPC.

82. See Harold R. Peat, *The Inexcusable Lie* (New York: Barse and Hopkins, 1923); "How Can We Wipe Out War?," Swarthmore Poster Collection, SCPC.

83. William James, "The Moral Equivalent of War," *William James: The Essential Writings*, ed. Bruce W. Wilshire (Albany: State University of New York Press, 1984), 355.

84. Marion H. Barbour, "Propaganda and Public," n.d., copy in folder general information, box 1, SG 1, National Committee on the Cause and Cure of War, SCPC.

85. Salvador de Madariaga, "Do War Books Help Peace?," *Reader's Digest*, n.d., condensed from the *New York Herald Tribune*, January 19, 1930, copy in folder 1930–34, Psychological Aspects of War and Peace, subject file 1, SCPC. For a more recent critique of using injury-themed photography as antiwar propaganda, see Susan Sontag, *Regarding the Pain of Others* (New York: Farrar, Straus and Giroux, 2003).

86. Major Sherman Miles, "Problem of the Pacifist," *North American Review* 217 (March 1923): 313–26, reprinted in *War—Cause and Cure*, ed. Julia E. Johnson (New York: H. W. Wilson, 1926), 74–75, 79, 83.

87. "Basket Cases Are Denied by the Authorities," *Syracuse Herald*, April 8, 1919, 11; "No Basket Cases in American Army," *Bedford [PA] Gazette*, April 18, 1919, 1. Also see assorted correspondence on the basket case search in entry 29, "1917–1927 General Correspondence (Surgeon General's Office)," box 387, record group 112, Surgeon General's Office, 1917–27, National Archives, Washington, DC.

88. "Reunion of the Fightin' 1st," *Kansas City Times*, March 18, 1920, 8; Derounian, 7.

89. "Radio Script," folder scripts of radio plays, dramas, box 1, subject file 1, Literature re: Peace, SCPC.

90. On the use of photographs of disabled people as "cautionary tales," see Rosemarie Garland Thomson, "Seeing the Disabled: Visual Rhetorics of Disability in Popular Photography," in *The New Disability History: American Perspectives*, ed. Paul K. Longmore and Lauri Umansky (New York: New York University Press, 2001), 335–74.

HAROLD RUSSELL

1. Harold Russell, with Dan Ferullo, *The Best Years of My Life* (Middlebury, VT: Paul S. Eriksson, 1981), 3, 16.

2. Ibid., 41, 163.

3. Richard Severo, "Harold Russell Dies at 88; Veteran and Oscar Winner," *New York Times*, February 1, 2002.

CHAPTER EIGHT

1. Keith Wheeler, *We Are the Wounded* (New York: E. P. Dutton, 1945).

2. Richard Seelye Jones, *A History of the American Legion* (Indianapolis: Bobbs-Merrill, 1946), 122.

3. Henry R. Luce, "The American Century," *Life*, February 17, 1941, 63, 64, 63. On the context and legacies of Luce's vision, see Andrew J. Bacevich, ed., *The Short American Century: A Postmortem* (Cambridge, MA: Harvard University Press, 2012).

4. Kenneth D. Rose, *Myth and the Greatest Generation: A Social History of Americans in World War II* (New York: Routledge, 2008), 7.

5. On postwar "victory culture," see Tom Engelhardt, *The End of Victory Culture: Cold War America and the Disillusioning of a Generation* (New York: Basic Books, 1995).

6. Michael C. C. Adams, *The Best War Ever: America and World War II* (Baltimore: Johns Hopkins University Press, 1994); Iris Chang, *The Rape of Nanking: The Forgotten Holocaust of World War II* (New York: Basic Books, 1997); Michael S. Sherry, *The Rise of American Air Power: The Creation of Armageddon* (New Haven: Yale University Press, 1987); John W. Dower, *Cultures of War: Pearl Harbor, Hiroshima, 9–11, Iraq* (New York: Norton, 2010); Michael Glover quoted in Chris Hables Gray, *Postmodern War: The New Politics of Conflict* (New York: Guilford Press, 1997), 110.

7. Terkel included the quotation marks because he believed "the adjective 'good' mated to the noun 'war' is so incongruous." Studs Terkel, *"The Good War": An Oral History of World War II* (New York: New Press, 1987), vi.

8. John M. Kinder, "The Good War's 'Raw Chunks': Norman Mailer's *The Naked and the Dead* and James Gould Cozzens' *Guard of Honor*," *The Midwest Quarterly* 47:2 (2005): 187–202; David A. Gray, "New Uses for Old Photos: Renovating FSA Photographs in World War II Posters," *American Studies* 47, nos. 3–4 (Fall–Winter 2006): 5–34.

9. James Jones, *WWII* (New York: Ballantine, 1975), 11.

10. Over the last two decades, the myth of the Good War has come under fire from a number of scholars. Representative studies include Adams; Rose; Philip D. Beidler, *The Good War's Greatest Hits: World War II and American Remembering* (Athens: University of Georgia Press, 1998); John Bodnar, *The "Good War" in American Memory* (Baltimore: Johns Hopkins University Press, 2010). A more thorough bibliography of the Good War's critics can be found in Rose, 258–59.

11. Quoted in Adams, 4.

12. George H. Roeder, Jr., "Censoring Disorder: American Visual Imagery of World War II," in *The War in American Culture: Society and Consciousness during World War II*, ed. Lewis A. Erenberg and Susan E. Hirsch (Chicago: University of Chicago Press, 1996), 48.

13. Tom Brokaw, "Remarks at the Dedication of the National World War II Memorial," in *The United States in World War II: A Documentary Reader*, ed. G. Kurt Piehler (Oxford: Wiley-Blackwell, 2012), 272.

14. Edward W. Wood, Jr., *On Being Wounded* (Golden, CO: Fulcrum, 1991), 80.

15. Adams, 102.

16. John W. Dower, *War without Mercy: Race and Power in the Pacific War* (New York: Pantheon, 1986), 298–99.

17. E. B. Sledge, *With the Old Breed: At Pelieu and Okinawa* (New York: Presidio, 2007), 271–72.

18. Roeder, "Censoring Disorder," 62.

19. Richard A. Gabriel, *No More Heroes: Madness and Psychiatry in War* (New York: Hill and Wang, 1987), 72, 74.

20. J. Glenn Gray, *The Warriors: Reflections on Men in Battle* ([1959]; repr. New York: Harper Torchbook, 1967), 104–5.

21. Adams, 95.

22. On the OWI's efforts to manage Americans' exposure to death and injury, see George H. Roeder, Jr., *The Censored War: American Visual Experience during World War II* (New Haven: Yale University Press, 1993).

23. Willard Waller, *The Veteran Comes Back* (New York: Dryden Press, 1944); Wilma T. Donahue and Clark Tibbitts, "The Task before the Veteran and Society," *Annals of the American Academy of Political and Social Science* 239 (May 1945): 1–9; Technical Information Division Office of the Surgeon General, US Army, "The Physically Disabled," *Annals of the American Academy of Political and Social Science* 239 (May 1945): 10–19; Donald Becker, "The Veteran: Problem and Challenge," *Social Forces* 25:1 (October 1946): 95–99; Roy V. Peel, "The 'Separateness' of the Veteran," *Annals of the American Academy of Political and Social Science* 238 (March 1945): 167–73.

24. Technical Information Division Office of the Surgeon General, 10.

25. David A. Gerber, "Heroes and Misfits: The Troubled Social Reintegration of Disabled Veterans in *The Best Years of Our Lives*," in *Disabled Veterans in History*, ed. David A. Gerber (Ann Arbor: University of Michigan Press, 2000), 73.

26. Technical Information Division Office of the Surgeon General, 10.

27. Rufus E. Clement, "Problems of Demobilization and Rehabilitation of the Negro Solder after World Wars I and II," *Journal of Negro Education* 12:3 (Summer 1943): 533–42; Elizabeth D. S. Stewart, "Post-College Achievement of Veterans of World War I Enrolled in the University of Colorado," *School Review* 54:10 (December 1946): 593–97; Walter V. Bingham, "'Start Climbing, Soldier!' The Army Program for Rehabilitating Casualties," *Annals of the American Academy of Political and Social Science* 239 (May 1945): 60–65; Evangeline Thurber, "Rehabilitation of World War I Veterans in District No. 12," *Pacific Historical Review* 15:1 (March 1946): 68–76.

28. Donahue and Tibbitts, 2.

29. Edna Yost, with Lillian M. Gilbreth, *Normal Lives for the Disabled* (New York: Macmillan, 1945), 269.

30. For a more detailed discussion of this literature, see Susan M. Hartmann, "Prescriptions for Penelope: Literature on Women's Obligations to Returning World War II Veterans," *Women's Studies* 5:3 (1978): 223–39.

31. Alexander G. Dumas and Grace Keen, *A Psychiatric Primer for the Veteran's Family and Friends* (Minneapolis: University of Minnesota Press, 1945), 6, 8, 9, 202.

32. Veterans Administration Visual Aids Division, *The Road to Decision*, 15:19, National Archives, College Park, MD (hereafter NACP). Other World War II–era rehabilitation films held at the NACP include *This Is Worth Working For* (1946), *What's My Score?* (1946), and *Where Pipe Dreams Come True* (1946).

33. On conversion narratives, see Lary May, "Making the American Consensus: The Narrative of Conversion and Subversion in World War II Films," in Erenberg and Hirsch, 71–102.

34. The GI Bill has been the subject of intense historical inquiry in recent years for how it both expanded and narrowed the class of state beneficiaries. See Stephen R. Ortiz, *Beyond the Bonus March and GI Bill: How Veteran Politics Shaped the New Deal Era* (New York: New York University Press, 2010); Suzanne Mettler, *Soldiers to Citizens: The G.I. Bill and the Making of the Greatest Generation* (Oxford: Oxford University Press, 2005); Nancy Beck Young, "'Do Something for the Soldier Boys': Congress,

the G.I. Bill of Rights, and the Contours of Liberalism," in *Veterans' Policies, Veterans' Politics: New Perspectives on Veterans in the Modern United States*, ed. Stephen R. Ortiz (Gainesville: University Press of Florida, 2012), 199–221.

35. Quoted in Aaron Glantz, *The War Comes Home: Washington's Battle against America's Veterans* (Berkeley: University of California Press, 2009), 72.

36. Margot Canaday, *The Straight State: Sexuality and Citizenship in Twentieth-Century America* (Princeton: Princeton University Press, 2009), 150.

37. Jennifer D. Keene, *Doughboys, the Great War, and the Remaking of America* (Baltimore: Johns Hopkins University Press, 2001), 205.

38. Clement, 533–42.

39. On "hypothetical Hiroshimas," see David Monteyne, *Fallout Shelter: Designing for Civil Defense in the Cold War* (Minneapolis: University of Minnesota Press, 2011), 1–34.

40. On Americans' anxieties following World War II, see Paul S. Boyer, *By the Bomb's Early Light: American Thought and Culture at the Dawn of the Atomic Age* (Chapel Hill: University of North Carolina Press, 1994); William Graebner, *The Age of Doubt: American Thought and Culture in the 1940s* (Prospect Heights, IL: Waveland Press, 1998); Engelhardt; John Fousek, *To Lead the Free World: American Nationalism and the Cultural Roots of the Cold War* (Chapel Hill: University of North Carolina Press, 2000); Mark Kleinman, *A World of Hope, a World of Fear: Henry A. Wallace, Reinhold Niebuhr, and American Liberalism* (Columbus: Ohio University Press, 2000).

41. William A. Ulman, "They May Be Disabled—But Man! Can They Work!," *Saturday Evening Post*, October 20, 1951, 30, 31, 216, 218; Hugh Morrow, "They Call *Him* Disabled?," *Saturday Evening Post*, April 11, 1953, 36–37, 88, 91, 95.

42. Alan Brinkley, "World War II and American Liberalism," in Erenberg and Hirsch, 326.

43. David Serlin, *Replaceable You: Engineering the Body in Postwar America* (Chicago: University of Chicago Press, 2004), 3.

44. On the concept of "patriotic orthodoxy," see Michael S. Sherry, "Patriotic Orthodoxy and American Decline," in *History Wars: The Enola Gay and Other Battles for the American Past*, ed. Edward T. Linenthal and Tom Engelhardt (New York: Metropolitan, 1996), 97–114.

45. Franklin Fearing, "Warriors Return: Normal or Neurotic?," *Hollywood Quarterly* 1:1 (Oct. 1945): 97.

46. Glantz, 71.

47. Rose, 242.

48. Leonard Quart and Albert Auster, "The Wounded Vet in Postwar Film," *Social Policy* 13:2 (1982): 26, 28.

49. Michael S. Sherry, *In the Shadow of War: The United States since the 1930s* (New Haven: Yale University Press, 1995), 124.

50. Robert J. Topmiller and T. Kerby Neill, *Binding Their Wounds: America's Assault on Its Veterans* (Boulder, CO: Paradigm, 2011), 50.

51. Ibid., 66, 49–72.

52. John S. Bowman, *Korean War*, updated ed. (New York: Facts on File, 2003), 120.

53. Paul M. Edwards, *The Korean War* (Westport, CN: Greenwood Press, 2006), 170.

54. Susan D. Moeller, *Shooting War: Photography and the American Experience of Combat* (New York: Basic Books, 1989), 268.

55. "Quadruple Amputee Now 'John Q. Civilian,'" *New York Times*, August 15, 1953, 17.

56. Edwards, 98.

57. Ibid., 167–75.

58. In a recent essay, Melinda Pash challenges the conventional view that links public apathy toward the war to the limitations of the Korean GI Bill. See "'A Veteran Does Not Have to Stay a Veteran Forever': Congress and the Korean GI Bill," in Ortiz, *Veterans' Policies, Veterans' Politics*, 222–40.

59. Howard A. Rusk, "Public Apathy to Korea GI's Slows Their Benefit Claims," *New York Times*, September 27, 1953, 4.

60. Lawrence M. Baskir and William A. Strauss, "The Vietnam Generation," in *The Wounded Generation: America after Vietnam*, ed. A. D. Horne (Englewood Cliffs, NJ: Prentice-Hall, 1981), 8.

61. Richard A. Gabriel, *The Painful Field: The Psychiatric Dimensions of Modern War* (New York: Greenwood Press, 1988), 79.

62. Quoted in "Oversight of Medical Care of Veterans Wounded in Vietnam," in *The Vietnam Veteran in Contemporary Society: Collected Materials Pertaining to the Young Veterans* (Washington: Veterans Administration, May 1972), III-23.

63. Nixon quoted in Moeller, 350; for a nuanced discussion of the various controversies related to media in Vietnam, see Moeller, 349–413.

64. Daniel Hallin, *The "Uncensored War": The Media and Vietnam* (Berkeley: University of California Press, 1986), 129–30.

65. Charles Child, "From Vietnam to a VA hospital: Assignment to Neglect," *Life*, May 22, 1970, 26.

66. Quoted in ibid., 28.

67. Lewis J. Sherman and Eugene M. Caffrey, Jr., introduction to *The Vietnam Veteran in Contemporary Society*, I-2.

68. Cecil P. Peck, "The Vietnam Veteran," in *The Vietnam Veteran in Contemporary Society*, IV-1.

69. Andrew E. Hunt, *The Turning: A History of Vietnam Veterans Against the War* (New York: New York University Press, 1999).

70. Ron Kovic, *Born on the Fourth of July* (New York: Pocket Books, 1976), 112, 130, 150.

71. Ibid., 180.

72. On the development of this discourse, see Gray, *Postmodern War*; Chris Hables Gray, *Peace, War, and Computers* (New York: Routledge, 2005). For a celebratory take, see George Friedman and Meredith Friedman, *The Future of War: Power, Technology and American World Dominance in the Twenty-first Century* (New York: St. Martin's Griffin, 1998).

73. Andrew J. Bacevich, *The New American Militarism: How Americans Are Seduced by War* (New York: Oxford University Press, 2005), 57, 58.

74. Michael Ignatieff quoted in Bacevich, 28.

75. Quoted Baskir and Strauss, 10.

76. James Fallows, "What Did You Do in the Class War, Daddy?" in *The Wounded Generation*, 28.

77. On the creation of the AVF, see Beth Bailey, *America's Army: Making the All-Volunteer Force* (Cambridge: Belknap Press of Harvard University Press, 2009).

78. Adrian R. Lewis, *The American Culture of War: The History of US Military Force from World War II to Operation Iraqi Freedom* (New York: Routledge, 2007), 340–63.

79. Veterans Benefits Administration, Office of Performance Analysis and Integrity Data and Information Services, "May 2002 Gulf War Veterans Information System, Briefing For National Gulf War Resource Center." Available at http://ngwrc.org/Resources/GWVISreportSeptember2002.pdf (downloaded June 12, 2007).

TAMMY DUCKWORTH

1. Peter Slevin, "After War Injury, an Iraq Vet Takes on Politics," *Washington Post*, February 19, 2006, available at http://www.washingtonpost.com/wp-dyn/content/article/2006/02/18/AR2006021801295_pf.html.
2. Quoted in Adam Weinstein, "Nobody Puts Tammy Duckworth in a Corner," *Mother Jones*, August 23, 2012, available at http://www.motherjones.com/print/188171.
3. Ibid.

EPILOGUE

1. Herbert Kaufman, "The Only Hopeless Cripple," *Carry On* 1:4 (October–November 1918): 22.
2. Ray Kurzweil, *The Singularity Is Near: When Humans Transcend Biology* (New York: Viking, 2005).
3. Quoted in Robert J. Topmiller and T. Kerby Neill, *Binding Their Wounds: America's Assault on Its Veterans* (Boulder, CO: Paradigm, 2011), 46.
4. Quoted in E. J. Dionne, Jr., "Rewriting The Record," *Washington Post*, September 10, 2004, A29.
5. Gilbert Burnham, et al., "Mortality after the 2003 invasion of Iraq: a cross-sectional cluster sample study," *The Lancet* 368, issue 9545 (October 2006): 1421–28.
6. Don Philpott and Janelle Hill, *The Wounded Warrior Handbook: A Resource Guide for Returning Veterans* (Lanham, MD: Government Institutes, 2009), 16–17.
7. David Vergun, "NFL, Army both work to combat traumatic brain injury," August 31, 2012 (available at http://www.army.mil/article/86544/NFL__Army_both_work_to_combat_traumatic_brain_injury/).
8. Linda J. Bilmes, "Iraq's 100-Year Mortgage," *Foreign Policy Magazine* (March-April 2008): 84–85; Joseph E. Stiglitz and Linda J. Bilmes, *The Three Trillion Dollar War: The True Cost of the Iraq Conflict* (New York: Norton, 2008).
9. Stacy Takacs, *Terrorism TV: Popular Entertainment in Post 9/11 America* (Lawrence: University Press of Kansas, 2012), 235. On the decline of network news coverage, Takacs notes, by December 2007, "the three major network evening newscasts (NBC, ABC, and CBS) dropped their average coverage of the war from thirty minutes per week to four, or less than one minute per day" (208).
10. Aaron Glantz, *The War Comes Home: Washington's Battle against America's Veterans* (Berkeley: University of California Press, 2009), 20.
11. Tom Vanden Brook, "Sexism Must Be Treated like Racism, Top Officer Says," *Military Times*, May 14, 2013, available at http://www.militarytimes.com/article/20130514/NEWS/305140024/Sexism-must-treated-like-racism-top-officer-says.
12. Topmiller and Neill, 170.
13. On the controversy surrounding Toles' cartoon, see Howard Kurtz, "Joint Chiefs Fire at Toles Cartoon On Strained Army," *Washington Post*, February 2, 2006, C01.
14. Quoted in Glantz, 157.

15. Dana Priest and Anne Hull, "Soldiers Face Neglect, Frustration at Army's Top Medical Facility," *Washington Post*, February 18, 2007, A01.

16. Glantz, 49–60.

17. James Dao and Dan Frosch, "Feeling Warehoused in Army Trauma Care Units," *New York Times*, April 24, 2010; Glantz, 56.

18. As of this writing, the United States Department of Veterans Affairs is facing yet another scandal about failures in veterans' healthcare. See David Lawder, Roberta Rampton, and Julia Edwards, "U.S. Veterans Health Problem Confirms Cover-Up of Care Delays," *Reuters*, May 29, 2014, available at http://www.reuters.com/article/2014/05/29/us-usa-veterans-investigation-idUSKBN0E824E20140529.

19. Glantz, 208, 210–11, 118.

20. Willard Waller, *The Veteran Comes Back* (New York: Dryden Press, 1944), 307.

21. Paul K. Longmore, "The League of the Physically Handicapped and the Great Depression: A Case Study in the New Disability History," in *Why I Burned My Book and Other Essays on Disability* (Philadelphia: Temple University Press, 2003), 58.

22. Andrew J. Bacevich, *The New American Militarism: How Americans Are Seduced by War* (New York: Oxford University Press, 2005), 1.

Index

Page numbers in italics refer to tables, photographs, and illustrations.

antiwar groups. *See* American League Against War and Fascism (ALAWF); Fellowship of Reconciliation; peace movement, interwar; Vietnam Veterans Against the War; World Peaceways

antiwar propaganda, injured soldiers in: aimed at and produced by youth, 240–45; attacks on rehabilitation/medical achievements, 226–27, *235*, 237; criticisms of, 249–52; devastation of the male body, 228–30; documentaries of the 1930s, 237–38; emphasis on seeing/visual culture, 230–39; false sightings of "basket cases," 250–51; function as form of ventriloquism, 227; Global War on Terror, 292; post–World War II era, *273*; stigmatization of disability, 221, 251–52, 292; ridiculing the benefits of military service, 221–28; symbols of national guilt during Vietnam War, 277–80. *See also* representations of disabled veterans

Argonne Day, 200–201

Argonne Village, 107

Armistice, 86–88

Armistice Day, 205–7, 226

Army and Navy Journal, 25

"Army Builds Men, The" (slogan), 58, 223, 241, 248, *273*

Army Day, 200

Army Medical Department, 121

Army Medical Museum, 37–38, 308n78

Arrears Act of 1879, 26

Atherton, Gertrude, 144

"atomic veterans," 272–73

Augustus, Caesar, 19

Auster, Albert, 272

Autry, Dave, 292

Avatar (film), 287–89

Babb, Nancy, 242, 337n69

Bacevich, Andrew, 281, 300

Backwash of War, The (La Motte), 54

Bagge, Christian, 1–2, 303nn3–4

Baker, Newton D., 73, 88, 100, 205

Bangs, John Kendrick, 96

Barber, Frederick A., 233–35, 237

Barbour, Marion H., 249

Barbusse, Henri, 248

Barthelmess, Richard, 112–14

Barton, Bruce, 220

"basket case," 215, 250–51, 292–93. *See also* quadruple amputee

Baynton, Douglas C., 31

Bennett, Michael, 268

Berkeley, Busby, 211

Berry, James, H., 29

Best Years of My Life, The (Russell), 255

Best Years of Our Lives, The (film), 255, 272

Big Island Veterans Camp, 175

Big Parade, The (film), 190–91

Billings, Frank, 133–34

Billings, John S., 41

Bilmes, Linda J., 290

Birch, Helen Ledyard, 104

Blighty wounds, 70

Blinded Veterans Association, 271

Bloch, Jean de, 42–43

Blondell, Joan, 211–*12*

Boardwalk Empire, 5

body bag syndrome, 282

Bonus Expeditionary Forces (BEF), 155. *See* Bonus March of 1932

Bonus March of 1932, The, 155, 180–84, 210

bonus. *See* adjusted compensation

Born on the Fourth of July (Kovic), 279

Bourrillon, Maurice, 119, 143

Bowerman, Guy Emerson, 69

Boyd, Thomas, 190, 193

Bring Home the Soldier Dead League, 193

Brinkley, Alan, 269

Brinton, John Hill, 37

Britten, Frederick A., 55

Brokaw, Tom, 261

Bruns, Paul, 37

buddyhood, culture of, 171–76. *See also* American Legion and Disabled American Veterans of the World War

Bureau of War Risk Insurance, 63, 104, 124, 132, 151, 167

Burgess, Gelett, 122–23

Burlingame, Roger, 91, 178

Meigs, Mark, 70
Memorial Day, 200, 202, 332n35
memory: benefits for disabled veterans, 194–95; cultural memory, 188–89; embodiment of, 195–96; emphasis on the dead, 193; forgetting as healing, 267; forgotten disabled veterans, 208–13; fraught relationship to disabled veterans, 193–97; future national security, 213–14; idealized memories of World War I, 192–93; living memorials, 192; memorial rituals, 198–200; memory boom after World War I, 189–94; memory studies, 188; public reassurances, 197–201; purposeful memory and veterans, 189, 213; "remembrance as principle," 205; social contract with veterans, 188; social processes of forgetting, 207; stakes for disabled veterans, 213; war memorials, 192–94, 331n11
memory boom. *See* memory
Men, The (film), 272
Mencken, H. L., 179
Meuse-Argonne Campaign, 78
Michael, Moina Belle, 201–2, 204
Miles, Sherman, 250
Milford, Lewis, 107
militarism, 39–41. *See also* antimilitarism
militarization of American society, 272
military medicine: advances after Civil War, 34–35; advances in Gulf War, 283; advances in Vietnam War, 275; advances in World War II, 263; media coverage, 3; Spanish-American War as medical triumph, 43–44; World War I as safe war, 61–62
military service as disability, 180–81
Miller, Nathan, 214
Mitchell, S. Wier, 31
Moeller, Susan, 73
"Moral Equivalent of War, The" (James), 249
Morgan, J. P., 198
Mosley, Clarence, 274
Mosse, George, 54
Mudd, Roger, 279

Murrow, Edward R., 274
mustard gas, 66
myth of American innocence, 51
"myth of the war experience," 54, 184

Nast, Thomas, *30*
National Blind Veterans, 154
National Circulating Library of Students' Peace Poster Contest, 242, 337n69
National Disabled Soldiers' League, 104
National Football League (NFL), 290
National Home for Disabled Volunteer Soldiers, 27
National World War II Memorial, 261
Neill, T. Kerby, 272, 291
Nesbitt, John, 224, 226
New Veteranology, 298–300
Nichols, Francis R. T., 29
Nixon, Richard, 275
No More War, 237
No More War Parade (1935), 248
nonbattle injuries, 67–68, 314n67
normal body, 31
Normal Lives for the Disabled (Yost and Gilbreth), 265
normalcy, cultural imperative of, 31, 35, 102–3, 110, 153, 184
Norris, George W., 55
"nostalgia," 24
"Nothing about Us without Us," 299
Nuclear Test Ban Treaty, 272

Office of the Surgeon General, 117: educational propaganda on rehabilitation, 139; support for rehabilitation, 121, 123–24
Office of War Information (OWI): 262–64
Okinawa, Battle of, 261–62
Ordronaux, John, 25
Ortiz, Stephen, 180
"Over the Top," by an American Soldier Who Went (Empey), 48–49, 311n1

Pace, Peter, 292
parades, 92–94

Red Cross Institute for Crippled and Disabled Men, *127*, 141–*42*
Red Scare of 1920–21, 98, 155
Reed, David, 168
rehabilitation: advocates of, 120–21; alternative to Civil War pensions, 120–23; association with progress, 144; attention to the psychological dimensions of disability, 129–30; benefits of, 121–24; complaints about facilities and instructors, 136–38; complicity in future wars, 145–46; concerns about inadequate training, 133, 136; concerns about women, 137–38; confidence during World War II, 265–67; declining participation following Korean War, 274; definition, 117; elimination of "waste," 123–24; establishment of government program in World War I, 124–26; facilities, 125–26; failures, 147–48; goal of making disability disappear, 145, 197; Harold Russell, 255; influence of foreign programs, 126; legacies for treatment of disabled veterans, 147; means of self-improvement, 122–23; messages to disabled veterans, 143–44; messages to employers, 141–42; messages to women, 142–43; mixed views of veterans' organizations, 167–86; numbers of participants, 130, 146; physical reconstruction as obstacle to demobilization, 90; problems in programs, 132–38; Progressives' support for, 120; propaganda following World War II, 265–67; publicity campaigns, 138–43; racial discrimination, 133–36; restoration of manhood, 122; segregation by type of injury, 128–29; stepping stone to class mobility, 130–31; two stages—physical rehabilitation and vocational rehabilitation, 124–25; vocational counselors, 129. *See also* end of war disability; McMurtrie, Douglas C.
Remarque, Erich Maria, 190
"Remember My Forgotten Man," 211

remembrance versus memory, 330n4. *See also* memory
Rentmeester, C0, 276
representations of disabled veterans: antiwar propaganda, 53–54; 221–28; concerns about emasculating vets, 164–65; designed to shock the public, 162–64; emblems of war's horrors, 230–39; focus on injured male bodies, 228–30; forgotten men, 224, 226; functions as symbols/lessons, 248, 251–52; Iraq War-era popular culture, 3, 291, 343n9; objects of ridicule, 224–25; OWI propaganda, 263–*64*; post–Vietnam War film, 281; post–World War II film, 272; pro-war spokesmen, 59–60, 75; Spanish-American War visual culture, 45
Resister, William Ellis, 188
responses to the World War I veterans' crisis: local, 97; state, 97; federal, 97–99
Restelle, William, 42
"return to normalcy" (slogan), 6, 86, 102–3, 111–12, 207. *See also* Harding, Warren G.
Ritchie, Albert C., 186
rites de sortie, 94
Road to Decision, The (film), 267
Robertson, Royal W., 182–83
Rogers, W. A., *29*
Roosevelt, Eleanor, *199*
Roosevelt, Franklin D.: campaign for vice president, 160; concerns about civilian casualties in World War II, 269; criticism of strategic bombing in World War II, 259; cuts to veterans' programs during New Deal, 168–69; Forgotten Man campaign, 210; paralysis (polio), 169; veto of bonus legislation, 184; White House garden parties, *199*
Roosevelt, Quentin, 55
Roosevelt, Theodore: celebration of war, 55; concerns about disabled veterans' health and welfare, 46; romantic view of disabled veterans and war injury,

46, 68; *Rough Riders, The*, 46; Spanish-American War hero, 46; support for rehabilitation movement, 4, 47, 120

Roosevelt, Theodore, Jr., 160

Root, Elihu, 40

Rough Riders, The (Roosevelt, Theodore), 46

Rozell, Garrett, 31

Rumsfeld, Donald, 289, 292–93

Rusk, Howard A., 274

Russell, Harold, 255–56

Russert, Tim, 289

Ryan, Mary, 92

"safe war," 60–63, 281. *See also* survivability of war

Salmon, Thomas W., 163, 207

Sands of Iwo Jima (film), 261

Sanford, James E., 136

Sanitary Commission, United States, 25

Saranac Lake, New York (sanatorium), 104, 108

Sargent, Dudley A., 31

Schnittkind, Henry T., 53

Scholastic, 241

Schwarz, Leon, 94

self-inflicted wounds, 72

sensationalism, 162

September 11, 2001 (terrorist attacks), 268, 289

"service-connected disability," 168, 328n81

Servicemen's Readjustment Act. *See* GI Bill

Sevareid, Eric, 240

Severo, Richard, 107

Shambles (Schnittkind), 53

Shapiro, Harold, 228–29

Sharp, John, 56

shell shock: American Legion activism on behalf of shell-shocked vets, 163; associations with social deviance, 101; common form of injury, 5; difficulties in rehabilitation, 133; disability worthy of public recognition, 165; etiology in World War I, 66; numbers of mentally traumatized US veterans

after World War I, 66–67, 112; shameful injury, 71–72; symptoms, 67; trauma of memory, 196; victims abandoned, 207; victims segregated in hospital, 128

Shepherd, Susan M., 224

Sherry, Michael S., 272

Sherwood, Isaac R., 55

Sitting Bull, 20

Sledge, E. B., 262

Slocum, Henry Warner, 28

Smith, Page, 51

Smith, Stephen, 35

Soldiers, What Next! (Mayo), 178–79

soldiers' homes, 19, 27

Soldiers' Pay (Faulkner), 209–10

soldiers' tales, 190–91

Solon, 18

Spanish-American War, 43–46

Sprague, A. A., 163

St. Elizabeth's Hospital, 24

Stallings, Laurence, 109–11, 190–91, 241

Stanley, Jo, 196

Stiglitz, Joseph, 290

Stoner, Elizabeth R., 85

"stopping power," 36

"Story of the Empty Sleeve" (Cary), 28

Stuart, Judson D., 62–63

Sturken, Marita, 195, 207

Summer School of Scientific Management, 118

Sun Also Rises, The (Hemingway), 108–9

supercrip, 285

survivability of war, 11, 17, 35, 60–63, 119

Sweet Bill, 151–52

Szymanski, Ludwig, 108

Takacs, Stacy, 291, 343n9

"Tale of the One Armed" (Credesly), 28

Taylor, John Thomas, 184

Tazewell, Charles, 227–28

technology as a cure for disability, 288–89, 292

Terkel, Studs, 260

Tet Offensive, 275

They Shall Not Die in Europe (Derounian), 250

Thomson, Rosemarie Garland, 75
Three Who Were Soldiers (Tazewell),
    227–28
Tibbetts, Clark, 265
Toles, Tom, 292–93
Tomb of the Unknown Soldier, 193
Topmiller, Robert J., 272, 291
Towne, Charles Hanson, 68
trauma, 7
traumatic brain injury (TBI), 290, 293
trench diseases, 64
Trudeau, Gary, 292
Truman, Harry, 268
Trumbo, Dalton, 229–30

ugly laws, 32
Unbeliever, The (film), 74–75
"Uncensored War," The (Hallin), 275
Uncle Sam Wants You (Shepherd), 224
Under-Fire Veterans Association, 79
Union veterans. *See* Civil War

Vance Cooke, Edmund, 226
Veteran Comes Back, The (Waller), 297
veteran racket, 176
veteranology, 297–98
Veterans Administration, United States,
    27, 258, 265–67, 273, 277
Veterans Affairs, Department of, 284
Veterans' Bureau, United States, 86,
    106–7, 126, 130–32, 148
Veterans of Foreign Wars (VFW): federal
    charter, 158; militancy, 160, 169; mixed
    veterans' group, 154; sale of "buddy
    poppies," 202–3, 332n35; support of
    veterans' bonuses, 181
Veterans of Future Wars, 241
veterans' organizations: attitudes toward
    bonus legislation, 181; cultivation of
    veterans' memory, 204–5; dedication
    to disabled veterans, 154; fraught
    relationship to rehabilitation projects,
    167–68; public suspicions of, 153; sale
    of remembrance flowers, 202, 332n37;
    three types, 154. *See also* American Le-
    gion; Disabled Veterans of the World

War (DAV); Veterans of Foreign Wars
    (VFW)
veterans' scandals (involving poor
    treatment): atomic veterans, 273;
    Global War on Terror—Afghanistan
    and Iraq Wars, 293–94, 344n18; World
    War I, 103–6, 207–8; World War II, 271;
    Vietnam War, 276
"victory culture," post–World War II, 258
Vidor, King, 190–91
Vietnam Veterans Against the War
    (VVAW), 277–*80*
Vietnam War, 4, 275–81
Vietnam War veteran as "new" veteran,
    276–77
vocational education. *See* rehabilitation
Vocational Rehabilitation Act of 1918,
    124–25

Wages of War, The (Severo and Milford),
    107
Waller, Willard, 297–98
Walsh, Joe, 285
Walter Reed Army Medical Center, 6,
    109–10, 125, 131, 151–52, 255, 284, 293–94
war: antidote to peacetime degener-
    ation, 40; American debates about
    war, 39; competing visions of Ameri-
    can war, 4, 12, 39; masculine proving
    ground, 58–60, 94; national addiction
    to war, 300; national war story, 11;
    new American way of war, 281; path
    to national progress, 38–41; recipe for
    injury, 41–43; war as impossible, 43
War against War! (Friedrich), 232–34,
    236–37, 248
war casualties, United States: all US
    wars, 22; Civil War, 22–24; Global War
    on Terror (Afghanistan and Iraq), 290;
    Gulf War, 283; Korean War, 273–74;
    Spanish-American War, 43–45; World
    War I, 5, 65–68, 78, 117; World War II,
    258, 261–63; Vietnam War, 275. *See also*
    World War I casualties
War Comes Home, The (Glantz), 294
War Cyclopedia, 73

War Department, 88, 96

war injury: conflicts over meaning, 3, 57, 155; efforts to rationalize/limit, 34–39; eugenicists' views, 42; facial, 48; fetishization of, 70; hierarchical view of, 70–72; intrinsic to war, 17, 296; medical views, 69; military views, 68; romanticized views, 68, 73; sentimental views, 75–76; sign of manly courage, 20, 28, 46, 60; symbol of sacrifice, 28–30; trauma, 7–8; unromantic injuries, 261; wounded solders' views, 69–72. See also disabled veterans

War Is a Racket (Butler), 239

War Labor Policies Board, 88

war memorials. See memory

War Risk Insurance, 63–64

War Time (Dudziak), 112

War—What For? (Kirkpatrick), 53

Warren, Harry, 211

Warren, Maude Radford, 102

warrior transition units (WTUs), 294

Warriors, The (Gray), 262

Washington Naval Conference, 218

We Are the Wounded (Wheeler), 257

Weber, Max, 308n67

Weightman, George, 294

"What Did You Do in the Class War, Daddy?" (Fallows), 282

What Every Young Man Should Know About War (Shapiro), 228–29

What the Employers of America Can Do for the Disabled Soldiers and Sailors, 141

Wheeler, Keith, 257

Whelan, Thomas J., 275

When the Boys Come Home (Hersey), 92

White Aryan Resistance, 293

White House garden parties for disabled veterans, 198–200

whiteness, 9

Wilson, Gill Robb, 205

Wilson, Woodrow: Armistice Day address (1923), 206; casualty of war (stroke), 79; Congressional war address (1917), 55; platform of nonintervention, 54; support for League of Na-

tions, 87; Sweet Bill, 152; war to make the world "safe for democracy," 57

Winter, Jay, 188, 196

Wister, Owen, 54

women in the military, 9, 268, 291, 304n15

Wood, Edward D., Jr., 261

Wood, Leonard, 160

Woods, Arthur D., 98–100

World Peaceways, 219–21, 224–25, 227, 241

World War I: American reluctance to fight, 52–53; antiwar culture, 53–54; apex of the Problem of the Disabled Veteran, 3–6; appeals of war, 57–60; Congressional war debate, 55–57; dangers/fighting conditions, 64–68; demobilization, 88–90; end of war, 88; fictional accounts, 190; myth of American innocence, 50–51; postwar disillusion, 217–21; postwar social upheaval, 96, 218; propaganda, 72–78; "safe war," 60–63. See also homecomings of troops after World War I; rehabilitation; World War I casualties

World War I casualties: disease, 64–65; European casualties, 78; hierarchy of injuries (heroic to shameful), 70–72; types of injuries, 65–68; US casualties, 5, 65–68, 78, 117; varying perspectives, 68–72. See also gas; nonbattle injuries; shell shock

World War I (disabled) veterans: female disabled veterans, 9, 304n15; historiography, 303n7; postwar hardships, 96–102; representations in 1920s fiction, 108–11; similarities with War on Terror veterans, 292–96; suspicions of criminality, 98–101; trapped in the past, 102. See also disabled veterans; veterans' organizations

World War II: brutality of the fighting, 261–62; decline of the Problem of the Disabled Veteran, 265–67; destruction/end of moderation, 259; "Good War," 260–61, 270–72; lingering anxieties about disabled veterans, 271–273;